**Shakespeare Performed**
Globe to Global

Founding editor: J. R. MULRYNE
General editors:
JAMES C. BULMAN, CAROL CHILLINGTON RUTTER

# Antony and Cleopatra

Manchester University Press

To buy or to find out more about the books currently available in this series, please go to: https://manchesteruniversitypress.co.uk/series/shakespeare-in-performance/

Shakespeare Performed
Globe to Global

# Antony and Cleopatra

Carol Chillington Rutter

Manchester University Press

Copyright © Carol Chillington Rutter 2020

The right of Carol Chillington Rutter to be identified as the author of this work has been asserted by her in accordance with the Copyright, Designs and Patents Act 1988.

Published by Manchester University Press
Altrincham Street, Manchester M1 7JA
www.manchesteruniversitypress.co.uk

British Library Cataloguing-in-Publication Data
A catalogue record for this book is available from the British Library

ISBN  978 1 5261 3249 9   hardback
ISBN  978 1 5261 9470 1   paperback

First published 2020
Paperback published 2026

The publisher has no responsibility for the persistence or accuracy of URLs for any external or third-party internet websites referred to in this book, and does not guarantee that any content on such websites is, or will remain, accurate or appropriate.

EU authorised representative for GPSR:
Easy Access System Europe – Mustamäe tee 50, 10621 Tallinn, Estonia
gpsr.requests@easproject.com

Typeset
by New Best-set Typesetters Ltd

For my big sister
Roberta Chillington Skelton
'A lass unparalleled'

# CONTENTS

|   | | |
|---|---|---|
|   | *List of illustrations* | *page* ix |
|   | *Series Editors' Preface* | xii |
|   | *Preface* | xiv |
|   | *Acknowledgements* | xix |
|   | Introduction: a play that 'approves the common liar' | 1 |
| 1 | 'That time? O times!': the Jacobean *Antony and Cleopatra* | 23 |
| 2 | 'Famous patterns of unlawful love': *Antony and Cleopatra*, 1677–1931 | 43 |
| 3 | 'Wogs exit nearest way': Glen Byam Shaw, Shakespeare Memorial Theatre, 1953 | 67 |
| 4 | 'By certain scales i'th' pyramid': taking the measure of *Antony and Cleopatra*, Royal Shakespeare Company 1972, 1978, 1982 | 92 |
| 5 | Boying greatness: the Citizens' Theatre (Glasgow), 1972, and Northern Broadsides (Halifax), 1995 | 149 |
| 6 | 'Back to Basics': Peter Hall, Olivier Theatre, National Theatre, 1987 | 179 |
| 7 | 'Some squeaking Cleopatra': Shakespeare's Globe, 1999 | 203 |
| 8 | Estranging the crocodile: foreign *Antony and Cleopatra* in Britain and abroad | 224 |

9   Restoring blackness: Josette Bushell-Mingo's Cleopatra, Royal Exchange, Manchester, 2005; Tarell Alvin McCraney's 'radical edit', Royal Shakespeare Company, The Public and GableStage, 2013   269

*Cast lists*   296
*Bibliography*   307
*Index*   316

# List of illustrations

1.1 Inigo Jones, costume design for 'A Daughter of Niger' in *Masque of Blackness* (1605) (© The Devonshire Collections, Chatsworth, reproduced by permission of Chatsworth Settlement Trustees / Bridgeman Images).    *page* 30

2.1 Playbill for *Antony and Cleopatra*, Theatre Royal, Covent Garden, 1813 (© Royal Shakespeare Company, by permission of the Shakespeare Centre Library).    56

3.1 Peggy Ashcroft as Cleopatra, Michael Redgrave as Mark Antony (photograph by Angus McBean, © Royal Shakespeare Company, by permission of the Shakespeare Centre Library).    76

3.2 Peggy Ashcroft as Cleopatra (photograph by Angus McBean, © Royal Shakespeare Company, by permission of the Shakespeare Centre Library).    85

4.1 Janet Suzman as Cleopatra, Richard Johnson as Mark Antony (photograph by Joe Cocks, © Shakespeare Birthplace Trust, by permission of the Shakespeare Centre Library).    101

4.2 Corin Redgrave as Octavius Caesar, Richard Johnson as Mark Antony (photograph by Reg Wilson, © Royal Shakespeare Company).    105

4.3 Alan Howard as Mark Antony, Glenda Jackson as Cleopatra (photograph by Joe Cocks, © Shakespeare Birthplace Trust, by permission of the Shakespeare Centre Library).    120

4.4 Alan Howard as Mark Antony, Glenda Jackson as Cleopatra (photograph by Joe Cocks, © Shakespeare Birthplace Trust, by permission of the Shakespeare Centre Library).    123

4.5 Richard Griffiths as Clown, Glenda Jackson as Cleopatra (photograph by Joe Cocks, © Shakespeare Birthplace Trust, by permission of the Shakespeare Centre Library).    130

4.6  Helen Mirren as Cleopatra, Michael Gambon as Mark Antony (photograph by Joe Cocks, © Shakespeare Birthplace Trust, by permission of the Shakespeare Centre Library). 140

4.7  Helen Mirren as Cleopatra, Josette Simon as Iras (photograph by Joe Cocks, © Shakespeare Birthplace Trust, by permission of the Shakespeare Centre Library). 143

4.8  Helen Mirren as Cleopatra (photograph by Joe Cocks, © Shakespeare Birthplace Trust, by permission of the Shakespeare Centre Library). 145

5.1  Jonathan Kent as Cleopatra, John Duttine as Antony (photograph by Diane Tammes, © Citizens' Theatre Glasgow, by permission of Scottish Theatre Archive, University of Glasgow Special Collections). 163

5.2  Angela Chadfield as Acolyte, Jonathan Kent as Cleopatra, John Duttine as Antony (photograph by Diane Tammes, © Citizens' Theatre Glasgow, by permission of Scottish Theatre Archive, University of Glasgow Special Collections). 164

5.3  Andrew Whitehead as 'Cleopatra', David Fenwick as 'Antony', Andrew Cryer as Caesar (photograph by Nobby Clark, © ArenaPAL). 170

5.4  Ishia Bennison as Cleopatra, Deborah McAndrews as Iras, Julie Livesey as Charmian, Andrew Cryer as Caesar (photograph by Nobby Clark, © ArenaPAL). 174

6.1  Judi Dench as Cleopatra, Anthony Hopkins as Antony (photograph by Donald Cooper, © Donald Cooper). 189

7.1  Mark Rylance as Cleopatra, Paul Shelley as Antony (photograph by Donald Cooper, © Donald Cooper). 211

8.1  Chris Nietvelt as Cleopatra, Marieke Heebink as Charmian, Frieda Pittoors as Iras, Hans Kesting as Antonius (photograph by Donald Cooper, © Donald Cooper). 250

8.2  Geraint Wyn Davies as Antony, Yanna McIntosh as Cleopatra (Melbar Entertainment Group in Association with the Stratford Festival). 258

8.3 Yanna McIntosh as Cleopatra, Geraint Wyn Davies as Antony (Melbar Entertainment Group in Association with the Stratford Festival). 260
8.4 Yanna McIntosh as Cleopatra, Jennifer Mogbock as Iras, Sophia Walker as Charmian, Antoine Yared as Mardian, E. B. Smith as Alexas, Andrew Lawrie as Messenger (Melbar Entertainment Group in Association with the Stratford Festival). 261
9.1 Joaquina Kalukango as Cleopatra, Sarah Niles as Charmian, Charise Castro Smith as Iras (photograph by Hugo Glendinning, © Royal Shakespeare Company). 283
9.2 Charise Castro Smith as Iras, Chivas Michael as Mardian, Joaquina Kalukango as Cleopatra (photograph by Hugo Glendinning, © Royal Shakespeare Company). 289
9.3 Chukwudi Iwuji as Enobarbus/Bawon Samedi (photograph by Hugo Glendinning, © Royal Shakespeare Company). 290

# SERIES EDITORS' PREFACE

Since this pioneering Series was first launched in 1984, the study of Shakespeare's plays as scripts for performance has grown to rival the reading of Shakespeare's plays as literature among university, college, and secondary school teachers and students. The aim of the Series remains today what it was then: to assist this study by exploring how Shakespeare's texts have been realised in performance, in a multitude of different ways by actors, directors, and designers, and in the various media for which the plays have been adapted.

The idea of what constitutes performance has itself changed considerably in the past few decades, promoted by cultural anthropologists who have defined performance as a more inclusive set of social practices than theatre historians ever envisioned, a continuum of human actions ranging from ritual, sports, popular entertainments and the performing arts to the enactment of social, gender, race, and class roles in everyday life. Advances in digital technology, too, have led to an expansion of what forms Shakespearean performance can take in various media – in theatres and less conventional playing spaces, in the cinema, and on the computer screen. They have also led to a fundamental questioning of what 'live' performance means – liveness being a basic tenet of performance studies – and to a better understanding of how viewers can become players in interactive performances. The rapid growth of media and digital technology, furthermore, has created a global market for Shakespeare that has not only encouraged intercultural exchanges by theatre companies, but also created new audiences for "local" adaptations of the plays in parts of the world that once would have had scant familiarity with Shakespeare.

Each contributor to the Series has selected a number of productions of a given play and analysed them comparatively. Drawn from different periods, countries, and media, these productions were chosen not only because they are culturally significant in their own right but because they illustrate how the convergence of material conditions can shape a performance and its reception: the medium for which the text is adapted; the language in which Shakespeare's text is spoken; the performance style and aesthetic decisions made by directors and whether they embrace or flout tradition; the production's set, lighting, music and costume design; the bodies – raced, gendered, aged, sized and shaped – and the abilities of the actors working individually but also in an ensemble; and the historical, political, and social contexts which condition audience responses to the performance.

We hope that audiences, by reading these accounts of Shakespeare in performance, may enlarge their understanding of what a playtext is and begin, too, to appreciate the complex ways in which a performance is a deeply collaborative effort. Any study of a Shakespeare text will, of course, reveal only a small proportion of the play's potential meanings; but by engaging issues of how a performance essentially translates a text into a work with cultural resonances and meanings beyond anything Shakespeare as author could have anticipated, our Series encourages a kind of reading that is receptive to the contingencies that make performances of Shakespeare an art unto themselves.

James C. Bulman and Carol Chillington Rutter,<br>General Editors

# PREFACE

The play that emerges through the chapters of this book is like the beast that Lepidus tries so vainly to pin down when he asks, 'What manner o'thing is your crocodile?' It evades definition. Instead, the four hundred years of performance history I chart here show *Antony and Cleopatra* as a series of what Jonathan Miller would call 'subsequent performances', 'becomings' that never fix its final form but rather re-perform Shakespeare's play to enact current topicalities.

In his own time, the story Shakespeare found in Plutarch (as translated by Thomas North) told of erotic seduction and martial delinquency on an unimaginable scale, Antony 'taken', 'ravished' by the 'companie and conversacion' of Cleopatra, whose 'discourse' was 'a spurre that pricked to the quick'. Fulvia might be embroiling Rome in civil wars. The Parthian army might be massed to invade Syria. 'Yet' Antony, 'as though all this had nothing touched him', 'yielded him selfe to goe with Cleopatra into Alexandria, where he spent and lost in childish sports ... and idle pastimes, the most pretious thing a man can spende ... and that is, time'. The word Shakespeare's Philo gives this folly is 'dotage', in the opening line of the play, 'Nay, but this dotage of our general's / O'erflows the measure'. From one angle, Antony is a study in 'dotage'. His 'fondness', another early modern term, enacted across the rest of the play in scenes of devastating self-exposure, is linked not just to infatuation but to senility. Time, for Antony, is running out. He's the 'old' lion 'dying', challenged by the 'lion's whelp', Octavius, who wants not just Antony's third of the empire but his grizzled head. 'Dotage', then, is a matter of primary political importance. Its issue is regime change, and Shakespeare follows Plutarch in plotting the mean-minded moves youth makes to dispose of power's geriatric hangers-on.

But where the subject of Plutarch's 'Life' is the Great Man, Shakespeare's is something new, the Great Couple. Alongside Antony he puts Cleopatra at the centre of things. Fully exploiting his theatre's ability to say 'this' and 'that' simultaneously, Shakespeare positions her to perform enigmatic self-contradiction (or a series of 'becomings' that enact self-representation oxymoronically).

She's both 'Egypt' and 'gipsy', 'queen' and 'tawny front', 'Eastern star' and 'boggler', 'triple turned whore' and 'lass unparalleled', foul-mouthed stand-up comic (not even Hamlet cracks better jokes than Cleopatra) and, via a soaring rhetoric that reaches for impossibilities, a maker of sublime imaginaries. Is she a type of female fickleness – or something of 'great constancy'? Is she Antony's ruin – or his rescue? Because from another angle, *Antony and Cleopatra* looks like a study of masculinity interrogated, dismantled and reconstructed to a new design. The male archetypes that early modernity inherited and cherished from the ancients – Hercules, Mars, Aeneas; hero, soldier, empire-builder – are played out in Shakespeare's play but simultaneously played *against* as though type and anti-type were theatrical doubles constantly enacting themselves as their own opposites. The Herculean hero is a sottish buffoon. The 'Mars' whose eyes glowed fire when he stood four-square to survey 'the files and musters of the war' runs flapping from Actium like 'a doting mallard'. The imperialist mocks the vast irrelevance of imperial ambition: 'Kingdoms are clay'. The triumvir daffs aside territorial conquest: 'Let … the wide arch / Of the ranged empire fall!' The man new-made by Cleopatra has found 'Here is my space!' Or is that finding a stupefying loss of self?

That question has fascinated productions of the play since Shakespeare. *Antony and Cleopatra* has been seen as the triumphant rendering of the greatest love story ever told, but also as the supreme tragedy of wrecked masculinity betrayed by wantonness. It's been played on massive stages with hundreds of extras, opulent costumes, fantastic scenery, interpolated scenes (including the arrival of Cleopatra down the Cydnus on her barge), but also in studio spaces and with a cast of seven. After 1606 it sat on a shelf for two hundred and fifty years, unstaged because 'unstageable'. When it finally returned to the theatre, the Victorians used *Antony and Cleopatra* to conduct an encounter with 'Egyptomania', to enact the 'exotic' – or what the white, British, imperialist imaginary fantasised as the 'exotic' – in the years after the Suez Canal was built and elite tourism began. This encounter was reprised in 1972 when Egypt went to London in the fabulous 'King Tut' exhibition at the British Museum, just at the moment when popular cheap travel became available to Brits, when 'abroad' became a real concept for British tourists lured by the exotic but fearful of the Other. The kinds of conflicted attitudes to foreignness that were reflected in class divisions in the 1970s (and after) show up time and again in reviews of *Antony and Cleopatra*. It's been a colonialist play that looked at history with white supremacist 'Roman' eyes, and a post-colonialist play that challenged the whiting-out of the black history that is central to Shakespeare's account. Its military culture has been located in antiquity, its warriors dressed in togas and leather-strapped tunics. But its battles have also been located much closer to the production's present, its soldiers put in pith helmets and khaki or in camouflage-coloured desert combat gear, the disciplines of these wars informed by 1914–18, 1939–45 or Afghanistan post-2001. The body of the warrior has been heroised – and unglamorously lampooned.

The play, too, has been a site where 'modernity' is on display (yet also significantly concealed, backstage). Given the design ambitions of some productions, ambitions that have tested the play's reputation for 'unstageability', theatre technology has raced to keep up with *Antony and Cleopatra*. And sometimes has out-run it. Machinery in the nineteenth-century theatre and sophisticated computer-assisted systems installed in theatres in the second half of the twentieth century took some productions of *Antony and Cleopatra* into the abstract realm of the 'tech', such that the set outplayed the scene, the spectacle, the actor, the visual, the voice. In reaction, other productions stripped back design concepts to the bare essentials. In them, modernity's fascination with gadgets yielded to a re-centring of focus on the actor's body – the body 're-tekhned' as Thomas Docherty puts it[1] – where 'infinite variety' properly belongs.

Is there a capital 'P' political play inside *Antony and Cleopatra*? Certainly, when foreign directors produce it, when they translate the text to make it local, when they align it to a critique of a current regime or design it to look askance at the fictions that legitimate power's self-representations, it becomes a 'Political' play. These productions occasionally threaten state apparatuses. In Moscow, Kiryll Serebrennikov's 2006 *Antony and Cleopatra* was raided by police urged on by political extremists who accused it of indecency. Much more dangerous than the sex it portrayed (video transmission from Cleopatra's bedroom onto a giant screen showed the 'dotage of our general's' in full orgasmic swing), however, was the challenge it offered Vladimir Putin's regime (Caesar was played as an unmistakeable parody of the Russian president) by locating the action in a place that looked like the contemporary Middle East but also evoked the present-day Chechen Republic, including a burnt-out scene of devastated school equipment that remembered the Beslan massacre.² More typically, however, on British stages the politics of *Antony and Cleopatra* play out at the level of the cultural and personal, of race and gender. The black representation of Egypt that Shakespeare so clearly imagines has been both asserted and occluded. The gender representation that sets Roman 'rule' v. Egyptian 'bend[ing]' and 'turn[ing]' has been seen as a power struggle that ambiguously explodes stereotypes only to confirm them: Cleopatra, 'the greatest courtesan that ever led man from the path of politics', as Beerbohm Tree made her in 1906 (quoted in Hodgdon 1998, 81), ends her life calling 'Husband, I come!' Before that, the play watches Antony turn with relief to the 'royal occupation', war, from the altogether more exhausting 'royal occupation' that is Cleopatra. Perhaps one of the significant cultural insights this performance history reaches as it observes the play across four hundred years is that for men, 'doing' war is so much simpler than 'doing' women.

As Vitaliy Eyber has discovered – along with many others who have written on the play, including actors – an 'entirely positive review' of *Antony and Cleopatra* on any stage anywhere 'is all but impossible to find'. That's the consolation Eyber offers Serebrennikov, reporting the drubbing from reviewers his production took in Moscow. Maybe the play doesn't satisfy because *it refuses to*, because it cocks a series of snooks at expectation. Shakespeare's *Antony and Cleopatra*, writes Eyber, seems designed with the 'odd and perverse objective of finding out how much it can get away with' (Eyber 2007, 147). Looking at the work of 'subsequent performance', the chapters that follow in this book ask, 'How much?' They respond, 'Let's see.'

## Notes

1 Thomas Docherty, personal communication responding to my draft of a chapter, May 2018.
2 For lack of materials, I have been unable to include a further account of this production in Chapter 9. An excellent review by Vitaliy Eyber on which I'm depending here is '"Let Rome in Moskva Melt": Antony and Cleopatra at Sovremennik'(Eyber 2007). Occasionally a very poor-quality pirated film of the production surfaces on the internet – only to disappear again. I accessed the film in the summer of

2018, but without Russian and without Eyber to break the visual code and make sense of the topical allusions, I was a spectator who could only see this film as a series of graphically imagined scenes designed to confront and disturb. Serebrennikov's habit as a film and theatre director of poking the bear is undoubtedly what prompted his house arrest in 2017 on trumped-up charges of embezzlement. In 2019 he was granted limited travel in Moscow. His trial continues.

# ACKNOWLEDGEMENTS

Nobody writes a book without help; in my case, a great deal of help.

I want to thank Thomas Docherty for reading all of my chapters in draft and pointing the way ahead with comments that challenged my thinking, and Jim Bulman for meticulous editing, almost curing me of my inveterate addiction to sentence fragments. But not quite. Bryony Rutter checked all my citations, compiled the cast lists and scoured the Citz (Glasgow) archives for production records – her attention to detail saving me from many errors. Ben Fowler frog-marched me to Amsterdam to see Toneelgroep at work, then advised on Chapter 9. Angela Ritter and Bernhard Klein translated Zadek reviews and Plessen's text, generously provided to me from the University of Munich's library by Betinna Boecker and Johanna Stowasser. Boika Sokolova alerted me to Serebrennikov's Moscow *Antony and Cleopatra*. Rowan Rutter talked me through gender representation and diversity in contemporary performance; and Ella McLeod, the politics of black hair. Archivists and librarians at a number of addresses have made work on this book pleasurable: Liza Giffin in Stratford, Ontario; Madelaine Cox and the collections team at the Shakespeare Birthplace Trust, Stratford-upon-Avon; and Claire McKendrick in the Special Collections Department of the University of Glasgow library, who arranged to have Havergal's rehearsal script photocopied and sent to me. Over the years, numbers of actors and directors have given me their insights into this play – as well as their performances: Janet Suzman, Judi Dench, Barrie Rutter, Josette Bushell-Mingo, Sorcha Cusack, Rakie Ayola and Terry Hands (who offered important comments on Chapter 4). I am extremely grateful to Tarell Alvin McCraney for sharing with me his 'director's cut' and for restoring Shakespeare's black Cleopatra to the English stage. His production made this book necessary.

Anyone who tries to write performance studies is indebted to generations of theatre reviewers and photographers who capture the ephemeral for the record in sharp eye-witness accounts (Ruth Ellis, Philip Hope-Wallace, Peter Fleming, Kenneth Tynan, Irving Wardle, John Peter, Michael Coveney, Michael Billington, Lyn

Gardner) and in snaps of the shutter (Angus McBean, Donald Cooper, Reg Wilson, Joe Cocks, Nobby Clark).

Anyone whose research is led by teaching must be grateful to students for asking awkward questions. Several years of Warwick University students have 'talked back' to my *Antony and Cleopatra* project. In particular I thank Irene Musumeci, Matt Armstrong, Gethin Roberts, Julian Richards and Stephanie Tillotson.

Much of this book was written in Venice, where Shaul Bassi, Susanne Franco, Mickey White, Pam and Kent Cartwright, Mauro Bondioli and Mariangela Nicolardi showed me the kind of hospitality, friendship and intellectual stimulation that provides welcome respite from the work of writing.

Practically the first scholarly voice heard in this book is Barbara Hodgdon's. And Barbara gets almost the last word, too. She was my friend. My mentor. My role model. She shaped how I think about this play. All of us who 'do' performance studies follow where Barbara led. I wish she'd lived to see the work of this, her latest collaboration, in print.

Looking back, I realise that this book began thirty-odd years ago. My four-year old daughter, sitting in the bathtub, probably at the end of a day when I'd neglected her while I struggled to match my wits to Shakespeare's in a lecture I was trying to write, looked up and asked, 'Mommy, who *were* Antony and Cleopatra?' My response: 'Do you want the long story or the short one?' 'The long story.' So we started back with Julius Caesar and Philippi, then got on to Cydnus, a Roman whistling to the wind in a marketplace, messengers, Actium, the monument, with plenty of costume details along the way. She, the daughter of an actor as well as an academic, listened seriously while more hot water went into the cooling bath, then asked, 'Mommy, who played the asp?'

'Who played the asp?' is one of the questions this book attempts to address.

# Introduction: a play that 'approves the common liar'

### Two epitomes

Her Herculean Roman is dead. She's been surprised by Caesar's thugs in the monument she thought was impregnable. The writing is on the wall. And she's backed up so hard against it that she can read it on her nerve endings.

So now what?

Facing desolation, Cleopatra turns to fabulous distraction. She performs an act of memorial reconstruction:

> I dreamt there was an emperor Antony.
> O, such another sleep, that I might see
> But such another man!

Ignoring attempts at interruption ('If it might please ye–'; 'Most sovereign creature–'), and under the sign of the dream-god Morpheus, god, too, of metamorphosis, Cleopatra makes her man more than a god. She makes him a proxy for the known universe:

> His face was as the heavens, and therein stuck
> A sun and moon which kept their course and lighted
> The little O, the earth.

She bodies forth this Antony in a monumental blazon: 'His legs bestrid the ocean; his reared arm / Crested the world; his voice …

/ ... his bounty / ... His delights / ... his livery ...'. She pauses to check the truth-content of her imagining –

> Think you there was or might be such a man
> As this I dreamt of? –

then rounds on Dolabella's 'Gentle madam, no' by denying the very incredulity she invited – 'You lie up to the hearing of the gods!' – only to switch again, instantly capitulating to her own gain-saying, hedging it in with hypotheticals:

> But if there be nor ever were one such,
> It's past the size of dreaming. (5.2.75–96, *passim*)[1]

Was Antony real? Illusion? Imagination? Flesh and blood? Lie? Is she remembering? Or fantasising? Cleopatra defers to sententiousness:

> Nature wants stuff
> To vie strange forms with fancy. (5.2.96–97)

That's true, as Cleopatra's own history has demonstrated when, at Cydnus, on a barge that 'Burned on the water', her 'own person' showed how 'fancy' could 'outwork nature' (2.2.202, 211). But the moment it's offered, this truth is withdrawn, the superior creativity of the imagination contradicted in a conclusion that explodes the separate categories of 'nature' and 'fancy' simultaneously to make and unmake Antony mortal:

> Yet t'imagine
> An Antony were nature's piece 'gainst fancy,
> Condemning shadows quite. (5.2.97–99)

In short, the Antony whom Cleopatra makes is an oxymoron, the rhetorical trope linking opposites. Structurally, oxymoron exclaims (from one side of the opposition or the other) 'You lie!', and I dwell on her exchange with Dolabella to offer it at the beginning of this book as an epitome of the whole play. From the outset, this is a play that traffics in oxymorons. Its regular business is to 'make defect perfection', to 'approve[ ] the common liar' (2.2.241, 1.2.61).

But something else is going on in this exchange with Dolabella. It, too, epitomises the play, for Cleopatra's memorial turn operates as narrative cover-story for another kind of 'turn' that she is performing as she tells her dream. Turning Antony into a monument, Cleopatra is turning Dolabella into a traitor. Cleopatra in Act 5 is Rome's captive, but here she takes this latest Roman captive (as she has how many before him?). She performs upon him a seduction.[2] Dolabella is the officer of Caesar's right hand sent to assume command from Proculeius, whose order was to take the queen alive, to tell her lies ('say / We purpose her no shame') to prevent the 'mortal stroke' that would 'defeat us' – Caesar – in the career-defining spectacle of humiliation that he's giddily imagining when he crows, 'her life in Rome / Would be eternal in our triumph' (5.1.61–66, *passim*). Dollabella enters 5.2 Caesar's man. He leaves it Cleopatra's servant. He doesn't just give the game away ('He'll lead me, then, in triumph?'; 'Madam, he will. I know't') so that Cleopatra sees through Caesar's subsequent hypocrisies ('we intend so to dispose you as / Yourself shall give us counsel'; 'He words me, girls, he words me', 5.2.108–190, *passim*). He also returns to discover to Cleopatra what he's just heard (off stage), Caesar's secret marching orders:

> I tell you this: Caesar through Syria
> Intends his journey, and within three days
> You with your children will he send before. (5.2.199–201)

Dolabella is a man who's tangled in Cleopatra's 'toil', whose new 'religion' is obedience to her 'pleasure'. And he knows exactly what he's doing:

> Make your best use of this. (5.2.202)

From now on Dolabella will play at 'Roman thought[s]'– 'I must attend on Caesar' (5.2.205) – but he'll perform Egyptian business. His beguiled 'Sir' will never penetrate his deception. It's Dolabella, ironically, who will be assigned, in the last lines of the play, in the play's final memorial turn, to arrange the funerals of Antony and Cleopatra ('Come, Dolabella, see / High order in this great solemnity', 5.2.364–365). Caesar thinks he's consigning Antony and Cleopatra to a grave and to history. But spectators realise that no grave will bury these lovers. Their grave is going to be a site of play, infinite play, 'play till doomsday' (5.2.231).

What, then, do these two epitomes give us? A play whose discursive business is to 'approve[ ] the common liar'. A play whose performative business is the same, continuously rolling out scenes 'Of excellent dissembling' that 'look / Like perfect honour' – but dissemble nevertheless (1.3.80–81). To borrow from *Macbeth*, it's a play in speech and act that 'lies like truth' (5.5.44). A play that constantly wrong-foots itself.

It is this last quality, I think, that most challenges *Antony and Cleopatra* in performance. How do you play a play that stages epic history but subjects it to a hard-boiled running revisionist commentary, that maps out a global structure but fills it with content that is frankly farcical? How do you play mythic figures like Antony, Cleopatra and Caesar, daunting enough if it were only their iconic celebrity to take on, but here selves constituted (also) of their opposites? As Cleopatra says of Antony, 'one way' he's 'painted ... like a Gorgon', 'The other way's a Mars' (2.5.116–117). So, too, Cleopatra. One way she's 'Rare', the other 'riggish' (2.2.228, 250). And Caesar. 'Sole sir o'th' world' one way, the other, puny, priggish 'boy' (5.2.119, 4.1.1).

The aim of this book is to see how performance has responded to the challenge Shakespeare issues in *Antony and Cleopatra*, beginning with an opening chapter that attempts to locate the play in its original Jacobean moment. In the chapters that follow, taking for granted that Shakespeare's plays 'mean' in performance, indeed, *only* but never *finally* 'mean' in performance, and that his plays are material for continuous cultural self-fashioning, each generation seeing itself in Shakespeare so that his plays (as Hamlet puts it) really do show 'the very age and body of the time' its 'form and pressure' (3.2.23–24), I will examine productions across four hundred years to see what meanings, what fashionings, have emerged as *Antony and Cleopatra* has been re-imagined by actors, directors and designers, and staged for new audiences bringing new eyes to its performance.

It's a performance history that begins as if mimicking its characteristic trope. It begins, that is, with theatrical wrong-footing, for after its first Jacobean performances, the play appears to have dropped off the stage for a century and a half. There is no record (except for six disastrous performances by David Garrick in 1759) of Shakespeare's play in the theatre until 1849, and then only in radically cut and rearranged versions. The Restoration didn't know what to make of *Antony and Cleopatra*. They performed John Dryden's *All for Love* instead, and as late as the 1830s what passed for *Antony and Cleopatra* was actually a mash-up of Dryden's play and Shakespeare's. If the Victorian theatre used Shakespeare's text, it used it as a pretext for staging its own imperialist fascination with Egyptology, archaeology and antiquarianism, played out with casts of hundreds and a text adapted to accommodate scene changes that made lavishly illusionist settings the background to glittering processions, 'authentic' Bacchic rituals, oriental ballets, projections of dissolving Sphinxes and, most sensationally, the arrival of Cleopatra and her lover on her barge, a stage history that peaked with Lillie Langtry's Cleopatra in 1890 and had run its course by the time of Beerbohm Tree's 'play pictorial' staging in 1906 (Hodgdon 2002). It wasn't until the 1920s when the writings of Harley Granville-Barker – in his *Prefaces* – took hold of directors like William Bridges-Adams at the Memorial Theatre in Stratford-upon-Avon (ironically abetted by austerity measures thrust onto the cultural industries by the Great Depression) that something very like the play Shakespeare wrote returned to the theatre.

This eventful history from Dryden to Bridges-Adams has been accounted for elsewhere and admirably in Richard Madelaine's *Antony and Cleopatra* (1998) and Barbara Hodgdon's *The Shakespeare Trade* (1998) and will only briefly be recapitulated here.[3] For my purposes, the modern history of *Antony and Cleopatra* in performance, which is also a history of its earlier histories partly remembered, not least (as we will see) in traces such as Cleopatra's 'authentic' red hair and costumes after Veronese or Tutankhamun, begins in 1953, at the Memorial Theatre in Stratford, directed by Glen Byam Shaw with Peggy Ashcroft as Cleopatra, Michael Redgrave as Antony and Marius Goring as Caesar.

Before turning to *Antony and Cleopatra* in performance, however, I want to use this Introduction to tease out from Shakespeare's writing a little more of the quality he builds into the theatrical DNA of the play, what I'm calling 'wrong-footing', to instance more of how this play operates as a theatre machine. *Antony and Cleopatra* gives every director, designer and company of actors who tackle it the same set of challenges to negotiate (and opportunities to explore). In the chapters that follow, we will see them working these challenges out, making decisions that make their production's meanings. Here, I want to anticipate their struggles under four headings: dramatic structure; scenic writing; characters and casting; and six deaths.

**Dramatic structure**

In or about 1606, the third year of James I's reign (King James having Caesarean aspirations, styling himself at his coronation the 'new Augustus')[4], Shakespeare returned to Plutarch's *Lives of the Noble Greeks and Romans* to write a sequel to *Julius Caesar*

(1599), to follow the story after Philippi, to see how the triumvirate who'd so efficiently mopped up the bloodbath of Caesar's assassination, who'd picked off enemies and routed the conspirators, managed the peace (North, 1579). That play fell neatly into two halves, 'jaw-jaw' and 'war-war', set tidily in two locations: a play built on handsome symmetries, with two murders (one at the hands of the politically motivated republican conspirators, the other, of the mindless mob), two funeral orations (the first, settling Rome, the second, rabble-rousing it to bloody mutiny), two hauntings (the eerie grave-opening storm in the first half echoed by the tent-apparition scene in the second); a formal play where characters spoke textbook oratory ('It must be by his death'; 'Friends, Romans, countrymen', 2.1.10, 3.2.74).

The sequel was altogether less measured. Indeed, 'measure' was in its iconoclastic sights from the play's opening speech.

From 'The Life of Marcus Antonius' Shakespeare wrote a play that both used (sometimes word for word) and confounded Plutarch's history, particularly Plutarch's view of Cleopatra (North 1579, 1009). It's almost as if Shakespeare, following Plutarch, applied the notion of the 'parallel life' to Antony himself, writing two Antonies – the Roman, the Egyptian – and a double life for him in the play, one authored squarely Roman, the other promiscuously Alexandrian. Taking the events of some dozen years sprawled across the 'ranged empire' (1.1.35), Shakespeare made no concessions to the map but framed the action in a narrative seemingly condensed to a few rushed days, employing a kind of time-lapse technique to synchronise two clocks, the one trying breathlessly to keep up with Roman imperial ambitions, the other slowed to the indolent half-pace of Alexandrian doldrums. In the Roman scenes of the first three acts, the play travels across time and space from Alexandria to Rome to Parthia, Misenum and Athens and back again. It brings the triple pillars of the world (Caesar, Antony, Lepidus) to a summit meeting, negotiates factions into alliance, spends a gaudy night in *Boy's Own* drunkenness on Pompey's galley, makes a political marriage (and wrecks it), then summarily disposes of allies and wife and liquidates rivals. Meanwhile, in intercutting scenes, it returns the focus three times to Alexandria to play out, as it were frame by frame, one slow-motion sequence in Egypt's quotidian domestic history that sees the notoriously unmarried queen taking the news of her just-widowed lover's remarriage.

Even as Shakespeare constructs a world 'past the size of dreaming' in *Antony and Cleopatra* he cuts it down to size (5.2.96). In Act 3, the epic battle that changed the course of Western history – Actium – is heard as dulled 'noises off'. (What spectators see staged as its proxy is an unseemly squabble about whether Cleopatra should lead her troops or not, which ends in a smutty joke.) The love affair whose 'bourn', it's said in Act 1, 'needs find out new heaven, new earth' shows itself first in scenes of maddening taunts and teases, then in increasingly sour, savage wrangles (1.1.16–17). (Antony finds the mood-swinging Cleopatra 'Whom everything becomes – to chide, to laugh, / To weep' fascinating in Act 1 (1.1. 50–51). In Act 3 such 'becoming' makes her a 'boggler' (3.13.115).) The 'death of the hero' moment that tragedy looks to for its generic culmination – compare *Julius Caesar* – is a botched farce made more grotesque when Antony's trussed-up body is raised cack-handedly into Cleopatra's monument, and it comes, anti-climactically, long before the end. Wrong-footing on a grand scale.

And then, structurally, in Act 5 Shakespeare does something extraordinary. He hands the play to Cleopatra. Reacting to Plutarch, who disposes of Cleopatra in a few paragraphs – 'Her death was very sodain' (North 1579, 1009) – he writes a final scene of some 430 lines, nothing remotely approaching it earlier in the play, a scene that never takes the focus off the queen and that manages, pushing relentlessly towards the inevitable ending that history records, to dice with an alternative ending. Astonishingly, he makes 'What is Cleopatra going to do?' the suspenseful question of the play's last act, audaciously keeping the dramatic tension strung to breaking point as he, the playwright, looks set to wrong-foot history: to tell the historian Plutarch, 'you lie!' In 4.15, her Antony a bloody corpse dead in her lap, she seems resolved to follow him, indeed, to 'rush' after him 'into the secret house of death', to do 'what's brave, what's noble' 'after the high Roman fashion' and make 'the briefest end' (lines 85–95, *passim*). But then she tarries. Meets Caesar. Presents her household accounts. Household accounts that appear to provide for a future very much alive.

Every production of *Antony and Cleopatra* is going to have to decide how to manage its emotional switchbacks and peripatetic moves, how to characterise location for instant legibility, how to negotiate the kind of kaleidoscopic scenic intercutting Shakespeare writes as continuous action in Acts 3 and 4 (given in modern textual editions as twenty-eight scenes, some of them only four lines long), how to place its sequences that arrest the action with story telling ('I will tell you. / The barge ...', 2.2.200–201), and how to stage its big 'production number', including taking a line on what that 'number' is showing. Shakespeare writes at least one such information-dense scene into every play: Capulet's ball in *Romeo and Juliet*; the sheep shearing in *The Winter's Tale*; the wedding masque in *The Tempest*; the apparitions and show of kings in *Macbeth*; the storm in *Julius Caesar* that anticipates 'Blow winds and crack your cheeks!' in *Lear* (3.2.1).[5] Here, the big 'number' is set on Pompey's galley in 2.7. Exclusively male, exclusively Roman, it's meant to be a feast celebrating a pan-peninsular alliance. But it plays out the ruptures that will shred it. From one angle there's the politic treachery that Menas proposes to Pompey, having the triumvirate at his disposal, to 'cut the cable', set the galley adrift, then 'fall to their throats' (lines 72–73). From another, there's the distraction, played out in front of our eyes, of the kind of voluptuary pleasure imported from Egypt that unmakes Romans and corrupts their duty. The lads invite a woman on board. Absent Cleopatra is located in the scene via her proxy, the 'strange serpent' the crocodile, who, like the queen, can be known only by reference to itself, 'shaped ... like itself' (lines 42, 49). Her absence tropes the action on the ship. As the drinking 'ripens towards' 'an Alexandrian feast', and men, told to 'Be a child o'th' time', raucously belt out a tune ('battery to our ears') to 'Plumpy Bacchus' while they 'dance ... the Egyptian Bacchanals', we see Romans travestied in a 'wild disguise' that, says Caesar, 'almost / Anticked us all' (lines 96–125, *passim*). Most of the Romans will survive this 'levity' with a bad hangover. The triumvirate won't. The scene spells out the 'pleasure' that 'lies' 'I'th' East' for Antony – and anticipates his Egyptian return (2.3.39).

## Scenic writing

Playwriting on this scale defeated eighteenth-century neoclassical decorum and nineteenth-century scenic illusionism (and as I've suggested, continues to challenge textual editors, including those of the First Folio, who simply gave up on its scenic arrangement one scene in). The Globe's open platform stage could take the traffic. At the Globe, play was continuous and scenes changed with actors' entrances: 'Welcome to Rome' (2.2.29). Indeed, that stage might have been purpose-built for the particular kind of scenic writing Shakespeare does in *Antony and Cleopatra* to set up a viewing economy that enacts dramaturgic wrong-footing: scenes built on the principle of looking twice, of seeing double.

We can see the strategy in action from the opening lines of the play. Shakespeare frames the scene to be viewed first with narrowed Roman eyes in tight close-up on two men. Philo is grousing to Demetrius who, evidently hot-foot from Rome, will shortly be staggered when Rome's messages are fobbed off. For the veteran Philo, this tour of duty in Alexandria has robbed Romans of their manhood. Egypt has 'turned' their general. They've lost him, once Mars, to 'dotage' and 'a gipsy'. 'Look where they come!' he urges, preparing Demetrius to look like a Roman, to see Antony, the 'triple pillar of the world', 'transformed / Into a strumpet's fool' (1.1.1, 10–13). But what do spectators see? Confirmation of Philo's disgust? The entrance of a debauched Alexandria? Shakespeare's Folio stage direction wants Cleopatra to enter '*with Eunuchs fanning her*' (through line numbering (TLN) 15–16).[6] How did the early modern theatre *do* eunuchs? What erotic culture, what pleasures or dangers are they there to signify? Or does this entrance put in view a vibrant, colourful circus that confounds Philo's sour disapproval in the fun it has staging and mocking its own hyperboles ('Let Rome in Tiber melt'; 'Excellent falsehood!', lines 34, 41)? With Antony and Cleopatra now in front of us, spectators are invited to look, wide-angle, with Alexandrian eyes. From the Alexandrian point of view, the point of view of revelry and sensuous indulgence, 'News ... from Rome' 'Grates' (lines 18–19). Politics are tedious, the empire no more than 'dungy earth', and Caesar a tetchy nag (line 36). Is this disdain magnificent? Or is it folly on a breathtaking scale? Where are Philo and Demetrius? They're watching. But from what angle? And what is their watching doing? How are spectators reading their silent faces? A mere fifty lines later, Alexandria exits and the scenic aperture closes down again. The scene ends once again in close-up on troubled Roman eyes.

This is just the first of many scenes written like this. In 2.2 the Roman generals stage their summit. They reach their politically expedient agreements and conclude a marriage to make them brothers. Job done. But shortly thereafter, the top brass exits leaving the subalterns centre stage. They remember an earlier summit meeting, when a Roman who thought he was the star of the imperial show, instead of being attended obsequiously by the local client queen, sat 'Enthroned i'th' market-place, ... alone, / Whistling to th'air'; then, 'barbered ten times o'er', went to a feast where 'for his ordinary' he paid 'his heart / For what his eyes eat only' (2.2.225–236, *passim*). Enobarbus's tale of Cydnus brings Egypt to Rome, makes Maecenas and Agrippa, hanging on every word, look with Egyptian eyes and situates for them a radical reassessment of what's just been transacted. The Roman deal newly brokered and sealed with Octavia's chaste body and with rehabilitated Antony's promise to keep 'my square' (2.3.6)? A mirage. Antony 'leave' Cleopatra 'utterly'? 'Never! He will not' (2.2.243–244). So much for 'Roman thought[s]'.

Most of these scenes of double viewing are set up to reframe the spectator's point of view, to offer another way of looking at things, such as the opening of 2.7, fifteen lines exchanged by two of Pompey's servants, true-bred Romans to their bootstraps, lines that act as curtain-raiser to the riotous night of reeling drunkenness to come. To be falling-down drunk, they say (as Lepidus is), if you're a great man (as Lepidus is supposed to be), is contemptible. You've been 'called into a huge sphere', but drunk, you're helpless 'to be seen to move in't'. That's like having 'holes where eyes should be', holes 'which pitifully disaster the cheeks' (lines 14–16). So much for drunkenness. So much for Alexandrian revels.

But some scenes are written so opaquely that they defy single meaning. In these scenes, games are being played, but it's hard to fathom exactly who's playing what to whom, with no help from the playwright's enigmatic non-disclosures. I offer three examples.

In 2.2 Agrippa stunningly proposes the marriage with Octavia, a marriage that he says will 'knit' the disaffected generals as 'brothers' with 'an unslipping knot'. Surely, even if this is a 'studied' thought, it's 'study' above Agrippa's pay grade (lines 133–134, 145). Surely he wouldn't spring it on Caesar mid-summit. Would he? (These are the kinds of 'surelies' that actors ponder in rehearsal.) The Caesar whom spectators have seen so far is always fully briefed. It's almost a joke: Caesar always has at hand the self-justifying 'writings' that show 'How hardly' he is 'drawn' into this move or that (5.1.76, 74). So have Caesar and his lieutenant worked out this scheme ahead of time? Caesar's wishful thinking, 'Yet if I knew / What hoop should hold us staunch ...', sounds like a rehearsed cue to Agrippa's naming the 'hoop' (2.2.121–122). But then, what's Caesar's aim? Is he cynically using his sister to bait a trap? Later, he'll reveal that he has 'eyes' in Antony's household, knows Antony's thoughts before he thinks them, 'his affairs' being brought to Caesar 'on the wind' (3.6.63–64). Is Octavia acceptable collateral damage en route to world domination? But then, if Agrippa's intentions are honourable, if he's sincere about the recuperative chances of this marriage, why is he the one voyeuristically lapping up Enobarbus's tale of Cydnus that follows after Antony has exited to meet his bride? Why is he the one ratcheting up the tale's salaciousness? 'O, rare for Antony!'; 'Rare Egyptian!'; 'Royal wench!' are all Agrippa's interventions, and he doesn't turn a hair when Maecenas's tight-lipped 'Now Antony must leave her utterly' is answered with Enobarbus's 'Never! He will not' (lines 215, 228, 236, 243–244).

In 3.12 comes another opaque scene. Thidias, on embassy from Caesar to Cleopatra, has been instructed to fake the part of ambassador, to corrupt her:

> From Antony win Cleopatra; promise,
> And in our name, what she requires; add more,
> From thine invention, offers. Women are not
> In their best fortunes strong, but want will perjure
> The ne'er-touch'd vestal. (3.12.27–31)

In 3.13, Enobarbus is on hand to hear Thidias do his message, to hear him give Cleopatra the constructively hypocritical diplomatic means to save her life by betraying Antony's, conveyed in the subtext of Caesar's message (which message is wholly invented by Thidias) that Caesar 'knows that you embrace not Antony / As you did love, but as you feared him' (3.13.59–60). Enobarbus is there to hear her answer: 'Oh' (Folio, TLN 2220). And then to hear her elaborate:

> He is a god and knows
> What is most right. Mine honour was not yielded,
> But conquered merely. (3.13.63–65)

Enobarbus sees the scene with Roman eyes, sees Cleopatra packing cards with Caesar, sees, that is, the scene that Caesar-the-misogynist scripted presumptively, a scene of weak female perfidy, in which Cleopatra's 'want', strung along with promises, will naturally be duped into treachery (3.12.30) – a scene Enobarbus needs to put a stop to. He exits, returns with Antony, then stands by grimly satisfied while Thidias is dragged off for flogging and Cleopatra is savaged: 'You have been a boggler ever'; 'I found you as a morsel, cold upon / Dead Caesar's trencher ...' (3.13.115, 121–122). But is Enobarbus's looking right? Is Cleopatra Caesar's stooge? Or is another scene being played here, one that Cleopatra is instantly improvising, cued by 'Oh' and the grotesque extravagance of 'He is a god', which makes Thidias a bit-player in Cleopatra's political carry-on? 'Oh' is uninterpretable until it's voiced. 'Oh' can make this a scene of devastating consciencelessness – or excellent dissembling. The rhetorical move that sums up this scene is 'Not know me yet?' (line 162). The question is put to Antony – and wrong-foots him. He doesn't answer. Perhaps he can't. But neither can spectators.

Finally, mid-way through 5.2, Seleucus, Cleopatra's treasurer, is summoned to hand over the inventory of her possessions to conquering Caesar and to audit her accounts – which Seleucus tells the Roman she's falsified. She has 'kept back', he says, 'Enough to purchase what [she has] made known' (lines 146–147). The queen flies into a rage, attacks the 'Soulless villain', protests that only 'lady trifles' have escaped the inventory, and rails against 'ingratitude' (lines 156, 164, 152). Caesar laughs off the deception. Indeed, he approves her 'wisdom in the deed', and in a grand gesture that appears to acknowledge that she's going to be needing her cash, he hands back to Cleopatra both what's been counted *and* what's been concealed: 'Still be't yours', for 'Caesar's no merchant to make prize with you / Of things that merchants sold' (lines 180, 183–184). So who's deceiving whom in this scene? Seleucus his mistress, exposing Cleopatra's fraud? Cleopatra dead Antony, hiding a hoard she'll use to bankroll a future in a new Roman settlement? Or Cleopatra Caesar (in collusion with her treasurer?) in the materialist currency Caesar understands, presenting a faked inventory to make it look as though she intends to live, so to buy herself time to arrange to die? Certainly, Caesar is lying. 'Still be't yours'? That's a sop to fool her trust. (When news in real history of Cleopatra's capture reached Rome, bank interest rates plummeted eight points to 4 per cent. Romans knew Caesar had every intention of despoiling Egypt, and that the spoils would enrich Rome.[7]) The dazzlingly tangled wrong-footings of this scene give spectators a Seleucus who's either a time-pleaser or selflessly faithful (and prepared to take a real beating to authenticate a scene of 'excellent dissembling'); a Caesar who's statesmanlike or a sleazy con-man; Cleopatra, a self-dramatising diva triple turned whore or a savvy politician, out-manoeuvring Caesar every step of the way by covering her tracks.

## Characters and casting

There's no one way of looking at such scenes in *Antony and Cleopatra*, or at the characters they portray: myths who 'inhabit "real" bodies' that in the act of performance 'demystify the myths they construct' (Hodgdon 2002, 245). And it's not just the super-sized characters from history who trail the kind of notoriety that makes every subsequent celebrity couple a 'squeaking' mini-version of their full-throated passion (5.2.219). For actors and directors trying to measure up to them, so too do the parts Shakespeare wrote. Their citational past – not just in previous productions of Shakespeare's play but in high, mass, alternative and counter-cultural representations in theatre, painting, opera, film, marketing – has loaded them with a vast baggage of expectation. Antony and Cleopatra are figures of history, but also of fantasy. Through them we explore not just events, world-shattering as they were, at the centre of the known world on the eve of that other world re-ordering event which the play declares 'is near', the 'time of universal peace' figured not just in Caesar's *pax Romana* but in the birth of Christ (4.6.5). We also use them to map our own psychic and erotic imaginaries. They are our 'play' space to experiment with power, politics, gender, glamour, grunge; iconoclasm, monstrosity, conformity; death. Where can we find actors to play them? One reviewer of the 1953 *Antony and Cleopatra* thought Shakespeare wrote 'the parts of the two lovers for the express purpose of ruining histrionic reputations' (*The Times*, 29 April 1953). Another, calling Cleopatra 'the sum and perfection of all that men, in their worst moments, have reckoned perfection in women', concluded that the part was 'almost unplayable by mortal woman' (*Birmingham Dispatch*, 29 April 1953). Laurence Olivier called Antony an 'absolute twerp' (1986, 162) while Glen Byam Shaw's initial character note on the part states simply 'This man is great' (1944).[8]

It's not just that these roles, as I've suggested, are anamorphs, the 'gipsy' who's also the 'lass unparalleled', the 'Mars', the 'man of men' who's also a sottish buffoon (1.1.10, 5.2.315, 1.1.4, 1.5.75). It's that they are also so many things in between. John Styan, writing about the 'endless possibilities' of Shakespeare's characters, long ago taught us to 'speak of the "parameter" of a part and the "tolerance" of a performance' (1979, 137). In *Antony and Cleopatra*, these are huge.

As Byam Shaw (NB 1944) saw him, Caesar, who appears in fourteen of the play's forty-three scenes, is the character who 'develops throughout the play more than any other' (but perhaps along a relentlessly single-minded line). He's a man the audience should find 'absorbing' as they watch him 'ruthlessly cutting his way through life, with all the intelligence, egotism, cunning and capacity for work' that mark the 'brilliance of his nature'. Work: that's his ethic. It's what marks him as so completely unlike Antony. Caesar's executive efficiency is staggeringly impressive. (Witness the incredible speed of his march into Egypt.) His success is magnetic. (Witness all the followers of Antony who revolt to Caesar. Clearly, in the political play *Antony and Cleopatra*, Caesar is man of the match.) More than a politician, he's a bureaucrat. Note his attention to dispatches, to paper trails, to sound bites. His face, Byam Shaw thought, should have a 'mask-like quality': the face of a poker player? And 'when he smiles one feels it comes from the brain & not the heart'. Caesar is never more opaque than when he's brokering his sister's marriage; never more foolish than when he's po-facedly resisting inebriation on Pompey's galley; never more attractive than when he's bidding Octavia tenderly farewell (and listening to whatever it is she needs to whisper in his ear); never more despicable than when, giving battle orders, he tells Agrippa to plant the soldiers revolted from Antony 'in the van', so that, attacking, Antony will have to kill his own men before he gets to Caesar's, will have 'to spend his fury / Upon himself': an order the revolted Enobarbus is on hand to hear (4.6.9–11).

If Caesar's part walks a straight line, Antony's rides a roller-coaster. He's first and foremost the soldier Caesar never has been, never will be; the kind of commander, Byam Shaw thought, who is loved by his men but the despair of the generals. Is going AWOL in Egypt just the most triumphant move he could make, the man of war staking his future life on love? Or is he a 'doting mallard' stupidly pursuing his hen on heat (3.10.20)? John Dryden subtitled his play *All for Love* 'or The World Well Lost'. Shakespeare's play keeps the betting open. We never get to see Antony in action. We see him hearing Caesar's refusal of single combat. (Caesar's no fool. Match himself against 'a sworder', even if the 'old ruffian' is twice his age (3.13.31, 4.1.4)? No chance.) We see Antony arm: an endearing 'domestic' scene, 4.4, that has Mars squired by Venus, Cleopatra turning bits of kit this way and that to see how they might fit on the soldier's body. But we never see him practising the 'royal occupation' that made his name (4.4.17). Instead we see him in scenes where he's bamboozled by politics: in the heavily freighted messages from Rome he finally hears in 1.2; in the summit (2.2) that has him contracting a Roman marriage he avows (in 2.3.1–9) and, in the same scene, *dis*avows (2.3.10–41). Just as Shakespeare never gives us Antony the soldier, so he never gives us Antony the lover. There are no scenes of intimacy between Antony and Cleopatra in *Antony and Cleopatra*. Like the Battle of Actium, the love affair is heard as 'noises off'. The first character note struck in the play's opening line by Philo's devastating 'Nay, but this dotage of our general's ....' serves to wrong-foot the lovers' huge passion. Dotage. Youngsters in love may dote, like Romeo doting on Rosaline before he meets Juliet (2.3.81) or Helena on that 'spotted and inconstant man', Demetrius, in *A Midsummer Night's Dream*: she 'dotes, / Devoutly dotes, dotes in idolatry' (1.1.108–109).[9] But the infatuations of youth that transform young lovers literally into fools can be indulged, generically 'corrected' by comedy. Age hardens attitudes towards 'dotage'. At Antony's age dotage looks grotesque, like pantaloonish delinquency, fumbling senility, or something worse, as Hector in *Troilus and Cressida* makes it, calculating the cost of 'keeping' another of history's infamous sirens:

> 'Tis mad idolatry
> To make the service greater than the god;
> And the will dotes that is inclinable
> To what infectiously itself affects,
> Without some image of th'affected merit. (2.2.56–60)[10]

'Affect'-ing Cleopatra, as the Trojans and Greeks 'affect' Helen, is Antony infected? In Cleopatra, is there any 'image' of 'merit' that would justify his 'service'? Is the rout at Actium a replay of the fall of Troy? Or in calling Antony's 'affection' 'dotage' is the Roman Philo massively wrong? Is it possible that in this latest rewrite of the soldier-turned-lover, Shakespeare in Antony is redefining masculinity, re-imagining epic achievement, locating it in a rejection of imperial conquest, finding it in a 'bourn' shrunk to the 'space' found 'here', in the beloved's body (1.1.16, 35)? If so, is Antony less the political has-been shoved aside by younger men whose enterprise is 'dungy earth', more the grizzled adventurer feeling his way across a landscape to 'find out new heaven, new earth' (1.1.36, 17)? As with so many other questions this play throws up, answers will be found in performance.

But if Shakespeare gives Antony scenes neither of love-making nor of war-making, what he does give this man who's perhaps the only character in the play totally without guile is scenes that register Antony wholly, unequivocally in the moment: deep-drinking on Pompey's galley (2.7); self-loathing after Actium (3.11); in mad rages (like his Herculean avatar) savaging Cleopatra one moment, embracing her the next (3.13); betrayed, as he thinks by Cleopatra (but really out-manoeuvred by Caesar's shrewd tactics), sitting in a moment of rare self-reflection, with his squire, the aptly named Eros, staring up at the sky watching the clouds make shapes – dragon, bear, lion – that 'thought' instantly 'dislimns', and analogising himself to the clouds: 'Here I am Antony, / Yet cannot hold this visible shape' (4.14.10, 13–14); then, hearing of Cleopatra's death, instantly capitulating from fury to heartbreak: 'Unarm, Eros. The long day's task is done … / Off! Pluck off! / The sevenfold shield of Ajax cannot keep / The battery from my heart' (4.14.35, 38–40).

It is, of course, the part of Cleopatra that marks this play's greatest distance from its prequel, *Julius Caesar*. In Cleopatra, history has to take on her-story. The initial actor's note must be, for starters, 'infinite variety' (2.2.246): gipsy, royal Egypt, boggler, eastern star. The key to this 'variety' is a self that is constituted of performances played to a rolling cast of spectators; a self, then, fundamentally unknowable? The grand theatre of Cydnus defers to fringe performances like the pleb-queen hopping forty paces through a public street, which defers to domestic farces such as the time she drank Antony to his bed, dressed him in her 'tires and mantels' (2.5.22) and strapped on (to her naked body?) his sword Philippan, or histrionic dramas such the farewell in 1.3 that has her out-Proteusing Proteus even as she accuses Antony of 'excellent dissembling': 'play one scene'; 'You can do better yet'; 'Look … / How this Herculean Roman does become / The carriage of his chafe' (1.3.79–86, *passim*). That word 'become' is, of course, Cleopatra's character signature, she, the woman in scene 1 whom 'everything becomes' (line 50), whose 'becomings' grow increasingly troubling to the political destinies of Antony and Egypt as they register perpetual motion, shifting-ness, constant inconstancy: the somersaulting and triple turning that defines (in Roman minds) the whore. Only in the final hundred lines of the play does Cleopatra's dazzling restlessness 'become' 'marble-constant' by 'becoming' her final form, queen ('Give me my robe. Put on my crown'); wife ('Husband, I come!'); and – Shakespeare's invention upon Plutarch – mother suckling the serpent which, like Cleopatra, *is* Egypt ('Peace, peace! / Dost thou not see my baby at my breast / That sucks the nurse asleep?', 5.2.239–309, *passim*). In this final form she re-imagines a triumvirate, a paradoxically female triumvirate, to mock Rome's, its feminine knowability decidedly ambiguous. By then of course she's played out her last 'turn', as straight-man to the 'rural fellow' who delivered a bucket of asps and with them reported a woman who, no longer than yesterday, died of 'the worm', its 'biting' being 'immortal'. She was, he said, 'a very honest woman, but something given to lie, as a woman should not do but in the way of honesty' (5.2.232–251, *passim*). In that vignette, the down-market Asp Man might be delivering the pop-cultural parallel to the 'Life of Cleopatra'.

Cleopatra puts in play erotic charge, sensuousness, sexual danger, but also sheer fun: she is the joker in the pack, the comic genius whose anarchy is devastating to Roman high seriousness, the personification of wrong-footing. Like Antony needing an actor who can play both Mars and mallard, who can move from volcanic rage to stunned broken-hearted grief, Cleopatra needs an actor not beautiful (Plutarch makes that point) but fascinating, and one who can move from scintillating temptress to raddled harridan in the space of a half line: 'He's married, madam' (2.5.72). One more point, which I will explore in the following chapter as I think about the Jacobean *Antony and Cleopatra*: Cleopatra is written black. This is an element of the script that has been almost entirely repressed in performance (while continuously represented in proxies), a history of 'whiting out' Cleopatra that can be traced from the Restoration, and here, from 1953; a history tentatively challenged in the UK with productions by Talawa in 1991 and at the Royal Exchange, Manchester, in 2005 (with Doña Croll and Josette Bushell-Mingo as Cleopatra) – while Cleopatras in North America were regularly cast black – before being utterly routed from mainstream theatre in the UK by Tarell Alvin McCraney's 2013 Royal Shakespeare Company (RSC) production. McCraney cast Cleopatra as Shakespeare wrote her, a black gipsy queen, and situated her and Alexandria inside a power struggle oppositional to the colonising forces that would destroy both Egypt – and Egypt.[11]

Writing three 'impossible' roles at the centre of *Antony and Cleopatra*, the playwright does give his players important helps. For one thing, while he keeps his three principals almost continuously present before spectators – they figure in all but eight of forty-three scenes; are off stage only for a mere 265 lines – he writes them from the outside, as 'exteriors'. They are never alone on stage, never made to account for the self's interiority in soliloquies. The only exception might be Antony's nine lines between messengers in 1.2 when he's conscience-stabbed at the news of his wife Fulvia's death – 'There's a great spirit gone! ... / The hand could pluck her back that shoved her on' – a mood of worthiness that Enobarbus minutes later punctures with laughter: '... dead ... dead ...' 'Fulvia?' 'Dead.' 'Why, sir, give the gods a thankful sacrifice' (1.2.129, 134, 163–168). Shakespeare makes these roles sites of performativity, but has their reputations rendered *beyond* performance by others. People constantly talk about each other in *Antony and Cleopatra*. Memorial turns abound. Enobarbus remembers Cleopatra as a tourist destination: 'a wonderful piece of work' which 'left unseen' 'would have discredited [Antony's] travel' (1.2.160–162). Enobarbus remembers Cydnus, a city that emptied itself to stand on the wharfs and gaze on a queen whose description in oxymoronic hyperboles nevertheless 'beggared' her actual self. Antony remembers Philippi when the 'boy' Caesar 'kept / His sword e'en like dancer' (3.11.35–36). Caesar remembers Antony's retreat from Modena, pursued by famine which he endured 'with patience more / Than savages could suffer', drinking the 'stale of horses', eating the 'roughest berry on the rudest hedge', and on the Alps consuming 'strange flesh / Which some did die to look on'; all endured 'so like a soldier that [his] cheek / So much as lanked not' (1.4.61–72, *passim*). Charmian remembers Julius Caesar. A certain Egyptian queen, to get his attention, had herself delivered to him rolled up in a carpet, which story the Romans remember too; as does Cleopatra – but she locates that memory in her 'salad days', when she was 'green in judgement, cold in blood' (1.5.76–77). Now, her memories are of Antony alive ('That time? O times!') and dead ('I dreamt there was an emperor Antony...') (2.5.18, 5.2.75). Such memories may function as reportage. They certainly function in the space of the imaginary, to frame reputations 'past the size of dreaming' – and to appropriate them (5.2.96). Modena 'then' is summoned to mind 'now' to reprove Antony's 'lascivious wassails' (1.4.57); Philippi, to hang on to what once *was* in the face of what now *is*.

Most helpfully, too, the playwright surrounds his principals with another thirty-odd named parts who all 'earn[ ] a place i'th' story' by giving perspectives on the main players (3.13.47). Enobarbus, built from just a name-check in Plutarch, the hard-bitten antidote to hyperbole and myth-making (so just the right rememberer of Cydnus), able to talk straight to both Antony and Cleopatra. He finally follows his head, abandons Antony and dies of a broken heart. Eros, Antony's squire (or, in a later war, his batman), who never leaves his master's service and plunges the sword Philippan into his own gut rather than Antony's. Ventidius, still on active duty (while Enobarbus appears to have traded in his combat boots for sandals), sent to Parthia on the mega-campaign that's supposed to be Antony's military business, where he's to proxy his general (and knows to take no credit for victory). The Soothsayer, a human stand-in for Antony's conscience. Antony's Schoolmaster, kept in his retinue as perhaps some kind of placeholder for childhood or bookishness, sent in sign of humility (or humiliation, the Romans think) as Antony's ambassador to Caesar in 3.12, a man 'of late as petty to his ends / As is the morn-dew on the myrtle leaf / To his grand sea' (3.12.8–10). Iras and Charmian: Cleopatra's 'girls', constantly in attendance, monitoring her performances, anchoring her volatility, writing her notices on their faces and visually composing the female triumvir before, fixing Cleopatra in her final form, she solely becomes it. Humouring. Needling. Talking of figs and male inches. Raunchy. Reverential. At the last, making defect perfection: 'Your crown's awry', says Charmian to her dead mistress. 'I'll mend it, and then play' (5.2.317–318). Her final words, however, wonderfully wrong-foot reverence. They flip the rare back to the riggish: 'Ah, soldier!' (5.2.327).

### Six deaths: tragedy becoming comedy

This play starts killing off its players long before the end. Fulvia is reported dead in 1.2; the corpse of Pacorus, heir to Parthian Orodes, is hauled off as victor's trophy in 3.1; the execution of Lepidus (by Caesar, on trumped-up charges) and the assassination of Pompey (by one of Antony's officers) are noticed in passing in 3.5 (as Antony walks in his garden furiously kicking the grass 'that lies before him', line 17); in 4.6, Enobarbus reports the 'pains' Alexas-the-turncoat took to ingratiate himself to his Caesar – which only got him hanged by this new master who's even now putting in his front lines the other men who've capitulated to him from Antony (4.6.15).

From 4.9, report turns to enactment, and the astonishing achievement of the last great arc of *Antony and Cleopatra* is not simply that Shakespeare writes six deaths and makes them uniquely significant from Enobarbus's last words 'O Antony!' to Charmian's 'Ah, soldier!' but that, by the time the final one comes, he has made us rethink death so thoroughly as to redefine genre (4.9.26, 5.2.327). In the final act, *Antony and Cleopatra* has more in common with *The Merchant of Venice* than with *King Lear*.

Leaving 4.6 'alone the villain of the earth' and seeking 'Some ditch wherein to die' (lines 31, 39), Enobarbus stands observed by sentries in 4.9 invoking the moon as 'mistress of true melancholy', wanting her to 'Throw my heart / Against the flint and hardness of my fault, / Which, being dried with grief, will break to powder / And finish all foul thoughts' (lines 15, 18–21). Antony leaves 4.12 like Hercules, 'The shirt of Nessus is upon me' (line 43). He enters 4.14 like Pliny reading natural philosophy in the clouds. These two deaths come closest to articulating the tragic in this play. Tragedy in *Antony and Cleopatra* is not loss of life, but loss of self, an Enobarbus 'infamous' in 'revolt', an Antony who 'cannot hold this visible shape' (4.9.22, 4.14.14). Antony may bring Eros to tears reminding him of his oath to 'Do't'; 'kill me'; 'The time is come'; and pushing on the death blow by imagining a scene, 'windowed in great Rome', himself led in triumph 'with pleached arms' and 'corrigible neck' 'bending down' (4.14.68, 73–74). If spectators are going to weep, this is where their tears are likely to fall. But then the mood swings. In a classic comic turn of events, the sworn servant spectacularly wrong-foots the master. Eros falls on the sword himself, dying for love. Antony has to cast about for a method to kill himself, follows the heroic pattern Eros has set, then discovers he's botched it. Shortly thereafter comes news that Cleopatra isn't dead. What response can there be but laughter? This is death as farce, and the logistics of the dying body hauled ingloriously up into the monument make that a scene of heroic death travestied. That's its point.

For Antony's death is the anti-masque to Cleopatra's last, wondrous performance. Dismissing her Alexandrian Dogberry (the Asp Man is surely Shakespeare's greatest clue to how he's writing Egypt's ending, a gamble, grounding it upon the groundling), Cleopatra begins the ascent to her final becoming. Her death, duping Caesar, is going to be the best of practical jokes. In her last moments of theatrical magic, the drama queen who moments earlier rejected her own medium, the public stage with its 'quick comedians' who can only 'boy' greatness like hers, self-consciously stages the spectacle of her death (5.2.215, 219). Where Antony dressed down for death ('Off! Pluck off!', 4.14.38), Cleopatra dresses up. She dresses to kill: 'Show me, my women, like a queen' (5.2.226). She dresses to re-enact her original seduction of Mark Antony: 'I am again for Cydnus' (line 227). Her jokes are still riggish: as she smuttily tells it, she needs to race after Iras, to overtake the girl who's just died upon her mistress's farewell kiss lest that 'girl' reach 'curled Antony' first and take from him 'that kiss / Which is [Cleopatra's] heaven to have' (5.2.300–302). But the ultimate triumph of her death is political: 'great Caesar' is 'beguiled'. He's proved an 'ass / Unpolicied' (5.2.306–307). Caesar gets the last lines of the play, appropriating the lovers and 'their story' to 'his glory which / Brought them to be lamented' (lines 360–362). But it's Dolabella who gets the last exit – an exit that remembers Cleopatra's last seduction and, in what it knows about how Dolabella has stage managed these 'High events' (line 359), an exit that performs *Antony and Cleopatra*'s final wrong-footing.

## Notes

1 All quotations of *Antony and Cleopatra* throughout this book are from John Wilders's edition of the play in the Arden Shakespeare Third Series (1995).
2 At least one director has read the scene as I am doing. In 1943 Glen Byam Shaw wrote in notes towards a future production that, as Dolabella listens to Cleopatra tell her dream, 'We must feel that he is completely under the spell of C., & that during this little scene he falls in love with her enough to risk his life for her sake.' See Chapter 3.
3 See too Deats (2005), Bevington (2005) and Escolme (2006).
4 See Yachnin (1991).
5 All quotations of *King Lear* are from Foakes 1997.
6 TLN, or through line numbering, was Charlton Hinman's editorial innovation in his Norton Facsimile of *The First Folio of Shakespeare* (1968). Only some of the plays in the 1623 Folio were marked up with act and scene divisions; and then only erratically. Whoever 'edited' the Folio *Antony and Cleopatra* put 'Actus Primus, Scœna Prima' below the title but thereafter marked no scene or act breaks.

Hinman in his facsimile gave every play 'its own through line numbering', starting with the title at 1 and numbering every line, half line, entrance and exit, and stage direction. Thus, writes Thomas L. Berger, 'there now exists ... a convenient system for referring specifically and accurately to a line, a word, or a piece of type in the text' of the Folio (T. Berger 1993, 196). Stage directions that appear in Folio *Antony and Cleopatra* have a particular authority, belonging to the original publication of the play.

7 Quoted from the RSC souvenir programme to Trevor Nunn's *Antony and Cleopatra*, 1972.
8 Unless otherwise indicated, all Shaw quotations are taken from these two sets of manuscript notebooks held by the Shakespeare Birthplace Trust, the 1943 notebooks catalogued as SBT MM/Shaw/6/8 and MM/Shaw/6/11, and the 1944 notebooks catalogued as MM/Shaw/6/2 and MM/Shaw/6/9. They are unpaginated. References in parentheses cite either the 1943 notebooks (NB 1943) or the 1944 notebooks (NB 1944). Transcriptions are my own. Shaw's abbreviations are expanded in square brackets
9 All quotations of *A Midsummer Night's Dream* are from Brooks 1979.
10 All quotations of *Troilus and Cressida* are from Bevington 1998.
11 See Chapters 8 and 9.

# 1

# 'That time? O times!': the Jacobean *Antony and Cleopatra*

One of the stories Shakespeare tells in *Antony and Cleopatra* is a political story of regime change, the *translatio imperii* that marks in geographical terms the progressive shift, historically, of the centre of geo-political and geo-cultural imperial power steadily westwards. Alexandria's fall is Rome's rise. Ordering his lieutenant, 'Go forth, Agrippa, and begin the fight', Caesar is announcing a new global settlement, 'The time of universal peace is near' (4.6.1,5) – prematurely, as it turns out, since, ironically, the battle he orders for 'tomorrow' as 'the last of many' that 'We mean to fight' (4.1.12–13) is one he loses (4.7.1–3).

Telling the past, Shakespeare is, as usual, telling the present. In 1606, the year of *Antony and Cleopatra*, Shakespeare, his playing company, London and the English were adjusting to their own experience of regime change. Indeed, Shakespeare's play, I want to argue, emerged out of the historical and cultural coincidences that forced those adjustments. To remember and recover these coincidences is a necessary work of recuperation, for they are the back-story to what Shakespeare was reading, thinking about, watching, responding to – and surviving – as he engaged in the process of 'wrighting' this play. If they ghost *Antony and Cleopatra* in shapes that can't finally be pinned down (allusive, fleeting, suggestive), they nevertheless remember the play's origins on the Jacobean stage.

First, there was a change in monarch. By 1606 Scottish James had been on the English throne for three years, the noise surrounding his peaceful accession to the throne occupied by English Elizabeth for forty-four years giving him initially 'on all sides' the reputation of 'a man of letters and of business, fond of the chase and of riding, sometimes indulging in play' (*CSPV* X, 22).[1] He was a man of an age with William Shakespeare, Richard Burbage and Robert Armin. (How odd this generational shift must have felt to subjects used to seeing their monarch an old woman.) He was a man with a young, teeming wife (seven pregnancies to date) and young family (three children under eight). A man whose personal loyalties might be interpreted by a playwright as aligning with his own. One of the first actions taken by the new order had been the release from the Tower of men put there by the old regime, co-conspirators who had fallen alongside that 'star of England', Essex, whom the playwright had so recently (and publicly) analogised to both 'conquering Caesar' and Harry, hero of Agincourt (*Henry V*, 5.0.28, 35).

Another change: within days of arriving in London in May 1603, King James, by letters patent and perhaps prompted by the personal patronage of his newest favourite, the young William Herbert, son and heir to the Earl of Pembroke and soon to be created Earl of Montgomery, made the Chamberlain's servants, Shakespeare's playing company, his own, the King's Men.

A week later, the Venetian secretary, writing to the Republic from London, noticed in a dispatch the sudden outbreak of plague in the city. Thereafter, he began noting the rising mortality in postscripts to his weekly dispatches home, from eleven dead in six infected parishes in May to 4,000 a week across all London's parishes in September (*CSPV* X, 55, 132). The playhouses were closed by order of the Privy Council. They would remain dark (barring a couple of weeks in spring 1604) until September 1604 – fifteen months – then again in 1605, throughout February and March and from October to December. Dark playhouses didn't need plays or players. From February 1603, a month before Queen Elizabeth's death (the latest possible date for *Troilus and Cressida*), to a year afterwards, 'Shakespeare may have written no new plays at all' (Barroll 1991, 125). That doesn't mean he wasn't thinking about them, however, absorbing from reading and the world at large ideas that would translate into theatre writing.

While a desperately uncertain future yawned for the players, their nominal 'master' was acting 'as yf this world wold last ever' – and as if he would have the spending of it (McClure 1939, I, 192). While he was King of Scotland, his pinched royal household allowed James Stuart to live only modestly, 'hardly like a private gentleman, let alone a sovereign'. Now, England's wealth beckoned him to adopt 'day by day' 'practices suitable to his greatness' (*CSPV* X, 46), as if he were the Antony Shakespeare would shortly write, able to 'drop from his pocket' titles, estates, pensions, favours, promotions: James granted 700 knighthoods in the first four months of his reign (*CSPV* X, 106), 'bountiful beginnings', wrote John Chamberlain, that raised 'all men's spirits and put them in great hopes, insomuch that not only protestants but papists and puritanes, and the very poets with theyre ydle pamflets promise themselves great part in his favor' (McClure 1939, I, 192). While infection in the city meant that the royal family's official entry into London would have to be postponed until March 1604, the king's coronation was eventually performed on St James's Day, 25 July 1603, in a gorgeous but limited ceremony. A sum of 200,000 francs newly paid by the King of France against a debt owed to England under Elizabeth was appropriated by the crown to bankroll the spectacle – but Londoners were denied the satisfaction of viewing it and told to stay away on account of infection (*CSPV* X, 73). Not insignificantly, but ironically given the measureless profligacy that was fast becoming habitual, James professed to model himself on 'measured' Octavius Caesar (whom Shakespeare in *Antony and Cleopatra* would imagine a finicky heir to *Measure for Measure*'s austere Angelo). Styling himself 'Augustus' presiding over a new empire, 'Britain', King James ordered his coronation medal to be inscribed 'JAC: I: BRIT: CAE: AVG: HAE: CAESARUM CAE.D.D': 'James I, Caesar Augustus of Britain, Caesar the heir of the Caesars' (Yachnin 1991, 1, 4).

Unlike Shakespeare's Octavius, however, the king was no bureaucratic swot. Indeed, his real double would have been Antony. From the first, James was impatient of royal chores. According to some, he set himself up as the 'arbiter of peace' in Europe (achieved with a controversial treaty with Spain in 1604: James negotiating as Octavius – or perhaps as a timorous Lepidus – a *pax romana*) only because he wanted 'to have no bother with other people's affairs and little with his own'. In effect, he handed the government over to Robert Cecil, his Secretary of State (whom he called his 'litle beagle'), while he followed his royal hounds, seeming 'to have almost forgotten that he is a King except in his kingly pursuit of stags, to which he is quite foolishly devoted' (*CSPV* X, 101). His 'dotage' on dogs, to some, 'o'er flowed' any 'measure'.

By December 1603 the appalling death toll in London looked to have abated, and the court, which had been continuously on the move out-running the infection, returned to town. The newly arrived Venetian ambassador, Nicoló Molino, wrote in astonishment that 'No one ever mentions the plague, no more than if it had never been. The City is so full of people that it is hard to believe that about sixty thousand deaths have taken place' (*CSPV* X, 175). On 2 December the King's servants gave a performance of 'one playe' 'before his ma*ies*tie' when 'the courte' was lodged at Wilton, the Earl of Pembroke's house (Chambers 1923, IV, 168). By Christmas, it seemed safe enough to hold the revels at Hampton Court, Shakespeare's company giving six performances between 26 December and 1 January. Still, the playhouses did not reopen. Ambassador Molino's dispatch had been premature. In January, alarm bells were again tolling. The state opening of Parliament intended for March was put on hold. The King's servants were awarded compensation, a 'free gifte' of £30 from his majesty 'for the mayntenance and releife' of the 'company being prohibited to p'sente any playes publiquelie in or neere London by reason of greate perill that might growe through the extraordinary concourse and assemble of people to a newe increase of the plague'. This 'gifte' aimed to keep the King's players 'till it shall please God to settle the cittie in a more p*er*fecte health' (Chambers 1923, IV, 168).

That wouldn't happen until September 1604. For while plague deaths in London remained comparatively low, they were sufficient to trigger closures based on the newly instituted Privy Council mortality rate of thirty fatalities per week. Besides, the plague hadn't gone away; it had simply shifted its ground. It had moved into the shires, ravaging cities, towns and villages. Provincial touring, for the players, wasn't an option.

Meanwhile, the King seemed 'to have sunk into a lethargy of pleasures'; would 'not take any heed of matters of state' except for his personal *translatio imperii*, his pet 'Great Britain project' which aimed 'to extinguish' the names of England and Scotland in a union that would put 'both Kingdoms ... under the one name of Britain' (*CSPV* X, 125, 132). He appeared not to notice the looming financial crisis consequent upon the 'absolute confusion' that had overwhelmed 'all public and private affairs' in a London where, wrote Ambassador Molino, 'No one will pay his debts, as he thinks his creditor must die one day or another'; where 'All orders on merchants have been recalled, all trade is at a standstill'; where 'Taxes, duties, customs bring in not a ducat in the whole City'; and where the 'Treasury is in confusion, without a penny in it' (*CSPV* X, 147). But though his coffers were bare, James's prodigal munificence flowed unstintingly. With Parliament dissolved in July 1604 without having voted the Crown a subsidy, the King applied to the City of London for a loan of 100,000 crowns – and was denied. He then resolved to issue under the Privy Seal bonds for 200,000 crowns in various denominations, to be offered to persons willing personally to advance the crown money. 'It is thought', commented Molino drily of the king finding himself 'in molta strettezza di denari', 'that many will decline' the invitation (*CSPV* X, 261). Secretary Cecil darkly observed of the Spanish treaty finalised that same month that 'Had the Crown not been in straits for money' the 'peace would not have been signed' – and he perhaps despaired at the gifts given to the treaty's commissioners at their departure home to Spain, a diamond worth 6,000 crowns; plate to the tune of 8,000 crowns; and solid gold vases weighing some 1,000 ounces (*CPSV* X, 261, 263). Observers at court must have looked on their king's erratic wilfulness, his fantastic refusal to grasp hard facts, as despondently as Scarus and Canidius would look on Antony's.

In November the finances of this king who was perpetually 'very hard up for money' were so straitened that he was considering farming out the customs and even more radically levying a tax on salt (*CSPV* X, 295). But looming insolvency didn't stop him, that same month, from disbursing £4,000 for 'a great maske' that Queen Anna had 'in hand against Twelftide', the first surviving notice of her designs being John Chamberlain's comment in a letter dated 18 December about a payment made 'a moneth ago' (McClure 1939, I, 198). In December, unquantified provision for 'maskes and revells' on St John's Day was also allowed 'against the mariage of Sir Phillip Harbert and the Lady Susan Vere'; £3,000 given to equip the Duke of Lennox on an ambassage for France and £4,000 as a gift to the Duke of Holst. £15,000 was assigned for expenses (not including 'two of the Kings best shippes to transport him') to Charles Howard, Lord Admiral, to carry the peace treaty into Spain (McClure 1939, I, 198). This was expenditure – magnificent, ruinous

– on a scale to rival Cleopatra's, except without her bottomless treasury to make it good.

For their part (if Leeds Barroll's chronology of this plague period is accurate), the King's servants may have reopened at the Globe in late September 1604. In November (at Hallowmas), December (St Stephen's and Innocents' Nights), January ('Betwin Newyers Day and Twelfe day') and February ('on Shrousunday' then 'againe commanded By the Kings Ma*i*estie' on 'Shroutusday') they appeared at court in seven plays by William Shakespeare, five of them – *The Comedy of Errors*, *The Merry Wives of Windsor*, *Henry V*, *Love's Labour's Lost*, *The Merchant of Venice* – plays that had appeared at the Globe before the plague closure. Two of these plays, however, were new to the autumn Globe repertoire, *Measure for Measure* and (more significant for my purposes) the play that would open the run of performances at Court, *Othello: The Moor of Venice*, staged 'att whithall' 'in the Banketinge house' on 'the first of Nouember' (Chambers 1923, IV, 171).

This packed entertainment schedule would climax with Queen Anna's 'great maske' on Twelfth Night. The masque was a project of Anna's own devising, and it built on the 'creative agenda for self-display' that she'd first put squarely in view a year earlier (Barroll 2001, 74). In Queen Elizabeth's court (and in Shakespeare's plays to date) such 'shows had been associated with men, not women', and with young blades like Romeo, Lorenzo and Benedick, not princes (Barroll 2001, 76). Anna's 1603 *Vision of the Twelve Goddesses* turned convention upside down. Appropriating the masque form, Anna stunningly reconfigured it to her own purposes of shaping a royal identity by putting herself (anticipating Shakespeare's Cleopatra?) and the most powerful women in England who served her at its centre. As Barroll writes, when Anna masqued, 'Royalty was dancing'. And royalty dancing 'raised the masquing stakes dramatically', allowing Anna not just to claim space for herself but to play out in public her personal rule in the symbolic patronage she bestowed upon men she made 'hers' by assigning them to her women as partners in the masque's 'taking out' sequences (Barroll 2001, 88, 87).

In 1603 the wordsmith appointed to write the text introducing the spectacle and linking its parts had been Samuel Daniel. In 1604 Anna commissioned as textual maker Ben Jonson, and put him to work alongside a maker of 'shows', Inigo Jones. It was their first collaboration. The queen's conceit, her brief to her wright-ers, was captured in the preface Jonson wrote to the 350-line printed text of the 'solemnities' of the *Masque of Blackness*:

> Pliny, Solinvs, Ptolemy and of late Leo the *African* remember vnto vs a riuer in *Æthiopia* famous by the name of *Niger*, of which the people were called *Nigritæ*, now Negro's, and are the blackest nation of the world. This riuer taketh spring out of a certain *lake*, east-ward, and after a long race falleth into the westerne Ocean. Hence (because it was her Maiesties will to haue them *Black-mores* at first), the inuention was deriued by me, and presented thus. (Herford and Simpson 1941, 169)

As the masque's conceit has it, the black Daughters of Niger (described in Jonson's note as 'the Masquers ... twelue Nymphs, Negroes' (Herford and Simpson 1941, 170–171)) thought they were beautiful until some 'braine-sick ... *Poets'* told them otherwise (Herford and Simpson 1941, 174). Now they've embarked on their own *translatio imperii*, journeying from east to west in search of 'fairness', which they're told they'll find in a land whose name ends in '*Tania*', whose ruler's 'light scientiall is', a sun-king 'Whose beames shine day and night, and are of force / To blanch an Æthiope' (Herford and Simpson 1941, 177). They discover their king in Britannia's James.

Thus narrated in the scene-setting dialogue between 'Niger' and 'Oceanus', Anna's masquers came forth and danced, performing the main business of the night, first in 'Their owne single dance', then in 'seuerall measures, and coranto's' which they 'danc'd with their men' before retiring to submit (off stage) to a blanching regime (Herford and Simpson 1941, 178). So ended the masque with the daughters of Niger still '*Black-mores*'.

Anna's performance on Twelfth Night caused quite a stir. The cosmopolitan Venetian Molino thought it 'beautiful and sumptuous' (*CSPV* X, 332), impressed perhaps with Inigo Jones's costume designs and, as a Venetian, no doubt familiar with the kind of 'guising' on display here that English eyes found alien. The women (wrote one English observer) were dressed 'strangely' – that is, exotically – 'in Barbaresque mantells to y$^e$ halfe legge' and 'buskins ... sett w$^{th}$ jewells' (Herford and Simpson 1950, 449). They were 'alike, in all', according to Jonson, 'without difference: the colours, *azure* and *siluer*'. Their 'hayre' was 'thicke, and curled vpright in tresses, lyke *Pyramids*', and at 'the front, eare, neck, and waists, the ornament was of the most choise and orient pearle; best setting off from the black' (Herford and Simpson 1941, 171) while in their hands they carried fans that, like their hair, alluded to Egyptian origins, each inscribed with 'a mute Hieroglyphick' chosen, wrote Jonson, as 'applying to that originall doctrine of sculpture which the Ægyptians are said first to have brought from the Æthiopians' (see 1.1). Another eye-witness, however, affected disgust at a 'sight' he called 'loathsome' (Herford and Simpson 1950, 449). His tone, to me, is more arch than outraged: he, Dudley Carleton, personal

1.1 Costume design by Inigo Jones for 'A Daughter of Niger' in *Masque of Blackness* (1605)

private secretary to the 'wizard' Earl of Northumberland, dabbler in alchemy and other scientific experiment, could hardly have been innocent to shock:

> Their Apparell was rich, but too light and Curtizan-like for such great ones. Instead of Vizzards, their Faces, and Arms up to the Elbows, were painted black, which was Disguise sufficient, for they were hard to be known; *but it became them nothing so well as their red and white, and you cannot imagine a more ugly Sight, then a Troop of lean-cheek'd Moors.* (Herford and Simpson 1950, 448; original italics)

As Carleton reports it, the real sensation Anna caused in *Blackness* was her decision to push even further the boundaries of masque convention that, in *Goddesses*, she'd stretched. Here, she would present blackness not by wearing 'Vizzards' or stocking masks but by blacking up cosmetically, like common players – like Richard Burbage when he'd played Othello at Whitehall two months earlier. Blackness associates in Carleton's snide report with sexual availability (dresses that make women 'Curtizan-like') which slides into carnality: the white impersonators are mocked as 'lean-cheek'd' (Herford and Simpson 1950, 449). Black women are fat, abundant, full-bodied. For Carleton, Anna's masquers are Octavias pretending to be Cleopatras.

'[I]t was her Maiesties will, to haue them *Black-mores* at first'. Why? To ask that is to ask a question that cannot be answered. Still, I want to pause on this statement of queenly 'will' to let it register. Anna's masque began with what today's theatre would call a design concept. What put it in mind? Something she'd seen? *Othello*, perhaps, with its fascinating black presence, its talk of 'fair' warriors, 'black' faces, 'extravagant' barbarians, Mauritania, Indian pearls tossed aside, the seduction of the 'strange', the 'passing strange'? Was it coincidence that two plays this revels season would put blackness so sensationally in view – or was it quotation?

The fact that all of these goings-on from Cecil's 'private' thoughts about the Spanish peace to Carleton's review of Anna's masque are on record demonstrates that court gossip was not contained as insider knowledge. It travelled in diplomatic dispatches as 'information'; it circulated in letters as 'news'; it was published in broadsheets: Carleton, in that letter written the day after the masque, stated that there was already 'a pamflet in press' that promised the full story (Herford and Simpson 1950, 449). So Shakespeare could have picked up reports of Anna's *Masque of Blackness* from any number of sources. Equally, since his company was performing at court 'Betwin Newyers Day and Twelfe day', his knowledge of the masque might have been first-hand. He might have witnessed it.

Setting out this Jacobean history, I'm patching together material to speculate on what may have lain behind Shakespeare's *Antony and Cleopatra*. Certainly, Shakespeare's own history lay behind it, in the play he'd written to open the Globe in 1599, *Julius Caesar*. But what a difference in treatments. Calling *Antony and Cleopatra* 'a kind of sequel' to *Caesar*, Michael Neill points to the 'considerable modification' Shakespeare's approach to his source took seven years later when he came again to material he found in Plutarch: 'Most strikingly, the hero of the new play' was 'a long way from either the frivolous playboy glimpsed in the early scenes' of *Caesar* 'or the ruthless machiavel who emerges following his patron's assassination' (Neill 1994, 8). Plutarch offered plenty of material for Shakespeare to pursue a ruthless Antony, but the playwright didn't follow that lead, putting the political focus instead on the 'pair of chops' that would 'grind' out Roman history, making the political agon of *Antony and Cleopatra* a contest between binaries, between two life types (3.4.13, 15). One Roman was magnanimous and bounteous (or ruinously wasteful, impulsive); the other, calculating, cold and brilliantly bureaucratic. In *Antony and Cleopatra* it's almost as though we're watching current Jacobean English politics on display, a shadow-puppet view of King James's imperialist fantasies managed by Robert Cecil.

Did topical sensitivity also lie behind the sequel? Did the 'story of a great soldier betrayed to his death by a queen' yield 'uncomfortable parallels with the story of Queen Elizabeth and her disgraced favourite, Essex, executed in 1601' (Neill 1994, 8, n. 1)? Certainly, at the time, Fulke Greville thought so. He burned his closet tragedy of Antony and Cleopatra because, he wrote, he was alarmed at potential (mis)interpretation: his play was 'apt enough to be construed, or strained to a personating of vices in the present Governors, and government'. The 'like instance' of Antony's fall might be seen 'not poetically but really fashioned in the Earl of Essex' (Neill 1994, 8, n. 1)). Theatre, that is, could cut too close to the bone, could get 'really' real, for if theatre speech, as Horatio says of mad Ophelia's half-sense, 'is nothing', still 'the unshaped use of it' can 'move / The hearers to collection', to 'botch the words up fit' to their own dangerous constructions (*Hamlet*, 4.5.7–10).[2]

Better reduce a script to ashes than leave it to the botchers. By 1606, however, such sensitivities were things of the past. The Essex faction was recuperated; the little earl, son to the executed traitor, was installed in Prince Henry's household as his 'henchman'. Antony might return to the stage.

Or did other matter much closer to home stand more immediately behind Shakespeare's sequel, matter he observed at court in the revels season 1604–05? Is it possible that Shakespeare's *Othello* in November 1604 taught Queen Anna to 'think black' in *The Masque of Blackness* (ten weeks later)? Is it possible, then, that the queen's masque, with its visible allusions to Egypt, taught *him* to 'think black' in the next play he wrote; taught him to re-read Plutarch and to 'think queen' (a queen able – as Anna was – to run rings around the men who were supposed to master her) in a play built to put on show a 'creative agenda for self-display' that opened with men gazing in disgust on a 'tawny front' which betrayed, they said, a 'gipsy's lust' (1.1.6, 10)?

Philo and Demetrius see in Cleopatra what Shakespeare wrote (whether indebted to court performance or not). Shakespeare's 'gipsy' Queen of Egypt is black. He was doing nothing new when he triangulated 'Egypt', 'gipsy' (an aphetic form of 'Egypt') and blackness. He was simply citing contemporary cultural 'knowledge'. All the Egyptians Shakespeare had imagined to date were black (in *Romeo and Juliet*, *A Midsummer Night's Dream*, *Othello*). Like Ethiopia, Egypt was known to Shakespeare's contemporaries as a 'black' nation, 'a country joined to Jewry', wrote Andrew Boorde in *The First Book of the Introduction of Knowledge*, where the 'people of the country be swart' (Boorde 1555, sig. N2v). Or they might be 'tawny of complexion' as George Sandys made them in his *Relation of a Journey Begun Anno Dom*ini *1610* (Sandys 1615, sig. L1r, published by the printer of Shakespeare's *Venus and Adonis*, Richard Field). They might be 'dun, or tawny, of which colour Cleopatra was observed to be', according to George Abbot's *A Brief Description of the Whole World* (1664, 162) – as were the fake 'English or Welsh' Egyptians, those 'counterfeit ... rogues', who, 'disguising themselves in strange robes', 'blacking their faces and bodies' and wandering 'up and down, and under pretence of telling fortunes', abused 'the ignorant common people' (Cowell 1607, sigs Bbl r–v). Egyptian blackness was inscribed in Herodotus. In Barnaby Riche's 1584 translation of *The Famous Hystory of Herodotus* Egypt was a 'lande ... continually voyde of rayne', where the 'swartness of the people' ('in cou*n*tenance ... black', their 'hayre ... fryzled') was accounted for 'by the vehement heat and scorching of the sunne' (fols 96, 75). Herodotus (via Riche) described the 'flower' of 'beauty' among the 'wom*e*n of Ægypt' as 'a fayre browne blew, tanned and burnt by the fyrey beames of the sunne' (fol. 85v). Oxymoronically, then, Shakespeare's Egyptian Cleopatra might be both fair *and* black.

Of course, it wasn't only Cleopatra whom Shakespeare wrote black. Egypt was black too. The political face-off between East and West that played out on the Globe stage before the eyes of Jacobean spectators was not just between Egypt and Rome. It was between black and white.

I need to pause at this point to ask a hard-headed question. The scheme I'm proposing fails if it wasn't practicable in production. Could the King's Men manage it with the sixteen actors who (normally) made up the company, casting *Antony and Cleopatra*'s forty-odd roles not just to cover doubling but to allow in that doubling for the added complication of actors blacking up? It would have taken careful plotting (along the lines of what was required of the Admiral's Men to stage George Peele's *The Battle of Alcazar* circa 1600).[3] But it could be done.[4] Cleopatra, Iras and Charmian are black parts that can't double. Mardian is black and unlikely to double (but he can certainly make up the numbers in the opening scene's carnival entrance of Cleopatra *'with Eunuchs fanning her'* (Folio, stage direction, TLN 15–16), Mardian being her chief eunuch, and he could undoubtedly take the part of the 'poor Egyptian' sent by Cleopatra to learn Octavius's 'intents' in 5.1.52 and 54). Black Alexas can double black Diomedes (and an Egyptian eunuch in the opening scene); the Egyptian Soothsayer can first appear as a eunuch and later return as Seleucus. Egypt, then, requires six blackface actors. That leaves ten actors to cover the remaining parts. Among the white Romans only Antony and Octavius are unlikely to double. Buffoonish Lepidus (last seen in 3.2) can return blacked up to play the clownish Egyptian Asp Man in 5.2, a 'goodly double' to occupy, say, the company's comic, Robert Armin. Enobarbus, dead in 4.9, can make up the numbers attending Antony's botched suicide in 4.14, and might even (ironically) double Dercetus, delivering Antony's sword to Caesar. Philo in 1.1 can return as Octavia in 2.3, a servant at the top of 2.7 and later in that scene the Singer before returning as Octavia in 3.2; after 3.6 this actor can double any number of parts (soldiers, sentries) in Acts 4 and 5. Along these lines 'is a play fitted' (as Peter Quince might put it) to my notional sixteen actors.[5]

Can we assign any of these parts to named actors? Perhaps, for although Antony is not among the roles attributed to Richard Burbage in the funeral elegy published after his death in 1619, which remembers him playing 'young Hamlett', 'Kind Leer, the greued Moore', it's safe to assume that the part was his in 1606, aged thirty-nine (Chambers 1923, II, 309). Certainly, he commanded technique that would have served his Antony well, especially in his last scene, a whole act before the play's ending. For he was an actor, wrote the elegist, able to 'do' death 'Soe lively' that 'spectators' and even the 'sad crew', his fellow actors, 'whilst he but seem'd to bleed, / Amazed, thought even then hee dyed in deed' (Chambers 1923, II, 309). Doing such a death, Burbage's Antony wouldn't have been forgotten, even though he might be absent in the last act.

What did the Jacobean Antony look like? Plutarch may have been consulted to 'design' Antony in Egypt, where he is supposed to have remembered his ancestor Hercules 'in the wearing of his garments': 'his cassocke gyrt downe lowe upon his hippes, with a great sword [the 'sword Philippan'?] hanging by his side, and upon that, some ill favored cloke' (North 1579, 971). In Rome he perhaps changed into the Jacobean version of regulation SPQR-issue army gear – or, not changed, stood out as the incorrigible maverick.

Shakespeare writes Antony-the-warrior without giving him any scene to put his reputation on display. There's no stage combat (massed or single-handed). But the playwright built into the part other physical challenges: to lead the drunken bacchanals on Pompey's galley; to inflict the botched suicide and, dying, suffer the awful, agonising lift into Cleopatra's monument, some fourteen feet above the platform stage; and most significantly, and characteristically, to perform the Herculean switch-backs Shakespeare writes for him, from insane fury to collected calm, from magnanimity to pettiness, from the maudlin to the magnificent, Mars to Gorgon to bereft loser. This Jacobean Antony looks written to interrogate contemporary ideas of masculinity, particularly identity framed by martial idealisation (like Essex's, like that of the child Prince Henry, who had schoolboy-sized armour made to fit). Was he the 'greatest soldier of the world' lost 'in dotage'? Or had he rewritten masculinity's code book, having found 'new heaven, new earth' in a 'space' that scorned martial conquest, that saw 'Kingdoms' as so much 'clay'? Did the Jacobean Antony, in a post-peace-with-Spain world presided over by a king who was reputed to dote so uxoriously on his wife that he would refuse her nothing, stunningly redefine the hero as anti-hero (*CSPV* X, 111, 513)? Did he interrogate the imperialist project ('Rome' a proxy for 'Britain') even as ambitions to empire were taking shape in the desiring imaginary of the king whose players played this play?

If Burbage played Antony, who in Shakespeare's all-male company played Cleopatra? For starters, he wasn't a 'boy' (leastwise, no one who today would be called a 'boy'), though Cleopatra herself has bamboozled some readers into making that mistake. But when in 5.2 she scathingly imagines the Egyptian 'puppet' show that will display her 'girls' and herself in Rome as exhibits in Caesar's triumph while on other platforms the 'quick comedians / Extemporally will stage us', casting 'Some squeaking Cleopatra' to 'boy my greatness / I'th' posture of a whore', she's not talking meta-theatrically about herself (5.2.190–220, *passim*). She's talking but about subsequent performance.[6] She's making a contrast, not a comparison. To her Cleopatra, to the *real thing*, every impersonation will be puny, a mere 'boy'.

On the Jacobean Globe stage, a 'squeaking Cleopatra' would have been a nonsense, not least because one of the things we know from experiments conducted over the past twenty years in London's reconstructed Globe is that a voice pitched higher than alto is a liability. Soprano voices simply do not go the distance in the open-air space. Neither do unbroken boys' voices. That said, I need to define what Shakespeare's contemporaries meant by 'boy', which turns out to have been a capaciously elastic concept. Henry Cuffe, whose *The Differences of the Ages of Man's Life* was published in 1607, a year after *Antony and Cleopatra*, reckoned that one was a child until the age of twenty-five, with infancy, up to the age of three to four, boyhood until nine or ten, 'breeching' at seven, 'our budding and blossoming time' following on, 'youth', up to the age of twenty-five, one's 'prime' at thirty-five or forty and manhood proper thereafter lasting until the age of fifty (Cuffe 1607, I3v, I4, I14v *passim*).[7] Grammar school lads were boys when they went up to university aged between fourteen and sixteen. So were apprentices in trades and guilds in London, normally taking up their apprenticeships at seventeen. They were still officially boys until they completed their minimum term of apprenticeship seven years later, which, according to the Statute of Artificers enacted by Parliament in 1563, would not expire (no matter what their age starting their apprenticeship) before they reached twenty-four. Male orphans subject to the Court of Wards reached their majority (and could claim their inheritance) aged twenty-one. Nathan Field, born in 1587, was still nominally a 'boy', aged twenty-six, when he left the Children of the Queen's Revels company in 1613, joining the King's Men around 1615.

My claim is that Shakespeare's first Cleopatra was an experienced adult player, a young man in his mid-twenties (so something short of Cleopatra's historic age), and probably, given the list of the 'Principall Actors in all these Playes' that appears as front matter to the First Folio, to have been one of three: Alexander Cooke, Robert Goughe or Nicholas Tooley.[8] He was a player who had the presence to carry the longest and most demanding part Shakespeare had yet written for a woman, and the voice to project it across the yard and into the galleries of the Globe playhouse. In modern editions – though not the Folio, where the play runs without act and scene divisions – Cleopatra appears in sixteen scenes (against Antony's twenty-two, several of which, however, in Acts 3 and 4 are only half a dozen lines long). She speaks 693 lines (against Antony's 839, Octavius's 403 and Enobarbus's 346). She is never off stage in the play's long final scene, driving its triumphant trajectory and speaking 225 of its lines (against 196 lines from everyone else collectively). We can glean something of what the Jacobean gipsy queen looked like, in that 'person' that 'beggared all description' (2.2.207–208). She talks of her 'tires and mantles' (2.5.22). She dresses to 'Appear' 'i'th' war' for a man (3.7.18, 16), perhaps remembering Elizabeth, famously addressing her troops at Tilbury, where she arrived down the river by barge, awaiting the Spanish Armada in a silver breastplate over a white gown (Arnold 1988, xiv). She has herself dressed 'like a queen' for death in her 'best attires', putting on robe and crown (5.2.226, 227). Most suggestively for design purposes, feigning swooning, because she can't breathe, she orders 'Cut my lace, Charmian ...' (1.3.72). Jacobean Cleopatra isn't dressed 'strangely' like Anna's Daughters of Niger in 'Barbaresque mantells to the halfe legge'. She's laced like an elite Jacobean female courtier into a 'pair of bodies', that is, into the close-fitted upper part of a woman's garment that we would now call a bodice (Arnold 1988, 360). Black, like Anna in 1605, she is 'Other'. Laced into a 'pair of bodies', she is 'us'. In the Jacobean Cleopatra, then, Shakespeare embodies the double focus that his stagecraft is setting scenically before spectators' eyes. In her he explores the exotic as also familiar. He explores paradox ('defect perfection') in one who is, after all, 'No more but e'en a woman' (2.2.241, 4.15.77). He explores female sexuality, sensuality and desire uncoupled from (Christian) marriage but implicated in maternity in a way completely new to his theatre writing.

Shakespeare's Jacobean *Antony and Cleopatra* emerged from and spoke to its original moment, an original moment that is gone. The historian of performance is wisely reminded by Barbara Hodgdon that theatre belongs to the present, that whatever topicality may have resonated in a 'play's first performances, that topicality cannot be re-performed.' 'All that can be played ... is present-day culture's preoccupations with a play's issues' (Hodgdon 2002, 245). Still, those 'issues' survive as trace memories of the play's origins. So the effort to read a play historically, contextually, by piecing together this and that (as I have tried to do here), to read diplomatically with and against Shakespeare's script, to recover something of a play's original topicality, what its 'issues' were and how its 'preoccupations' hit the nerve endings of its first audience, is not labour lost. What the following chapters will find is how subsequent performances of *Antony and Cleopatra* have re-performed topicality for a new present, how they have used this script to stage conversations with audiences about the things they have on *their* minds.

## Notes

1 As recorded by the Venetian secretary, Giovanni Carlo Scaramelli, who had been forced by the coincidence of Elizabeth's death to remain resident in London, in a dispatch to the Republic: 'Il Re per quello che s'intende da ogni parte è huomo di lettere, di practica, di caccia di cavalli, et talvolta anco di giuoco' (Venice, Archivio di Stato, Senato, Dispacci, Filze, Pezzo 2, fol. 113v, calendared in Horatio F. Brown, ed., *Calendar of State Papers Venetian* (1900; hereafter *CSPV*), 24 April 1603. Scaramelli, marooned by diplomatic protocol, is our best witness to the regime change, and further references in this chapter to *CSPV* are quoting from Scaramelli's dispatches which

end in December 1604 when Nicoló Molino arrived as ambassador from Venice. References are to document numbers.
2. All quotations of *Hamlet* are from Thompson and Taylor 2006.
3. See Foakes's notes on casting in Foakes and Rickert (1968, 329–330); see also Bradley (1992).
4. I take it that one of the things we understand from the end of *Masque of Blackness* is that the technology for 'quick change' out of blackface had not yet been developed (though within a few years it would be: the black gipsies who reappear metamorphosed 'white' in the final scene of Ben Jonson's 1621 masque, *The Gipsies Metamorphosed*, tell spectators that 'what dide [that is, dyed] our faces was an oyntment' simply 'fetcht of with water and a ball' (Herford and Simpson 1941, lines 1481, 1485). In the doubling I'm proposing, then, I assume that so far as the Jacobean *Antony and Cleopatra* is concerned, white can subsequently double black but black cannot subsequently double white.
5. Imagining this doubling, I am consulting T. J. King (1992, 230–235). 'Twelve men', he writes, 'can play nineteen principal male roles, and four boys play four principal female roles'; but then another thirteen men and three boys are needed, says King, to play thirty-seven small speaking roles and the fifty-eight mutes. This is fanciful casting, for the Jacobean King's Men simply did not have such numbers at their disposal, although if they had wanted to make a mass entrance for Egypt in the opening scene they could have pressed into service other playhouse personnel, as the Admiral's Men did in 1597, recruiting the gatherers – who collected the admission money at the playhouse door – as walk-ons to bulk up the end of *Frederick and Basilea* (Rutter 1984, 111–113). Here, to propose doubling scaled to actual Jacobean practice, I am consulting Northern Broadsides's director, Barrie Rutter, who shows me how the play can be cast with a company of sixteen actors *and* with Egypt black. I gratefully acknowledge his expertise.
6. It is important to acknowledge David Kathman's seminal work identifying players (Kathman 2004a, 2004b, 2005, 2015). But not uncritically. Observing that contemporaries talked about 'female roles being played by "men", "young men", and "youths", terms which are sometimes used interchangeably with "boy" by the same author on the same page', Kathman nevertheless states that 'From the sixteenth century right up [... to] the early 1660s, women were played by teenagers or young men no older than twenty-one' – though he later recognises how few firm birth dates we have for actors that could make us secure in such a claim (2005, 221). Asserting that 'No person identifiable as an adult, let alone a sharer, is ever shown playing a female role' he must be ignoring the entry in the Admiral's

Men's account in Philip Henslowe's *Diary* (Foakes and Rickert 1968) laying out nine shillings 'to geue the tayller to bye tensell for bornes womones gowne the j of desember 1597' (fol. 37), which can hardly have been a mistake since the entry is repeated on fol. 43v: '... for bornes gowne'. William Borne (also styled 'Bird') was a sharer in the Admiral's Men. The payment on 1 December comes between payments on 25 November for 'clothe of gowlde for the womones gowne in branholwlte' and another on 8 December 'for the bodeyes of a womones gowne to playe allce perce' (fol. 43v). Either of these could have been 'bornes womones gowne', but the costume ordered for *Alice Perce* might just as well have been designed for John Pyg, Edward Alleyn's apprentice who'd been a member of the company since at least the provincial tour of summer 1593 (Foakes and Rickert 1968, 282). A duplicate entry on fol. 37v records that on the same day 'tafetie & tynsell' were ordered 'to macke a payer of bodeyes for a womones gowne to playe allece perce', more was laid out 'the same tyme for makynge & a payer of yeare sleavse of the bodeyes of pyges gowne'. In December 1597, then, Pyg may have been playing the title role in *Alice Perce*. Six months earlier, he'd been playing Andreo in *Frederick and Basilea*, whom Kathman terms 'a youth', though on what evidence is unclear since the play doesn't survive except in a plot (Foakes and Rickert 1968, 328–329). Kathman does not connect 'allece perce' to 'pyges gowne' although the entries on fol. 37v follow each other. What he does assert is that it appears 'that Pig [sic] was playing some substantial female roles, or had recently done so, around the same time that he was playing minor male roles', a claim he bases solely on an inventory of costumes belonging to the Admiral's Men taken in March 1598 that lists 'j red sewte of cloth for pyge, layed with whitt lace'; 'Pyges damask gowne', 'j harcoller tafitie sewte of pygges', 'j white tafitie sewte of pyges' and 'j littell gacket for Pygge' (Kathman 2005, 230; Foakes and Rickert 1968, 321, 323). But how do these costumes identify themselves as clothes for 'substantial female' roles – or for 'minor male' roles? Admitting that 'we are dealing with several levels of uncertainty', Kathman can still confidently find consistency in this uncertainty, viz. 'these ages are entirely consistent with what we saw earlier' (Kathman 2005, 230). This same sort of incoherent (to my mind) run of argument turns up when Richard Madelaine (1998, 23–25) first calls Shakespeare's Cleopatra a 'boy'; offers conjectures on the 'status of boy actors as apprentices'; assigns to 'boys' with 'unbroken voices' 'unimportant roles, female and male'; thinks 'maturer boy actors were trained to speak major female roles in a voice [like Cordelia's in *King Lear*, 5.3.270–271] "ever soft, / Gentle, and low" ...' [*sic*: on the open platform stage at the Globe?]; then concludes that the 'first actor of Cleopatra ... was almost certainly a youth rather than a boy' before, on the following page, continuing to conjecture the 'costuming of the boy Cleopatra'. For Madelaine, the 'one [sic] costume payment' that I cite for 'bornes womones gowne' is 'of doubtful significance'. I disagree. Documentary evidence is always significant. Thus I can't respect Kathman's determination, reiterating in 2015 his arguments from 2005, to ignore it: 'It has been suggested that adult male actors sometimes played older women ... but as I discuss ... evidence for such a practice is scant to non-existent' (2015, 248, note 5). Leaving aside the puzzling notion of a scale that runs from 'scant to non-existent', I argue that even where evidence is scant – perhaps particularly where evidence is scant – it needs to be considered seriously, not daffed aside. As for speculations about voice and maturity, Judi Dench in her dressing room at the National Theatre London in 1987 once growled at me, 'No *boy* ever played this part!' I'm with Dench.

7 But the treatise must have been written at least half a dozen years earlier. Cuffe was one of the Earl of Essex's secretaries; implicated in the so-called 'Essex rebellion' of February 1601, he was hanged, drawn and quartered as a traitor a couple of days before his master was executed.

8 For the following biographical information on these three players I am depending on Kathman (2004a), but where I query Kathman – over Robert Gough – I rely on my own knowledge of the performance records in Foakes and Rickert (1968). Alexander Cooke was made free of the Grocers' Guild in 1609 (it not being uncommon for players also to follow trades). His likely birth date, therefore, was 1583. A 'principal player' in Ben Jonson's *Sejanus* (1603), he may have played Lady Would-Be in *Volpone* (1605–06). In his will dated 1614 he named John Heminges 'my master'. Presumably, then, he had been Heminges's apprentice in the Lord Chamberlain's company. Robert Goughe is conjectured to have played Juliet opposite the twenty-eight-year-old Richard Burbage for the Chamberlain's Men circa 1595. But if he is the 'Ro. Go' who appears in the plot to *Frederick and Basilea* for the Admiral's Men in June 1597, it's hard to see how he could have done so. Or how he could have been the 'Ro Go' who played Aspatia and Philomela in *The Second Part of the Seven Deadly Sins* which David Kathman assigns to the Lord Chamberlain's Men in 1597–98 – unless that play marked his move from one company to the other (Kathman 2004b). Goughe was certainly with Burbage and what was now the King's Men by July 1603 when he was named a legatee in Thomas Pope's will. Nicholas Tooley (born 'Wilkinson' in late 1582 or early 1583) was apprenticed, it appears, as a boy to Richard Burbage whom he called his 'master'

and whose will he witnessed in 1619. He may have followed Burbage to the Chamberlain's Men when that company re-formed in 1594, and he was certainly with the company when it was elevated to the King's Men in 1603, receiving a legacy from Augustine Phillips who called him his 'fellow' on 4 May of that year (see Kathman 2004a). On balance, given working relationships and rehearsal practice, I'd opt for Tooley, Burbage's one-time apprentice, as likeliest casting for Cleopatra, though if Cooke indeed played Lady Would-Be he would have enjoyed certain preparation for the exorbitant gipsy queen.

# 2

# 'Famous patterns of unlawful love': *Antony and Cleopatra*, 1677–1931

### 'After Shakespeare'

What became of *Antony and Cleopatra* after Shakespeare's lifetime? For readers, the tragedy survived in print, being published in 1623 in the First Folio (along with fifteen other never-before-printed Shakespeare plays), where it was placed just after *Othello*. For spectators, however, there is no record of the play in the theatre for the next 150 years. It was among the pile of 'old' plays assigned at the Restoration to Thomas Killigrew in that notional 'division of the kingdom' that divvied up the pre-Commonwealth repertoires and licensed two royally patented playing companies in 1660 to reopen London's theatres along imported continental lines (which included putting the first women actors on the English stage). But *Antony and Cleopatra* does not appear to have been performed at all by Killigrew's 'new' King's Men. Instead, Killigrew's company waited seventeen years for the play to be written that would displace *Antony and Cleopatra* from the stage until the early nineteenth century, John Dryden's *All for Love, or The World Well Lost*. In this chapter I will examine Dryden's play as a Restoration stand-in for Shakespeare's, but I will also recognise its long after-life, traces of it persisting in further adaptations for the next two centuries. Then I will briefly observe the return of Shakespeare's play to performance, but in a theatre that wasn't much interested in the writing or dramaturgy. Instead, it used the script as a vehicle for more and more dazzling spectacle, playing some of Shakespeare's scenes but not in Shakespeare's order. These were productions that put 'Egyptomania' and Britain's increasingly bullish imperial ambitions on stage. Finally, this chapter will conclude with *Antony and Cleopatra*'s arrival in Stratford-upon-Avon, where the fag-end of the Edwardian theatre age, lying in the rubble of the Great War, was being cleared away by new theorists of Shakespeare who were also theatre practitioners. Only in the 1920s was Shakespeare's *Antony and Cleopatra* restored uncut to the English theatre.

By the time *All for Love* appeared on stage in 1677, Dryden (collaborating with William Davenant) had already made a musical version of *The Tempest, or The Enchanted Island* (1670). Later, he would adapt *Troilus and Cressida, or Truth Found Too Late* (1679), removing what he called 'that heap of rubbish' that 'wholly buried' its 'excellent thoughts' (quoted in Bevington 1998, 90). *All for Love* was a wholly different undertaking from either of these, not an adaptation, but a new play that used Shakespeare as its source the way Shakespeare used Plutarch as his source – although to call Shakespeare's play a 'source' might be something of an anachronism. According to Dryden's most recent editors, connections between the two plays were not commonly drawn in the eighteenth century and really only 'dated from Sir Walter Scott's Dryden edition, published in 1808'. Dryden's immediate prompt to writing *All for Love* is likely to have been topical: to put on stage a robust, pro-monarchical answer to Sir Charles Sedley's pro-republican *Antony and Cleopatra* that had been premiered the year before at the Duke's Theatre with Thomas Betterton as Antony. But whether Shakespeare was a 'source' or not, Dryden drew attention to the fact that he was writing 'after Shakespeare' – meaning both 'in the wake of' and 'in imitation of'. As he put it in his 'Preface' to the published play, it was because 'The death of *Antony and Cleopatra*' had been 'a Subject which has been treated by the greatest Wits of our Nation, after Shakespeare', that he aspired to claim a place 'amongst' this 'Crowd of Sutors', to 'try' the 'Bowe of Ulysses'. But, while he aimed to 'imitate the Divine *Shakespeare*', he would also 'use the priviledge of a poet' to 'take my own measures' (Novak *et al.* 1984, 'Preface', 10, 18).

Those 'measures' are what reveal *All for Love* to be very much a play of its own time, but not just of its own time. Given its persistence as a theatrical substitute for Shakespeare's *Antony and Cleopatra* until 1813, it's instructive to look in some detail at what Dryden presents to get a sense of what audiences across those years expected from a story of characters called 'Antony' and 'Cleopatra'. Theatre politics aside, Dryden's narrative 'motive' for rewriting Shakespeare, he said, was 'the excellency of the Moral' which derived from the 'chief persons represented': 'famous patterns of unlawful love'. Their 'crimes of love', committed by 'both' and 'wholly voluntary', meant that 'their end accordingly was unfortunate': a moral equation that Thomas Rymer, whom Dryden cites, would shortly theorise as 'poetic justice' (Novak *et al.* 1984, 'Preface', 10).

But given terms like 'crimes' and 'unlawful', seemingly loaded with opprobrium, the playing out of this 'Moral' would arrive at some paradoxical conclusions about a 'world well lost', not least because positional paradoxes littered the political landscape in an England whose Restoration was, in 1677, barely seventeen years old. The restored monarch, Charles II, had been a married man since 1662. But, flagrantly promiscuous, the nation's new role model and aristocratic tone-setter placed a French woman, whom he made 'Duchess of Portsmouth', at the centre of his court, thus enraging the country – if not the town: London reputedly seethed with seducers who brazenly masked their rapes with wit. (The actress Nell Gwyn, another royal mistress, is supposed to have distinguished herself from Portsmouth as the King's 'Protestant whore'.)[1]

Given his own proclivities, Charles Sedley – aristocrat, notorious rake, partner in crime with the Earl of Rochester and erstwhile playwright – might have been expected to support the king. He didn't. But it wasn't the king's continuous round of 'lascivious wassails' that Sedley objected to, nor even his extravagant expenditure (paid for by general taxation) on a series of high-class mistresses (who produced numbers of royal bastards while 'the married woman', Queen Catherine, succeeded only in miscarrying royal heirs). It was rather the suspicion that Charles, who'd spent some years of his exile in France, had sold out Protestant, Commonwealth England to the Catholic, autocratic French. Opposing what looked like Francophile Crown policy, Sedley sided with the poet Andrew Marvell, and with Shaftesbury, Buckingham, Wharton and Salisbury – Parliamentarians who'd all been sent to the Tower for speaking out, as the title of Marvell's 1677 pamphlet put it, against '*the Growth of Popery and Arbitrary Government in England*' (Novak *et al.* 1984, 375, n. 52). Sedley's pro-republican *Antony and Cleopatra* was another intervention in this war of words. In it, 'Antony fights for the return of the Roman Republic and the power of the senate', and even 'Cleopatra's suicide may be viewed as her defiance of Roman tyranny' (Novak *et al.* 1984, 374). By contrast, Dryden, who, it appears, wrote admiring verses entitled 'On the Dutchesse of Portsmouths Picture', seems to have intended *All for Love* to reframe national politics as a politics of a newly defined personal heroism such that Antony and Cleopatra, losing 'all for love', proxied Charles and Portsmouth. Dryden's editors propose that his aim was, by idealising Cleopatra and sensual love, to connect that 'idealization and the Duchess of Portsmouth', to suggest 'a parallel between Cleopatra loved by great leaders and Portsmouth loved by Charles II'. His play would show 'how sensual passion on the level of a monarch and his mistress might be viewed as an heroic emotion', a 'world well lost' (Novak *et al.* 1984, 373, 375).[2] But where, one wonders, does that leave Egypt/England – or their peoples?

As for the play itself, taking his 'own measures' in *All for Love* Dryden 'disincumber'd' himself of his regular poetic form, rhyming couplets, to write in freer, Shakespearean blank verse. He observed the neo-classical unities, setting the action on a single day following the Battle of Actium, but allowed himself some licence, for the 'Models' of 'the Ancients', which had crossed the Channel from the French theatre when the exiled monarchy was restored to England, though admirably 'regular', were 'too little for *English* tragedy; which requires', wrote Dryden, 'to be built in a larger compass' (Novak *et al.* 1984, 'Preface', 18). He reduced the cast to twelve. Stunningly, he cut Octavius Caesar and Enobarbus altogether, along with the Asp Man, but introduced 'Antony's two little Daughters' and a stand-off scene between Cleopatra and Octavia. Thus, matter he'd inherited from Shakespeare – imperial history, state politics, carnivalesque comedy and 'tragedy that turns on manlike aims and passions rather than on strained points of honour' – was out, pathos and idealisation were in.[3] Fashioning his play for the first of Thomas Killigrew's Theatres Royal on Drury Lane, Dryden was, of course, working in a theatre radically different from Shakespeare's, an indoor playhouse seating about a thousand spectators arranged on backless benches in the 'pit', surrounded on three sides by boxes, with two tiers of galleries above, facing an apron stage some twenty feet deep where the acting was set. Behind the actors, masked by the proscenium arch, a new technology for framing 'scenes' had been introduced, apparatus to enable moveable scenery. Painted 'wings' and 'shutters', trundled into position along grooves in the stage floor, could set individual scenes and establish new locations – and feed the spectator's eye with visual variety. But this scene shifting took time. This was no stage capable of handling Shakespeare's constant cross-cutting in *Antony and Cleopatra* between sequences of continuous action – those forty-two scenes marked in modern editions of the play. Dryden resolved Shakespeare's scenic bustle by laying out just five scenes (as five acts) set in a single location against a single 'scene', 'The Temple of Isis'.

Thus condensed and focused, *All for Love* presented a domestic drama for a formally 'correct' but personally licentious age, a psychomachia conducted across a series of two-handed debate scenes. Who, or what, would prevail with Antony? Honour? Love? There's a clue in the title. In the play's final minutes Dryden would finish things off by recuperating licentiousness and endorsing Antony and Cleopatra as 'famous patterns of unlawful love'. To make this 'a play about truly great lovers in adversity' he would construct a final stage picture of the two dead 'Lovers' sitting side by side 'in State together, / As [if] they were giving Laws to half Mankind' (5.1.508–509), leaving Cleopatra's priest Serapion to pronounce the final verdict that 'No Lovers liv'd so great, or dy'd so well' (line 519). Before that, however, he would present scenes of highly wrought tussle where the outcome was by no means inevitable.

Act 1 gives us Antony. Divided from his name, his reputation, his soldiership, his very 'self' in defeat after Actium, Antony is reported literally playing out that self-division. Sometimes he 'defies the World and bids it pass'; 'Sometimes ... gnawes his Lip, and Curses loud / The Boy *Octavius*' then 'draws his mouth / Into a scornful smile, and cries, *Take all, / The World's not worth my care*'. Sometimes, in Timon mode, he sees himself 'turn'd wild, a Commoner of Nature' living 'forsaken' in some 'shady Forrest's Sylvan Scene' (1.1.120–124, 232–234). When heroic Ventidius (the type of the hardened soldier) enters, returned from campaigning in Parthia, honour gets a voice. Ventidius rails against Cleopatra. She 'has quite unman'd' Antony; he's 'Unbent, unsinew'd, made a Womans Toy' (lines 174, 177). Before 'Love misled' Antony's 'wandring eyes', he was, the soldier tells his general, 'the chief and best of the Human Race' (lines 403–404):

> Fram'd in the very pride and boast of Nature,
> So perfect, that the gods who form'd you wonder'd
> At their own skill, and cry'd *A lucky hit*
> *Has mended our design.* (1.1.405–408)

Antony was the man to whom the gods had 'intrusted Humankind', putting '*Europe, Africk, Asia* ... in ballance'. But now, all that 'wonder' is 'weigh'd down by one light worthless Woman!' (lines 370–372). At the end of Act 1, roused by Ventidius's rhetorical whip-cracking, Antony is 'fir'd': his 'Soul's up in Arms'; 'noble eagerness of fight has seiz'd' him'. Antony and Ventidius exit 'Like Time and Death' to take on Caesar once again, to 'Begin the noble Harvest of the Field' (lines 438, 440, 450, 453).

Act 2 undoes Act 1. Honour's voice fails against Love's. Antony has refused to countenance any muttering against the Egyptian queen, has put it beyond argument that Cleopatra 'deserves / More World's than I can lose' (1.1.369–370). Now, the focus is on this woman for whom the world might be 'well lost'. She enters Act 2 wailing, 'What shall I do, or whither shall I turn?' Antony reanimated in warrior mode is 'Antony ... lost' to her. 'If once he goes' there is 'no more to lose', and so she yields to her Eunuch's ploy to engineer an 'accidental' farewell meeting with Antony. (Ventidius furiously objects: 'see her'? Then 'Y'are in the Toils; y'are taken; y'are destroy'd: / Her eyes do *Caesar's* work' (2.1.1, 11, 13, 225, 222–228). By the end of the scene, Cleopatra has talked Antony round, not least by showing him a letter in Octavius's hand offering her Egypt and Syria if she'll betray Antony – an offer she's refused (line 390). Then, in as close to full-throttle diva mode as Dryden allows her, she performs what her protests aim to prevent, urging her 'Soldier' to go, 'leave me', 'leave me dying' (lines 410–411). (To see how 'polite' this drama queen is, we need to compare Shakespeare's Cleopatra in 1.3, cracking lewd jokes and mocking the 'greatest soldier of the world' as its 'greatest liar', lines 59, 39–40.) 'He melts', observes the Eunuch Alexas '*aside*', 'We conquer' (line 407). Act 2 ends with Antony capitulating, scorning 'This Rattle of a Globe', this 'Gu-gau World'. The gods can give it 'to your Boy, your *Caesar*.' Antony's resolution is fixed. He'll 'not be pleas'd with less than *Cleopatra*' (lines 445–446, 444, 447).

Act 3 brings on a big production number, '*A Dance of Egyptians*' (no choreographic clues in the stage directions indicating the character of this dance except that Roman 'trumpets' are answered by Egyptian 'timbrels'). It celebrates the coronation of Antony in laurel victory. He's won a battle against Caesar. On the back of what Ventidius knows is just a momentary setback for Rome, the old campaigner proposes Antony seek peace with Caesar, and he knows just whom to employ to broker the deal. Enter Octavia, the wife, leading their two little girls. She's the image of dignity. She won't beg or howl or nag. She states her conditions simply: her brother pursues his war against Antony as a vendetta on her behalf. She will tell Octavius, 'we are reconcil'd; / He shall draw back his Troops', and Antony 'shall march / To rule the East.' As for Octavia, 'I may be dropt at *Athens*' (3.1.300–303). Tugged by honour, Antony wonders rhetorically 'which way shall I turn?' while Octavia urges the daughters, 'Go to him, Children, go; / ... pull him to me, / ... from that bad Woman'). Once again he's 'vanquish'd' by a woman: 'take me, Octavia, take me, Children, share me all' (lines 335, 350, 354–355, 362–363). They exit, but Octavia re-enters to confront Cleopatra – the stage direction indicates Octavia 'bears up to her' (line 416) – a face-off between Antony's 'Houshold-Clog' (as Cleopatra calls Octavia) and 'his ruine' (as Octavia terms Cleopatra) that begins as a wittily 'civil' slanging match, ends with Cleopatra protesting she'd 'lose' her 'life' 'For him I love', and Octavia drily riposting as her exit line, 'Be't so then: take thy wish' (lines 424, 451, 465–466). (We should note that with Octavia Dryden is inventing a major new role, establishing how audiences would see this part for the next two hundred years.)

Antony's vacillations play out across another two acts engineered around the 'same again' sexual politics of 'will he go or will he stay?' His lieutenant Dolabella (the type of male friendship) is set up as a stooge by Cleopatra's Eunuch in Act 4 to make Antony jealous. Though the general has renounced Cleopatra he can hardly brook his 'betrayal' by the younger man, who's reputedly been adopted her new lover. The ploy works; Antony wavers; Octavia storms out; the peace treaty is dead in the water; the act ends with recriminations of mutual betrayals, with Cleopatra protesting her innocence and the 'lovers' edgily exiting 'severally' (line 598). The highly condensed fifth act pits personal despair against political ruin while keeping the actual politics removed: noises off signal the invasion by sea of Octavius's navy and the rout of Cleopatra's sails, which fly to fall in behind the Roman galleys. Then there's the retreat into the monument and news sent of Cleopatra's death; the botched suicide; the lovers' farewell in each other's arms; and in the final hundred lines of the play, the death of Cleopatra, dressed again for Cydnus as 'the Bride of *Antony*' seated 'in State' beside her 'Lord' (lines 463, 508, 494).

Dryden's is not an inconsiderable play. The iambic pentameter is frequently sinewy. The confrontations are energetic. But despite the 'Temple of Isis' setting that backs them, they seem to be conducted in drawing rooms, not somewhere 'past the size of dreaming'. Certainly, there is more of melodrama than tragedy or triumph in the ending ('my eye-lids fall, / And my dear Love is vanish'd in a mist. / ... O ... lay me on his breast' (lines 497–500)). Dryden gives his audience a Cleopatra who is, Michael Neill observes, 'little more than a sentimentalized version of that stock Restoration type, the cast mistress' (Neill 1994, 25), plaintively seeing herself simply 'meant' by 'Nature' for 'A Wife, a silly harmless, household Dove' (4.1.91). The great swells and troughs of emotion, of blistering rage followed by euphoria or edgy calm in Shakespeare's play are reduced in Dryden to the near-comedy of the 'strangely "disturbed motion" that characterizes Antony's physical presence on stage', at 4.1.27 for example, where Antony *'Goes to the door, and comes back ... goes again to the door, and comes back ... Goes out and returns again'* (Neill 1994, 26; stage direction, 4.1.27, 31, 36).

In the 1677 casting of Dryden's Cleopatra, spectators would have seen nothing of Shakespeare's riggish queen who could hop forty paces through a public street or, in his Antony, Shakespeare's lugged bull. As sex criminals go, Elizabeth Boutell would have been more likely to be served a police caution than arrested on suspicion. She was familiar to audiences from Wycherley's *The Country Wife* two years earlier, when she'd played the gormless Margery Pinchwife. Although she was a 'considerable actress', according to 'Edmund Curll' in *The History of the English Stage* (1741), his description of her doesn't suggest a Cleopatra: she was 'low of Stature' with 'very agreeable Features', had 'a Childish Look', and her 'type' was 'the young, Innocent Lady whom all the Heroes are mad in Love with'.[4] As white as Millamant in *The Way of the World* and nearly as well bred, this Cleopatra wouldn't have dreamt of putting an asp to her *breast*. The snake made it only as far as her forearm. Charles Hart, a Civil War veteran, had more promising credentials for Antony. An actor before the war, he enlisted on the royalist side and saw action at Naseby and perhaps Edgehill. Opposite Boutell in *The Country Wife*, he played Horner: how curious to consider Margery and Horner recast as Antony and Cleopatra. Hart also inherited parts Burbage first created, among them Brutus and Othello, prompting Richard Flecknoe to propose that what 'Burbage was once' 'such Charles Hart is now' (quoted in Gurr 2004, 229). But just as there is little of the 'gipsy's lust' in Dryden's Cleopatra, so there is little of the Bacchic reveller in his Antony. The 'crimes of love' committed by this Antony and Cleopatra are not of the 'dungy' earth; they're crimes of rarefied erotics, refined, sublimated into what Dryden termed 'Heroique Passion', passion he fully intended to 'Prove ... [a] fit' subject 'for Tragedy' (Novak *et al.* 1984, 'Preface', 10, 371). Counterintuitively, then, if the story's moral, headlined in the title, sounds oxymoronic, as though the playwright-as-prosecutor were presenting evidence for the defence, it turns out to be so. The world these criminal 'patterns of unlawful love' lost 'all for love' was, Dryden asserts, '*well lost*'. This left his contemporary John Dennis railing. The 'Design' of Dryden's play was not just 'pernicious' and 'criminal', Dennis wrote, but, being so, exposed the corrupt politics of the age that it was sycophantically serving. For 'Certainly never could the Design of an Author square more exactly with the Design of White-Hall, at the time when it was written, which was by debauching the People absolutely to enslave them'.[5] Dryden's 'Heroique Passion' was, to Dennis, a cynical royal project, by dissipation to deaden the political intelligence of the people.

This, for Dennis, then, constituted the politics of Dryden's play. But there were more politics to it than just its audience reception, for in spite of *All for Love*'s near-exclusive focus on the lovers' 'Heroique Passion', the play did venture into political 'chat', skirting around its edges ideas that royalist and republican sympathisers might by turns have found objectionable. It's probably predictable that political ambiguities would rise to the surface of its action. After all, this play, which ends with regime change, was written in the wake of the most traumatic period of regime change that England had experienced since the Reformation. Parliament's revolutionary challenge to the monarchy, the execution of Charles I, the Civil War, the Commonwealth – or Interregnum, depending on whose side you were on – and the Restoration all stood behind it, and turning the political world upside down every twenty years or so was hardly likely to produce political consensus or the end of discursive ambiguity. No wonder, then, that we get the feeling that Dryden might be talking as much about England as about Egypt in incidental speeches that give off the whiff of political non-conformity. One of these comes just forty-five lines into the opening scene. What Cleopatra's High Priest, Serapion, has to say about regime change and the fickle masses who are swept like flotsam and jetsam in its tidal wakes – the play opens, we remember, *after* Actium – sounds, if not exactly treasonous, hardly like solidarity. The Eunuch Alexas wonders whether Serapion has 'invent[ed]' his 'horrid' prophecy of Egypt's doom, to 'frighten our *Ægyptian* Boys withal' (1.1.32–33). No, says, the Priest. The truth of the matter is that 'Our faint *Ægyptians* pray for *Antony*; / But in their Servile hearts they own *Octavius*' (1.1.44–45).

Is Serapion right? As political critique, maybe this needs unpacking. Are the '*Ægyptians*' faint? Are they servile? Or, 'own[ing]' Octavius, do they just want what the governed always want, better government? Should the people have to accept whatever government – Antony's, Caesar's; Cromwell's, Charles II's – is visited upon them? The 'ranged empire': is it better off under the management of Antony or Caesar? Is Egypt more prosperous pursuing an economy of profligacy or austerity? At war? Or peace? Administered by the bureaucrat or the soldier? (One wonders whether Alexas is talking about Antony, too, when he calls Ventidius 'This downright fighting Fool, this thick-scull'd Hero / This blunt unthinking Instrument of death' (3.1.378–379). And further, whether perchance these (political) views on the military class are Dryden's, who'd been a spectator on the English Civil War.)

Dedicating the published play to Thomas Osborne, Earl of Danby, Dryden declared his own politics. He was anti-Republican. That put him on the same side as Danby, the Lord Treasurer who had restored the restored king's 'embroyl'd' treasury which he had found 'not only disorder'd, but exhausted' and who now stood as an 'Isthmus betwixt the two encroaching Seas of Arbitrary Power, and Lawless Anarchy' (Novak *et al.* 1984, 'Dedication', 31, 5). Both 'Nature' and 'Reason', Dryden wrote, had 'bred' in him 'a loathing to that specious Name of a Republick' which he called a 'mock-appearance of a Liberty'. (But constructing that binary – 'Lawless Anarchy' v. 'Arbitrary Power' – wasn't he doing something that compromised his own political position, for while 'anarchy' was the business Sedley and the republicans were accused of, wasn't 'arbitrary power' the complaint the republicans made against the king?) Perhaps personal experience had contributed to Dryden's 'loathing': he was eighteen years old when the Commonwealth was declared and came to manhood during the 'personal rule' of Oliver Cromwell. Anti-republican, he was also anti-imperialist – because (it appears) he was proto-capitalist. 'The Situation of our Country, and the Temper of the Natives', he thought, made Great Britain 'An Island ... more proper for Commerce and for Defence, than for extending its Dominions on the Continent' (Novak *et al.* 1984, 'Dedication', 6). Murmurs of these matters make it into Dryden's play. The obnoxiousness both of tyranny and imperialist conquest are topics of a single exchange, sixty-five lines into *All for Love*. Serapion mutters darkly that whichever way the cards fall, it's going to be bad for Egypt. Whether Antony

>                                 be vanquish'd,
> Or make his peace, *Ægypt* is doom'd to be
> A *Roman* province; and our plenteous Harvests
> Must then redeem the scarceness of their Soil.

The Eunuch Alexas responds:

> Had I my wish, these Tyrants of all Nature
> Who Lord it o'er Mankind, should perish, perish,
> Each by the others Sword.

But, he continues, *real politique* must kick in. 'Since our will / Is lamely follow'd by our pow'r, we must / Depend on one' – that is, Antony (1.1.63–66, 71–75). On this exchange – which articulates the absolute need to keep militarised Antony dug in in Egypt – hangs all the political plotting the Egyptians do over the course of Dryden's otherwise domestic passion play. These gestures are limited, but not insignificant, particularly as they nod towards the incipient topic of imperialism. As later chapters will show, *Antony and Cleopatra* is the Shakespeare play which subsequent productions have used to stage their culture's current take on imperialism and how they see the imperialist project of putting 'Europe, Africk, Asia ... in ballance', including to whom they propose 'Humankind' should be 'intrusted'.

## After Dryden

No one until David Garrick attempted to revive Shakespeare's play for the stage. But after spending five months preparing the play with 'fine Scenes', 'all new Dress'd', Garrick produced a flop (Richard Cross, diary, 3 January 1759, quoted in Madelaine 1998, 32). The production that opened in January 1759 survived only six performances. A rather tight-lipped Richard Cross, the theatre's prompter, wrote in his diary on opening night: 'This play ... did not seem to give y$^e$ Audience any great Pleasure or Draw any Applause.' Garrick later implied that Antony, if not *Antony and Cleopatra*, had defeated him: although 'it gain'd ground Every time it was play'd ... I grew tir'd, & gave it up, – the part was laborious' (Burnim 1961, 69, 71). Ten years later, his bad luck with the play would be repeated when the pageant he planned as part of the 1769 Shakespeare Jubilee celebrations in Stratford-upon-Avon had to be cancelled. He'd intended to stage a procession through the town's streets featuring dozens of Shakespeare's characters, among them Antony and Cleopatra, who'd be attended by 'blacked up and turbanned' Egyptians, including 'eunuchs' in 'long "oriental" robes carrying fans and parasols' (Madelaine 1998, 32).[6] The parade, however, was rained off.

After Garrick, we can fast-forward to 1844 via 1813 and a selection of playbills that not only instance the durability of Dryden's play but give a sense of what variety was on offer in a theatre where the evening's entertainment was bulked up with popular farces, pantomimes and hornpipes that aimed to appeal to all segments of an audience (who, it must be supposed, found nothing bizarre in Dryden's Cleopatra sharing the bill with Irish milk-maids):

> 22nd of March [1766]
> Theatre Royal Drury Lane
> *All for Love; or, The World Well Lost*
> Antony: Mr Powell; Cleopatra: Mrs. Yates
> 'In Act III, a *Dance* incident to the *Play* By Sig. and Signora Giorgi'.
> '*End* of the *Play*, a dance call'd the *Irish* Milk-Maide'
> 'To which will be added, *The DEUCE is in HIM*'
> 'Part of the Pit will be laid into the Boxes'
> 'Ladies are desired to send their Servants by Three oClock'[7]

When *All for Love* was performed ten years later, this time at the Theatre Royal, Covent Garden, an interval after Act 3 was filled with 'a Grand Ballet, called RURAL LOVE'. After Act 5 came 'a grand Pantomime Ballet ... The WAPPING LANDLADY', the landlady played cross-dressed by 'Mr. Miles', followed by a 'Double Hornpipe' and an 'English Burletta', its parts cross-cast with bit players from top of the bill. In 1790 'ALL FOR LOVE; Or, THE WORLD WELL LOST' finished the evening with 'AN HARMONIC FESTIVAL, Consisting of the following favourite Songs, Glees, &c in which the Performers of the Concert of Ancient Music have obligingly offered their assistance': 'The Wooden Walls of Old England'; 'As I saw fair Clora'; 'September 13th, or the Siege of Gibraltar' rounded off with 'Grand Chorus, "Bless the true Church and save the King", HANDEL'.

Not until 1813, when John Philip Kemble produced 'ANTONY AND CLEOPATRA' with Harriet Faucit as the Egyptian queen, was 'Shakspeare's Play' once again advertised in the theatre, being staged at the Theatre Royal, Covent Garden. Still, even this version was enhanced 'With Alterations, and with additions from DRYDEN' (see 2.1). The production's playbill trails some of its scenic interpolations: '*In Act III The SEA FIGHT at Actium*' and after Act 5, 'The grand FUNERAL OF ANTONY AND CLEOPATRA'. Thus Garrick's 'fine scenes' were now being elaborated into grand spectacles. But even grand spectacles, wrote George Odell, couldn't make this 'a pretty dish to set before the king'. It was disappointing in its 'admixture ... of unworthy selections from Dryden' and its casting, 'Mrs Faucit' being a 'rather prosaic' actor for 'the Nile-serpent' (Odell 1966, 70).

Thirty years later, in October 1849, Shakespeare's play finally returned, Dryden-free, to the stage. Sadlers Wells offered 'for the First Time at this Theatre the Tragedy of ANTONY AND CLEOPATRA FROM THE TEXT OF SHAKSPERE', 'with Antony: Mr [Samuel] Phelps' (also billed as 'the theatre manager') and 'Cleopatra: Miss [Isabel] Glynn' [sic]. Spectators were promised '*NEW SCENERY, DRESSES AND DECORATIONS*', the 'Scene' being 'Dispersed in several parts of the Roman Empire'. But even restored 'from the text', Shakespeare's tragedy couldn't avoid entertainment add-ons: the evening would 'conclude' with 'a Farce', 'entitled The MISTRESS OF THE MILL' cast from *Antony and Cleopatra*.[8]

Very little detail survives about these productions, but enough to suggest how Cleopatra was being performed. Kemble's Cleopatra in 1813 was no serpent or gipsy but a queen who dressed *à la mode*. An 1814 engraving shows Harriet Faucit looking as English as Jane Austen in a neoclassically cut empire gown.[9] It suggested her 'exotic' qualities only in some design details, which may have owed something to world events, to Egyptomania set off by Napoleon's Egyptian campaigns, Nelson's victory in the Battle of the

THEATRE ROYAL, COVENT-GARDEN
This present MONDAY, Nov. 22, 1813,
Will be acted (4th time) *Shakspeare's* Play of

# Antony and Cleopatra

*With Alterations, and with additions from* DRYDEN.
The Overture, Marches and Act-Symphonies new, by Mr. WARE.
Marc Antony by Mr. YOUNG,
Octavius Cæsar Mr. ABBOTT, Emilius Lepidus, Mr. BARRYMORE,
Dolabella, Mr. HAMERTON, Ventidius Mr. TERRY,
Enobarbus, Mr. EGERTON, Canidius, Mr. TREBY, Diomedes, Mr MENAGE,
Thyreus, Mr. MURRAY, Mecænas Mr. CRUMPTON,
Agrippa, Mr. CRESWELL, Proculeius, Mr. JEFFERIES, Alexas, Mr. CHAPMAN
Philo, Mr. Brook, Eros, Mr. Grant, Attendant on Antony, Mr. Platt
Messengers to Antony, Messrs. Atkins & Norris, Officers to Antony, Messrs. Lee & Heath
Messengers to Cæsar, Messrs. Howell & Daunfet Messenger to Cleopatra Mr. Claremont
Male Attendant on Cleopatra, Mr Sarjant, Ambassador, Mr. King,
Egyptian Attendant Mr. Louis, Officer to Cæsar, Mr. Yarnold.
Octavia by Mrs. M'GIBBON, Charmion, Miss COOKE, Iras, Mrs WATTS
Cleopatra by Mrs. FAUCIT.

In Act III
*The* SEA FIGHT *at* Actium.
End of Act V.
The grand FUNERAL of ANTONY and CLEOPATRA,
WITH AN
*E P I C E D I U M,*
The MUSICK *new, composed by* Mr. BISHOP.
The principal vocal characters by
Mr. INCLEDON, Mr. SINCLAIR, Mr TAYLOR, Mr. BROADHURST, Mr. SLADER.
Mess. Everard Higman, Linton, Montague, J Taylor, J Terry, Tett, S Tett, Tinney, Watton, Williams
Miss MATTHEWS, Miss RENNELL, Miss BISHOP, Mrs STERLING, Miss LOGAN,
Mesdames Adams, Bologna, Bologna, Bishop, Carew, Coates, Cox, Decker, Feeney, Findlay, Grimaldi, Heath,
Herbert, Hibbert, Iliff, Lefevre, Louis, Norman, Ryall, Standist, Tuthe, Watts, Whitmore.
To which will be added the Melo-Dramatick Romance of

# A L A D D I N;

*Or, The Wonderful Lamp.*
ALADDIN by Mrs H. JOHNSTON,
TAHI TONGLUK (Cham of Tartary) Mr CRESWELL,
KARAR HANJOU (his Vizier) Mr. BOLOGNA,
KALIM AZACK (the Vizier's son) Mr. BOLOGNA, Jun.
ABANAZAR (the African Magician) Mr. FARLEY,
KAZRAC (his Chinese Slave) Mr. GRIMALDI,
The PRINCE'S BALROULBOUDOUR, Miss BRISTOW,
AMROU and ZOBYAD her chief attendants Miss TREBY and Mrs. PARKER,
The Widow Ching Mustapha, Mrs. DAVENPORT,
Genie of the Ring, Mrs WORGMAN.
Olrock, Genie of the Air, Mr. JEFFERIES,
☞ *NO ORDERS CAN BE ADMITTED.*
Macleish, Printer, 2, Bow Street, London.

Those numerous parties who have not yet been able to secure Boxes for the performances of Miss
STEPHENS, are respectfully informed that her other nights of acting will be
Tomorrow, Wednesday, Friday and Saturday next.
Tomorrow, the Serious Opera of ARTAXERXES.
To which will be added the Farce of The SLEEP WALKER.
And the new Melo-drama of The MILLER AND HIS MEN.
On Wednesday, will be performed The BEGGAR'S OPERA.
On Thursday, Shakspeare's Play of KING HENRY the FIFTH; *or, The Conquest of France,*
King Henry, Mr CONWAY.
To which will be added the revived musical Entertainment of The DESERTER.
On Friday, the Comick Opera of The DUENNA.
With the Melo-Drama of The MILLER and HIS MEN.
On Saturday, the Serious Opera of ARTAXERXES.
To which will be added a favourite Comedy, reduced into three acts, called
I'LL LY AS IT FLIES.
The Publick are respectfully informed that
Shakspeare's Play of ANTONY and CLEOPATRA, with alterations, and additions from
DRYDEN, was honoured throughout its third representation with the most flattering approbation
and applause, and will be repeated every Monday till further notice.

2.1 Playbill for the 1813 production of *Antony and Cleopatra* at the Theatre Royal, Covent Garden, when 'Shakspeare's Play' returned to the stage after an absence of two hundred years, but still 'with additions from Dryden'.

[ 56 ]

Nile in 1798 and the opening of William Bullock's Egyptian Hall in Piccadilly in 1812. Twenty years later Egyptian exoticism appeared to have made it from the costume onto the body of the part. Played by Louisa Anne Phillips at Drury Lane in William Charles Macready's 1833 production, Cleopatra was distinctly 'Other': if not exactly 'swart', then perhaps 'tawny', 'her complexion' coloured an 'artificial brown'. Even so, reviewers complained that she 'was still much too fair, especially when contrasted with her mulatto attendants' (*Morning Chronicle*, 22 November 1833, quoted in Madelaine 1998, 41). Their comments ('much too fair', 'mulatto attendants') seem to suggest that Hanoverian spectators (like Jacobean viewers before them and Garrick in the Jubilee pageant) expected their Egyptians to be black.

Another decade on, a surviving engraving of Isabella Glyn's Cleopatra published in the *Illustrated London News* in 1849 shows her looking somehow both 'Other' and 'us', both foreign and uncannily familiar.[10] That production restored most of Shakespeare's Cleopatra to the stage for the first time since 1606, though twelve scenes – most of them Shakespeare's military or political scenes – were cut to accommodate interpolated spectacle (Wilders 1995, 18). It also made Cleopatra darkly 'eastern': her skin tawny, her head adorned with something resembling an 'authentic' Egyptian headdress and her skirt decorated with hieroglyphic patterns. Yet at the same time, the *Illustrated London News* engraving shows her presenting something comfortably close to home – for her figure has the sturdy shape of the matronly Queen Victoria. Playing the part for twenty years in three celebrated productions and in numerous platform recitations, Glyn would 'attempt to cover the full range of the role, including the sexual implications of the "undulations of the Eastern form"' (Madelaine 1998, 44). Those 'undulations' sexualised the part in disturbing (and exciting) new ways. It may be possible to get a sense of how audiences looked at Glyn in Lucy Snow's reaction when she 'comes face to face' with a portrait of Cleopatra 'in a picture gallery' in Charlotte Brontë's *Villette* (1853). Gazing at 'this huge, dark-complexioned gypsy queen', at her 'affluence of flesh', flesh which strikes Lucy Snow as 'very much butcher's meat', the young, prim, pale Englishwoman, writes Adrian Poole, 'is not impressed'. Cleopatra, he comments drily, 'made most Victorians nervous' (Poole 2004, 109).

If Glyn's performance restored erotics to *Antony and Cleopatra*, the 'NEW SCENERY, DRESSES AND DECORATIONS' in Samuel

Phelps's production exploited the full resources of the Victorian theatre to push the play's spectacular-isation beyond Garrick's boldest attempts at approximating materially what Shakespeare had imagined in poetry. The Egyptian views, wrote *The Times*, were 'decorated with all those formal fantasies with which we have been familiarised through modern research' (Madelaine 1998, 49). This 'modern research' was not unconnected to current events, including, first, the furnishing of an Egyptian court in the Crystal Palace when it was removed to Sydenham in 1853, thus transforming the Great Exhibition of 1851 into a popular tourist destination and giving Egyptomania to the masses. And second, the construction of the Suez Canal (starting in 1859 and taking a decade to complete), a project which inscribed British imperialism on the map of the Mediterranean while opening up Egypt to tourism, English minds to orientalism and art collections to the acquisition of Eastern treasures. In productions directed by John Douglass, George Vining, Frederick Chatterton, Lewis Wingfield and Frank Benson (who first took the play to the Memorial Theatre in Stratford-upon-Avon), the Victorian interests of the time found expression in *Antony and Cleopatra*. These interests included highly wrought spectacle rendered with pictorial accuracy to reproduce on stage the cultural opulence that had been discovered by archaeology; the allure of oriental exoticism (including dark female sexuality wholly absent from dramatic narratives centred on that Victorian domestic icon, the 'Angel of the House'); and most assertively, empire. How remote, now, is Dryden's anti-imperialism. How quaint his notion must have sounded to Victorian ears, that Britain was 'An Island ... more proper for Commerce and for Defence, than for extending its Dominions on the Continent'.

A puff in the *Daily Telegraph* (8 September 1873) announcing Frederick Chatterton's production for October that year showed how far *Antony and Cleopatra* had travelled in the direction of visual consumerism at the expense of Shakespeare's writing. It quoted Chatterton's opinion that, for 'A Play to be acceptable to all classes in a large theatre like that of Drury Lane', which had been remodelled in 1812 (after numbers of enlargements) to *reduce* its audience capacity by 500 to a still-staggering 3,060 seats in pit, stalls and galleries, it 'must appeal to the eye and the senses as well as to the understanding': the 'action must be accompanied by spectacle, and the play itself must be adapted to the dramatic fashion of the time in which we live' (quoted in Madelaine 1998,

57). Chatterton's adaptation consisted of compressing five acts into four; 'Thirty-three Scenes' into twelve; and, to accommodate the stagehands, eliminating Shakespeare's scenic cross-cutting. All of Acts 1, 3 and 4 were set in Egypt, Act 2 in Rome. The spectacle advertised on the playbill was designed to astonish. Scene 3, billed 'CLEOPATRA'S BARGE', staged her arrival at Cydnus, noting scrupulously that while this event occurred in 'a period antecedent to ... Shakspeare's Play', it was 'here transferred to Egypt in order that so magnificent a scene may not be lost', including (sensationally) the effect of 'The Perfume ... Produced by Means of Rimmel's Persian Ribbon'. Act 3, set 'on the sea shore', gave spectators the 'Naval Battle between the Roman and Egyptian Ships of War' – the theatre being equipped with hydraulics reportedly capable of discharging 39 tonnes of water. Then it took them to 'THE TEMPLE OF ISIS' for Cleopatra's death (Bradby *et al.* 1981, 103). A farce ('The Straight Tip') finished off the evening with a cast including 'a fortune Hunter', 'a solicitor' and 'a Tippling Sporting Tipster': a nicely ironic re-view of the night's main attraction? Chatterton's Antony, James Anderson, complained of the savagely cut script that this show couldn't count as 'a tragedy'. It was 'spectacle ... made up of scenery, processions, ballet, gaud and glitter' that, he bitterly reported, was nevertheless applauded 'with maddening demonstrations of approval by the pit and galleries' (quoted in Madelaine 1998, 58). The *Times* reviewer remarked with vast understatement how 'widely different' the play had 'become ... from that which years ago Mr Phelps produced at Sadlers Wells' (22 September 1873).

What Shakespeare lost to rewriting in Dryden he now lost to the scene painters and shifters in Chatterton *et al.*, including at the Princess's Theatre in 1890, a production by Lillie Langtry. Multiply married, a former mistress of the Prince of Wales, the 'Jersey lily' was a woman as notorious as the one she played. Her playbill featured an archaeologically accurate Sphinx and 'Cleopatra's needle', one of which had been erected in London twelve years earlier. Her Cleopatra costume (shown on souvenir postcards) gives a high-society impression of pharaonic dress. Slated by critics, snubbed by royalty, giving off the aphrodisiac scent of scandal, Lillie was adored by the masses who made her American tour of *Antony and Cleopatra* a storming success. The girl from the Channel Islands who'd left home on a yacht arrived in her production's opening scene with her Antony sailing down the Nile on her barge.

The popularity of this sort of eye-popping spectacle crested with Beerbohm Tree's Edwardian *Antony and Cleopatra* at His Majesty's Theatre in 1906. As Barbara Hodgdon's closely observed account of Tree's production argues, what he did, as producer and actor playing Antony opposite Constance Collier's Cleopatra, was to put 'squarely into view' a 'theatrical heart of darkness where "Shakespeare" rubs shoulders with low culture and the feminine becomes readable along a colonial-imperial axis' (Hodgdon 1998, 81). For Tree, this was the 'tragedy of a world-passion', and Cleopatra was 'the greatest courtesan that ever led man from the path of politics – the eternal feminine that "beggared all description" and that ruled and undid empires and emperors' (quoted in Hodgdon 1998, 81). Tree inherited from the Victorians the discourses of Egyptology and antiquarianism that he reanimated here; but additionally, in December when his production opened, Egypt was in the news, having been put there by the Denshawai Incident, which, in June, had started with a scuffle and, thanks to British military overreaction, let to mass arrests and executions, escalating further into anti-imperialist struggle in the region. Six months later its aftershocks were still making headlines.[11]

Tree filled his stage with materials to reify the imperial imaginary (so recently stamped with hegemonic brutality upon the colonised 'subject peoples' of Denshawai): 'palatial sets decorated with gaudy gold, their walls bearing monstrous figures, their rooms filled with silken canopies'. He put 'dancing girls, "flamingoes" holding their outstretched phoenix-wings aloft, Nubians, incense bearers, dimpled Cupids, and hordes of court attendants' on stage, and Collier appeared in six extraordinary gowns that would later be copied for fancy-dress balls (Hodgdon 2002, 242–243). Like Langtry's production, Tree's show opened (after the image of the Sphinx projected on the front cloth gauze dissolved) with an enactment of Enobarbus's account of Cydnus, the lovers arriving in view on Cleopatra's barge. Thereafter, Tree cut so much of Shakespeare's text that the *Speaker* dubbed this 'a raree show' merely 'tagged with Shakespearean phrases' (2 January 1907, quoted in Madelaine 1998, 61).

Over the next decade, war in Europe and the slide into worldwide economic depression would put an end to theatrical extravagance on this scale. In parallel, the publication of Harley Granville-Barker's *Prefaces to Shakespeare*, the second series in 1930 containing his chapter on *Antony and Cleopatra*, revolutionised how directors saw

Shakespeare's text as a script for the theatre. These essays had the effect of sweeping theatrical extravagance into the dustbin. 'Here', Granville-Barker wrote of *Antony and Cleopatra*, 'is the most spacious of the plays ... it has a magnificence and magic all of its own, and Shakespeare's eyes swept no wider horizon'. But, he stated firmly, producers had to stop directing the play from editions of a text 'distorted by editors' (or adapters) and 'grievously misunderstood by critics'. They must 'start afresh from the untouched text' and 'must read' that text 'in the light of a clear understanding of the stage of its origin'. Thus Granville-Barker tackled head-on the matter of editorial act and scene division in *Antony and Cleopatra*, noting first that there is 'no juncture where the play's acting will be made more effective by a pause' and, second, that 'On the contrary, each scene has an effective relation to the next, which a pause between them will weaken or destroy' (Granville-Barker 1951, 126, 127, 139). For Granville-Barker, then, *Antony and Cleopatra* was a play that needed to be played straight through with no interruptions.

Granville-Barker's play was not yet available to spectators, certainly not in Stratford-upon-Avon, where Frank Benson and his touring company had, since 1886, been servicing what had started in 1879 as an annual week-long Birthday Festival at the Shakespeare Memorial Theatre. Benson's company brought to Stratford productions already in their repertoire, productions that returned, year in, year out, with costumes, properties (including the stuffed stag in dozens of *As You Like It*s), heavily cut texts and business in performances that audiences knew by heart. Three *Antony and Cleopatra*s appeared between 1898 and 1912.[12] They had pictorial aspirations (though scaled to the cramped limits of the Memorial Theatre's festival stage), but few other ambitions. The state of play on the Memorial stage as darkness fell across the dying years of the Edwardian age is perhaps best captured in an anecdote. The 'new' production and Birthday Play for 1912 (by which time a three-week summer season had been added to the April Festival) was *Antony and Cleopatra*, revived from fourteen years earlier, 'new' only in featuring a 'new' Cleopatra, the twenty-six-year-old Dorothy Green. By the time of the dress rehearsal, Benson, playing Antony, 'had still not rehearsed any of the scenes' between himself and Cleopatra. When Green protested, he 'agreed to run through the scenes with her at six o'clock on the morning of the first night. He then travelled up to London, spoke at Shakespeare celebrations on the South Bank, returned to Stratford, and went on' (Beauman 1982, 56).

When the festival resumed in 1919 after a three-year interruption during the Great War, the Benson era was finished; the thirty-year-old William Bridges-Adams was the newly appointed artistic director – and not only was he reading Granville-Barker, he was anticipating Granville-Barker insights, not least in giving 'the plays straight and as uncut as may be' (*Westminster Gazette*, 25 July 1921). Bridges-Adams would produce *Antony and Cleopatra* four times between 1921 and 1931 (in spring and summer seasons that offered spectators a repertoire of ten plays, each of them allocated, by strict Memorial Theatre governors' budgets, three rehearsals). Even working to this insane production schedule, Bridges-Adams would restore Shakespeare's *Antony and Cleopatra* to the stage relatively uncut, played at a pace that left reviewers marvelling, his productions taking their cue, perhaps, from Granville-Barker's observation that if this were Shakespeare's 'most spacious' play, it was also his 'most business-like'. Thus the reviewer for *Truth* magazine called Bridges-Adams 'a wonderfully fine and sympathetic producer of the plays' who had 'thought out their every detail' with 'real vision' which he had 'been able to stamp ... upon the minds of others' (10 August 1921). Chiefly to be recognised, wrote a somewhat astonished and seemingly grateful *Truth*, was that he 'remains faithful to the order of [the] scenes' and that his 'innovations' – reducing scenery to a minimum and using draw curtains to cover scene changes – 'gave an almost continuous performance without annoying waits' while producing 'delightful stage pictures of studied simplicity without bizarre extravagances' (*Stratford-upon-Avon Herald*, 2 September 1921). Dorothy Green played Cleopatra, with somewhat more rehearsal than Benson had given her in 1916, and was singled out as the triumph of the production. W. A. Darlington in the *Daily Telegraph* called her 'quite out of the common': 'She has exactly the majesty of style without which Cleopatra sinks to a petulant, spoiled child'; 'in all her changing moods' this Cleopatra 'never forgets that she is a queen; and what is more, she always looks like a queen' (18 July 1921).

Green played the role twice more for Bridges-Adams, in 1924 opposite Basil Holloway as a 'strong, rugged soldier' Antony whose 'force and vigour and dignity' saved him from 'being the scented amorous fool he might easily be made' (*Birmingham Post*, 17 July 1924); and in 1927, opposite the 'finely picturesque and manly Antony' of Wilfrid Walter (*Birmingham Mail*, 13 July 1927). Green's Cleopatra was again 'perfectly the woman of Shakespeare's imagining', her voice 'rich as fruit cake but not so cloying, speaking verse as verse and yet with all the meaning of all the lines' (*Birmingham Mail*, 13 July 1927; *New Age*, 10 July 1924). Reviewers say almost nothing about what the productions looked like, how they were costumed, what happened on stage – except for some stray, tantalising observations: 'Mr Bridges Adams' is 'at his very best as a master of lighting and an expert at making the best of scant scenic resources'; Cleopatra 'almost throttles the half-naked Nubian [a blacked-up role?] who tells her of Antony's marriage'; 'The expression on their faces' – Iras: Edith Johnson; Charmian: Lydia Sherwood – 'are plays, and at times even poems, in themselves. Watch these two ladies when they wait on Cleopatra, and see how intensely dramatic can be inaction' (*Birmingham Mail*, 13 July 1927; *Birmingham Post*, 17 July 1927; *Stratford-upon-Avon Herald*, 15 July 1927).

Ironically, most of what can be known about the look of these productions has to be inferred retrospectively, by comparison with Bridges-Adams's final *Antony and Cleopatra* in 1931, his only production for which the promptbook survives.[13] It shows him living up to his soubriquet, 'Unabridges-Adams', playing all of Shakespeare's scenes in the right order and making internal cuts of two lines here, ten lines there, many of them aimed at what looks like 'decency'. Enobarbus lost his bawdy back chat with Antony in 1.2. Antony wasn't allowed to be remembered drinking the stale of horses and eating strange flesh in 1.4. Cleopatra didn't 'Hop forty paces through the public street' in 2.2 and didn't ask the question 'For what good turn?' or get the answer, 'For the best turn i'th' bed' in 2.5. Her dream of Antony was trimmed (5.2.96–99), and the final lines of the play cut from line 334 ('Bravest at the last …') to line 357 ('She shall be buried by her Antony'). The final stage picture had 'Caesar's attendants: 'All draw swords – raise in salute & lower slowly' as 'Act Drop'. But then, at the curtain 'Calls', other tableaux were produced as last images to be absorbed by spectators: '1 Picture' 'In front of Tabs': '1. Caesar, Agrippa' then '2. Caesar', followed by: 'Open tabs on picture of: – Cleopatra on couch Charmian Iras Antony on double shield' (promptbook). The final *final* stage picture, it appears, settled on a tableau of monumental death, Cleopatra laid out on her 'couch', Antony, on his shield.

But that reference to the 'couch' is significant. This Cleopatra – played by Dorothy Massingham (Dorothy Green having been poached to play the part in John Gielgud's current production at the Old Vic), died lying on a bed, not seated on her throne, her head adorned with the cobra crown of Egypt. And that decision was connected to thoughts Bridges-Adams was expressing elsewhere. In an interview in April given just as that year's Birthday Play, *King Lear*, was opening, he told the *Observer* that *Lear* couldn't 'be put on the stage' unless the producer bore 'in mind the Elizabethan conditions in which the playhouse was released from time and space'. *Lear* was 'no good against a natural background' (5 April 1931). Such 'Elizabethan' ideas were also introduced into *Antony and Cleopatra* – Bridges-Adams's own instincts perhaps being given even greater prompting by the 'Preface' to the play that Granville-Barker had published only months before. *Era* reported as the new festival season opened that Bridges-Adams was looking 'forward to several of the plays being produced with the freshness attaching to a new play'. New play? How revolutionary! 'For example, in *Antony and Cleopatra* the Roman dressing will be subject to an admixture of costume contemporaneous with the poet' (8 April 1931).

Only a handful of studio portraits survives in the Shakespeare Birthplace Trust archives for this production. They show Gyles Isham's Antony in regulation Roman gear: peplum, toga-style cloak thrown across one shoulder, feathered helmet strapped beneath his bearded chin, sandals laced up to the knees. Massingham's Cleopatra, however, is costumed as a slightly Wagnerian Tudor: heavy fabric, full skirt, Brunhilda-esque shield-like medallions clamped onto the bodice. The *Stratford-upon-Avon Herald* was disturbed by what it saw:

> In few other plays does dress take so important a place ... The costumes, even more than the settings, symbolise the character of their wearers, and illustrate the gulf between austere Rome and burning Egypt. It was disturbing, therefore, in the present performance, to find Cleopatra and her women in Elizabethan garb.

The reviewer conceded that 'In Shakespeare's day this may have been done, but surely on those occasions the whole company, Romans and Egyptians, would appear in the dress of the period.' Without wanting to reject Bridges-Adams's innovations or 'to condemn an experiment on sight', the *Stratford-upon-Avon Herald* reviewer could 'not see the advantage of a Cleopatra weighed down with the habiliaments of Good Queen Bess'. 'Happily', however, Massingham's 'splendid' Cleopatra dressing for death 'was allowed the traditional [i.e. what the festival audiences expected to see, and had, it appears, seen in earlier Bridges-Adams's productions] headgear and robes of Egypt' (8 May 1931).

Interestingly, none of these reviews remarks on what later audiences and theatre house managements would surely have balked at: the announcement in the programme that 'The play will be given in five acts, with an interval of ten minutes after Act II' – that is, a single interval placed just after Cleopatra in 2.5 sends Alexas away to grill the Messenger on Octavia, to 'Bring me word how tall she is' (line 118). Ten minutes' interval – with more than three big acts to follow. The programme does not, unfortunately, give the running time of the performance. But that single 'interval of ten minutes' is perhaps the best marker of the shift from Dryden's theatre across three hundred years into the twentieth century, from the introduction and then dominance of the entre'acte – with its interruptive 'matter' not just covering scene changes but progressively displacing the script – to the reassertion of the headlong surge of acts and action as the playwright wrote it, and from interpolated spectacle to the performance of Shakespeare's writing.

There would be two more *Antony and Cleopatra*s in Stratford in the next twenty years, neither of them distinguished except for some movie star casting. After Bridges-Adams in 1931, Shakespeare's script would wait until 1953 to 'find out new heaven, new earth' with Peggy Ashcroft's Cleopatra and Michael Redgrave's Antony, directed by Glen Byam Shaw.

## Notes

1 See 'Nell Gwyn', *Wikipedia*, https://en.wikipedia.org/wiki/Nell_Gwyn (accessed 11 December 2019).
2 The 'Picture' of Dryden's verses is now lost, but in a later painting by Pierre Mignard, Portsmouth figures as a proxy Cleopatra. She is attended by a sumptuously dressed little black girl whose neck is collared in a pearl choker. The child proffers Portsmouth a bowl of pearls. See http://www.npg.org.uk/collections/search/portrait/mw05102/Louise-de-Keroualle-Duchess-of-Portsmouth? (accessed 8 December 2019).
3 R. H. Case in the 'Introduction' to his 1906 Arden edition of *Antony and Cleopatra* is making a comparison between Sedley's play of

1676 and Dryden's, which is 'still influenced ... by the love and honour scheme of the heroic play' (xxxviii).

4 'Curll' was Thomas Betterton's pseudonym; quoted in Novak *et al.* 1984, 377.

5 Novak *et al.* 1984, 376–377. Novak *et al.* comment: 'Dennis viewed Dryden's tragedy as deliberately directed toward inculcating a message that combined libertinism and absolutism' as if to write a play 'on the orders of the court of Charles II' 'that exalted the libertine manners of the monarch and placed his values and actions beyond the reach [of] ordinary political and moral judgments'.

6 The description of this pageant gives us evidence to show that the 'orientalising' of the play with black 'extras' started very early.

7 Performances in London theatres at this time regularly began at 3 p.m. All of the information in this section is extracted from playbills held at the Shakespeare Birthplace Trust, Stratford-upon-Avon, catalogued as Playbills/1700–/ANT.

8 Catalogued as Playbills/1700–/ANT, Shakespeare Birthplace Trust, Stratford-upon-Avon.

9 Accessed at shakespeare.berkeley.edu: 'Mrs. Faucit as Cleopatra, 1814' (accessed 8 December 2019).

10 See Rhodes College Digital Archives, Farnsworth Shakespeare Print Collection, http://hdl.handle.net/10267/9307 (accessed 8 December 2019).

11 This 'incident' began as a dispute between British officers stationed at Denshawai and villagers angered by the occupiers shooting for sport pigeons they'd reared for market. A scuffle escalated; a village woman was shot; an officer collapsed and died (probably of heatstroke); officials, worried about growing Egyptian nationalism, reacted; the British army moved in, arresting fifty-two villagers identified as the 'mob' who were tried by a court of British and Egyptian judges. Four were sentenced to death (one hanged from a gallows set up in front of his own house), and the rest given either life sentences or periods of penal servitude and flogging. The incident, which led to a rise in nationalism and to anti-colonial struggle in Egypt during the Great War, marked a turning point in British colonial rule in Egypt

12 Sally Beauman in *The Royal Shakespeare Company: A History of Ten Decades* is still the authority on these formative years that made the modern RSC. About Benson's years – and festival audiences – she writes, 'When Benson played Caliban in a scaley suit with a dead fish in his mouth in his 1891 Birthday production of *The Tempest*, audiences were delighted. They were still delighted by it in 1916' (Beauman 1982, 33).

13 This promptbook is held at the Shakespeare Birthplace Trust, Stratford-upon-Avon.

# 3

# 'Wogs exit nearest way': Glen Byam Shaw, Shakespeare Memorial Theatre, 1953

A pencilled note in the deputy stage manager's promptbook helps situate the production of *Antony and Cleopatra* that Glen Byam Shaw directed in 1953 at the Stratford-upon-Avon Memorial Theatre with Michael Redgrave and Peggy Ashcroft in the title roles. After 'Speak not to us' (1.1.56) the deputy stage manager has scored through half of the editorial stage direction – 'Ant & Cleo exit ~~with their train~~' – to indicate that the twenty-seven assorted Egyptians who'd massed, at a run, for the star couple's first entrance ('Look where they come!' (1.1.10)) should remain behind on stage. Then the DSM adds: 'As soon as they're off all wogs jabber. Philo shouts at them – wogs exit nearest way.'[1]

This was the first post-war *Antony and Cleopatra* in Stratford. The one just before it, directed by Robert Atkins, opened on 23 April 1945, when Hitler still had another week to live and when Victory in Europe was still a fortnight off. Resolutely 'post', Shaw's *Antony and Cleopatra* nevertheless carried into the 'post' distinct traces of the 'pre'. 'Wogs', for one thing; and a view of Egypt in its mob aspect as an infantilised space of unintelligible 'jabber'. Shaw had worked as an actor and director with John Gielgud in London in the 1930s before being commissioned to the Royal Scots in 1940. Wounded in Burma in 1942, he ended his war in 1945 in India making training films. At that point, the British Raj still controlled India (if under mounting political pressure). The British still occupied Egypt. The 'subject races' of both colonies were, as Lord Cromer had put it thirty-five years earlier, *'in statu pupillari'* (quoted in Said 1978, 36–37). Or more demotically, to the class of white colonial supremacists who hadn't learned Latin at school (unlike Cromer, who attended Eton) – and even to many who *had* (like Shaw, who went to Westminster) – the natives encountered on location as Shaw encountered them were just 'wogs'.

'Wogs', then, tropes this *Antony and Cleopatra* as a product of residual colonialism. Just as certainly, though, it was a product of global war fought on an East–West axis, of civilisations in genocidal conflict, and of Shaw's time in the military. He later wrote that what 'made the play particularly fascinating' was 'the unusual situation' he'd found himself in when he 'read *Antony and Cleopatra* for the first time': 'I was in the East, and I was in the Army'. It would be the collision of these two huge repositories of personal, political and cultural meaning that would come to define his 1953 production. He'd 'had a lot of time … to get to know the play' while he spent eight months recuperating in an army hospital where by chance his big brother, also wounded, pitched up and suggested, as a kind of occupational therapy, that Glen start making notes towards a future Shakespeare production (Walton 2008, 38). The earliest of these notes, undated but probably from 1943, are recorded in pencil in octavo-sized notebooks now preserved in the Shakespeare Birthplace Trust, later expanded in a second series, dated April 1944.[2] In them, the army, its codes, conduct, camaraderie and service, provide the terms for profiling the Romans. Antony is 'a great leader. A dashing Cavalry Offi[cer]', someone 'who can drink all night & fight all the next day & win the battle!'; 'The sort of Offi[cer] who is enormously popular with his troops, but not so popular with the Generals' (NB 1943). Enobarbus is 'a soldier through & through'. 'Men in the Services are his friends. Politicians to him are scum that floats on the surface of life'. Eros is 'the perfect batman'; Scarus, 'A winner of V.C.s'; Thyreus, 'the perfect young Guards off[icer]' (NB 1943).

This 'male caste' (as Shaw revealingly writes them throughout) of military men is put against his descriptions of the East and the Egyptians in character notes that he could have lifted straight from Cromer's two-volume *Modern Egypt* (1908), published four years after Shaw's birth but still the default text providing the standard British classification of 'the Oriental': 'devoid of energy and initiative', constitutionally gullible, apt to 'fulsome flattery', 'lethargic and suspicious'; and, since his 'mind' 'easily degenerates into untruthfulness', an inveterate liar (quoted in Said 1978, 38–39). This isn't far off Shaw's notes on Alexas and Mardian. The first is 'A wicked devil'; 'Eastern to his finger tips. Lecherous, indolent, obsequious, cunning, vicious; in fact utterly immoral, but very attractive', a man who 'gets what he deserves & is hanged by Caesar' (NB 1943, NB 1944). The second is 'absolutely Oriental'. 'Fat, lazy, crafty, suspicious, inquisitive, superstitious, timid' – and giving off 'that unpleasant impression of a Eunuch, & old (50–60)'. Since he's 'been with Cleopatra ever since she was a child', 'there's nothing the old wretch does'nt [sic] know about what goes on in the Palace'. Still (and here we hear the authentic voice of colonial paternalism kicking in), he 'is a wonderful musician & in spite of all the failings of his nature, a good & loyal servant' (NB 1944). As Shaw saw them, 'All the Eastern characters must be in strong contrast to the Romans. They must look different, move differently, & speak in a different tone. And most important of all, they must think differently' (NB 1944). He didn't say how his notional actors were supposed to 'think themselves into an Eastern state of mind' out of which 'the outward appearances of that state' would 'automati[cally] follow' (NB 1944). But he did mark the way Egypt's 'becomings' would show Romans 'turned' from 'pillars' of martial masculinity to gipsy toys. Some of them would 'go native'. He imagined Antony, for one, to have 'become slightly Egyptian looking'. When 'he gets back to Rome he looks unusual, almost like a foreigner, & feels out of place' (NB 1943). Dare Shaw say it? A 'wog' Antony?

The 'pre', then, survived conceptually in the 'post'. But it also survived practically, in the complex of inter-related working lives that Shaw drew on to put his production team together in 1953: actors, directors and designers who'd first worked together twenty years earlier and whose careers had kept criss-crossing; colleagues who could be tapped for casting, costumes, set design. In 1935 Shaw had played Benvolio in John Gielgud's unforgettable *Romeo and Juliet* with Laurence Olivier and Peggy Ashcroft as the star-crossed lovers and Edith Evans as the Nurse (a production developed from their work on the play three years earlier at Oxford University that introduced the Motley design team: Margaret (Percy) Harris, her sister, Sophie, and Elizabeth Montgomery Wilmot). In 1937 Shaw joined Ashcroft, Michael Redgrave, Rachel Kempson (all of whom he'd direct in 1953) and Anthony Quayle (who'd play his Enobarbus in Shaw's 1946 *Antony and Cleopatra*) for a four-play season at the Queen's Theatre (including *Richard II* and *The Merchant of Venice*) directed by Gielgud, Tyrone Guthrie and Michel Saint-Denis. Redgrave and Kempson (who'd married in 1935) were brought to the Old Vic by Guthrie in 1936. The following year Redgrave, aged thirty-one, played Orlando to Edith Evans's forty-eight-year-old Rosalind. The Munich Crisis changed all these lives. Tony Quayle enlisted in the Royal Artillery, rose to the rank of major, left an administrative job in Gibraltar to learn to parachute, then joined Albanian partisans behind German lines. Shaw went to Burma. Redgrave was called up in 1941 as an ordinary seaman but discharged the following year on medical grounds. Ashcroft, recently married and newly a mother, went into semi-retirement, campaigning for her husband's election to Parliament in 1945 and having a second child the following year. She would not return to the stage until 1947. The previous year, de-mobbed and back in London, Shaw had joined Saint-Denis and George Devine to set up the Old Vic Theatre School.

That same year, in the West End, he had his first shot at *Antony and Cleopatra* – and ignored almost everything he'd put down in his little blue notebooks three years earlier. Tony Quayle as Enobarus (after Albania) was certainly equal to Shaw's conception of 'a soldier through & through'. But for the rest, there was nothing of the voluptuous, indolent, jabbering East in Shaw's 1946 production. Instead, either because, newly recruited to the Old Vic, he was loyally following the 'revolutionary' step Harcourt Williams had taken in that theatre in 1930 (followed the next year by Bridges-Adams at Stratford) of putting the play in Renaissance dress-after-Veronese (which Harley Granville-Barker had first proposed in his preface to the play published that year), or because he was consciously reacting against the faux-Hollywood Egyptianising of the play in the two most recent Stratford productions (Ben Iden Payne casting a glamour couple to play the leads in 1935; Robert Atkins casting an American movie star as Cleopatra in 1945), Shaw in 1946 directed *Antony and Cleopatra* as an Elizabethan play (Neill 1994, 36; Rutter 2001, 68–75).

Designed by Motley and building on scenography that Motley had first devised to allow continuous action in Gielgud's *Romeo and Juliet*, the production was staged on a permanent set, a stunning novelty for this play, that, perhaps gesturing at a more recent

Rome, had the four-square squatness of fascist architecture. It jutted 'forward like a flattened and enclosed Elizabethan "heavens" with a tower on top for the monument' (Rutter 2001, 68). Godfrey Tearle's stolid Antony was in doublet and hose. So were the Egyptians. Edith Evans's Cleopatra was a frowsy matron in a heavyweight farthingale and a red, Queen Elizabeth look-alike wig that made her appear alarmingly raddled. (This was her third attempt at the 'lass unparalleled'. Her first Cleopatra had been Dryden's in a revival of *All for Love* in 1922. Her second, Shakespeare's in 1924, was played when she was forty, a year off the Egyptian queen's age at death.) Although reviewers agreed that the Evans–Tearle double act was technically brilliant at delivering Shakespeare's lines, they didn't think much of the casting at the level of character. There was, wrote Anthony Cookman in the *Tatler* (December 1946), 'as little' in Tearle 'of the reckless amorist' as there was in Evans 'of the gipsy'. Still, in 1946, given the actors available, the 'next casting' of Cleopatra wasn't obvious. Or of Antony. Particularly considering Shaw's demanding view that 'the whole play, literally, rests on' Antony and that while 'Cleopatra is a greater part than Antony', Antony is 'a more important part than Cleopatra' (NB 1944).

Within months of Shaw's production closing, Tyrone Guthrie recruited Shaw's Enobarbus to the Memorial Theatre in Stratford: Anthony Quayle took over as artistic director in 1948. Meanwhile, the visionary programme of the Old Vic Theatre School having collapsed, Shaw resigned that appointment in 1951. He was available, then, when Quayle summoned him to Stratford the following year to direct *As You Like It* and *Coriolanus* with Quayle playing Jacques and Caius Martius. They would share the artistic directorship of the Memorial for the next four years.

Shaw was now in a position to put everything in place for the *Antony and Cleopatra* he'd had in mind since he'd been 'in the East' and 'in the Army'. He'd thought about the characters in explicit detail:

> Cleopatra: 'the greatest woman's part ever written'; 'It has everything in it'; 'The most important quality needed is that of voice'; 'She must captivate & hold the audience spellbound by what she says & how she says it' (NB 1944).
> Octavia: 'This woman is very beautiful, serious, & good, but lacks vitality & is rather cold, &, I'm afraid, dull' (NB 1943).

Octavius: 'I want the cleverest young actor of the day for this part. Here is the first Roman Emperor, ruthlessly cutting his way through life, with all the intelligence, egotism, cunning and capacity for work, & brilliance of his nature. This man would'nt [sic] throw away a kingdom for love, but he comes suspiciously near throwing love – that of his sister, whom he professes to love more than anyone – away for a kingdom' (NB 1944).

Lepidus: 'This is the old type of Politician. They seemed to be exactly the same in Shakespeare's time (& in the time B.C.) as they are now! A man with education, tact, & breeding, but a time server. Too old for the position that he holds, too much used to it to give it up … The M<sup>r</sup> Chamberlain of the time' (NB 1944).

The triumvirate: 'I can't help seeing a certain likeness between Antony, Caesar, & Lepidus on the one hand, & Mussollini [sic], Hitler, & Chamberlain on the other … if the three actors gave one the impression of those three present day characters, the play would be very much alive, & not far out, from the "balance" point of view' (NB 1943).

The ensemble: 'Compared to the characters already sketched the rest of the male caste [sic] seem completely unimportant, but this is only so by comparison, & the actors must not be allowed to feel this comparison too sharply. In other words the Director must build up in the mind of each actor the importance of his part' (NB 1943).

To clarify this last point, Shaw went on to 'say this: – Even in comparison to Winston Churchill I don't think myself unimportant. The Public obviously would, & so might Mr Churchill, but I don't. Why? Because first & foremost my mind is full of my own life, which <u>must</u> be the most important thing to me.' That importance was what 'the smaller part Actors should be made to feel' (NB 1943).

But Shaw had also thought about design concept, going scene by scene in his notebooks giving blockings and even line readings. 'The Chief point' that had arisen from his 'study of the play' was 'that one doesn't want a <u>Big Production</u>': 'there are wonderful characters in the play, & the audience must be allowed to focus on <u>them</u>, & not on Crowds, attendants, slaves waving fans etc' (NB 1943). ('Big', of course, is a relative concept. By 'Big Production' did he mean the 'cast of thousands' extravaganzas of, say, Beerbohm

Tree's 1906 production at Her Majesty's Theatre? If so, his *Antony and Cleopatra* might be small in comparison. In 1953 Shaw would have forty-five actors playing seventy-two parts.) He aimed to achieve focus by cross-casting named parts as (also) the dozens of messengers who network the play and by cutting supernumeraries. ('Supernumeraries': that was another relative concept. In 1953 Caesar would be flanked by six soldiers; Antony, by nine; Cleopatra would have fifteen slaves variously in attendance.) Such economies 'would tighten things up' and achieve what 'The Palace' needed: 'to be very exclusive'. 'Odd Messengers popping in & out' would 'lower[ ] the status of the "Important Characters". (After all you ca'nt [sic] just run into Buckingham Palace, however important the news you bear!)' (NB 1943).

'This business of not having a **Big Production**' applied 'to the sets too'. He wrote in his earliest notebook that he had 'tried to cut them down by making all the scenes in the Palace take place in the ante-room to A&C's private apartments. (It fits very well, I think) & also by putting a certain number of scenes in tents' (NB 1943) that could be erected in seconds with canvas and poles on the forestage as actors entered. The palace 'must be exquisite. The sort of beauty that grows, the more you see it, not the kind that hits you in the eye!'; 'Outside it is blazing hot'; inside, 'it is cool by comparison & very quiet & still' (NB 1944). Later, 'The battle Field Scenes ... should be on an empty stage. (Sky back-cloth & wings)'. This would 'open up the size of the play & give the audience a rest from "interiors" before the Monument scenes' (NB 1943).

Shaw's notebooks continue with more and more pages of this sort of detailed description before pausing for breath with an 'anyhow': 'Anyhow, the outcome of all this is that the production is visualised by me as being "intimate" with all the focus on the Play & Players & not on the production', because 'If the beauty & intricacy of the verse & the subtlety of the playing & great characterisation can't hold the audience, a lot of slaves waving wands wo'nt [sic] do it' (NB 1943). Then he reminds himself of the limits of imaginative projection: 'as I said before, this cannot really be done on paper, as it were, without expert advice' (NB 1943).

In 1953 that 'expert advice' came from Motley. For twenty years, constantly updating their work, the Motley collective had been practitioners of the 'new stagecraft' influenced by what they'd seen of the 'unified concept' design of Diaghilev's Ballets Russes and Theodore Komisarjevsky's productions of Chekhov in the 1930s.

They raided Renaissance painting for colours, textures and shapes (but were willing to make up costumes in modern materials like duckcloth, flannel and rayon). Convinced that Shakespeare should be played at speed, with no interruptions for scene changes, they aimed at set design that would allow continuous play, and they sketched out costumes that, as material constructions, would do all the things that actors do: take up space, have weight, move. Motley design wasn't 'decoration' loaded 'on top of the play'. It emerged 'out of the play'. It was simple, practical for actors to use and move in, and supportive of their performances. Motley costumes 'provided the close-up of individual characterization'; design *evoked* a time and place but didn't *reconstruct* it (Rutter 2013, 132, quoting Mullin).

In 1953, like Shaw, and again in partnership with Shaw, Motley's Margaret Harris was having a second crack at the play. Like Shaw, she threw out everything she'd created in 1946. She designed costumes that extended Shakespeare's writing into clothing, dressing Antony and Cleopatra like walking oxymorons. Amazingly, she made a triumphant virtue of the too-wide, too-low proscenium-framed Stratford stage that others had complained of as modelled on art deco picture houses. Did the Memorial stage make spectators think of cinema screens? Harris used that screen to wide-angle effect to map the 'wide arch /. Of the ranged empire' (1.1.34–35) between two elegant columns across empty spaces spectacularly backed by a cyclorama – Shaw's notional 'Sky back-cloth' – that changed colour with lighting – purple, orange, red – to merge sea and sky, air and water. She did away with the notion of the 'interior'. In Egypt, a yellow canopy and billowing swags suggested heat and undulating femininity; a drape pulled back revealed Cleopatra as the voyeuristic object of the Roman gaze. In Rome, a drop curtain that stretched the width of the stage produced the effect of architecture in its massive ceiling-to-floor pleats, held in place by the talons of the raptor-sized eagle that perched, wings outspread, on its mounting, stamped with the empire's global brand, 'SPQR', the initials of the *senatus populusque Romanus*. A curve of five steps sweeping the width of the stage and down onto the forestage allowed for dynamic movement in a depth of field upstage/downstage, and for striking stage pictures in a world where private moments were all public. Paradoxically, Motley's design also achieved the intimacy that Shaw in his notebooks intuitively craved. Its spare minimalism threw the whole attention onto bodies in space uncluttered by superfluous stuff, making them look larger than life. With this design, Margaret Harris swept away the pre-war: here was modernist Shakespeare designed for what had just opened elsewhere in Britain, the second Elizabethan age.

1953 was coronation year. The twenty-six-year-old Elizabeth Windsor inherited the throne in February 1952. Sixteen months later 'visitors from around the world, particularly from the Commonwealth's so-called "White Dominions" of Australasia, came in droves to celebrate' (Rutter 2001, 70), including, as the *Coventry Evening Telegraph* headlined, 'Jap Crown Prince Here for Coronation' (28 April 1953). In Stratford, the celebrations were double, acknowledging not just the coronation, but the 'coming of age' of the Elizabeth Scott-designed Memorial Theatre, which had been opened twenty-one years earlier on Shakespeare's birthday by the new queen's uncle, then Prince of Wales (whose spectacular erotic delinquency and abdication – all for love – was the messy family business that had propelled Elizabeth to the throne). In April 1953 the flags of eighty-two nations would be unfurled along Stratford's Bridge Street (including Japan's, for the first time in post-war Britain), and fifty-six nations would be represented by sixteen ambassadors, twelve ministers, four high commissioners. 'William Shakespeare, Esq' would receive a telegram 'c/o the Mayor' wishing 'Happy birthday, you old fraud', signed 'Francis', i.e. Bacon (*Coventry Evening Telegraph*, 23 April 1953). Shaw's *Antony and Cleopatra* would be presented as the birthday play. There in the theatre, spectators would see played out on the stage some of the cultural contradictions ('faultlines', as Alan Sinfield would later call them) that were walking the town's streets. On the one hand, those international guests from former colonies showed just how 'post' the 'colonial' was in a Britain shorn of empire. (Did spectators see Britain's ruined ambitions ironically ghosted in Octavius's relentless imperialism? Was there any consolation for the Brits, watching Antony shrug off empire as the 'world well lost'?) On the other hand, in post-war, austerity Britain, where rationing wouldn't end for another two years and where life was still stuck in grim black and grey, Motley's modernist design and bold claim for colour might also be read as laying down markers for a vibrant British future.

Shaw's opening scene reportedly took spectators' breath away (see 3.1). (The headline in the *Daily Herald* on 29 April 1953 shouted, 'CLEOPATRA'S ROBES MADE THEM GASP'.) Looking like nothing out of Veronese *or* Hollywood, Peggy Ashcroft's Egyptian queen

3.1 'Look where they come!' (1.1). Antony (Michael Redgrave), Cleopatra (Peggy Ashcroft) and Egypt.

arrived on stage in a 'Flame silk jersey dress, trimmed with gold spots'. 'Gold gauze and net hip belt. Gold gauze cloak'. 'Gold kid sandal boots'. 'Black & gold feathered headdress, turquoise front spray'. 'Black & gold snake necklace' (all are itemised in the production's wardrobe plot).[3] Most definitely neither kitsch Hollywood Egypt nor Renaissance Veronese but sassy Audrey Hepburn, Ashcroft's wig was styled in a 'Light red pony tail and fringe'. (That word 'ponytail' had only entered the Merrian-Webster American dictionary in 1951.) No wonder spectators gasped. She had Michael Redgrave's Antony literally in her 'toil' (5.2.347), tugging him into the scene lasso-ed by a 'wreath of lotus flowers' (promptbook).

Here was Egypt in full Eastern colour. Alongside Cleopatra, Jean Wilson's Charmian was in a 'Pink shantung pleated dress, trimmed with white painted spots and gold' and 'Dark blue green wool crêpe drape'; Mary Watson's Iras, in a 'Pale blue jersey dress, trimmed with gold spots' and 'Wine wool crêpe drape'. Both of them wore Eastern gold: earrings, bracelets, anklets and circlets. Their wigs were 'Long black Egyptian'. One attendant 'Slave' (George Hart) wore a 'Lemon rayon short skirt. Red, black and gold shoulder collar and belt. 4 anklets. 2 bracelets'. Another (David King), 'Pale pink pleated jersey short skirt. Black felt shoulder collar, trimmed [with] silver and gold paint ... red jersey trunks. Gold earrings. 2 gold anklets. 3 gold bracelets'. Mardian (Mervyn Blake), bulked up with 'Body padding' presumably to fit Shaw's notion of the 'absolutely Oriental ... Fat, lazy ... unpleasant ... Eunuch' (NB 1944), wore a 'Pink turban', '7 bracelets', a 'Blue rayon tabard, trimmed gold', 'Red gauze hip drape, white stripes, gold fringe'. Like all the other palace 'Slaves', Mardian was barefoot.

Orientalism, then, was clearly on display, and the colour was not just in the costumes. It was written onto bodies. Shaw's Egypt was black: Cleopatra's 'Slaves' as well as her named attendants from Iras and Charmian to Alexas, Mardian, Seleucus and the Soothsayer were marked by 'Long black Egyptian' wigs or 'Black curly negro' wigs, but also by cosmetics. Not a single black actor was cast – 'naturally'. In 1953 Britain there was apparently only one black Shakespearean actor – and he was currently otherwise engaged playing an 'Attendant Lord' in *The Merchant of Venice* at the Old Vic (Howard and Rogers, 2016). The 'wogs' had to be artificially constructed, the stage manager sending a production memo instructing the cast on the 'Provision of Bole': 'Would members of the cast please ask Mrs. Audrey Sellman for bole, and please provide their own containers', working to a calibrated scale of negritude:

**COLOUR NO. 1** (Culliford [Slave], Malone [Slave], Glendenning [Slave], Sherry [Slave], Duguid [Slave], Graham [Slave], Clinton [Slave])

**COLOUR NO. 2** (Miss Jean Wilson [Charmian], Miss Mary Watson [Iras], Miss Marigold Charlesworth [Dancing Girl], Mr Richard Martin [Slave], Mr David O'Brien [Slave, Eros])

**COLOUR NO. 3** (Mr David King [Slave], Mr Jerome Willis [Slave], Mr Charles Gray [Slave], Mr Mervyn Blake [Mardian], Miss Diana Chadwick [Nubian Slave Girl])

**COLOUR NO. 4** Mr. James Wellman [Clown]

In production photographs the 'bole' on Diana Chadwick's 'Nubian Slave Girl' face is so thick that the stage lighting bounces off its surface.

To contrast with hot, vibrant, 'dark' Egypt, Margaret Harris dressed Rome in grey, 'Silver grey' for Octavius (Marius Goring) in his 'knee length' and 'ground length' 'flannel kilt[s]'; plain grey for the Roman subalterns and Lepidus. Even Lepidus's wig was 'short grey Roman'. The most colour Rome achieved was in Caesar's 'Fair short Roman' wig, 'Gold laurel leave [*sic*] circlet' and 'Purple wool drape' – imperial flashiness reined in, perhaps, by the 'Double grey' belt. Grey Rome was populated by white bodies – exclusively white bodies.

Rome: monochrome. Egypt: technicolour. Redgrave's Antony straddled these two visual worlds: below the belt, a Roman in standard issue Roman 'kilt' (though this kilt had gone 'off', was no longer grey but 'rust'); above the belt, Dionysian Hercules, bearded like his avatar, 'massy' as his club and dripping gold, a 'superhuman spendthrift' as Kenneth Tynan would call him in a review (*Evening Standard*, 1 May 1953). Where Roman Octavius's tunic encased him to the neck, Egyptian Antony's flame-coloured slashed jacket exposed him to the waist. In Rome, though, that broad expanse of naked chest would be buttoned up behind a fish-scale-patterned leather breastplate. Beside him, Harry Andrews's Enobarbus, in a 'khaki knee length velvet jersey kilt', showed a soldier too long on assignment in Egypt. His 'Black suede tunic' was studded with non-regulation gold and decorated with a necklace of golden shells. His kit was 'broken down'; his shirt, 'torn'. He was literally 'enobarbus' in a 'Red curly short wig, beard + moustache', which connected him to red-ponytailed Cleopatra, and he'd clearly learned something of oriental luxury: he wore '4 [non-u] bracelets'.

Visually, then, the *translatio imperii* that plays out in Shakespeare's script was boldly staged in Shaw's production as a contest between East and West, black culture v. white, imperialist v. wog. But for one stunning exception, an exception that located oxymoron at the centre of the show: Ashcroft's Cleopatra. Back in 1943 Shaw had written of Cleopatra that 'She must be completely Oriental' (NB 1943), then added: 'A foreigner to look at (though pray heaven she can speak English clearly!)'. That parenthetical remark is a show-stopper. Was Shaw imagining actually *casting* a 'foreigner' in the part, anticipating the comments on Cleopatra that the reviewer Kenneth Tynan would make in the *Evening Standard* of 1 May 1953 when he'd observe that Cleopatra, as one of the 'great sluts of world drama', was a role that had 'always puzzled our girls'; that the only part 'English actresses' were 'naturally equipped to play' was Octavia, 'the girl "of a holy, cold and still conversation"';

that making his heroine an 'inordinate trollop', Shakespeare ensured 'that we should never see the part perfectly performed – unless, by some chance, a Frenchwoman should come and play it for us'; and that, he concluded, 'An English Cleopatra was a contradiction in terms'? Of course, in 1953 it might not have been so hard to square Shaw's 'completely Oriental' 'foreigner' Cleopatra with Tynan's 'Frenchwoman' Cleopatra: as the common English adage had it, 'The wog begins at Calais'.

In the event, however, the actor Shaw cast in the role kept no appointments with Mrs Audrey Sellman, dispenser of bole. Egypt's black court was presided over by a 'whitely', 'ghost-pallid', 'snowy-skinned' Cleopatra (as reviewers saw her); an 'English' Cleopatra 'without tincture of the East' (a phrase that perhaps ironically codes the 'stain' on other characters' bodies?) (Ivor Brown, *Observer*, 3 May 1953; Peter Fleming, *Spectator*, 8 May 1953; Philip Hope-Wallace, *Time and Tide*, 8 May 1953). She looked 'as English as Lily Langtry', even perhaps 'too English' (*Royal Leamington Spa Courier*, 1 May 1953). This Cleopatra was one that Ashcroft consciously modelled on the frontispiece of the Temple edition that the production was using for its prompt copy, which showed Ashcroft a Cleopatra as 'a Macedonian Greek, like Alexander, without a trace of Egyptian blood' (quoted in Rutter 2001, 69). But if she displayed no 'tawny front', 'whitely' Ashcroft nevertheless managed to put squarely in view the 'serpent of old Nile' (1.5.26). She was never without her signature 'Black & gold snake necklace' that coiled around her throat, its head lying between her breasts. Arriving in 1.5 reclining on a couch carried shoulder-high by 'Slaves', she might have been a crocodile sunning itself, in a yellow-green dress that clung to her shape, a flash of pink across the belly and sinuous black cords lashing the folds to her body, a dress no 'whitely' Englishwoman could have imagined in her wardrobe.

(Mis)cast, as reviewers saw it, in a part they thought Ashcroft was 'obviously not born to play' since to date she'd been typecast as 'the gentle lady cooed at over the matinee tea-tray' (*Daily Mail*, 29 April 1953; *Daily Express*, 29 April 1953), Ashcroft would develop 'new arts', even 'black' arts, to play Cleopatra, 'a trick of dropping her jaw low' and 'widening' her 'lips into a snarl' to talk through 'teeth clenched' (*Daily Express*, 29 April 1953). Of course, as Shaw had imagined the part back in 1943, 'The most important quality needed' for Cleopatra was the 'voice': 'She must captivate & hold the audience spellbound by what she says & how she says it' (NB

1943). (Had he been reading North's Plutarch? It wasn't Cleopatra's 'beawtie' that 'did enamor men with her'. It was 'the good grace she had to talke and discourse', 'her voyce and words', 'for her tongue was an instrument of musicke to divers sports and pastimes' (North 1579, 982). Casting Ashcroft, Shaw cast one of the best voices in the business. Reviewers constantly remarked on Ashcroft's ability to speak 'verse with magnificent feeling' that 'shaded off into fine meaning'; her 'instinctive appreciation of the value of every line' (*Birmingham Mail*, 29 April 1953); her 'incomparably musical diction' 'plucking out a line of Shakespeare and holding it up beautifully' (*Daily Express*, 22 June 1960); the way she made 'speech ... the primary medium' for her 'character effects' (*Stratford-upon-Avon Herald*, 1 May 1953). But in casting Ashcroft Shaw cast something else, as Kenneth Tynan shrewdly observed (correcting his laddish review of only a month before (1 May 1953) when he'd trivialised her performance as a 'Cleopatra from Sloane Square'). Ashcroft, he wrote, was an actor who had an 'ability to convey, on the stage, an intelligent interest in sex' (*Evening Standard*, 30 June 1953).

Some of this is captured in the suspended animation of a black and white production photograph showing the opening exchange between Redgrave's Antony and Ashcroft's Cleopatra (which T. C. Worsley in the *New Statesman* of 1 May 1953 described live: 'They whirled in a flurry of passion unsatisfied down the long steps bathed in a hot, sandy light'; 'the imperial whore prods and goads, and the magnificent wreck of a bull is blinded with desire'). The still catches them in a full-length portrait shot where their bodies fill the frame. He towers over her, planted four-square yet somehow tentative as though stopped in his tracks, a boyish grin above the grizzled beard, a shock of tousled hair falling across his brow, the bare chest dressed with a heavy gold chain hung with a medallion. Stray lotus flowers are caught in his sleeves, and a twist of paper (the 'news from Rome' that the promptbook indicates he 'snatches' at line 16) is ignored in one hand as he gazes, rapt, into Cleopatra's eyes. In profile, she lifts her chin as if to rise to his 'inches' (1.3.41), the strength of her powerful jaw-line counter-poised to the liquid grace of her arm outstretched with its hand caressing the Roman's face in a gesture that works like lotus flower bondage, white fingers forging invisible fetters of erotic magnetism. She is exotic, oozing 'completely Oriental' (NB 1943) sexuality like some hieroglyphic human–animal composite in her 'Black & gold feathered headdress' with its 'turquoise front spray' (wardrobe plot). She is a shimmering thing against the bulk of Antony: her 'Gold gauze cloak' presents her from her first moment on stage as 'thou day o'th' world', the 'great fairy' Antony will celebrate in 4.8 who can 'Leap ... attire and all, / Through proof of harness to my heart, and there / Ride on the pants triumphing' (4.8.12–16). In this production photograph they 'stand up peerless' (1.1.41) as though alone in Egypt, each fixed solely on the other, finding out 'new heaven, new earth' (1.1.17).

It's a compelling image – but it's also something of a mirage as shown in a second production photograph. This one reframes the couple's glorious self-absorption by paradoxically confirming and confounding it. In it, the camera has pulled back to give a wide-angle shot of the whole stage where Antony and Cleopatra are now seen not alone, but at the centre of a scene crowded with near-naked figures, black bodies, slaves wearing collars and crouching for employment; female attendants with their eyes fixed on their mistress; two Roman soldiers, one having moved up the first tier of steps as if to approach Antony, the other, down right at the edge of the frame, clutching his helmet, jaw set in profile, aloof. Yet for all the notice the Egyptian queen (glowing as if incandescent, dead centre stage) or her 'man of men' (1.5.75) takes of them, the retinue might as well be human wallpaper. This Antony and Cleopatra are performers locked in an exquisite double act surrounded by spectators whose riveted attention is both constitutive of the performance – and irrelevant to it. A couple of years earlier T. C. Worsley had written of Ashcroft in the *New Statesman* that she had 'more than any other actress the power of touching us simply by her posture' (29 June 1950). Here, the 'posture' on display is both teasing and calculating, helped by the 'Gold gauze and net hip belt' that wraps sensuously into her groin over the folds of the silk jersey cascading alluringly to the ground, presenting a woman, as a reviewer would comment, expert in 'the arts of those who trade in love without the least fear of being thought vulgar'. This Cleopatra's 'physical passion' was unashamed, on public display 'without fastidiousness' (*The Times*, 29 April 1953).

And what did that 'tentative' posture of an Antony who appears wrong-footed in this opening scene reveal? A conflictedness that belonged as much to the actor as the part. Years later Redgrave would observe that since Frank Benson's productions of *Antony and Cleopatra* at the Shakespeare Memorial Theatre between 1912 and 1927, 'no actor's reputation' had ever 'been enhanced by playing Antony', a comment that he immediately followed with an apparent *non sequitur*: 'No creative artist is complete without a fatal flaw. In life, as in art, he is paradoxically only at full strength when his spirit grapples with this flaw. He may not be aware of it – indeed, he must not be too aware of it. But the battle has begun' (Redgrave 1983, 206–207). The 'battle' Redgrave here owns only obliquely was something reviewers had long before spotted in his work and located 'at the centre of his being', as a profile of the actor in the *Sunday Times* on 15 March 1953 put it, writing of a conflicted family history. The great-grandson of a Drury Lane tobacconist who (also) touted theatre tickets, the son of actors, Michael was a lad who'd 'very nearly' been 'side tracked into becoming an intellectual'. (His first job out of Cambridge, where he read modern languages, was schoolmastering at Cranleigh.) He appeared to have been marked, even perhaps crippled, by the age he was born into. As the profile diagnosed him, as he grew up in the early 1930s, 'a touch – often more than a touch – of the earnest, shrinking guilt, the determined harping on the nerves which characterised the poets and critics of that fretful period … stamped almost all his work'. If the Prospero he'd played in Stratford in 1951 had become, 'with great effort' a 'wizard almost painfully lacking in self-confidence', his Antony two years later would reveal deep fissures of inner conflict, a man 'writhing in invisible bonds', 'a first-class fighting animal' but one 'suffering from the inner ravages made by his dissoluteness, vanity and overworked charm' (*The Times*, 29 April 1953).

In the event, Redgrave made more of Antony than Shaw's 'dashing Cavalry Offi[cer]' (NB 1943), and Ashcroft, much more of Cleopatra than the 'wonderfully vile woman' she herself had called her (David Lewin, 'Spotlight', *Daily Express*, 29 April 1953). In this production, the play in performance out-classed the play in mind – certainly the play that reviewers and spectators had in mind, and it was gloriously bound to, as Ruth Ellis shrewdly observed, because conventional preconceptions simply didn't stack up to Shakespeare's actual achievement in this play. A puckish Ellis wrote in the *Stratford-upon-Avon Herald*:

> One major pitfall of this play has always been – for stage, stalls, and study alike – that so many people thought they knew what it was all about before they ever got to Shakespeare. A Great and at least Goodish man was betrayed by a Bad Woman into neglecting his duty to rule the world. They were punished by ruin and death and the world was left to carry on under the Man Who Knew his Duty

and did it. It is true that this satisfactory, eminently classifiable view became extra-ordinarily difficult for those with ears for verse when assaulted by Shakespeare's. The Bad Woman, in fact, seemed to be leading them a dance that couldn't be classified and didn't all the way fit in with any conceivable notions of badness. (1 May 1953)

But Glen Byam Shaw, wrote Ellis, had approached the play 'through Shakespeare', not history, and had directed Ashcroft to find a 'woman with a natural grace and effortless dignity and no need for seductive art'.

Other reviewers – conditioned to find in Cleopatra's 'infinite variety' 'the sum and perfection of all that men, in their worst moments have reckoned perfection in women' (*The Times*, 29 April 1953) – saw in Ashcroft's Cleopatra 'a dark, over-blown harpy'; 'royal courtesan'; 'tigress' who 'gloats', eyes 'blazing' with 'greedy delight'; a 'hell-cat' without 'beauty and allure' who was all the more shocking to those used to seeing Ashcroft in scenes of 'domestic affliction and the tranquilities of homespun tragedy' (John Barber, *Daily Express*, 29 April 1953). That she could 'crack[ ] wit like a Dekker' (as A. V. Coton had written of her Beatrice, *Theatre*, 30 June 1950) and show 'tyrannical caprice and a loose-mouthed, lickerish dominion over her Antony' (Ivor Brown, *Observer*, 3 May 1953) made her Cleopatra a 'terrible creation' (John Barber, *Daily Express*, 29 April 1953). This 'tyrannical' Cleopatra 'stops him' (as the promptbook records) when 'Ant tries to kiss her' on 'Here is my space!' (1.1.35) and 'won't take letter' when Antony offers her evidence of 'Fulvia's death' (1.3.57). When Charmian twits her about 'brave Caesar! ... valiant Caesar!' (1.5.70, 72), tiger Cleopatra leaps from the litter where she's been reclining, 'takes Char face in her R[ight] hand'; 'pushes her ½ down steps'; 'Char grovels at Cleo's feet'; 'Cleo kicks Char down' (promptbook). When the Messenger brings news from Rome of a marriage, the blazing Cleopatra 'advances', 'hits his shoulders (both hands)'; 'takes him by his hair'; 'Throws him off'; '(on her knees) holds his head'; 'grabs dagger from Alexas belt. (Mardian cowers ...). To messenger (dagger above head to strike)'. As the Messenger 'scutters off (while speaking)' Charmian and Iras 'scream', a 'scream' that 'stop[s] her'. On 'I will not hurt him', 'Cleo puts right hand out with dagger' and is disarmed: 'Alexas in and takes it' (promptbook).

As the moves in the promptbook record, there was plenty of the 'Bad Woman' in Ashcroft's Egyptian queen. But plenty, too, of Ellis's dazzling dancer who eluded classification by 'sheer acting', playing the writing Shakespeare gives her, making the 'illuminating speech' the 'primary medium of the "grave charm", "the strong toil of grace" of the "triumphant lady"'. It is Ashcroft's 'approach to the text' that 'lights up the whole play' for Ellis, the way, hearing Antony report Fulvia's death, she 'is genuinely and profoundly shocked by his callousness' and hearing of his Roman marriage is a 'woman cut to the heart by ... betrayal'. 'I am paid for't' (2.5.108) 'pricks the heart', wrote Ellis (*Stratford-upon-Avon Herald*, 1 May 1953). 'Within the privacy of her retinue' she turned 'for a moment into an old disillusioned woman' (*The Times*, 29 April 1953), a 'helpless victim of the love game' (Barber, *Daily Express*).

The enigma of Cleopatra's 'Oh!' responding to Thidias's corrupt invitation to collude with Caesar in 3.13 ('He knows that you embrace not Antony / As you did love, but as you feared him' (lines 59–60)) is not disclosed in the theatre records of this production (see 3.2). But if the promptbook gives no indication of how Ashcroft spoke her line, comments in his notebook of 1944 perhaps indicate how Shaw directed it. He saw 'disloyalty' in the exchange, writing: 'It is difficult to justify Cleopatra's disloyalty to Antony, but we must realise that all her life she has been interested in Great men & has used her power over them. Here is a new Conqueror to be conquered ... She cannot be judged by ordinary standards for she is not an ordinary woman'. 'Also', of course, 'we must'nt [*sic*] forget that she is Eastern' – so, remember, an 'inveterate liar'. Did Ashcroft embody these notes? Perhaps not – or not fully. A production photograph shows the moment in performance, Cleopatra sitting on her sunburst throne extending a hand to the kneeling Roman youth. No emotion is discovered on her inscrutable face. Behind her, her women stand stiff, visibly tensed.

Later, though, the equally enigmatic Seleucus scene (5.2.135–174) *is* disclosed by pencilled notes in the promptbook that show Ashcroft playing a different Cleopatra to the one Shaw imagined in 1944. Originally, he'd intended a straightforward betrayal of a momentarily wrong-footed queen. Shaw's notes are worth quoting in full to observe how meticulously the director was thinking through each scene by playing it out on a mental stage:

> On line 'Here my good Lord,' she turns swiftly to the table L, opens the casket & takes out a scroll. Caesar says 'you shall advise me in all for Cleopatra' as she is doing this. She turns back again & presents Caesar with the scroll, which he looks at casually. The

3.2 'Give me grace to lay / My duty on your hand' (3.13). Thidias (William Peacock), Cleopatra (Peggy Ashcroft), observed by Mardian (Mervyn Blake), Charmian (Jean Wilson), Iras (Mary Watson), Nubian Slave Girl (Diana Chadwick), and Dancing Girl (Marigold Charlesworth).

only treasure that Caesar is really interested in, at present, is Cleopatra herself; the rest will follow in due course.

'Where's Seleucus?'

'Here madam.'

There is a slight pause. Cleopatra had not noticed him before & did not expect to find him among Caesar's followers. But she recovers herself in a moment.

When Seleucus – who is obviously telling the truth – publicly exposes Cleopatra as he does, she becomes speakless [sic] with rage. She immediately realises the trap that has been set for her. Caesar, of course, is not in the least surprised by Seleucus's statement, for the Treasurer has already deserted to Caesar, & the Emperor is in possession of all the facts.

[As they exit] Cleopatra turns her back on them as they go & stands absolutely still, tearing the scroll, slowly to pieces, & letting them flutter to the ground, speaking her next two lines as she does so. (NB 1944)[4]

In Ashcroft's performance, however, while it looked as though her treasurer was betraying her to Caesar and making her a laughing-stock ('Caesar smiles'), it was she who was the joker (and the whole fandango with her treasurer was a set-up to sting Octavius). Dismissing Seleucus before Caesar's face with 'go hence, / Or I shall show the cinders of my spirits / Through th'ashes of my chance', Ashcroft half-turned to her girls: 'Cleo gives women a crafty side-long glance' (promptbook).

Ashcroft's Cleopatra was savvier than Shaw's. She knew exactly what Caesar had in store for her – 'He words me, girls, he words me' – which she registered in the long 'look after him' that she cast as he exited (5.2.190). Her end had been on the cards since the monument scene, an aloft space that rose hydraulically from the main stage to give a platform that the women entered 'through trap in lift' (promptbook). Brought to Cleopatra dying, Antony 'reaches up' but 'Cleo can't quite touch him', so she urges her women 'Let's draw him hither', using for tackle the silk 'scarfs' that 'Cleo and Charm take off', lowering them so that Antony's guards can loop them under the body (4.15.14). The stage direction 'women haul' and a stick figure diagram in the promptbook register the effort and physical awkwardness of the sequence, the way Iras and Charmian had to 'manage his legs' and retrieve the 'left foot' that 'hangs over d[own]/s[tage] edge of lift', the way Cleopatra, desperate to 'Quicken with kissing', hugged Antony 'face into bosom' (4.15.40). In his 1943 notebook Shaw intended this manoeuvre to 'be difficult & should appear so'. 'The picture' he had in mind was 'the descent from the cross by Botticelli', and he wanted 'the positions of A & C and the two women' to 'remind' spectators of that 'heavy sight'. But he also wanted 'For the remainder of the scene until A dies the same feeling of complete detachment by A&C ... as there was in Scene I Act I only now it is far greater. Nothing exists for them except each other' (NB 1943). When it came, Antony's death registered simply as his 'L[eft] hand drops over D[own]/S[tage] edge of lift' (promptbook).

The anti-climax was striking in an Antony who, 'shock-headed, wide-eyed, hot-headed in war as he was hot-hearted in love', had launched himself through most of the play 'like a great eager boy bursting with a zest for life, rather than a voluptary [sic] insistently seeking his pleasure' (C.L.W., *Birmingham Mail*, 29 April 1953). Shaw's production was self-consciously 'virile' (*Daily Mail*, 29 April 1953), and Redgrave's Antony was 'a soldier who, though just past his prime and tinged with autumnal regret for glorious summer spent', was 'still so rich in sap' that 'his crisis' was 'the crisis of middle age': 'It is now or never for him', and 'though vainly he may wish that he had never met the enchanting queen his sense of the present is too urgent for him to break her strong enchantment' (*The Times*, 29 April 1953). This performance, *The Times* continued, made it 'perfectly clear' that the 'bonds which cling unshakably to this once great captain are sensuality and despair of his own will power', and it was best 'in the later reaches', Alan Dent thought, when 'shame overwhelms Antony up to the neck' (*News Chronicle*, 29 April 1953). The bonds that fettered him were visible every time he stepped away from Cleopatra's wrangling (as on 'I'll leave you, lady'), only to be tugged back with a new 'toil of grace' ('Courteous lord, one word': 1.3.87, 88)). As they'd left 1.1 together, so they exited 1.3 'holding hands', finished 3.11 (after Actium) 'cheek to cheek' and ended the explosive scene that had Thidias dragged off for whipping (3.13) with 'Ant onto knees' in front of Cleopatra, declaring 'I am satisfied' (line 172), his 'head in [her] bosom', the two 'Hold[ing] each other' before exiting, once again, as a couple (promptbook).

The ruin of this magnificent soldier was choreographed in the aftermath of Actium, the defeat signalled by a 'supreme stroke' of Anthony Hopkins's music, when the composer 'turned the momentarily empty stage into an eerily echoing cavern of sound that made almost superfluous Enobarbus's cry of despair at the chaos of the disastrous sea fight' (*Royal Leamington Spa Courier*, 1 May 1953). Then 'short and long bursts of trumpet' off stage heralded the lonely entrance of Antony and Eros – the general's 'perfect batman' stopping in their tracks the soldiers who began to move into view behind them, attempting to mask Antony's humiliation – but in vain. The promptbook indicates that his men watch 'Ant stu[m]ble on top step – onto knees'; 'only Eros helps Ant up' and 'steadies him', but then Eros is 'push[ed] ... down front steps' to 'exit (running)', only pausing to 'glance[ ] at Ant when centre stage'. The soldiers who now 'move on ... slowly' 'exchange looks' when their general commands them to 'make your peace with Caesar' (3.11.6) then 'exit slowly', only the 'Old Sold[ier]' remaining behind to watch abandoned Antony 'fall onto pros steps (face down)' (promptbook), where Cleopatra finds him, seeking her 'Pardon, pardon!' (3.11.68) and getting in return 'kisses' that repay 'All that is won and lost' (3.11.70).

The tragedy of this *Antony and Cleopatra* was Antony's, his ruin grounded in the performance of Harry Andrews's soldier-of-soldiers Enobarbus and written onto the faces of the 'male caste' who had to observe it. Andrews certainly fulfilled Glen Byam Shaw's aspirations for the part, playing him as a 'hardened campaigner', a 'careful watcher of generals', a 'hearty roisterer' and 'wise old soldier who walked in leather and lived by steel' (T.C.K, *Birmingham Post*, 29 April 1953). There was not an ounce of sentiment in him. Telling a story of a barge that burned on some water and of 'gentlewomen, like the Nereides' (2.2.216) who crewed the craft, he sat down unceremoniously on the 'Pros. steps & pull[ed] Agrippa down' beside him. But if he had no illusions, he was yet capable of dis-illusion. Watching Antony capitulate yet again and Cleopatra's household triumphing yet again in her feminine spoiling of his general (Charmian and Mardian exited 3.13 '(laughing) up front steps'), Andrews's Enobarbus had to 'seek / Some way to leave him' (3.13.205–206), and doing so, died of a broken heart, falling 'head down steps' in 4.9, 'O Antony!' (4.9.26) the last words on his lips (promptbook).

By contrast, Ashcroft made Cleopatra's death a triumph. In his notebooks, the monument Shaw had in mind was something 'bare and unlived in': 'There must be something very sad about this set. It should l̶o̶o̶k̶ be a̶ like a prison … The door must look very heavy and strong. The two windows small' (NB 1943). In performance, Motley produced instead a monument that was gravely gorgeous. Centre stage, Cleopatra's winged throne towered at twice her height, made of fanned feathers, like some splendid re-invention of Rome's screaming eagle, wings metamorphosing into flames leaping skyward. The Queen who had been seen in acid yellow and crimson silk was now dressed in royal blue; invested by her women with a 'Peacock blue wool drape' and shrouded in a 'Black and gold brocade cloak, lined [with] red felt' (wardrobe plot), decorated at the shoulders with nuggets of gold that shot illumination into the gathering darkness of what was turning into a tomb, making it rather a 'feasting presence full of light' (*Romeo and Juliet*, 5.3.86). When Ashcroft spoke 'Give me my robe. Put on my crown' (5.2.279), *The Times*'s reviewer heard her reaching an ending that 'stills the stage with its slow beauty' (29 April 1953). With 'Husband, I come!' (5.2.286), Ruth Ellis saw Ashcroft's Cleopatra achieve 'the last great pageant of immortality' (*Stratford-upon-Avon Herald*, 1 May 1953). Typically, the promptbook recorded the scene much less reverently:

'Cleo takes an asp & sits on throne. Puts asp in bosom. Goes to take another – but first one does the trick.' When Charmian closed her eyes and straightened her crown, the 'No more but e'en a woman' (4.15.77) Cleopatra was fixed as a monumental icon. Entering behind Dolabella, who carried a lantern that illuminated the whole space but that came too late to discover anything but what his tactical delays meant would be found, Caesar surveyed the scene dispassionately.[5] As Marius Goring played him, he fulfilled Shaw's character brief, there being 'something attractive & yet unpleasant about his face', having 'a maske like quality': '& when he smiles one feels it comes from the brain & not the heart' (NB 1944). For reviewers, he was 'the perfect patrician'. 'The pale face, the incisive speech, and the tight lips' were 'indexes of a cold, calculating mind', the 'boyish haircut, bright blue eyes and toga' combining 'to suggest a keen young saint in a hurry'. This was a man who, throughout, had made spectators 'aware of a compelling occasion', his face permanently 'turned outward to some horizon of personal destiny' (T.C.K., *Birmingham Post*, 29 April 1953; *Punch*, 13 May 1953; G.R.A., *Coventry Evening Telegraph*, 29 April 1953). At the end, he praised Antony and Cleopatra, 'now that they [were] dead and safely out of his way'. But he could not 'resist, also, praising himself'. Shaw's notebooks imagine the final stage picture after Caesar's exit:

> The room is left in semi-darkness.
> We hear muffled drums. The door centre has been left open
> & outside we see the sky, streaked with red.
> The drums die away.
> From far away we hear Cleopatra's trumpet call.
> It is answered by Antony's call,
> trumpets distant but triumphant as the Curtain falls. (NB 1943)

The promptbook, however, gave a different ending: 'DRUMS to cover exit of Cae[sar] – then Antony trumpet in extreme distance'. On the final lines of the play – 'Come, Dolabella, see / High order in this great solemnity' (5.3.364–365) – Caesar's lieutenant ignored the order to 'Come'. Rather, with Caesar gone, he played out the after effects of the seduction Cleopatra had performed upon him when she'd dreamt her Antony:

> Dolabella stops on Pros[cenium] steps R.[ight]C.[entre]
>   – looks back – & exit
> Dolabella's EXIT SLOW CURTAIN DOWN

For reviewers, Shaw's production staged the magnificent, doomed, follied contest among three larger-than-life personalities who embodied duty, delinquency and desire – the lotus-flower rope of the opening scene emerging as a trope for the geo-political tug of war that ensued. A few reviewers observed in the production evidence of their own post-war times. As Teddy Boys (with their quiffs, flick-knives, crêpe soles and working-class London origins) were being first reported in the media and Marlon Brando in *The Wild One* was answering 'What are you rebelling against?' with 'What've you got?', Stephen Williams saw in this *Antony and Cleopatra* not empire 'kissed away' (3.10.7) but a battle across what the 1960s would call 'the generation gap': 'the pitiful, heartrending struggle of age against youth – a struggle which, deplorably enough, can have only one issue: between the smug, complacent, beardless Caesar ... and Antony, in which Michael Redgrave harrows our hearts with the picture of a man whose youth has faded and yet who is still, helplessly and humiliatedly, tortured by the impulses of youth' (*Evening News*, 29 April 1953). Most read apotheosis in the lovers' ending. 'As he lies dying in the monument', the 'grizzled old ruffian' ('almost another Falstaff in his debauchery') 'becomes the godlike Antony once more', his 'grossness' 'purged into poetry and the last kiss stamp[ing] immortal love instead of the moment's lust'. After him, 'The golden girl, dead on her throne, has the look that the dying often have, the smile of recognition that love and death may be the same thing in the end, the answer to life's riddle' (E.R.A., *Nottingham Guardian*, 30 April 1953).

But what of the 'wogs' who 'jabber[ed]' in the opening scene, who 'scatter[ed] to let Ant[ony] thro'' when he brought on the map to plan the Battle of Actium, who 'ease[d] on' when defeated Antony, improbably victorious in the next battle, returned to hug his 'nightingale' (4.8.18) and followed when he gestured them to make 'one other gaudy night' to 'mock the midnight bell' (3.13.188, 190) (promptbook)? Not a single reviewer noticed the 'absolutely Oriental' Egypt that had literally been embodied by the dozen blacked-up actors on Glen Byam Shaw's stage. A couple of notices made snide imperialist supremacist comments about Cleopatra that nodded at the production's racial configuration, remarking that although she 'dazzles us at close range we are not allowed to forget that from a distance she was, like a more recent ruler of her country [King Farouk], a music-hall joke' (Peter Fleming, *Spectator*, 8 May 1953); that 'If Miss Ashcroft does not satisfy Occidental concepts of regality' it 'must be remembered that this is a corrupt and half barbarous Oriental court' (*Scotsman*, 30 April 1953). Exceptionally, the *Birmingham Post* noticed that Iras and Charmian 'attended Cleopatra with the patient attention of the oriental' (T.C.K., 29 April 1953). But the (other) black bodies that constructed this production's orientalism were invisible. As it happened, then, the most spectacular survivor of the pre-war in the post-war on display in Shaw's production was this: that in *Antony and Cleopatra*, Britain simply didn't see its 'wogs'.

## Notes

1 This promptbook is held at the Shakespeare Birthplace Trust, Stratford-upon-Avon.
2 References in parentheses cite either the 1943 notebooks (hereafter NB 1943) or the 1944 notebooks (NB 1944). See Introduction, n. 8.
3 This wardrobe plot is archived with other records relevant to Shaw's production at the Shakespeare Birthplace Trust, Stratford-upon-Avon. All subsequent costume notes are quoted from this plot.
4 But ambiguously, he also notes of this scene, 'Cleopatra is utterly insincere with Caesar. She, already, knows what he means to do with her, & she is simply playing for time. Only someone as self-centred as Caesar could be taken in by such flagrant flattery. Caesar is a master in the art of deception, but he has found his match in Cleopatra!' (NB 1943).
5 As Shaw wrote, anticipating this moment: 'Dolabella enters. What he sees is no surprise to him but of course he has to put on an "act"' (NB 1943); and: 'Dolabella enters with a lantern. He knows what he will find, but must, of course vain [*sic*, for 'feign'] ignorance' (NB 1944).

# 4

# 'By certain scales i'th' pyramid': taking the measure of *Antony and Cleopatra*, Royal Shakespeare Company, 1972, 1978, 1982

### Up-scale Egypt: 1972

In an essay titled 'Past the Size of Dreaming' first published in 1977 (too late to be of any use to the recently appointed artistic director of the RSC, Trevor Nunn, as he was planning *Antony and Cleopatra* for his 1972 season), Bernard Beckerman asked, 'What are the dimensions of *Antony and Cleopatra*? Is it truly "a vast canvas" depicting the clash of empires?' Or is it as 'delicate as porcelain, fragile as a lyric of elusive affection'? (Beckerman 1979, 209). Twenty years earlier, when the play had last been staged in Stratford, Glen Byam Shaw knew the answer to Beckerman's question. For the ex-army officer-turned-director, the play certainly wasn't 'delicate' or 'fragile'. But it *was* intimate. 'One doesn't want a Big Production', Shaw mused in notes to himself. 'There are wonderful characters in the play, & the audience must be allowed to focus on them, & not on Crowds, attendants, slaves waving fans etc' (Shaw, NB 1943). Two decades on, those 'Crowds, attendants, slaves' were very much in Trevor Nunn's sightline. 'You can't really do' *Antony and Cleopatra*, he told an interviewer, 'with fewer than 50 people in the company' (Tierney 1972, 25).

He'd come to the RSC as a twenty-four-year-old in 1964, had a disastrous couple of seasons directing flop after flop and fully expecting 'Peter [Hall, the company's artistic director] to fire me' (Tierney 1972, 24), then pulled off a stunning triumph with *The Revenger's Tragedy* in 1966 – and found himself hand-picked as Hall's successor when his boss left the RSC in 1968 to head, eventually, the National Theatre. In 1969, working with his creative partner and closest collaborator, the designer Christopher Morley, Nunn directed *The Winter's Tale* in what famously became known as the 'white box season'. Built on the principle of 'the empty space' – a seminal notion borrowed from Peter Brook, whose book of that title was published the year before – the 'permanent design condition' for that season of late plays turned Brook's theory into practice to offer the stage as a sounding board for 'ritual resonance', 'sacred resonance'. But by putting in view the stage's technical workings, the lighting rig and so on 'in a very overt ... way', it also acknowledged itself 'a theatre space, a place for performance, a place for celebration of text' (quoted in Dunbar 2010, 85). This 'big white void', whose walls climbed so far up into the flies that there was a 'soaring, cathedral-like height to the dimension', was right for a set of plays that, said Nunn, 'were going to be looked at for their psychological, psychiatric content, their symbological content, and their hieratic content', not their 'social, realist' or 'naturalistic' content (a sideways glance at the repertoire and house style Peter Hall had institutionalised at the RSC over the previous decade (quoted in Dunbar 2010, 86–87); thus Morley's design for Nunn's *Tale* set Sicilia in a mind-space, a child's nursery, and at its centre, Mamillius's larger-than-life-sized rocking horse). Almost counter-intuitively, this 'big white void' functioned also as an old-fashioned Kodak box camera.[1] It set actors in a chamber where they were the 'most important object on the stage'. It worked 'within the scale of the individual actor – to make his words, thoughts, fantasies and language seem important' (Ansorge 1970, 17). The innovations of 1969 provided the groundwork for Peter Brook's life-and-theatre-changing white box *A Midsummer Night's Dream* the following year, which began its iconoclastic life in Stratford and then toured the world for the next three years, revolutionising global theatre's idea of what a Shakespeare play was all about and emptying out 'deadly' redundancies from props cupboards, costume skips, wigs departments and set workshops as it went. But it also provided the prototype for a complete re-design of the Royal Shakespeare Theatre that Nunn would undertake three years later.

By 1971 Nunn was consciously looking to produce a season that would stamp his authority (and vision) on the RSC as definitively as *The Wars of the Roses* had Peter Hall's in 1963–64 when the *Wars* cycle, a trilogy adapted from the *Henry VIs* and *Richard III*, was judged by reviewers the most 'valuable' thing 'done for Shakespeare in the whole previous history of the world's stage' (Harold Hobson, *Sunday Times*, 14 April 1963).[2] Hall had taken over the company from Glen Byam Shaw in 1960, barely post-adolescent, aged twenty-nine, and in the following three years had transformed the company's structure. He acquired for it a London venue and new name (gone, the lugubrious 'Memorial' from the title; 'Royal' signalling a new populism, that the RSC 'virtually belongs to the Nation'[3]). He re-designed the stage, equipping it with a rake and a fourteen-foot thrust that propelled the actor downstage into a shared space with the audience. He gained for the RSC its 'first Arts Council grant, discovered Brecht as a model for theatrical aesthetic', and, in partnership with another young turk, the designer John Bury, 'settled into the image that would define its visual house style for the rest of the decade', most importantly discovering in Shakespeare's history plays 'political Shakespeare', 'a Shakespeare who articulated "the pressure of now"': a Shakespeare 'who anatomised power (institutional, oppositional, personal, renegade), and so anticipated the concerns – and rhetoric – of the militant 1960s' (Rutter 2006, 55).

It was this 'political Shakespeare', Shakespeare influenced by the Berliner Ensemble and presented in a style 'of "epic" heightened naturalism' (quoted in Dunbar 2010, 86), that Nunn was consciously reacting to with his 'hieratic' theatre of 'ritual'. And it was Hall's trajectory that, consciously or not, Nunn was shadowing.

For 1972 he announced his own cycle of linked plays, going one better than Hall's *Wars* trilogy. Nunn and Christopher Morley would create a permanent white box set to stage Shakespeare's four Roman plays, played in historical (but reverse compositional) sequence from *Coriolanus* (Shakespeare's last tragedy) through *Julius Caesar* and *Antony and Cleopatra* to *Titus Andronicus* (his first) to tell a story not of politics but of civilisation: 'the birth, achievement, and collapse of a civilisation' (Rutter 2001, 75).

Nunn's audacity was breathtaking. Or lunatic. No creative partnership had ever been solely responsible for a whole season of work at the RSC. The challenge was magnified by the fact that Nunn was not just undertaking the exploration of four massive texts, two of which had no recent production history, not having been seen in Stratford since the 1950s, but that he was also commissioning Morley to undertake a complete re-design of the stage, to extend the thrust by another two feet and to install hydraulic machinery, lifts, and dimmers that could transform the configuration of the space and its lighting at the press of a button.

Could Nunn's 'hieratic' theatre escape politics? 1968 had been intoxicating. 1972 still hadn't shaken the hangover. In 1968 Anglo-American youth culture found radical politics on the streets of London, New York and LA. In the UK, anti-Vietnam war protests staged in front of the American Embassy in Grosvenor Square turned violent. The Women's Liberation Movement took two assertive steps forward: the Abortion Act came into effect, and women sewing machinists at Dagenham went on strike for equal pay. The Theatres Act ended censorship in the theatre industry by abolishing the historic role of the Lord Chamberlain to license plays for performance. Almost immediately, the anti-establishment US rock musical *Hair* opened in London. The last lingering connection to Britain's trans-Atlantic slave trade ended when cotton trading at the Royal Exchange, Manchester, ceased. (The final day's business is preserved high on the wall of what is now a theatre, on the exchange's trading board – those numbers functioning as tribute, memory, indictment). The Race Relations Act went into effect, making it illegal to refuse housing, employment or public services to people in Britain because of their racial background, addressing the immigration 'problem' that Enoch Powell made explosive in what was tagged his 'Rivers of Blood' speech in April. In Northern Ireland, though banned, the first Civil Rights marches took place, protesting (sectarian) discrimination in housing policy, employment and electoral law; within months, the marches became violent as the Irish Republican Army stepped up its campaign of direct action.

Four years later, none of this had been resolved. US involvement in Vietnam staggered on; Bloody Sunday in Derry/Londonderry left thirteen dead; the Tory government persisted in its policy of internment without trial in Ulster; Uganda expelled 40,000 resident British Commonwealth Asians, thousands of whom took refuge in Britain; the first edition of *Spare Rib* rolled off the press, giving a popular voice to Women's Lib and ideas that Germaine Greer had articulated in *The Female Eunuch* (1970); labour relations nose-dived in January when the National Union of Miners took its members out on strike, leading first to power-cuts as coal supplies fell, then to a three-day working week and a national state of emergency. In Washington DC there was a break-in at the Watergate Hotel; in London, the first 'gay pride' parade; in Cambridge, the first admissions of women undergraduates to three formerly all-male colleges.

In Stratford-upon-Avon, Trevor Nunn was trying to figure out where the RSC stood, institutionally, in all this. Was Shakespeare above politics? Or implicated in them? The strikes that nearly shut down Britain in January certainly had an impact on the RSC, threatening Morley's theatre refurbishment. Only days before the first preview of *Coriolanus*, the season's opening production, the *Birmingham Post* reported seeing 'just a huge hole where the stage used to be, in which dim figures moved, hammering, sawing and throwing planks of wood to each other' (22 March 1972). A month later, members of Nunn's Roman Season led by his feisty assistant director, Buzz Goodbody, one of the first women to direct at the RSC, used the Shakespeare birthday celebrations to stage a street protest against political repression in Greece. Mark Dignam (a.k.a. Julius Caesar) held up a placard reading:

> ~~Aristophanes~~
> ~~Aeschylus~~
> ~~Sophocles~~
> Shakespeare?

According to the *Coventry Evening Telegraph* Nunn 'would have been taking part' in the protest 'if he had not already been committed to rehearsals' (22 April 1972). So: was Shakespeare's *artistic director* above politics? Or implicated in them? Or ducking them? One might turn to The Boss in Günter Grass's *The Plebeians Rehearse the Uprising* to gloss the interview Nunn gave the *Coventry Evening Telegraph* in August when he confessed:

> I frequently fret about the dichotomy I feel between the kind of theatre company which morally and politically I have been impelled to form and the kind of company the Royal Shakespeare Company must be.

On the one hand, he said, 'Shakespeare is not a propagandist'. On the other, he 'does challenge us to examine our social and political views'. That means that a director has to read a Shakespeare play 'as if it is completely new and has just dropped through your letter box that morning. That means looking at it in the context of all that is happening in the world around you'. But against that, 'You must use the most thorough scholarship'. (Presumably 'you' used this 'scholarship' to get in touch with an 'authentic', 'original' Shakespeare, Shakespeare of his 'age', the Shakespeare who underwrites 'the kind of company the Royal Shakespeare Company must be'.) Paying attention to the play discovered by 'scholarship' meant, said Nunn, that 'it isn't possible for the Royal Shakespeare Company to be a revolutionary company or a Maoist company or a Marxist company, because its house dramatist won't respond to that'. In this, we can hear Nunn juggling a topical, political, even radical Shakespeare with a universal, conservative, notionally 'academic' Shakespeare – before he concludes by dropping all his rhetorical balls into a scuttering heap and managing simultaneously to advocate and repudiate politics: 'But sometimes I have to stop myself from taking an intransigent position. Because Northern Ireland and Vietnam and the American elections are there it's not enough to say, "I care about all that but they have nothing to do with my work". That is the worst kind of English liberalism' (*Coventry Evening Telegraph*, 3 August 1972). Nunn, it might be concluded from this, wanted his 'dichotomy' both ways.

Certainly, if he aimed to sidestep politics by strap-lining his Roman Season 'the birth, achievement, and collapse of a *civilisation*', as against, say, 'an empire', he hedged his bets by what he put on stage. Each of the four productions opened with a 'hieratic' massed entry to code 'civilisation' at the present moment. In *Coriolanus*, a masked procession numbering thirty-odd (accompanied by the 'biggest battery of percussion outside Tschaikovsky's *1812*' (Peter Lewis, *Daily Mail*, 12 April 1972)) marched down steep stairs onto the forestage. These 'bronze-faced automata' had no 'human attributes' but carried aloft 'a huge bronze idol of the She-Wolf' (B. A. Young, *Financial Times*, 12 April 1972), icon of Rome's mythic, barbaric origins, to whose bronze teats white-robed patricians raised two children, a ritual that briefly replayed Romulus and Remus while also suggesting human sacrifice (Peter Lewis, *Daily Mail*, 12 April 1972). *Julius Caesar* opened barely a month later to another deafening tattoo of drumbeats that accompanied the unrolling of a wide red carpet the full length of the stage and a march-down of six files of Roman elites (twenty-seven actors plus eight banner carriers and four drummers) flanking their cynosure, Caesar, who was crowned with laurel in a mime performed by Brutus (promptbook)[4]. But for all the performative ritualism, neither ceremony totally exempted politics: Cominius kicked aside a plebeian who was left dead in his wake as the procession moved on; the raised arm salute to shouts of 'All hail, Caesar!' deliberately mimicked Nuremberg and, closer to home, the National Front.

By the time the third production in the season opened in August, reviewers had grown weary of this sort of 'Sam Spiegel' treatment placed above the credits (so to speak) as an over-determining prologue (Benedict Nightingale, *New Statesman*, 21 April 1972). They'd always been dubious about its reference to the actual play scripted by Shakespeare. Irving Wardle, for one, noted that the plebs who appear in Shakespeare's 'own first scene' wouldn't stand for a moment the contemptuous kicking delivered by Cominius *et al.*, being 'anything but cowed by their betters' (*The Times*, 12 April 1972). And what was to be understood, given the aftermath of Shakespeare's opening scene, by *Brutus* crowning Caesar in Nunn's prologue?

Reviewers had also seen enough of hydraulic gimmickry. Originally, they'd been 'dazzled' – John Barber's term, in the *Daily Telegraph* (27 March 1972) – by the 'marvellous box of tricks' – as Irving Wardle put it in *The Times* (12 April 1972) – that Morley had installed at a cost of £90,000. Reviewing *Coriolanus*, Wardle wrote:

> The stage is an unbroken continuation of auditorium contracting to a precise focus. The bare stone chamber with its towering walls then recedes to reveal its secrets. The floor is mined with hydraulic lifts. For the first crowd entry the stage swings down to form a rake. A flight of steps grows out of the level; followed by walls to form a skin-festooned market place, and then by narrower side walls for fire-lit palace interiors. The effect of Christopher Morley's settings is of inexhaustible flexibility: endless geometrical rearrangements within the compass of the bare cube. It is a marvellous box of tricks, and in its present hands there seems no danger of its being used as a toy. (*The Times*, 12 April 1972)

John Barber wasn't so sure. Though 'dazzled' back in March when reviewers were first shown the refurbishment, in April, seeing how the 'box of tricks' would be used in an actual performance, he found the 'merry-go-round' of scene changes – 'walls rise or fall, unexpected flights of steps appear, and even flaming furnaces sprout from nowhere' – 'all very distracting' (*Daily Telegraph*, 12 April 1972). Harold Hobson in the *Sunday Times* (16 April 1972) was frankly scathing. Spectators were no longer paying 'much attention to the actor' in this space because 'all eyes are riveted on the convulsive performance of the stage itself'. The RSC was now putting 'its trust, not in men and women, not in passion, wit, or ideas, but in machinery' and the 'epileptic tricks' it could perform.[5]

Morley's set design for *Antony and Cleopatra* evidently responded to such criticisms. Hydraulics shape-shifted the stage only sparingly. For what the production records called the '1st' and '2nd Senate' scenes (1.4, 2.2), a massive map of Rome's imperial ambitions in Europe and the Mediterranean seemingly inscribed on stone flew in, providing the back wall to the meeting of the triumvirate that was held in a white space, its floor a grid of over-sized stone tiles like a monochrome chessboard. Out of the stage surface, bench lifts raised austere forum-style seating (set at right angles), while up from the grave lift came a huge clinical slab of a council table, as if by Habitat, purveyors in the UK of 1970s minimalism, here giving a monumental version of straight-line functionality. Rome was entirely colourless, stony, whitewashed. In Act 5, Cleopatra's monument emerged structurally, walls moving, stairs appearing, surfaces angling, then the façade opening up to give the death-chamber interior, a 'magnificent transformation', wrote Peter Thomson, into something that 'was so genuinely a fortress, so visibly impregnable, that its capture by the Roman soldiers achieved the status of a major event' (Thomson 1974, 148). For the rest, the stage (mostly) stayed put and handed the acting back to the actors.

That said, Nunn's production made no concession to the reviewer who wailed, 'I do not want opening tableaux – obligatory at Stratford just now' (J. C. Trewin, *Birmingham Post*, 16 August 1972). *Antony and Cleopatra* opened with the most dazzling walk-down he'd yet devised, requiring five pages of diagrams in the deputy stage manager's promptbook to plot. Most significantly, however, unlike the two earlier processions, this walk-down didn't put Rome on display. Rather, it paraded the civilisation Rome would have to destroy in order to become ROME. Nunn gave spectators Alexandria – in vivid colour, roiling with bodies and cultural superiority, 'the full MGM' treatment (*Daily Mail*, 16 August 1972). Ironically, this opulent Other even *displaced* Rome: the pre-set map of Roman conquest that faced spectators as they were taking their seats in the auditorium flew out when the lights dimmed before coming up on the spectacle of Alexandria's burnished world.

Nunn was inspired, undoubtedly, by what was happening elsewhere in the UK. This was the year the fabulous Tutankhamun exhibition arrived in London – and 1.7 million queued outside the British Museum to see the 'wonderful things' Howard Carter had brought to light when he discovered and opened the pharaoh's tomb in 1922: golden slippers, a gold pectoral, the boy king's gold-and-lapis-lazuli-inlaid death mask.[6] Reviewers who, like Felix Barker in the *Evening News*, suspected Nunn in Stratford of raiding the exhibition for props and costumes (or at least for ideas for them), had a point. Nunn's opening procession was a spectacle in gold that put some thirty-five actors on stage (including those playing six client kings and four eunuchs) advancing like a chorus line on the audience. Richard Johnson's Antony wore an 'orange silk frock, edged with gold trim and bright blue braid' topped by a 'Fawn and Gold lurex cloak' and a 'gold jeweled collar'; Janet Suzman's Cleopatra (in the shoulder-length square-cut black wig institutionalised by representations of the Egyptian queen on film), a 'gold mesh dress ... with lilac chiffon under-layer, decorated beaded belt attached to dress ... hem ... fringed with gold', a 'gold mesh over cloak decorated with a gold tissue border and a gold fringed edge', and on her head, a 'small gold fillet'; around her neck, a 'gold jeweled collar' (production records). Antony carried a gold 'flail & scepter'; Cleopatra, an 'ankh and sistrum' (production records). Their attendants, kitted out with lotus fans, scarab jewellery and pharaonic signifiers, processed under a massive, undulating blue canopy to music 'played on stage on flute, harp and great curving brass instruments, which look[ed] as if they might have been filched from the Tutankhamun exhibition' (*The Times*, 16 August 1972). There were 'golden bird head-dresses, tinkling cymbals, negro eunuchs and the lapping of the waves on the Alexandrian shore', and at the centre, 'a dusky, raven-haired denizen of the Eastern Mediterranean'. It was, said the *Daily Mail*, 'an eyeful' (16 August 1972).

When this spectacle dispersed, it left Philo and Demetrius literally marginalised, downstage, grousing about the transformation of their general from 'Mars' to 'strumpet's fool' (1.1.4, 13) as, centre stage, 'domestic' Alexandria was busily assembled under the mottled lighting that would come to characterise the changeability of Egypt. Tent poles erected a 'flame[-coloured] canopy' that shadowed a carpet where Cleopatra reclined 'like some luxurious, amused cat' (Benedict Nightingale, *New Statesman*, 25 August 1972) among soft furnishings ('3 carpets – rolled, 12 orange cushions, 2 gold cushions': production records). Behind her were set '1 tray & 3 goblets, 1 basket of figs'. And '1 hookah'. Thus, Alexandria was coded hot, sensual, supine, addicted to pleasure – and other drugs. Against these odds, Demetrius, hot-foot from Rome with messages (and conspicuous in the black leather uniform of the police state he was representing), attempted to play out 'The Audience' (as the scene was titled in the promptbook). First he had to watch a domestic travesty (as if playing out the cross-dressing frolic that Cleopatra remembers in 2.5) in which Suzman's Cleopatra wielded Antony's sword ('If it be love …' (1.1.14)) and Antony, in a look-alike Cleopatra wig, 'wig[gled]' like a girl and 'simper[ed] in reply': 'There's beggary in the love that can be reckoned' (1.1.15) (*New Statesman*, 25 August 1972). Then, when Antony rebuffed him, declaiming 'Let Rome in Tiber melt' (1.1.34) 'in the manner of an official proclamation' (see 4.1), Demetrius was forced to suffer the indignity of having the 'Egyptian wig' crammed onto *his* head, which sent him, 'girled', downstage 'to sulk and glare at the great man gone native' (J. C. Trewin, *Birmingham Post*, 16 August 1972).

This opening put squarely in view the stakes of the global contest Nunn's production would play out. Rome was a place of 'brazen

4.1 'Here is my space!' (1.1). Antony (Richard Johnson), Cleopatra (Janet Suzman) and Egypt.

trumpets, cold calculation and white knees'; Egypt, of 'voluptuous opulence' where people moved 'drowsily under billowing Felliniesque canopies' (Michael Billington, *Guardian*, 16 August 1972). For Billington, Rome evoked 'the sordid world of political intrigue from which Antony [sought] refuge in individual feeling'. Egypt evoked lewd laughter. Antony and Cleopatra were 'utterly frivolous and careless of their responsibilities' as they played 'at majesty' (B. A. Young, *Financial Times*, 16 August 1972) to a gallery of gawping 'eunuchs, serving maids and debauched soldiers' (Charles Lewsen, *The Times*, 16 August 1972). They may, Lewsen wrote, have staged their encounters 'as highly conscious public performances', but the business of such performances was numbingly puerile, silly – like 'Egypt' tickling with her big toe the ear of 'Mars' (*The Times*, 16 August 1972). Which of these worlds was preferable? Between the sot and the ascetic, between 'the great man gone native' (*New Statesman*, 25 August 1972) and 'the Bobby Fischer of the ancient world' (*Punch*, 24 August 1972), between the 'rowdy opportunity-monger' whose 'main stimulant' was 'self-gratification' (*Financial Times*, 16 August 1972) and the 'teetotal politician' (*Daily Express*, 16 August 1972) who, with 'a dictator's fanaticism burning in his eye' (*Daily Telegraph*, 16 August 1972), made 'the prospect of universal peace seem a threat' (*Daily Express*, 16 August 1972), there wasn't much to choose.

Nunn had clearly cast his principals to bring on stage their reputations and performance histories. Richard Johnson was an Antony cut from Glen Byam Shaw's cloth, an 'Offi' who'd served in the Royal Navy from 1945 to 1948. He'd made his film debut in *Never So Few* (1959), a World War II story – overlaid with sex, intrigue and imperial ambition: shades of *Antony and Cleopatra* – shot in Burma. He was first casting for James Bond in the original film series but turned the part down, instead playing Bulldog Drummond (an 007-type character) in *Deadlier than the Male* (1967). On stage he appeared in *Cymbeline*, Peter Hall's first production at the Memorial Theatre in 1959, and was among the first group of actors Hall appointed as 'associates' to the new RSC in 1960. Forty-five years old in 1972, full-bearded, with a shaggy head of unkempt grizzled hair (that marked him as belonging to the 'yoof' of the *Hair* generation) and 'tall as a tree with a tree's towering presence', he was the alpha male among adolescent pygmies whose entrance as Antony in *Antony and Cleopatra* (for spectators watching Nunn's Roman Season in sequence) must radically have reframed what they thought of the Antony they'd seen exit *Julius Caesar*. At the end of that play, the 'scarce-bearded' Octavius, having just invited Antony 'To part the glories of this happy day' (5.5.82),[7] didn't wait for a response but turned smartly on his heel and exited stage right. Alone on stage, Antony 'shook his head slightly, and slowly walked off *left*' (Thomson 1974, 145).

Between that exit and his next entrance, in scenes Shakespeare didn't write, Roman Antony had been 'translated' by a 'Faery Queen' as sensationally as Athenian Nick Bottom was in an earlier Mediterranean play. Not only had Antony 'translated' himself geo-politically, repositioned as triumvir in charge of Rome's Eastern territories and setting up house in Athens; he'd experienced Cydnus, which had 'translated' him from captor to captive. 'Enthroned i'th' marketplace' – where the big-wig Roman had summoned a local client queen – he'd sat alone, 'Whistling to th'air', the entire city having 'cast / Her people out' upon the 'wharfs' to gaze at a barge that, incredibly, burned on the water, an elemental translation into impossibility, as Cleopatra sailed into view (2.2.223–226). After Cydnus, Mark Antony would never be the same. After Cydnus, he was Egypt's conquest. Richard Johnson's Antony dressed his willing capitulation: orange his signature colour; silk his fabric; 'frocks' the cut of his clothes; gold braid the trim, sewn with chunks of what looked like lapis lazuli along the hems (production records). His part in Egypt was to play the straight man to Cleopatra, the butt of her jokes ('Why did he marry Fulvia and not love her?' (1.1.42)) or else, 'his brain fuming', her 'libertine' prisoner, kept 'Tie[d] … up in a field of feasts' (2.1.22–24). Antony's order to Enobarbus, 'I must with haste from hence' (1.2.139), was staged as the slurred end to a long night's drinking that produced lockerroom jokes ('a wonderful piece of work') and boys-in-short-trousers guffaws ('the *business* you have broached here … especially of Cleopatra's') (lines 160–161, 180–181). But when his audience was his soldiers – as in 3.7 – the 'diminution' they observed in their 'captain's brain' (3.13.203) was contemptible. They were gazing at wreckage.

Opposite Johnson's ageing dotard boyed by love, Corin Redgrave's lanky Octavius was a 'caustically humourless youth' who'd evidently never been 'a child' (Geoffrey Parsons, *Morning Star*, 18 August 1972). Like Trevor Nunn, Redgrave was just over thirty and had been a contemporary of Nunn's at Cambridge (along with Ian McKellen and Derek Jacobi). He was also heir presumptive to a theatrical dynasty now in its third generation. As a child twenty years earlier, he'd sat behind his dad in the car driving up from London to Stratford, where both parents were rehearsing Byam Shaw's 1953 *Antony and Cleopatra*: Rachel Kempson (Octavia), the mother he adored; Michael Redgrave (Antony), the father he both loved and loathed for qualities shared with 'the old ruffian' (4.1.4). Corin remembered being so sick with the kind of uncomprehending dread that children feel for adults they suspect aren't really grown-ups that, as a prophylactic for the doom he anticipated overwhelming his father, he memorised all his dad's lines in the play.[8] Perhaps, this vignette suggests, Redgrave *fils* had built into his DNA the Octavius he would play in 1972, an Octavius who knew nothing of childhood. Blond, white-kneed, pink-skinned, a Roman Malvolio in a starched white toga and monastic haircut (without even a 'scarce' beard on his baby's bottom smooth chin), perhaps his Octavius was not just a character efficiently hunting to death Richard Johnson's 'old ruffian' (4.1.4), but an actor treating the louche 'masquer and reveller' (*Julius Caesar*, 5.1.61) as a surrogate to play out the conflicted dynamics of another domestic relationship, one whose contours uncannily mapped onto Shakespeare's fiction.

One reviewer saw Redgrave as an Octavius-after-Gibbon. The historian had observed of the historic Octavius that 'A cool head, an unfeeling heart and a cowardly disposition prompted' him 'at the age of 19 to assume the mask of hypocrisy, which he never afterwards laid aside' (Derek Mahon, *Listener*, 24 August 1972). On Redgrave, the mask was both stony and, intermittently, horribly mobile, like a skull flashing into life. He had a trick of pursing his lips as though tasting sour grapes then stretching them into a razor-sharp smile that flicked across his face as if it aimed to cut someone's throat. In Rome, there were only two seats at the council table. Redgrave's Octavius sat at the far end, as distant as could be measured from Antony opposite. (Antony had, at least, dressed as a Roman for the occasion, in toga and purple sash; see 4.2.) On Pompey's galley (2.7), he drank – but expressed disgust that the wine made his 'tongue' 'Split[ ] what it speaks' (lines 123–124). The 'distaste' of this 'killjoy and lubricious puritan', wrote Thomson, was 'palpable': he was the kind of man who'd enter Egypt 'in the hope of finding blue films to confiscate' (Thomson 1974, 147).

In the '3rd Senate' scene (3.6), now wearing regulation black leathers, he sat (evidently oblivious to irony) enthroned centre stage. In his hand were fistfuls of 'Documents' that he consulted to tell

4.2 'Welcome to Rome' (2.2). Octavius (Corin Redgrave), Antony (Richard Johnson), observed by Lepidus (Raymond Westwell) and Enobarbus (Patrick Stewart).

'the manner' of Antony's public outrages in Alexandria – where the reprobate, Octavius fumed, had 'enthroned' himself and Cleopatra 'I'th' market-place' (3.6.2–5). He was never crueler than now, seeing his sister return to Rome. In her terms, she was an ambassador; in his, a 'castaway' (3.6.41). He savaged her, making Antony's wrong her fault – but also his occasion. 'Where is he now?' was a taunt at her naïve stupidity, more brutal because he'd already signalled that he knew what Antony was up to: 'I have eyes upon him, / And his affairs come to me on the wind' (3.6.63–65). 'You are abused' (line 88) was no consolation; rather, the legitimating fiction for the mobilisation already afoot. This same mentality, which ruthlessly objectified sister and soldiers alike, making them so many expendable pawns in his endgame, issued the order to Agrippa in 4.6 not just to 'Go forth ... and begin the fight', 'Our will' being that 'Antony be took alive', but to 'Plant those that have revolted [from Antony] in the van / That Antony may seem to spend his fury / Upon himself' (4.6.1–11, *passim*). At the end, this Octavius was incurious of 'the manner' of Cleopatra's death (5.2.336). Nunn cut the play's last line, in which Octavius instructs Dolabella to arrange a double funeral and to 'see / High order' in its 'great solemnity' (lines 364–365). Octavius and his army would attend the funeral.

[ 105 ]

But now that he was 'Sole sir o'th' world' (5.2.119), his mind was already headed elsewhere: 'to Rome' (line 364). Caesar's 'Rome' got the last word in Nunn's production.

Corin Redgrave's Octavius was a calculating hypocrite. But so too was Janet Suzman's Cleopatra. In the twenty years since Ashcroft had played the Egyptian queen as an 'expert in "the arts of those who trade in love without the least fear of being thought vulgar"' (above, p. 81), 1960s Women's Lib had politicised that 'trade', claiming for women's bodies autonomy, not dependency: a sexual revolution – thanks to the contraceptive pill – that made promiscuity as freely available to women as to men. Suzman's Cleopatra was unashamedly a female philanderer, a sensualist. But her body was the seat of her political power as well as her pleasure, a dichotomy equally topical in the world outside the theatre and still disturbing to a generation just learning to assert a separation of those spheres while experiencing the lived reality of their overlap. Suzman's Cleopatra, in line with the times of the women in the audience who were watching her (some no doubt approving, others no doubt aghast), was a 'liberated woman' testing the problematic power of promiscuity and the misogynistic taxonomy of female sexual activity. Was she a 'prick tease' (in the common demotic), a 'clog' (Dryden's term) or, in the language of the play, a 'trull', 'boggler', 'morsel' left 'cold' upon a dead man's 'trencher' (3.6.97, 3.13.115, 3.13.121–122)? Could she yet be, for all that, a 'lass unparalleled' (5.2.315)? And how did her sensuality square with her political power? Could the player queen of the opening acts who played Antony for a fool in an endless repertoire of sex jokes and footling masquerades ever be taken seriously as the Roman Empire mobilised for war? Suzman's Cleopatra kept her options open. She was a watchful Cleopatra. And what she watched was her advantage.

As an actor, Suzman almost qualified as the 'foreigner' Cleopatra whom Kenneth Tynan longed for in 1953: not a Frenchwoman, so perhaps not sufficiently 'sluttish' for Tynan's tastes, but a privileged South African of Jewish parents (her father, a wealthy tobacco importer) in a family of political campaigners who opposed South Africa's apartheid regime. Potentially, then, this Cleopatra would have opinions about colonialism, imperialism, and white supremacism. Born the same year as Corin Redgrave, Suzman arrived in London in 1959, aged twenty, to attend the London Academy of Music and Dramatic Art (LAMDA). Peter Hall cast her in his *Wars of the Roses* (1963) as Joan la Pucelle – crop-haired, loose-limbed, a 'girl' in chain mail and breeches who could beat to a pulp any arrogant comer who chose to challenge her. Her senior (and mentor) in the company was Peggy Ashcroft (playing Margaret of Anjou). They became life-long friends (and sharers of notes on Cleopatra). Thereafter followed RSC casting as Ophelia, Portia, Kate, Beatrice, Rosalind and, on film, Alexandra in *Nicholas and Alexandra*, released as rehearsals for the Roman Season were getting under way, a performance that garnered Suzman a Best Actress nomination at that year's Oscars. Three years earlier – just after Trevor Nunn was appointed the RSC's artistic director – Suzman and he married, she giving him the kind of full style make-over that Astrid Kirchherr had a few years earlier applied to the Beatles: 'fab' Nunn acquired his moptop, his Che Guevara facial hair and the full-length leather coat that he afterwards wore like a uniform. Suzman, then, could bring to Cleopatra a woman expert in the semiotics of representation.

As Cleopatra, Suzman looked magnificent: if a cat, then out of Africa, not Puss-in-Boots. Only half a head shorter than her Antony, well built, her ample chest displayed in every costume (each described by the wardrobe department as 'based on net bra'), she presented the voluptuousness of a warrior queen, Athena, say, or Spenser's Britomart. But she was hardly a workaday warrior; rather, the kind of icon that Homeric heroes had Vulcan beat into the decorative ironwork on their shields. Dressed for Actium, she wore 'Armour' made of 'copper leaves sewn on to a bodice corselet' and 'buckled on the sides', a 'beaded hanging belt' 'with scarab motif' that, like all her other belts, fell suggestively between her legs, and plenty of gold: '1 gold scaled collar', '1 gold headdress with 3 Asps & coin falls at side' (production records). She looked, then, like power on display.

But how Cleopatra acted was curiously at odds with her looks – at least to begin with. Reviewers called her 'childish', 'trivial' (*Financial Times*, 16 August 1972), a 'gypsy tomboy' who 'in this age of Women's Lib' 'sits, legs apart, as ungainly as a hippie' (*Gloucester Citizen*, *Evening News*, both 16 August 1972). Mocking Antony in the opening scene ('Hear the ambassadors' (line 49)), her honeyed sarcasm raised roars of laughter from her retinue. By turns arch, sullen, strident, petulant and flouncing, she was an adolescent bully running rings around her bull-headed Antony even as she whipped up her gaggle of eunuchs, servants and hanger-on kings into a pack of yelping hounds. Even her farewell in 1.3 – 'Your honour calls you hence; / ... Upon your sword / Sit laurel victory' (lines 99–102) – was spoken ironically, as if set in quotation marks. Alone in Alexandria (serviced by her staff of dozens) she passed the time with manicures, massages and lubricious memories ('That time? O, *times*!' (2.5.18; Suzman's emphasis)) or with equally self-indulgent unsightly tricks, savaging the messenger who, Cleopatra-like, sucker punched her with a joke she didn't see coming ('He's bound unto Octavia'; 'For what good turn?'; 'For the best turn i'th' bed' (2.5.58–59)). Later reunited with her 'man of men' (1.5.75), she was dressed gorgeously for war but was in no other way prepared, carelessly echoing the intonations of Antony's silliness (delivered by Johnson sing-song) when he announced he'd fight Octavius 'by sea': 'By sea – what else?' Why? Because 'he dares us to't' (3.7.28–29). The lingering kiss they indulged in as they exited to Actium left reeling the soldiers who had to endure it as spectators. Antony had lost his mind. And Cleopatra was the succubus who'd sucked it out through his lips.

Observing the first half of the play, Jeremy Kingston in *Punch* thought Suzman was a Cleopatra who 'Possibly ... does not love the "old ruffian" as much as she did' – but was increasingly 'interested in manipulating him':

> She lies there, casually leaning on an elbow, her hand cupped beneath her chin, looking formidable and even rather masculine, the Ptolemaic equivalent of your modern emancipated woman. You would expect to catch her reading *The Female Eunuch* rather than dallying with male ones. (24 August 1972)

But Kingston also shrewdly observed how, in this production, 'as Antony declines' and 'acquires a thicker speech and an unsteadier gait in the face of shame', 'Cleopatra grows', 'a girl in the process of becoming a queen'. He noted one 'sublimely perfect moment when Cleopatra is kneeling beside their couch concealing her mouth behind her hand'. Looking up at Antony, 'her gaze memorably combines cool appraisal of the past with calculation for the future' (*Punch*, 24 August 1972).

Calculation was certainly the name of the game in 3.13 when Octavius's messenger arrived with offers that would 'perjure / The ne'er-touch'd vestal', never mind Cleopatra (3.12.30–31). Her response to his treacherously recuperative gambit – Caesar 'knows that you embrace not Antony / As you did love, but as you feared him' – was a sharp rush of breath – 'Awwwwwwww' – that raised her from reclining on her couch to sitting up and listening. 'He is a god and knows / What is most right' contained no irony. On 'Mine honour was not yielded / But conquered merely', she lifted and elongated 'conquered' flirtatiously and thrillingly even as her hand went out to pat the space beside her, inviting the messenger to sit while she hugged her knees and leaned into his face, coyly asking, 'What's your name?' (3.13.59–65, 76). She sat impassive as, surprised by Antony, Thidias was dragged away for whipping, taking full-on the brunt of Antony's Herculean fury: 'You were half blasted ere I knew you' (3.13.110). Was her flirtation with Thidias great acting, 'excellent dissembling' (1.3.80) – or a calculated manipulation of the 'body politic' to secure Egypt's future? And the bland poker face she showed Antony: was that innocence? Or brazenness? Yet again the scene, like so many before, dissolved into effeminate embraces, Antony 'satisfied' with her assurances ('Not know me yet?'), new 'hearted, breathed', vaunting that with '[his] sword' he'd yet 'earn our chronicle', and bellowing, on the eve of battle, 'Let's have one other gaudy night': 'Fill our bowls once more. / Let's mock the midnight bell' (3.13. 162–190, *passim*).

What ensued was a sorry replay of that original 'gaudy night' on Pompey's galley (2.7). Drunken Antony lurched into the arms of his soldiers, trying to remember the steps of 'the Egyptian bacchanals' but missing his footing as his queen, who'd earlier embraced carousing ('It is my birthday./ ... since my lord / Is Antony again, I will be Cleopatra' (3.13.190–193)), stayed sober, watching. Written on her face was a line from another play: 'I know thee not, old man' (*King Henry IV, Part 2*, 5.5.46).[9]

It was not until Antony lay dead in her arms that Suzman's Cleopatra stopped prevaricating and grew up. Arching her 'head to the skies' and letting out 'a heart-wringing cry of grief' that came 'from every fibre of her body' – 'I can hear its echo yet', wrote Michael Owen (*Evening Standard*, 16 August 1972) – she was 'No more but e'en a woman' (4.15.77), a woman acknowledging what she'd always hedged before, that she was a woman in love. Still, her greatest scene of 'excellent dissembling' was yet to play (1.3.80). Dressed in black, like a widow, she knelt before Octavius. She brought her treasurer Seleucus forward to present the inventory of her possessions. Then, evidently betrayed, humiliated, she bowed to Caesar's proffered care: 'be cheered; / ... For we intend so to dispose you as / Yourself shall give us counsel' (5.2.183–186). Only, as he exited, she growled *sotto voce*, 'He words me, girls, *he words me!*' (Suzman's emphasis), incredulous that he could be such an 'ass / Unpolicied' as to imagine his hypocritical performance a match for hers (5.2.190, 306–307).

Her end crowned all. Robed in gold encrusted with lapis lazuli, encased in a vulture-headed hood whose wings framed her face with feathers made of gold, seated on a golden throne etched with hieroglyphics, she staged her apotheosis, diva made dea. As the asp she almost tetchily urged to its business bit and 'her eyes glazed, a moment that communicated the sudden stopping of her pulse', one reviewer confessed to being 'held in something like awe' (Charles Lewsen, *The Times*, 16 August 1972). Geoffrey Parsons in the socialist daily *Morning Star* (18 August 1972) was slightly more grudging. Cleopatra 'is the world's greatest actress, admired for her skill by all except Antony' who wants 'a reality', a reality he locates in love, 'frustratedly demand[ing] through their love a reality which both achieve only in the consummation of death'. It was, wrote Parsons, finally Suzman's achievement as Cleopatra to 'convince[ ] us that this reality is there'.

Question: where was 'the birth, achievement, and collapse of a civilisation' in all of this? Nunn's *Coriolanus* had seen 'civitas' wrested from barbarism and political institutions born from civic debate; *Julius Caesar*, the assassination of the tyrant who would usurp those institutions then the deaths of the liberators who, operating anarchically, themselves grew tyrannous, a threat to 'civitas'. But was *Antony and Cleopatra* anything more than a *folie à trois*, or more graciously in Bernard Beckerman's terms a 'lyric of elusive affection'? Given the scenes Shakespeare writes from 3.8 to 3.11 that move from 'Yon ribaudred nag of Egypt' (3.10.10) turning tail and fleeing the fight to 'O, whither hast thou led me, Egypt?' (3.11.51) and from 'Forgive my fearful sails' (3.11.55) to 'Fall not a tear, I say; one of them rates / All that is won and lost' (3.11.69–70), is it possible to see the Battle of Actium in Shakespeare's version as the clash of civilisations that will determine the future history of the world? Or is Actium just white noise behind a cult of erotics and crushing shame recuperated by kisses? The reviewers who called Suzman's Cleopatra a 'hippie' and 'the Ptolemaic equivalent of your modern emancipated woman' did allude – even if snidely – to a politics of the moment (its rallying cry: 'the personal is political') and to the notion of Nunn's that a director has to read a Shakespeare play as if it has 'just dropped through your letter box that morning'. But where were the capital 'P' politics in Nunn's *Antony and Cleopatra*?

One answer: they were literally marginalised, perhaps spotted fleetingly out of the corner of an eye by those reviewers who saw Antony and Cleopatra 'playing at majesty' and staging 'highly conscious public performances' to an onstage throng of 'richly clad courtiers, soldiers, musicians' and 'negro eunuchs'. For it was this cast of 'supers' crowded around the periphery of the action that constituted the immediate politics of Nunn's production – a politics visible in the theatre but almost totally unacknowledged by reviewers, a politics of representation which Nunn fitted (ultra-conservatively, perhaps predictably) to the narrative of Shakespeare's play but which belonged much more significantly (in the world of actors and rehearsals) to the offstage work that the production was doing *as radical labour*. In what way? No one should miss the significance of the fact that Trevor Nunn, in the Roman Season, employed the largest number of black British and Asian actors ever to appear at the RSC (see Howard and Rogers 2016). Seven of the eight (in a company of forty-four actors) were cast in *Antony and Cleopatra* in parts they might 'naturally' play as a 'veritable negro'[10] alive in the classical world – 'authentic' casting that wouldn't disrupt any white audience assumptions in 1972. Joe Marcell was Eros, Antony's freed 'bondman' (as the progamme made him); Calvin Lockhart, Octavius's 'lieutenant' Thidias (evidently recruited to an otherwise all-white Rome from some African colony). In Cleopatra's household, Darien Angadi was Alexas, her 'grand vizier'; Jason Rose, Seleucus (also playing a eunuch); Loftus Burton, 'her bodyguard' Diomedes (doubling Pacorus of Parthia); Joseph Charles, the harassed Messenger; and Tony Osoba, 'first servant'. Further swelling this corps of 'genuine dark-skinned servants and lieutenants' (*Oxford Mail*, 16 August 1972) and marking Egypt as a black nation, Cleopatra's retinue of near-naked and hairless eunuchs led by Sidney Livingstone as Mardian along with Cleopatra's 'girls', Charmian (Rosemary McHale), Iras (Mavis Taylor Blake) and two further waiting women, were covered with dark body makeup. Indeed, the company used so much of the stuff that Guerlain cosmetics were credited separately in a programme note (Rutter 2001, 81).

More sensational was the statement of racial politics located at the centre of Nunn's production. Suzman's Cleopatra was a queen of Egypt who, if not 'black / And wrinkled deep in time' (1.5.29–30), certainly presented a 'tawny front' (1.1.6).[11] But just as reviewers didn't remark on Cleopatra's black Egypt, so they didn't acknowledge her 'front', except perhaps for Peter Lewis in the *Daily Mail*, who called her (in language of the time that is certainly racially coded) 'dusky', a 'raven-haired denizen of the Eastern Mediterranean' (16 August 1972).[12] As in 1953, then, Britain in 1972 turned a (colour-) blind Western eye on Shakespeare's East. Perhaps that was understandable given the 'dichotomy' that was fretting *Antony and Cleopatra*'s director that April, a 'dichotomy' that perhaps propelled him to political evasion; in any case, a 'dichotomy' that was stunningly visible in the souvenir programme that elaborated his production.[13] There, under the title 'Contest for the World', Cleopatra was constructed not just as racially Other, but as powerfully racially Other: 'hated in Rome, and feared as the queen of the East, an older, richer, more mysterious and still potentially greater civilisation'. On another page, the one devoted to locating Cleopatra 'In History', her racial Otherness was whited out, a move that was only possible by producing for her a genealogy that ignored the maternal line. According to this write-up, Cleopatra 'In History' 'had no Egyptian blood – she was a Macedonian Greek, like Alexander'. The illustration placed alongside this text, however, told a different story. It showed 'a bas-relief carved at the time of Cleopatra in the temple at Dei el Bahri, Egypt', the 'real' Cleopatra. And this 'real' Cleopatra was black.

### Down-scaled Egypt: 1978

In 1972 Trevor Nunn calculated the dimensions of *Antony and Cleopatra* on a grand scale. Six years later, Peter Brook re-sized the play. He staged it on the RSC's main stage but effectively cut that stage in two, using only the downstage half and locating the play inside a chamber. This chamber wasn't a box – like the set of his *A Midsummer Night's Dream* – but a shell of four opaque perspex panels framed in wood, set at slight angles with gaps between allowing multiple entrances, roofed in perspex panels like a geodesic dome, a world not 'wide ... range[d]' and 'triple pillar[ed]' but caught inside a bubble (1.1.34–35, 12). Nunn put forty-two actors on stage; Brook, twenty-eight.

For months before it opened the production was hyped – ironic, given what would face viewers on opening night, an almost monastically chaste production. As Robert Cushman in the *Observer* (15 October 1978) wrote, alluding to Brook's *Lear* in 1962 and *Dream* in 1970, 'Mr Brook is now generally felt to have a historic function at Stratford: about once a decade, he arrives and changes everything'. Thus, 'by general consent', the opening of *Antony and Cleopatra* was being 'regarded as the most important first night in the British year' (Sydney Edwards, *Liverpool Daily Post*, 5 August 1978), arousing 'hopes of a landmark production in the class of his *Lear* and .... *Dream*' (Irving Wardle, *The Times*, 11 October 1978). But as Bernard Levin observed about 'expectation', Brook 'precedes expectation': 'it is never any good looking for him where he was last seen, for he will always have moved on' (*Sunday Times*, 15 October 1978). And Levin read the 'moving on' that Brook was doing in *Antony and Cleopatra* as the director's fundamental reconsideration of the play's subject, size and style, a decisive 'break ... with the voluptuous tradition that reached its apogee in [Glen Byam] Shaw's 1953 production'. Levin continued: 'But Mr Brook is not in the business of breaking with tradition simply *pour épater les bourgeois*; he has something to say about the play, and deserves an attentive hearing when he says it'.

That last, with its rather sniffy tone, implies diplomatically what other reviews after the opening night stated outright: disappointment in the production's 'Finite Variety' (as one headline put it) that left audiences 'underwhelmed' (*Observer*, 15 October 1970). Audiences were warned: 'Anyone visiting the show in hopes of spectacular novelties' would 'sit through its three and a half hours in vain' (*The Times*, 11 October 1978). But 'spectacular novelties' were not what Brook had in mind for this *Antony and Cleopatra*. Rather, the reverse. The intimate play that Byam Shaw intuited (but ultimately didn't direct) and that Trevor Nunn had no time for, given his own imperial ambitions, was the play Brook now attempted to stage, setting it inside that oh-so-fragile, oh-so-narrow, oh-so-self-contained-and-self-absorbed perspex bubble.

Brook had working with him a production team he'd collaborated with at the RSC over the past fifteen years, on *Marat/Sade* (1964, filmed 1967), *Theatre of Cruelty* (1965), *US* (1966) and *A Midsummer Night's Dream* (1970): the designer Sally Jacobs and the composer Richard Peaslee. His Cleopatra was an actor he had brought to the RSC in her twenties to play Charlotte Corday in *Marat/Sade*, Glenda Jackson; his Antony, Alan Howard, had just finished a three-year stint touring the world as Theseus/Oberon in Brook's *Dream*, cast in that double-act on the back of his decadently erotic and monstrously magnetic Lussuriosso in *The Revenger's Tragedy*

(1966). Directing for the RSC for the first time since the *Dream*, Brook said that he was 'returning to a basic line of work'. He hadn't been gone. He looked on his work with the RSC 'as an unbroken chain'. What he did in between, he said, related 'to Peter Hall's big contribution to the whole theatre. [Hall] insists Shakespeare is the mainstream and that his directors and actors also do other work and then return to the central and most difficult challenge: Shakespeare, never to be mastered, never to be conquered' (*Evening Standard*, 15 September 1978). One aspect of that 'basic line of work' on Shakespeare had been shrewdly spotted by Peter Fiddick, reviewing *A Midsummer Night's Dream* in the *Guardian* eight years earlier. What Brook seemed 'driven to work on' was 'not merely his own concept of Shakespeare's ... text – the concept, that is, of a man in the vanguard of modern European theatre – *but his audience's concept*' (my italics). In *Antony and Cleopatra*, as review after review indicates, Brook challenged his audience's concept of the play head-on, the 'received idea', as Irving Wardle put it in *The Times*, 'of a tragic love affair between two doomed, great-hearted principals ranged against a cold-blooded political adversary'. But, Wardle continued, since 'Brook's approach to Shakespeare has always been that he gives you more from moment to moment than any other dramatist', moments that tug insistently against, even pull the rug out from under, any 'received idea', he had 'gone out of his way' with *Antony and Cleopatra* 'to point up all the things that do not conform to the myth of the world well lost' (11 October 1978).

There was no gold in this production; no scarabs or animal-headed priests; no cinema-inspired wigs (rather, a Cleopatra in a severe Eton crop); no togas; no gang of court hangers-on. Nothing exotic. Nor what historically had coded the 'exotic' for this play: there was not a black body in sight. Alexandria was a square of red carpet on a honey-wood floor where Cleopatra and her 'girls' (Charmian: Paola Dionisotti; Iras: Juliet Stevenson), their near-isolation throwing their relationship into high relief, presented a female triumvirate to match the men's. Rome was a woven mat (replacing the carpet) and four plain wooden benches set in front of the perspex panels, three of the benches pulled up to the sides of the square when the 'triple pillar[s] of the world' (1.1.12) met, positioning them literally to square off opposite each other while a 'crowd' of four looked on. (Barring a couple of black leather upholstered stools that looked like capstans, one of which would serve as Cleopatra's 'throne', there was no other furniture on Brook's stage.) The lighting design, using white light, involved 'scarcely more ... than a straightforward increase or diminution of wattage' (*Sunday Times*, 15 October 1978).

Equally unfussy and looking mostly made up from Egyptian linen, Sally Jacobs's costumes used a gravely muted colour palette and simplicity of design: for Cleopatra, tube dresses in black and brown stripes or Aegean blue topped with black stoles and head-dresses reminiscent of Yasser Arafat. Indolent, Antony wore a 'Striped Blue/Orange Arab Robe' tied at the waist (production records); in action, a fawn suede tabard over black leather breeches and knee-high black boots; for the Roman summit, a full-length white linen over-tabard covering the leather, belted at the waist, edged with a red stripe that made him 'Other' than the Romans (Octavius: Jonathan Pryce; Lepidus: Paul Brooke) who were in long white gowns flashed with blue. Brightness was Cleopatra's backdrop: Iras in sun-yellow spotted with black and tied with an orange woven belt; Charmian in a gauzy custard-yellow and grey striped strap dress. Kitted out for Actium, Cleopatra appeared in a black shift with a voluminous over-mantle in bold black stripes on a deep rust background, the dressing of which started at her head, covering her brow, then was pinned at the back of her neck, framing her high-cheekboned face, wide mouth and narrowed eyes before falling to the ground. She was the walking image of the Sphinx. (It could be supposed that Brook and Jacobs used this costume here for the same kind of mischievous, iconoclastic business that the Mendelssohn 'Wedding March' had been put to in *A Midsummer Night's Dream*, accompanying Bottom en route to Titania's bower.)

The effect of this scaling down was, as Michael Billington wrote in the *Guardian*, to 'domesticate the tragedy; to present it as a play of private emotion rather than public rhetoric' (11 October 1978), where the emotion had more to do with personal power than with erotics. Spectators caught the first glimpse of this in the opening moments of the production. Philo (John Bowe) and Demetrius (David Lyon) appeared upstage in the centre gap between the perspex panels, the deputy stage manager's note telling them simply to 'stand there' while they talked in muted voices about the transformation of their general from 'plated Mars' to 'strumpet's fool' (1.1.4, 13). Hearing him coming and seeing shadow shapes massing behind the scene (the panels being translucent but not transparent, giving a 'world beyond' of indistinguishable forms), they moved downstage, to the edge of the carpet, not stepping on it, waiting. The 'big entrance', when it came, brought just seven bodies onto the stage. The full extent of any ritual which that entrance might have been performing was briefly choreographed as a slight Bacchic moment: entering, Enobarbus, Charmian and Alexas were, the promptbook indicated, 'All [to] spin twice', a sign perhaps of Egypt's giddiness, or its queen's propensity for turning. In their wake, Antony and Cleopatra entered, Cleopatra riding 'on Antony's back' (promptbook).

That entrance epitomised their relationship. Where Richard Johnson in 1972 played Antony the broken-down sot, Alan Howard played Antony's virility. This Antony was the veteran of innumerable military campaigns, a believable survivor of that terrible retreat from Modena recounted by Octavius when, his army facing starvation, he drank the 'stale of horses' and ate 'strange flesh / Which some did die to look on' (1.4.63, 68–9). He entered here as a Hercules carrying empire lightly on his back – not unlike the actor himself, whose current reputation was Herculean. In the RSC season just gone he had played the title roles in *Henry V* and the three parts of *Henry VI* in repertoire before adding as the final production in the season *Coriolanus*, all directed by Terry Hands. *Coriolanus* was still running as *Antony and Cleopatra* rehearsed. After Brook's production opened, Howard commuted between performances in London and Stratford-upon-Avon, not just, as an actor, moving between two massive parts, but, as two characters, showing on alternate nights, heads and tails, the opposite sides of the Roman coin that Shakespeare minted in his theatrical exchequer.

Mounted on him, *enthroned* on him, Jackson's Cleopatra was a woman who instinctively used men as human furniture; proleptically, an imperious Maggie Thatcher (already leader of the Tory Party and who next year would become Britain's Prime Minister). Brook may have intended to cast Charlotte Corday as Cleopatra, the childlike narcoleptic committed to the French Revolution-era Parisian asylum in Peter Weiss's *Marat/Sade*. A melancholic, her post-adolescent body dropping randomly into sleep, Jackson's Corday projected a vulnerable sensuality, its open availability entirely without intent, while her extraordinary voice, pitched lower than most men's, was, against the physical image of fragility, stentorian. But since her apprenticeship under Brook in 1964, Jackson had played very different women: on film, Gudrun in Ken Russell's

*Women in Love* (1969, for which she won an Oscar); Queen Elizabeth in the BBC mini-series *Elizabeth R* (1971); and, in the theatre, Hedda in *Hedda Gabler* (RSC, 1975, directed by Trevor Nunn; subsequently filmed) – parts that put centre stage the qualities that now wrote Jackson's actorly signature in bold capitals: 'blazing intelligence, sexual challenge and abrasiveness' (McFarlane 2003, 339). If Janet Suzman played Cleopatra the cat, Glenda Jackson played Cleopatra the hieroglyph, as hard-edged as inscriptions on a stele, and just as unreadable. In an *Observer* interview published a week before Brook's production opened that asked 'previous' Cleopatras to reflect on the Egyptian queen, Suzman had observed that 'the eternal teasing question', the 'chiefest stroke of Shakespeare's genius', was 'just how much in love' with Antony Cleopatra 'really was' (interview with Judith Cook, 8 October 1978). The 'eternal ambiguity' that Suzman had played in 1972 with such emotional nuance of intonation and gesture, Jackson's performance in 1978 registered as a blank. Her Cleopatra was detached, emotionally unplugged, a Cleopatra whom reviewers would find 'stupendous and utterly unmoving' (*The Times*, 11 October 1978); 'sardonic to the point of contempt' (*New Statesman*, 20 October 1978); 'mannish', 'an ironic observer of male emotions' (*Listener*, 16 October 1978). The 'danger' of her 'succumbing to absolute passion' was 'no closer than Mrs Thatcher's likelihood of weeping at Cabinet meetings' (*Evening Standard*, 11 October 1978). Jackson was, in short, a Cleopatra for a deeply post-romantic, post-idealist world; a Cleopatra to challenge the 'received idea' of *Antony and Cleopatra* as the greatest love story ever told.

Not insignificantly, their first entrance gave the principals no eye contact. It established a relationship that was literally intimate but only functionally so. It showed their gaze cast elsewhere: a sign of things to come, for this Antony and Cleopatra would be most themselves when apart. It was as if the 'elusive affection' (Bernard Beckerman's phrase) that mostly eluded them as a couple could only reveal itself displaced onto other objects, other intimacies, sometimes monstrously inverted, as in 3.13 ('you have been a boggler ever' (line 115)). That was the scene that Johnson had used to unleash the full fury of Antony's rage upon Suzman's Cleopatra, physically assaulting her, sending her sprawling. By contrast, Howard's Antony attacked Caesar's messenger, and in such a way as to make that body Cleopatra's stand-in. The promptbook records his moves: 'Grabs hold of Thidias &

lifts him up'; 'Throws Thidias down R[ight] of Cleopatra'; 'kicks Thidias'.

The self that Jackson's Cleopatra revealed when she was alone with her girls in Egypt was a self-sufficient self. Did she, as Enobarbus argued (not without lewd imputation), need an Antony to manage 'the business ... broached' in Egypt, 'especially that of Cleopatra's' (1.2.180–181)? It appeared not. Early in her career Jackson had played an Ophelia that the critic Penelope Gilliatt (1971) thought ready to play the Prince himself.[14] Now she was a Queen of Egypt to out-Caesar Caesar, to make the Roman triumvirate redundant. There was nothing in her Alexandria of the 'Ptolemaic glee-factory' that reviewers had come to expect in productions of this play (Benedict Nightingale, *New Statesman*, 20 October 1978). As their review discourse discovers, still lugging the baggage of received ideas into the theatre with them and still burdened with pre-1960s attitudes to women, stereotypically anchored on the semiotics of women's hair, reviewers groused that they saw nothing in Brook's production of 'swinging Egypt': there were 'no guests to have fun, nor any fun to have guests'. Instead, Jackson's Cleopatra and her girls sat perched 'upright on lonely cushions, hair cropped short, like girls in a boarding school of somewhat butch tendencies' with 'not so much as a picnic of crisps and lemonade ... to soften the austerity of their midnights' (*New Statesman*, 20 October 1978). Reviewers weren't expecting the kind of Cleopatra who played the actual rhythms of the writing Shakespeare gives her – or the Cleopatra who is made from those clipped lines:

> You must not stay here longer; your dismission
> Is come from Caesar; therefore hear it, Antony.
> Where's Fulvia's process? – Caesar's, I would say.
> Both? (1.1.27–30)

> Cut my lace, Charmian, come!
> But let it be; I am quickly ill and well –
> So Antony loves. (1.3.72–74)

> I do not like 'But yet'. It doth allay
> The good precedence. Fie upon 'But yet'! (2.5.50–51)

Nor were they expecting the savage self that was released by the news of the Roman wedding. On 'Madam, he's married to Octavia' (2.5.60), the promptbook has: 'X [cross] to Messenger & grabs him by the hair'; 'kicks him to C[entre] L[eft]', 'grabs his hair & drags him to D[own] C[entre]'; 'shakes him by the hair'; 'draws a knife from Messenger's costume & threatens him with it', while the eunuch Mardian (Philip McGough) stood 'pressed up against R[ight] screen' trying to make himself invisible (promptbook). Given that Richard Griffiths, playing the Messenger, would easily have made two of Glenda Jackson, her manhandling of him was not just impressive; it was shocking, not least to Michael Billington in the *Guardian*, who found her 'the most ferocious' Cleopatra he had ever seen. A boggler? 'A Bugner would be more like it' (11 October 1978). As if to rewind the coils of violence she'd released and to regain the self whose loss of self Charmian chastised – 'keep your self within your self' (2.5.75) – this Cleopatra had to enact more violence. On 'Melt Egypt into Nile' (2.5.78) the promptbook records 'circles on spot'. Her frenzied spinning recalled, in over-drive, the opening moments of the play. It would return in 3.13 after Thidias stumbled out, leaving behind a 'satisfied' Antony and a Cleopatra who, declaring 'since my lord / Is Antony again, I will be Cleopatra' (3.13.172, 191–192), would 'spin[ ] on the spot & keep[ ] spinning until she gets giddy & collapses C[entre] of carpet', and again in 5.2 when, having punished Seleucus's betrayal ('shakes Seleucus'; 'throws him on floor'; 'starts kicking him') and endured Octavius's 'adieu ... Adieu ('Kisses Cleopatra's hands'; 'Kisses Cleopatra on the cheeks'), she moved to 'U[p] C[entre] of carpet & dances a few steps' before snarling 'He words me, girls, he words me' (lines 189, 190) (promptbook).

In contrast to this solipsistic Cleopatra, Alan Howard's Antony was a man who craved the human touch. In the opening scenes in Egypt it is he, in the promptbook, who makes the moves: 'kisses her' (1.1.38 on 'to do thus'); 'gives her letter (1.3.66 on 'Fulvia's death'); 'takes hold of Cleopatra' (1.3.57 on 'I go from hence'), then, when she 'throws letter on floor', moves away, and 'sits', 'crouches' next to her. A production photograph captures this last moment, showing Antony kneeling, mid-speech, holding one of Cleopatra's hands in both of his, his eyes locked on her face before, in the next frame, his head falls onto their clenched hands. She sits, back ramrod straight, the arch look on her frozen face seeming to say 'excellent dissembling ... / You can do better yet, but this is meetly' (1.3.80, 82) (see 4.3). Her other hand, however, registers most in the image. It faces the camera, held flat, rigid, fingers straight and clamped together like a saw to cut through Antony's asseverations, or like one of those two-dimensional pictograms on a pharaoh's

4.3 'You can do better yet, but this is meetly' (1.3). Cleopatra (Glenda Jackson), Antony (Alan Howard).

tomb. It was Antony who brought her finally into an 'embrace' before his 'Away!' ordered – with masterful paradox untinged by irony – a going that he said would be a staying, a 'separation' that would be a 'residing', a 'fleeting' that would yet 'remain' (1.3.107, 104, 105, 106). His Antony, then, was full of the kind of idealism that never entered this Cleopatra's ken. Or maybe he was just full of poppy-cock.

Certainly, he was much more at home among men: just how much was registered in 1.2. Now he was listening to the 'News ... from Rome' (1.1.18) that he'd daffed aside earlier: insurrection in Syria; faction in Rome; civil war; and then, from Sicyon, 'Fulvia thy wife is dead' (1.2.124). He sent the messenger away, stood facing out, alone in the scenic bubble, a lop-sided half-smile on his face as he mused, 'There's a great spirit gone!' (line 129). (As he spoke it, the line was an epitaph.) 'She's good, being *gone*' (line 133). (That line with Howard's emphasis on 'gone' was a confession; it was a truth, though a truth *escaped* into utterance, not intended for other ears.) But then, when the next thought arrived in his mouth, another escapee from his mind, it caught him, arrested him with a further truth – and its utterance registered self-reproach: 'The hand could pluck her back that shoved her on' (line 134). Here was Antony recoiling from dotage, getting 'holy': 'I must from this enchanting queen break off' (line 135). Just then Enobarbus (Patrick Stewart, having his second go at the part, more grizzled but less cynical than in 1972) entered. Carrying cushions. He reacted to Antony's new puritanism ('I must with haste from hence' (line 139)) with lewd jokes, the two of them lounging on the cushions until Antony suddenly stood and cut him off with the line he intended would be the gob-stopper; only it wasn't:

> Fulvia is dead.
> Sir?
> Fulvia is dead.
> Fulvia?
> Dead. (1.2.163–167)

Pause (promptbook). That silence, interminable in the theatre as the two eyeballed each other, was finally broken with a whoop, marked in the promptbook against 'Why, sir, give the gods a thankful sacrifice' (line 168): 'Enobarbus yells with delight & embraces Antony, spinning him around', then crouching next to him to dissolve Antony's high-mindedness in conspiratorial gags about men's chances: 'If there were no more women but *Fulvia* then had you indeed a cut ...' (lines 172–174). The moment was laddish but also bursting with sheer sensual pleasure, an animal pleasure that Antony never shared with Jackson's Cleopatra, for as Irving Wardle noted, 'Direct human affection of the Roman kind' was 'the one thing' he could 'not get' from her (*The Times*, 11 October 1978). It was there, though, with other men.

With the 'boy Caesar' for one. As Jonathan Pryce played him – against the grain of 'received ideas' and against the grain of his own disposition to snarkiness on stage: to wit, the obnoxious yob Petruchio that Pryce was playing opposite Paola Dionisotti's Kate in that same RSC season – Octavius emerged as the great revelation of Brook's production. With his page-boy hairstyle that took years off his back, his habit of sitting like a schoolboy with his hands folded neatly in his lap and his endearing beakiness, he was not 'the usual ice cold schemer' but 'a man of reckless passion', 'unstinted affection for his sister' and 'delight in revelry' (*Guardian*, 11 October 1978). Wardle saw the attachment between this 'gentle, sweet-natured Octavius' and Antony as 'more than an onerous political duty'. There was 'straightforward human love between the veteran and the young man'. After their first parley in Rome, when each side put 'his point with the slow vigilance of a chess player', the 'reconciliation [was] sealed with a delighted embrace' (*The Times*, 11 October 1978) and later with a raucous knees-up on Pompey's galley.

It was a *Boy's Own* party, the flip side to the 'boarding school' atmosphere of Alexandria. And in the theatrical memories of veteran RSC watchers it must have stirred images from John Barton's 1968 *Troilus and Cressida*, when Achilles, played by a younger Alan Howard, upstaged the party that he was hosting for the visiting Trojans in the Greek camp – another *Boy's Own* event – by appearing at the height of its drunken revelry in drag, cross-dressed as Helen of Troy. The night on Pompey's galley had the same abandon, the same celebration of animal manliness, the same edginess and the same citation of the absent iconic woman. Cleopatra and her crocodile shadowed these 'Egyptian Bacchanals' (2.7.104), brought to Rome like souvenirs of decadent life in Alexandria. Billington described the scene as a 'magnificent piece of voluptuous staging':

> The drunken world leaders enter with the faintly exaggerated tip-toe care of people half-cut. With the introduction of Richard Peaslee's music the tempo of the Bacchanal slowly increases. A boy singer is rather suggestively whirled around Antony's waist like an Apache dancer [a move that recalled Achilles-as-Helen spun by Hector, naked legs clamped around the Trojan's waist]; pillows are flung and benches overturned as the dancers circle the stage in leaps and bounds like minor Baryshnikovs; and eventually the floor cloth rises into into [*sic*] the air and becomes a huge sail to the furls of which Antony precariously clings. (*Guardian*, 11 October 1978)

Pryce's Octavius genuinely looked up to Antony. He gave his adored sister (Octavia: Marjorie Bland) to him in marriage sincerely, and he showed more affection in the kisses he exchanged with her in the 'betrothal' scene (2.3) than Antony did. Antony planted a remote kiss on her hand as he owned up to his reputation – 'blemishes' that he admitted were blazoned in 'the world's report' – which, in

4.4 'O thou day o'th' world, / Chain mine armed neck! Leap thou, attire and all, / Through proof of harness to my heart' (4.8). Antony (Alan Howard), Cleopatra (Glenda Jackson).

a kind of pre-nuptial contract, he promised to reform ('I have not kept my square, but that to come / Shall all be done by th' rule' (2.3.5–7). In the moment, Antony sincerely meant those words (just as, earlier, he'd sincerely meant those words to Cleopatra about 'fleeting' and 'residing').

Exiting, Pryce's Octavius gave no sign of seeing the Soothsayer (David Bradley), the Egyptian brought to Rome in Antony's retinue who was standing just inside the scene, far right, in the shadow of the bubble, observing this betrothal. But Antony, centre stage, did. He'd been studying his own hand (promptbook). (Was he still feeling the cool pressure of Octavia's flesh upon it? Was he searching a future written on his palm? Or having just given this hand away, was he calculating his betrayal, if that's what it was, of the woman in Egypt – who was only a gipsy, after all?) Antony looked up and saw the Soothsayer, who crossed to him, took that studied hand (promptbook) and sealed a new deal ('O Antony, stay not by his [Octavius's] side': 'Make space enough between you' (2.3.17, 22)). After the Soothsayer's exit, the promptbook records Antony's brief turmoil: 'paces L[eft] & R[ight]'. Then: 'Stops D[own] C[entre] on 'I will to Egypt'. Pause. 'And though I make this marriage for my peace' (pause), 'I'th' East my pleasure lies' (2.3.37–39). There was that same wry half-smile on his face (rueful or cynical, Alan Howard was capable of suggesting both simultaneously) as when he'd honoured a 'great spirit gone'. This new marriage was over even before it began. And in the long pause that followed, one calculation that might have been imagined passing through Antony's mind was how little women figured in the traffic between men, for his silence was broken only when he turned and saw Ventidius waiting to receive his commission to Parthia. Oh blessèd reprieve from uncomfortable thoughts! War! How much simpler was 'war' than 'women'. The two soldiers exited together.

It was because both Pryce's Octavius and David Suchet's Pompey idolised Antony 'as a senior partner by whom they have always felt outclassed' – a view, Irving Wardle shrewdly observed, 'Antony shares' – that when the defeat at Actium came, it was met with 'incredulity on both sides' (*The Times*, 11 October 1978). Howard's Antony staggered into 3.11 (titled in the promptbook 'Antony's retreat'), sank to his knees, covered his eyes *and wept* (promptbook) at his 'unbelievable humiliation', while Octavius, from the moment of that unbelievable triumph, began 'to lose his innocent charm and develop into the icy calculating demigod of the later scenes'

(*The Times*, 11 October 1978), and more dangerously, into the petulant adolescent martinet who'd make a laughing stock of the man he'd once worshipped. Pryce's Octavius was never nastier nor more childish than when he entered 4.1 running, bleating 'He calls me boy' as he swung Antony's letter around his head 'in a state of delirious frenzy' (*Guardian*, 11 October 1978) before making a paper kite of it and dismissing Antony with a mock: 'Let the old ruffian know / I have many other ways to die; meantime / Laugh at his challenge' (4.4–6).

Ugly but accurate, Octavius's jibe set the tone of this Antony's end, an end that would mark the death of a soldier rather than a lover, for, as Billington observed, it was 'the agony of his humiliation and defeat in a fighter's world' that moved spectators 'more deeply than ... the strength of his love for Cleopatra' (*Guardian*, 11 October 1978). But his end was also, in the botched suicide, farcical. His scene with Eros (Hilton McRae), persuading his freed slave to honour the promise made at his enfranchisement to kill his general if the time came when Antony's honour could only be saved in death, was more nearly a love scene than any that Howard's Antony played with Cleopatra.

That end started as far back as 4.10 (Antony: 'Their preparation is today by sea' (line 1)), staged simultaneously with 4.11 (Octavius: 'But being charged, we will be still by land' (line 1)), the generals standing just outside the perspex bubble, their backs to the audience, gazing upstage at the battle beyond. Those parallel scenes ran straight in to 4.12, Antony remaining 'onstage looking toward the fight' until, on 'All is lost!' (4.12.9), he hurled 'his sceptre away &' moved back inside the bubble (promptbook), into the world of tangled personal destinies. He handed his helmet to Scarus, already by this gesture starting the stripping away of his soldiership that would culminate in his quiet conversation with his Eros.

But before that, he would unleash his final Herculean rage when, bellowing 'Eros, Eros!', the 'eros' who entered was Cleopatra (4.12.30). This time she was innocent of the betrayal he accused her of. But as she'd said earlier of another innocent, innocence is not necessarily a defence, particularly against elemental forces: 'Some innocents 'scape not the thunderbolt' (2.5.77). Now that thunderbolt hit her square in the face with 'Ah, thou spell! Avaunt!' (4.12.30).

Alan Howard was the most technically brilliant and emotionally attuned speaker of Shakespeare of his generation – or any since;

an actor who *embodied* Shakespeare's writing, negotiating its pitch and toss, riding its lyrical curves, its stutters; finding its extended arguments that swing from line to line, its binary thinking spoken in antithesis, its meaning-making through metaphor, the rhythm of its rhetorical process. His voice was unmistakeable. Metallic. Reviewers described it as 'braying', but that wasn't right. Rather, it was a voice that seemed to come through gritted teeth and narrowed eyes, sometimes beguiling but frequently menacing, always conveying an edge. It was a voice that younger actors parodied the way they parodied Olivier (as much in awe as jest, minnows mocking Triton). Howard's 'Have we no *wiiinne* here?' from *Coriolanus* (1.9.91) was as idiosyncratically imitable as Olivier's 'Now is the win-tah of our *dis-con-tent...*' (*Richard III*, 1.1.1).[15] It was a voice that spanned a huge range. (The Welsh soprano Dame Margaret Price was 'amazed' at the end of Howard's performance as Henry V: 'He uses more octaves than we [opera singers] do.')[16] It was a voice that matched Cleopatra's tribute to Mark Antony:

>                               propertied
> As all the tuned spheres, and that to friends;
> But when he meant to quail and shake the orb,
> He was as rattling thunder. (5.2.82–85)

But more than an actor's instrument, Howard's was a voice that 'did' Shakespeare's writing, 'doing' that can be tracked across his Antony's last savaging of Cleopatra:

>                          ...Ah, thou spell! Avaunt!
> Vanish, or I shall give thee thy deserving
> And blemish Caesar's triumph. Let him take thee
> And hoist thee up to the shouting plebeians!
> Follow his chariot, like the greatest spot
> Of all thy sex; most monster-like be shown
> For poor'st diminutives, for dolts, and let
> Patient Octavia plough thy visage up
> With her prepared nails! (4.12.30, 32–39)

'Ah' was a growl emitted from deep inside Antony's bowels; 'thou spell!', a punch felt on the solar plexus, Antony ambushed by Cleopatra. 'Avaunt' was a catching of the breath, summoning breath to go on. In the next line 'Vanish' extended the ideas of witchcraft that were colliding in his thoughts and carried Antony across the alternative threat (marked by 'or': 'or I shall give thee thy deserving') into the next line, where the violence was shocking. Though it wasn't the threat contained in that word 'blemish' that was the greatest shock – the suggestion that Antony would 'blemish' Cleopatra's body the way he'd 'blemished' Thidias's. Rather, it was what came next, at the metrical turn of the iambic pentameter line and at the syntactical period of the sentence: 'Caesar's *triumph*'. There. It was said. Antony admitted defeat. Octavius had triumphed. But Octavius's 'triumph' wasn't just Antony's defeat. Triumph for Antony meant something specific. It meant *Roman* triumph, that civic display of martial supremacy and humiliation staged for the plebs that brought Rome's captives home to Rome, bound as slaves chained to the conqueror's chariot wheels or displayed to the gaze as abjects in Rome's self-glorifying victory parade. With 'Let him take thee / And hoist thee up to the shouting plebeians', Antony was putting into Cleopatra's mind the monstrous image of that travesty of greatness that she would re-imagine later, played upon a scaffold (or a playhouse stage): 'Mechanic slaves ... shall / Uplift us to the view ... / The quick comedians ...' (5.2.208–215, *passim*). Technically, what Howard always did so brilliantly as an actor was to follow the instructions of Shakespeare's writing, where he gives the actor longer and longer periods, requiring bigger and bigger breaths delivering larger and larger thoughts until the five lines of 'Follow his chariot ... monster-like be shown ... plough thy visage up' came out as a roar on a single breath.

And then his rage was gone. In his next scene, with his last loyal adherent ('Eros, thou yet behold'st me?' (4.14.1)), Howard's Antony sat quietly contemplating, of all things, the sky, the way clouds form and re-form in shapes across its surface, sometimes a shape 'that's dragonish' or 'like a bear or lion', sometimes a 'pendent rock' (lines 2–4). Antony-the-lost-soldier had become Antony-the-natural-philosopher, ambling laconically across a territory that seemed remote from present circumstances, but eventually apposite. He drew a moral from the clouds' shape-shifting. He was like them, he told Eros. Howard's lop-sided half-smile was enigmatic as ever: 'Here I am Antony, / Yet cannot hold this visible shape' (4.14.13–14). But as one reviewer observed, even now, at his most still, Howard was not 'afraid of the big effect': 'witness' the way, musing on how those 'pageants' 'mock our eyes with air' (lines 7–8), he reached out a hand to Eros who took it (promptbook), man and boy wandering hand in hand across the rest of the speech, 'a walk prefiguring' the 'celestial encounter with Cleopatra' that Antony would shortly imagine, in a 'haunt' that would 'make the ghosts gaze' (lines 55, 53). Or 'witness' him sitting cross-legged on that capstan-chair, impassive as a Buddha, holding his sword Philippan gently in his arms like a votive waiting for the death stroke: 'witness his voluptuous caress of the blade that will kill him' (*Guardian*, 11 October 1978).

Antony's death was Cleopatra's turning point.

Beginning rehearsals with Brook back in August, Glenda Jackson had admitted she'd 'never seen' *Antony and Cleopatra* nor 'even read it all the way through' (Sydney Edwards, *Liverpool Daily Post*, 5 August 1978). But Peter Brook had. And whether he directed the wail of anguish that Jackson's Cleopatra gave, head thrown back, when dying Antony went limp in her arms, or whether the reflex was irresistible, the culmination of the rising hysteria Shakespeare writes for Cleopatra here ('Noblest of men, woo't die?'; 'Hast thou no care of me?' (4.15.61–62)), that wail exactly reproduced Suzman's from 1972. For Brook, it was '"The death of Antony [that] transforms Cleopatra", and from capricious variety "she becomes simpler and simpler"' so that in the final sequence of the play Jackson achieved 'a stunning transformation-in-death' (Warren 1980, 178; *The Times*, 18 October 1978). Brook conducted her there by a route that astonished reviewers. He brought on the Clown.

Shakespeare's Act 5 Asp Man with his bucket of 'immortal' worms (5.2.246) had always baffled those who came to the play burdened with the 'received idea' of what a tragedy should be and that *Antony and Cleopatra* was one. To wit, Felix Barker in the *Evening News* (11 October 1978) acidly commented that in his 'innocence' he 'did not realise until last night that *Antony and Cleopatra* was a light-hearted comedy'. He went on: 'Came the *awesome moment* when the *sinister stranger* arrives at the *tomb* carrying the *deadly asp* with which Cleopatra is to *kill herself*', and on comes a 'routine of grotesque comedy', so that 'just when *the tragedy* should be *breaking our hearts*', Cleopatra goes 'gaily to her death'. (The italics are mine, emphasising all those 'received ideas' that hung like albatrosses around the reviewer's neck – or better said, clung to his eyes like cracked goggles, allowing him to view the play only through those lenses.) Barker concluded: 'The break in tension was complete.'

But that was the point of the scene – which point Glen Byam Shaw had puzzled out back in 1953. Shaw was never afraid to confess to his notebooks his occasional bewilderment of Shakespeare's ways and means. Of Diomedes he wrote, 'Why is he introduced into the play so late? I can't think'; and of Euphronius, the Schoolmaster whom Antony sends as ambassador to Octavius in 3.12 to negotiate the terms of his defeated future: 'I don't understand why this character is introduced, or what effect he is meant to create. Is it that Shakespeare is handing a bouquet to the loyalty of scholars as opposed to that of soldiers? I don't know' (Shaw, NB 1944). With the Asp Man Shaw felt himself on surer footing. He was Nick Bottom come to Alexandria. He was a knock-knock joke (like the Porter in *Macbeth* or the Ambassadors at the end of *Hamlet* who enter to announce 'That Rosencrantz and Guildenstern are dead' (5.2.355)). He arrived to tip the play vertiginously into the grotesque (as Jan Kott characterised it in *Shakespeare Our Contemporary*, 1965) and into the carnivalesque (as Shakespeare applied and Mikhail Bakhtin (1984) theorised it). He was, wrote Shaw, 'an English yokel dressed up in Eastern clothes'; 'impossible to make him into a real Egyptian as he is absolutely English'; one who is 'fascinated by C[leopatra], though he does'nt [*sic*] know who she is'. Shaw saw the 'clown's job' clearly: it was 'to bring an atmosphere of rock bottom reality on to the stage, with his basket of asps'. And Shaw knew that Shakespeare knew exactly what he was doing with his Dogberry-ish Asp Man: 'Shakespeare makes the audience smell the earth before it rises to heaven on the poetry that follows' (Shaw, NB 1944).

Shakespeare's Clown, then, is what makes nonsense of the kind of mindlessness that boggles Michael Billington's mind (in an otherwise wonderfully observed review) when he calls *Antony and Cleopatra* 'crucially flaw[ed]' and identifies as its fatal 'structural fault' 'its limping refusal to come to an end'. Shakespeare, he complains, 'assumes that two deaths are better than one': so, having 'reached a magnificent climax with the expiration of Antony at the end of Act IV, the play itself expires, so that Cleopatra's death seems like an anti-climax' (*Guardian*, 11 October 1978). But Brook showed that the Clown is exactly why Cleopatra's death isn't an antic-climax; that bringing on the Clown was Shakespeare's brilliant theatrical device to prepare the space for the second death that the first death *needs*; that validates and triumphantly *finishes* the first, to produce an *Egyptian* 'Roman triumph' that will mock the out-manoeuvred Roman gaggle of gawpers that will arrive shortly to view it. (What does Antony's death add up to without Cleopatra's? For that matter, can the play be imagined without her death?

Cleopatra surviving to breed crocodiles in an Augustan empire where the 'boy' Caesar's self-inflated political ambitions haven't been punctured and put in their puny place by her mocking laughter?) As Brook directed him, Shakespeare's Clown cleared away the monumental rubble of Antony's 'magnificent climax' to place Jackson's Cleopatra at ground zero to begin her own climax, smelling the dungy earth of mortality before she worked her apotheosis by poetry.

Thus Richard Griffiths's Asp Man was like nothing spectators had seen before – not in *Antony and Cleopatra* anyway, a circus clown straight out of Barnum and Bailey via Samuel Beckett (see 4.5). He was dressed in a striped undergarment, a sarong tied around his bulky waist. A hat, shaped in rope like a capsized

4.5 'Hast thou the pretty worm of Nilus there / That kills and pains not?' (5.2). Cleopatra (Glenda Jackson), Clown (Richard Griffiths).

Egyptian solar ship, covered his ears. His eyes were heavily kohled. And smack in the middle of his hang-dog face was an out-sized nose in bright red plastic. That nose remembered the one stuck on Bottom-as-Ass in Brook's *Dream* (and marked their kinship in clownage). That nose would be what reviewers remarked on and what spectators remembered. It's interesting, then, that it may have been an after-thought. The stage manager's rehearsal notes for 29 September – just a week before opening – adds a pencilled message to the wardrobe department: 'Pockets both sides Clown costume'; 'Red nose needed for Richard'. That late-coming red nose went on to code Griffiths's performance (and how Jackson's Cleopatra responded to it), Clown and queen performing a Beckettian double act like some silent routine out of *Endgame*.[17] First Cleopatra served as his stooge in a three-dimensional version of three-card monte, where the asp basket kept turning up in the wrong hands. Then, when the Clown had it back under control and moved to deliver it, which meant stepping onto the red carpet that he'd so far skirted, he stopped, foot suspended in mid-air. (The gesture remembered John Bowe's Philo in the opening sequence of the play, not daring to step into Cleopatra's space.) The prompt-book next records a kind of 'fort-da' game between Cleopatra and the Clown, she kneeling in front of him, a spell-bound spectator riveted to his every move as she had been to no one else's, not even Antony's, while the Clown was a master of serpentine focus-pulls, false exits and wrong-footings:

Takes one shoe off
Takes other shoe off
Picks up shoes & puts them on his hands, then picks up basket
Moves to C[entre] of carpet, holding basket with shoes on hands
Puts basket on floor. Cleopatra to Clown [on 'Get thee hence', line 257]
Clown returns to R[ight] of carpet
Clown off pros[cenium] R[ight] behind C[entre] R[ight] screen to C[entre] R[ight] entrance, then to R[ight] of Cleopatra and kneels
Clown turns away from Cleopatra as if to leave again [on 'not worth the feeding', line 269]
Cleopatra goes to touch basket – Clown stops her [on 'Will it eat me?', line 270]
Clown takes lid off basket, still with shoes on hands [on 'mar five', line 276]

> Cleopatra takes basket, looks in it, turns it upside down, there is nothing in it. Clown takes R[ight] shoe off his hand + produces snake – puts it in basket. Takes 2nd snake from gown & puts it in basket
> Produces last snake from within his costume [on 'Yes, forsooth', line 278] Puts lid on basket & exits pros[scenium] R[ight] [on 'joy o'th' worm', line 278][18]

With this routine, which saw the carnivalesque utterly confounding portentousness, Brook revealed *Antony and Cleopatra* as containing both Antony's tragedy and Cleopatra's triumph, for now the Clown, exiting, crossed Iras and Charmian as they entered, bringing 'clothes and crown' to 'dress Cleopatra' (promptbook). And now, for the first time, Brook's stage *dazzled*. Cleopatra was made into a thing of gold. But more significantly, Jackson found for Cleopatra not Jack Tinker's silly notion of gaiety but a profound celebration at her end.

In rehearsal, Jackson had identified the 'hardest thing' about playing Cleopatra: 'genuinely to make the words do the work'. Shakespeare's verse, she said, 'is made alive by artificial means. But if you don't get *inside* the verse, it doesn't work' (Judith Cook, *Observer*, 8 October 1978). In the final fifteen minutes of Brook's production, the Clown having opened the door, so to speak, this Cleopatra found her way into the heart of Shakespeare's writing, achieving that 'stunning transformation-in-death' that Brook required by becoming 'simpler and simpler'. This ending 'existed on a higher, more moving level than anything before' (Warren 1980, 178).

Not everyone thought so. In his review, Bernard Levin wrote 'only' about 'my thoughts', 'nothing about my emotions' because, given the 'detachment' he'd observed 'on stage', he'd *felt* very little. He called this a production 'for collectors and connoisseurs, rather than those who feel' (*Sunday Times*, 15 October 1978).

But other reviewers found in it things to celebrate. Its 'greatest merit' for Robert Cushman in the *Observer* was its 'unremitting concentration on the text', and he marvelled that all its 'startling moments' were located 'in the acting' (15 October 1978). And, given Peter Brook's cool directorial hand and the simplicity of the design, no one missed those moments of consummate theatricality which this production put squarely before spectators' eyes, such as the way the set's multiple entrances allowed startling juxtapositions, scenes crossing scenes, most strikingly, for John Elsom, 'where

Brook switches from Pompey's party, dangerous and erotic in its brutal comradeliness, into the battle on Syria's plains, another kind of orgy altogether' (*Listener*, 16 October 1972). In Shakespeare's 3.1, set in Syria, Pacorus is already dead. Brook had him butchered before spectators' eyes (shades of Brook-the-anti-war-director of *US*, remembering the activist 1960s) so that 'the Parthian war scene' erupted 'through the gaps in the screen to defile the sanctuary itself' – this bloody rout coming hard on the heels of the laddish antics on Pompey's galley, 'a true Bacchanal' (Bernard Levin, *Sunday Times*, 15 October 1978).

Billington admired in 'this most cinematic play' Brook's use of a 'technique of fades and dissolves so that one moment melts into another often with great poignancy. No sooner has Octavius at the end of one scene cried "poor Antony" than we see the tottering hero entering for the next propped up by Enobarbus' (*Guardian*, 11 October 1978). The Battle of Actium was a study in isolation, produced as a focus on the lone figure of Patrick Stewart's Enobarbus. He stood in silhouette far upstage, outside the bubble with his back to the audience, looking out on ruin, his only accompaniment being the sound of the rise and fall of distant waves. Since no machinery was used in this production, and no changes were ever made to the fixed set, the hoisting of dying Antony into Cleopatra's 'monument' – the square of red carpet the only signifier of that monument – was managed as a *trompe l'oeil*. The wounded Antony staggered to the edge of the carpet and collapsed along its width. Cleopatra and her girls threw downstage the ends of their sashes, which his men looped under the body then tossed back. The women hauled mightily on the 'silken tackle' (2.2.219) to roll the body upstage, an illusion that 'saw' the wounded Roman rising to meet Cleopatra's arms. Perhaps most memorably of all, the battle sequence of Act 4 was simply stylised, and over in seconds, with shadowy figures running around the backs of the screens, throwing water balloons at their surfaces. When they hit the panels, they exploded. They were full of blood that splattered in terrible bursts, then ran down the panels, like a Jackson Pollock mural of death. Just so did the 'world beyond' impact the 'great lives' played out on the forestage. There was no finer illustration than this of Glenda Jackson's observation (doubtless quoting Brook) that *Antony and Cleopatra* is 'not ... at all' 'an epic play'. 'They are epic people but they are ... acting out their lives in private rooms. You get this tremendous sense of millions of people outside, pressing against doors and windows, whose lives depend on these extraordinary beings', those 'millions of people' figured here only in blood (*Observer*, 8 October 1978).

All that said, it remained the case that in *Antony and Cleopatra* Peter Brook failed his 'historic function at Stratford', which was to arrive 'about once a decade' and 'change[ ] everything'. Ironically, however, he might have succeeded, *stunningly* succeeded, if RSC spectators had seen the play it appears Brook had very early discovered in the rehearsal room. Benedict Nightingale leaked to readers of the *New Statesman* that 'According to the RSC's in-house Deep Throat, the eminent director of *Antony and Cleopatra*' 'was so delighted by the initial rehearsals with his five or six leading players that he rang head office, suggesting that the remaining 30 or 40 parts be cut' (20 October 1978).[19] *Antony and Cleopatra* played by six actors at the RSC? Now, that really *would* have cut the epic play down to size. And perhaps might have 'change[d] everything'.

### Egypt in a tin hut

Is it possible that four years later the task Brook began of killing off 'received ideas' of this play was completed by Adrian Noble? Two bits of theatre record drawn from the performance archive show just how far Noble's 1982 *Antony and Cleopatra* had moved on (or perhaps away) from Brook's.[20] The first is a production photograph illustrating James Fenton's review in the *Sunday Times* (17 October 1982). It shows Michael Gambon's rough-bearded Antony crouching, bending into the lips of Helen Mirren's Cleopatra as she's stretched out on the floor on her back, legs splayed, arms extended behind her head which is thrown back, neck stretched, mouth anticipating Antony's offer, spine voluptuously arched to meet his hand as it travels down her hips. A speaking picture in itself, this production image says even more in archival context, for as it happens, Fenton's review, pasted into the RSC's press cutting book held at the Shakespeare Birthplace Trust, is folded into another review of an exhibition that opened that same week at London's Tate Modern, a review that was also illustrated. The coincidence of that fold juxtaposes the two illustrations, making them suggestively inform each other: it puts Mirren's Cleopatra alongside one of Lucien Freud's abundantly sprawling female nudes, creating an erotic diptych where Freud glosses Shakespeare.

The second is a memo sent by Bronwyn Roberts, theatre administrator, to the RSC's top brass on 28 September 1982, 'Subject: Antony and Cleopatra Production Budget', reporting 'The financial position on the above production ... as at today's date':

| | |
|---|---:|
| Costumes (materials and labour) | 2,435 |
| Vinyl (for floor covering) | 588 |
| Transport of above from London | 75 |
| Misc. scenic materials | 150 |
| Blacks (for back wall, upper level) | 200 |
| Worms (for asp) | 15 |
| Furniture and props | 98 |
| Musicians overtime? | |
| | £3,561 |

'This', the memo continued, 'takes us £1,000 over the original budget of £2,500', the over-spend occasioned by the fact that while '[w]e were fortunate enough to get a large amount of free cotton jersey for the T-shirts and togas', it shrank 'widthways and lengthways when washed, and so, when draped on the actors, required a larger amount than we'd bargained for'. The worms who'd been cast to play asps, too, were proving more costly than originally budgeted. A fortnight earlier they'd been itemised as 'Slow worms and tank 11.50'.

Item one – the production photograph – suggests the sheer uninhibited sexual charge of Noble's production. There was going to be nothing of Brook's boarding-school-girls-behaving-primly in Noble's Alexandria. Item two – Roberts's memo – suggests the production's scale. If Brook had re-sized the play by setting it on half the RSC's main house stage, Noble down-scaled it even further, taking it out of the Royal Shakespeare Theatre altogether and moving it up Waterside past the Dirty Duck to The Other Place (TOP), the corrugated 'tin hut' (as it was affectionately known to actors and audiences) converted in 1974 from a no-frills rehearsal room into a no-frills 200-seat black box studio space. (Audiences and actors used the same entrances and exits and shared the same toilets in the interval.) TOP was home to the company's most risk-taking experimental work – and to its greatest box-office risks, plays such as *Arden of Faversham* or *The Roaring Girl*. In budgetary terms, TOP had to scrounge. In 1982, main house productions (Terry Hands's *Much Ado About Nothing*, Adrian Noble's *King Lear*) were budgeted at £120,000. TOP productions had a budget of

£2,500. And they had to stick to it. Otherwise, as an exasperated production manager wrote in a tetchy response to Roberts's request for authorisation to over-spend on *Antony and Cleopatra*, 'Play 6 at The Other Place will be left with peanuts'.

Some reviewers thought that what Noble was doing was perverse, casting *Antony and Cleopatra* with a paltry nineteen actors and putting the play into a studio space whose only claim to the spectacular was its shabbiness, where the production's 'design concept' would amount to black vinyl floor covering, and the costumes, to hand-me-downs raided from the hire wardrobe (admittedly dressed up with a couple hundred yards of 'fine mercerised knitted cotton', a.k.a. T-shirt fabric). Michael Coveney in the *Financial Times* grumbled about the extravagant 'indulgence of presenting Helen Mirren and Michael Gambon, a coupling of immeasurable box office appeal, in one of the greatest plays ever written, for the benefit of a small audience in a Nissen hut' (14 October 1982). But perhaps Noble's aim was not self-indulgent. Maybe it was riskily experimental, to test to the limit Brook's intuition (that he'd only half-realised on half a stage) that *Antony and Cleopatra* was not at all the 'spectacular play' of common 'misunderstandings'; that '[t]here is no pageantry'; that '[e]verything concerns personal relationships'; that it 'consists of 45 or so short scenes of intimate behaviour'; that '[t]he Empire may be tottering' but that Shakespeare 'keeps' that empire 'out of sight' (*The Times*, 18 October 1978). Glenda Jackson's sensation of 'millions of people outside, pressing against doors and windows', looking in on 'these extraordinary beings' on 'whose lives' they 'depend' was literally so at TOP, where the theatre's spectators stood in for those 'millions of people', 'so close to the action that metaphorically they could bathe their feet in the water of the Queen of Egypt's Nile' (*Yorkshire Post*, 15 October 1982).

Adrian Noble was still in his apprenticeship at the RSC, having joined the company two years earlier, just turned thirty, on the back of an award-winning *The Duchess of Malfi* at the Royal Exchange, Manchester (1980), with Helen Mirren as the Duchess and Sorcha Cusack (whom he would cast as Charmian in 1982) as Julia. As assistant director at the RSC he honed his craft under Terry Hands, directing his first solo production, Alexander Ostrovsky's *The Forest*, followed by a beautifully judged *A Doll's House*, both at TOP, the Ibsen garnering him a Theatre Circle Award. In 1982 he was given his first main house production, a *King Lear*-after-Jan-Kott, stunningly designed by Bob Crowley on a huge spatial canvas that domesticated the European grotesque to a place near Dover and that produced, in the double act between Michael Gambon's Lear and Antony Sher's Fool, two of the most heartbreakingly memorable performances of those roles ever seen in Stratford. After that Lear, it's no wonder that Gambon was Noble's first casting for Antony.

Noble was on a roll. If he was taking a risk stripping away everything 'theatrical' from *Antony and Cleopatra*, hanging everything 'on the actors and the text' (as Irving Wardle wrote in *The Times*, 15 October 1982), it was no doubt a decision his Cleopatra fully supported. Helen Mirren had arrived at the RSC in 1967, aged twenty-two, via the National Youth Theatre, to be directed by Trevor Nunn in *The Revenger's Tragedy* as Castiza opposite Alan Howard's Lussurioso and by John Barton in *All's Well that Ends Well* as Diana, two 'chaste maids' that belied Mirren's growing reputation (in a fashion era when two-dimensional Twiggy reigned supreme in a body that was the antithesis of Mirren's delicious curvaceousness) for cornering the market in performances of 'sluttish eroticism'.[21] At the National Youth Theatre in 1965 she'd already played her first Cleopatra. Grown men who were spear-carrying lads at the time remember crowding the wings, hoping to see bits of her 'equipment' fall out of her costume. In 1968 Barton cast her as Cressida in a body-conscious production of *Troilus and Cressida* that would become famous, or infamous, not least for Alan Howard's camp Achilles. In the 'morning after' scene, 4.2, Mirren's Cressida appeared clothed only in a bed sheet that, exiting, she let fall, momentarily naked as she spun into the wings – a performance that made at least one schoolboy spectator decide on a future in Shakespeare studies.[22] Then, in 1972, the trajectory she appeared fixed on, as classical theatre's sex goddess, radically changed direction. Having 'been working non-stop for four years' and becoming 'very wearied by the theatre in England' because nothing she did seemed to be 'progressing', she dropped out, into Peter Brook's International Centre for Theatre Research, touring to North Africa and the western states of the United States for two years with him and a company of actors chosen because they had nothing in common with each other, conducting experiments that moved between public streets, work spaces, tribal commons and rehearsal rooms, eventually creating *The Conference of the Birds*.[23]

Returning to the RSC in 1974 to play Lady Macbeth directed by Trevor Nunn, Mirren was evidently informed by the experience of Brook. There was a new seriousness of purpose in her work, a focused sense of where the 'art' of her craft lay, reflected in a highly publicised letter to the *Guardian* that minced no words, criticising the RSC and National Theatre for wasting money on production expenditure that was 'unnecessary' and, worse, 'destructive to the art of the Theatre'. 'The realms of truth, emotion and imagination reached for in acting a great play', she wrote, 'have become more and more remote, often totally unreachable across an abyss of costume and technicalities' (Beauman 1982, 322). Her letter appears to have made some impact: when *Macbeth* transferred to the Aldwych, Irving Wardle reported in *The Times*:

> Gone are John Napier's heavy ecclesiastical furnishings, the traverse curtain shadow plays, spot lit asides, coronation pageantry, and the witches swinging on chandeliers. In their place, Trevor Nunn bases his production on the naked physical properties of the stage. It is like moving from an Italian cathedral to a primitive Methodist chapel. (6 March 1975)

If there was one Cleopatra who would sign on to the 'abyss'-free *Antony and Cleopatra* that Adrian Noble had in mind, it was Helen Mirren – but a Helen Mirren whose actorly body, beyond all else, couldn't help but code uninhibited sexuality, sexuality reviewers such as Stanley Wells (*Times Literary Supplement*, 29 November 1982) and John Barber (*Daily Telegraph*, 15 October 1982) would connect to a spontaneity that was by turns 'bewitching' and if 'not quite coarse, ... shop soiled', making her an 'awesome' Cleopatra who showed the part to be 'unequivocally great' when played by an actor of, beyond spontaneity, 'intelligence, imagination and technical mastery', an actor who moved like 'a dancer' but spoke 'with the precise but imperceptible control of a musician'.

Noble used the limited space at TOP to significant effect. At ground level spectators were arranged around the postage-stamp-sized playing space on three sides. Above, a shallow gallery ran around the theatre, one end reserved for the action, the rest for two rows of spectators. This allowed Noble and his designer Nadine Baylis to set scenes on two levels, 'Egyptian dalliance concentrated downstairs where Cleopatra and the girls disport themselves', while 'Upstairs ... Caesar and Agrippa launch political objectives, Cleopatra has her tomb and Antony dies' (*Financial Times*, 14

October 1982); also where, in the drunken galley scene, the 'boy' singer of 'Come, thou monarch of the vine' (2.7.113) positioned himself before launching a swan dive into the revellers' arms below.

Shifting spectators' sightlines from below to above and back again allowed Noble to effect the kind of scenic juxtapositions, cross-cuts and fades that reviewers had so admired in Brook's production; further, to give a sense of Egypt and Alexandria 'eavesdropping on each other' (Victoria Radin, *Observer*, 17 October 1982). The spatial constraints of the room allowed him to accelerate the pace of the action. At two hours and fifty minutes playing time, this was an *Antony and Cleopatra* that came in forty minutes under Brook's. Such speed made sense of the 'sudden rushes of blood to the head' that Michael Billington saw determining the decisions made by Gambon's Antony (*Guardian*, 14 October 1982) or of the way Mirren's 'barefoot Egyptian nymph', with 'the charming naivety of Princess Diana' (who'd married the Prince of Wales in a fairy-tale wedding the previous year), raced 'from one emotional whirlpool to another' (David Roper, *Daily Express*, 14 October 1982). But Noble's direction also made room for the languid, the reflective. That mysterious scene among the common soldiers (4.3) who hear 'the god Hercules whom Antony loved' abandoning him was set on the gallery above while below, the music 'Under the earth' (4.3.21, 17) came from among 'the lovers and their entourage' who were 'stretched out in slumber' – comatose – 'after that "one other gaudy night"' (*Financial Times*, 14 October 1982). Later, Mirren delivered Cleopatra's memorial reconstruction of dead Antony as 'a dream-like fantasy', one of the production's 'finest touches', according to Billington.

Her Cleopatra's relationship with Gambon's Antony registered in their first entrance: he, grizzled, leonine, seeming 'twice the size of any other character', his 'habit of cupping his friends' heads in a single massive hand' serving 'to shrink the object of his affection'; she, 'a feather to his oak' (*Times Literary Supplement*, 22 October 1982), no 'statuesque Egyptian enchantress' but utterly 'un-Egyptian', with Garbo-length blonde hair, in clinging cotton jersey dyed in rainbow colours knotted at one shoulder, and 'tiny' (*Guardian*, 14 October 1982, *The Times*, 15 October 1982). Nevertheless, she dragged him in on the end of a scarf, and they played their opening exchanges as a game of tug-of-war that she had every intention of winning, the cloth stretched orgasmically taut between them,

4.6 'Fie, wrangling queen, / Whom everything becomes' (1.1) Antony (Michael Gambon), Cleopatra (Helen Mirren).

a teasing sign of their aroused emotional life (see 4.6). This scarf would return throughout, the only 'propertied' object in the production: she would invest him in it for the Battle of Actium; he would cast it away, thinking she'd betrayed him, then, hearing she was dead, wind it around himself, preparing himself to die (promptbook). It would be the 'tackle' used to hoist him into Cleopatra's arms, and, blood-stained, it would drape her shoulders as she prepared her own suicide. The scarf was equipment for play 'in the sensuous intimacy of the Egyptian court where blazing rows' changed 'into childish games' under the 'lightning emotional reversals' of a queen whose mercurial giddiness repeatedly left Antony 'like a bewildered bull plagued by swarms of flies' and where 'protocol comes and goes like a carnival mask' (*The Times*, 15 October 1982). There was little 'queenly' in this queen; little to distinguish rank, status or deference. But as Victoria Radin shrewdly observed, the scarf was also 'a noose ... a symbol of the killer instinct that lurks in obsessive sexual love' (*Observer*, 17 October 1982). And obsessive it was, in Radin's view. In the first four acts of the play she saw Mirren's Cleopatra as 'a desperately insecure Lolita to Michael Gambon's fly-blown general' who knew he was 'wriggling off the hook' while she was 'wild to keep him' on the line.

For Irving Wardle, the first half of the production was 'a marvellously agile blend of politics and sexual comedy' that drew 'a firm distinction' between the bewildering 'becomings' of Egypt and the 'severities of Rome', presided over by Jonathan Hyde's Octavius. This 'saturnine watcher with the features of an Aztec mask', whose silences conveyed 'volumes of indignation and regret', revealed himself to be 'grimly puritanical' on Pompey's galley, where, 'in the manner of puritans' letting themselves off the leash, he outdrunked the drunks and leered hungrily upward at the girl-pallid near-naked body of the boy who sang of 'plumpy Bacchus' (*The Times*, 15 October 1982). There was, wrote Stanley Wells drily, a suggestion that, in the 'gay' abandon of these revels, which saw Clive Wood's Pompey stripping off his shirt and baring his alpha male chest to Antony, then kissing him, 'the abundant sexuality of these warriors' sought 'satisfaction whatever the circumstances' (*Times Literary Supplement*, 29 November 1982). Wells's carefulness is telling: cultural performances like this one that normalised what a distant generation had called 'Greek love' were currently in the process of creating the climate of anxiety among conservative 'establishmentarians' (whose hero-soldiers were even then fighting the Falklands War) that would produce, six years hence, the Thatcher government's notorious 'Section 28' legislation making it illegal for any local authority to 'promote homosexuality', to 'publish material with the intention of promoting homosexuality' or to 'promote the teaching' in school 'of homosexuality as a pretended family relationship'. Still, Hyde's Octavius was a man infinitely tender of his sister (Penelope Beaumont); a man who, when Antony's sword Philippan was placed in his hands, stained with the blood of his 'mate in empire', broke down and wept (5.1.43). Similarly bipolar, Bob Peck's Enobarbus was, on the one hand, a phlegmatic Northerner who gave the barge speech 'like a police report' which nevertheless 'almost reduced [him] to silence' (*The Times*, 15 October 1982); on the other, a broken-hearted self-confessed 'master leaver' who, 'amazingly', found 'voice for high tragic rhetoric in the moment before death' (*Guardian*, 14 October 1982).

Strong but understated performances like Hyde's and Peck's left the centre of this 'chamber play' *Antony and Cleopatra*, as Mirren put it, to a 'domestic story of what happens to two people' (*Evening Standard*, 24 September 1982), not 'demi-gods but fallible mortals' (*Guardian*, 14 October 1982), though played by actors who were prepared in a narrow room 'to push the temperamental polarities' of their parts 'well beyond the usual limits' (*The Times*, 15 October 1982). For Gambon, wrote Wardle, this meant 'a contrast between the public behaviour of a demi-god and a private life in which he regresses to the total sensuous dependence of infancy', his dotage making him a 'big baby fondling his plaything' (*The Times*, 15 October 1982); while for Mirren, said Wardle, the contrast took 'the form of policy' since, apart from the fact that her 'one aim' was 'to possess' Antony, everything else was 'either megalomaniac emotion or masterly guile' (*The Times*, 15 October 1982), as when, learning of his Roman marriage, she responded with 'almost certifiable hysteria' (*Guardian*, 14 October 1982). Gambon's presence was massive, his voice almost too big for the space, his rages and raptures huge. Production photographs capture him variously embracing Cleopatra ecstatically or shaking her like a rag doll and hurling her to the ground, while the stage manager's reports record a number of injuries to Cleopatra due to over-energetic manhandling: on 21 December, a badly grazed knee; on 23 February, a bruised bottom and an injured leg. (Once, oh sweet role reversal, the stage manager reports that 'Mr Gambon fell flat on his back while trying to kick Miss Mirren. He sprained his wrist and upper hand' (16 May 1983).)

'What happens to two people' codependent in a volatile affair – the one a 'grizzled bear and man of startling doubts and contradictions, impulsive yet curiously melancholic', the other 'histrionic, hysterical, sly, funny', her 'lightning mood swings' never differentiating between the 'artificial and genuine' (*Financial Times*, 14 October 1982; *Times Educational Supplement*, 22 October 1982) – was here as abusive as it was elevating. Radin in the *Observer*, pointing to the 'teasing disjunction' that Shakespeare's text offers 'between the shabby behaviour of the pair and the grand claims made for them by other people', asked, 'What are we to believe?' Her answer: 'Noble's suggestion is that they grow into their own greatness'.

Certainly in the last act, with Antony gone, Mirren's Cleopatra moved onto a different plane of being. Her sweetest moments had been with her girls, bodies entangled, rolling around on the floor like a litter of puppies, using each other's hips, bottoms and backs as pillows, remembering 'That time? O times!' (2.5.18). Their Egypt was accurately captured in Enobarbus's 'infinite variety', a stunningly colourful place where women regularly 'Hop[ped] … through the public street', played games, mocked Roman hierarchies in an alternative re-gendered triumvirate. For Cleopatra's 'girls', as Sorcha

Cusack remembers, 'her pleasures were ours, her griefs ours, not in a subservient way but in a way of being more intensely alive'.[24] Cusack's Charmian, her hair plaited tight against her head in cornrows, and Josette Simon's Iras, her casting reanimating the now tired stereotype of the black body shadowing a white Cleopatra – an iconic proxy for 'oriental' Egyptian or African 'Otherness' – were dressed identically with their mistress in slightly different combinations of the rainbow (see 4.7). They watched her back; were her intimates (see Rutter 2001, 63–64). If, as Billington thought, the male frolics on Pompey's galley strongly hinted 'that these world leaders spend the night in each other's beds' (*Guardian*, 14 October 1982), it appeared just as likely that these women bedded down

4.7 'He's speaking now, / Or murmuring "Where's my serpent of old Nile?"' (1.5). Cleopatra (Helen Mirren) with Iras (Josette Simon) behind.

together, too, though not for the kind of groping the men on the galley got up to but for the sheer fun of sharing giggles in the dark.[25] Production photographs catch Cusack's smiling Charmian gazing indulgently upon Cleopatra, seeing her always as a 'lass unparalleled' (5.2.315). It was she who ministered to Cleopatra at the end.

The queen entered 5.2 dressed as a widow in black, crazed with grief, her hair trapped tight against her head inside a skull cap, her face dirty with penitential ash streaked with tears that left ugly tracks down her cheeks. Here, Seleucus (Nigel Harrison) was played as a traitor, his scene in front of Octavius reducing Cleopatra to a final 'frantic humiliation by the embarrassed confession of her treasurer' (*The Times*, 15 October 1982). Once the Romans were gone, she simply knelt in front of a basin and quietly washed. The face she turned upon the 'rural fellow' (5.2.232) who interrupted her ritual of cleansing was radiant: this Cleopatra was ready for the worm whose biting was 'immortal' (line 246), a Cleopatra who 'live[d] like a woman but dies like a queen' (*Guardian*, 14 October 1982).

At the end of Noble's production, the 'general question' Irving Wardle was left contemplating was 'whether *Antony and Cleopatra* ranks as a tragedy at all' (*The Times*, 15 October 1982). He'd registered as 'wholly comic' the effect of Cleopatra's *volte-faces* from 'megalomaniac emotion' to 'masterly guile'; comic, too, was her 'pampering the messenger of Antony's marriage with cushions and drinks before flying at his eyes' or her raising a laugh on 'He words me, girls, he words me' (5.2.190). Wardle's further comment that the 'production does not contract into tragic focus in the second half', that the death speech of Peck's Enobarbus was 'the only tragic sound to be heard', was meant as criticism. But maybe Wardle was wiser than he knew. Maybe *Antony and Cleopatra* doesn't rank as a tragedy. As played by Helen Mirren, Cleopatra's 'joy o'th' worm' (5.2.278) was just that – *joy* (see 4.8).

The final thought Michael Coveney was left grumpily contemplating was the gross disservice Noble had done by shrinking into the cramped broom cupboard of TOP Shakespeare's epic play, his 'past the size of dreaming' play (to recall Beckerman, where this chapter started). Coveney wanted epic restored. He wanted 'to see the whole show re-directed and re-designed for next season in the main house'. *Then* 'we would catch the full force of the electric partnership between Mirren and Gambon' (*Financial Times*, 14 October 1982). Some such plan may have been seeded. A tight-lipped

4.8 'Will it eat me?' (5.2). Cleopatra (Helen Mirren).

note from the RSC's executive director to Adrian Noble (copied to other administrators), dated 7 March 1983 as the production was transferring to the studio theatre in the Barbican, reads:

Subject: Antony & Cleopatra: London

I've had a call from Nadine Baylis' agent suggesting that you intend a complete re-design on A&C for The Pit.

What's all this then?

No re-design was done. No compromise of the production's impact was made by aggrandisement. Noble achieved what Brook had aspired to: he located the heart of the play in a little chamber, in a domestic story. What's more, even on a shoe-string budget, Adrian Noble looked after his actors. Another memo dated 2 March

1982 headed 'LIVE ANIMALS AT THE BARBICAN CENTRE' informing heads of department 'of the intended use of two slow-worms in the RSC's production of "Antony and Cleopatra" to be given in The Pit Theatre from 6th April to 7th July' assured them: 'Only one slow-worm is used per performance and it is in the care of Stephen Dobbin the assistant stage manager who then takes the creature home after the performance'. Now there, certainly, is 'elusive affection' after Beckerman's own heart.

## Notes

1 Irving Wardle, *The Times*, 12 April 1972, writes of the spectator's experience, taking his seat in the re-designed Royal Shakespeare Theatre: 'the impression is of looking into the inside of an old Kodak'.
2 Nunn's dynastic ambitions were read as such at the time. See Nicholas de Jongh announcing the up-coming 'Stratford season of Rome' as 'A challenge to the Wars of the Roses in 1964' (*Guardian*, 2 February 1972).
3 David Addenbrooke (1974, 48) records that 'From 1961, all RSC press releases and theatre programmes began to carry the following statement "Incorporated under Royal Charter, with the Queen as Patron, it [the RSC] virtually belongs to the Nation".'
4 The promptbook and production records quoted in this chapter are held at the Shakespeare Birthplace Trust, Stratford-upon-Avon. A film of Nunn's stage production was made in 1974, videotaped for television distribution by ITV in the UK, directed by Jon Scoffield. It is now available on DVD.
5 Hobson's further comments might usefully have been recalled as *déjà vu* when the next major refurbishment of the RSC took place between 2006 and 2010 under Michael Boyd: 'In the past week hints have been given to Mr Nunn not to overdo this sort of thing. But that is sheer nonsense. The nation has helped to buy this expensive toy for Mr Nunn. Therefore, since the thing is done, let him fool around with it as much as he pleases. Otherwise nobody will be satisfied. But if the good of the theatre had been what matters, it would have been better if the Arts Council had been able (as under its code it is not) to fob him off with a model train, which he could have taken home and played with to his heart's content.' It's uncanny how pronouncements from 1972 that talk about how the refurbishment aimed to create a 'one-room relationship between the actor and the audience' that would establish 'the immediacy of Shakespeare's platform stage' were echoed thirty-five

years later, word for word. Dispiriting, too, how rapidly, in both cases, the innovative technologies (Morley's hydraulic lifts, Boyd's flying apparatus) were dropped.

6  The phrase 'wonderful things' is what has been popularly reported of Carter's diary entry for 26 November 1922 when, having made a 'tiny breach' in the boy king's tomb wall, and being struck dumb with amazement at the 'strange and wonderful medley of extraordinary and beautiful objects heaped upon one another' that he saw in the interior, he could only answer the anxious enquiry of others standing by, 'Can you see anything?', 'Yes, it is wonderful'. See Carter's diary, 26 November 1922, in *Tutankhamun: Anatomy of an Excavation. Howard Carter's Diaries and Journals*, Griffith Institute, Oxford, http://www.griffith.ox.ac.uk/discoveringTut/ (accessed 8 December 2019).
7  All quotations of *Julius Caesar* are from Daniell 1988.
8  Redgrave remembered this personal history making his speech to the annual birthday celebrations in Stratford-upon-Avon in 2005 accepting the Pragnell Shakespeare Prize.
9  All quotations of *King Henry IV, Part 2* are from Bulman 2016.
10 That term is Coleridge's, from a lecture on *Othello* in 1819. See Coleridge 2004, 231.
11 'We were', Suzman told me years later, 'all meant to be black', as is evident in the filmed version of the production shot in 1974 (personal communication, 2001).
12 This sort of coded language among reviewers, which has travelled forward from Tynan *et al.* in 1953, will continue on its way in, for example, Milton Schulman's *Evening Standard* review of 11 October 1978. 'Glenda Jackson', he writes of Peter Brook's production, 'is one actress who ought to have resisted the temptation of trying her hand at Egypt's bewildering temptress. Her looks and gestures are so stubbornly anglo-Saxon that it makes nonsense of genetics to suggest that she could ever project the essence of a dark-haired African queen. Surely 'dark-haired' is here a proxy for 'dark-skinned'?
13 The souvenir programme for this production is held among other production records at the Shakespeare Birthplace Trust, Stratford-upon-Avon.
14 Penelope Gilliatt's 'Making *Sunday Bloody Sunday*' (1971) was published originally as the introduction to the United States publication of the script.
15 All quotations of *King Richard III* are from Siemon 2009.
16 Personal communication from Terry Hands, January 2018.
17 For an excellent analysis of the moves recorded in the promptbook see Hodgdon 2016, 10–11.

18 This beautifully marked-up promptbook was the work of the production's deputy stage manager, Trevor Williamson. It's a gift to any who aims to write performance studies. Additional production records for this production, including the stage manager's reports and photographs, are held at the Shakespeare Birthplace Trust, Stratford-upon-Avon.
19 Brook evidently had no notion of the production that Giles Havergal had staged at the Citizens' Theatre, Glasgow, six years earlier. See Chapter 5.
20 The production records, including the stage manager's reports, promptbook and photographs, for this production are held at the Shakespeare Birthplace Trust, Stratford-upon-Avon.
21 In a television interview that has since become notorious as a demonstration of 1980s sexism, Michael Parkinson introduced Mirren by quoting comments (supposedly from reviewers) who called her an 'amorous boa constrictor', an actor who was 'especially telling at projecting sluttish eroticism'. While the video of the interview itself is currently blocked, a report of its content can be accessed at http://thetab.com/us/2016/08/22/sexist-questions-49398 and at https://www.huffingtonpost.co.uk, where, while the video is shown, the audio is captioned (both accessed 8 December 2019).
22 I owe this personal history to Peter Holland.
23 See Mirren speaking both in voiceover and direct to camera in the documentary made by the International Centre for Theatre Research of Brook's research towards *The Conference of the Birds*, now archived on YouTube at https://www.youtube.com/watch?v=7UhPlba_QQA. See also http://en.wikipedia.org/wiki/International_Centre_for_Theatre_Research and http://www.grotowski.net/en/node/1861 (all sites accessed 8 December 2019).
24 Personal communication, August 2017. I am grateful to Sorcha Cusack for talking me through the women's play.
25 The female space of Egypt was feminised in a way that one reviewer found unaccountable unless the women's intimacy was sexualised. So Peter McGarry in the *Coventry Evening Telegraph* wrote that 'Charmian and Iras are overt in a lesbian relationship and attempt to encompass Cleopatra. She is unsure of her feelings there, as she is towards the motherly protectiveness of her eunuch'. When I read her this review, Sorcha Cusack responded with laughter.

# 5

# Boying greatness: the Citizens' Theatre (Glasgow), 1972, and Northern Broadsides (Halifax), 1995

### Extemporal stagings

Rousing her women to assist her to do 'what's brave, what's noble' (4.15.90), Cleopatra re-imagines for Iras the scene that Antony has fixed in her mind in 4.12, of the Egyptians led in Caesar's triumph, herself 'hoist ... up to the shouting plebeians' (4.12.34) and 'windowed' in Rome (4.14.73):

> Thou an Egyptian puppet shall be shown
> In Rome as well as I. Mechanic slaves
> With greasy aprons, rules and hammers shall
> Uplift us to the view. In their thick breaths,
> Rank of gross diet, shall we be enclouded
> And forced to drink their vapour (5.2.207–212)

Worse, the Egyptians will be translated, travestied:

> The quick comedians
> Extemporally will stage us and present
> Our Alexandrian revels; Antony
> Shall be brought drunken forth; and I shall see
> Some squeaking Cleopatra boy my greatness
> I'th' posture of a whore. (5.2.215–220)

This future, the high drama of her 'greatness' captured for low comedy and coarsened to the tastes of popular culture, is one she doesn't live to see. But her prediction is right. 'Vulgar fame' hasn't been able to keep its greasy fingers off Antony and Cleopatra.

In 1866 F. C. Burnand, the prolific scribbler of some 200 farces, burlesques and pantomimes with titles like *Ixion; or, the Man at the Wheel* and *Helen; or, Taken from the Greek* (tributes, if dubious, to his Eton and Trinity College Cambridge education), offered his public 'A Grand New and Original Burlesque', *Antony and Cleopatra; or, His-tory and Her-story in a Modern Nilo-Metre* (Wells 1978). It has Lepidus, 'incog', entering Cleopatra's palace through 'the Back Door'. His 'mission', expressed in jingle-jangle rhyming couplets, is to find Antony, 'catch him, / And then from Cleopatra's chain detach him' (Wells 1978, 143). The palace 'Interior' is 'full of exotics'; 'Sphinxes support the roof'; a 'dark slave' enters 'bearing drinks', and 'Antony is discovered' as a bizarre cultural tourist retaining tastes from home, 'sipping chocolate' (Wells 1978, 147). He's in Egypt 'finishing [his] education', trying to learn Egyptian, but it's hard-going:

> The Egyptian language one rather wishes
> Had fewer of these birds, and beasts and fishes.
> Ideas drawn on walls by stupid niggers,
> Which bother one, for I'm no hand at figures. (Wells 1978, 148)

Cleopatra's barge is an 'elegant poney carriage'; her attendants, 'Assyrian Blues and Black Guards'; her 'girls', 'dark-looking little creoles' found 'listening at the keyholes' (Wells 1978, 162, 164). When she blows her top reading a letter from Octavius, she begs excuse for 'getting hot and fireish':

> Excitement often runs me into Irish.
> There's some connexion can be traced in full
> 'Twixt the Assyrian and the Irish Bull. (Wells 1978, 162)

At the end, the finale, 'Hunkey Dorum', is marked to be sung by the London branch of the blackface Christy's Minstrels (Wells 1978, 190).

Thus, *His-tory* mobilises a full assortment of Victorian imperialist stereotypes and white supremacist gags patronising John Bull's colonies both east and west to deliver 'squeaking' Cleopatra and louche Egypt in low-comic blackface. This travesty reached a mass audience. Throughout the 1860s and 1870s Burnand's burlesques were performed in theatres such as the 1,200-seat St. James and the Adelphi; his *Black-Eyed Susan* ran for 400 nights at the 650-seat Royalty Theatre, and *Ixion* raked in for him £3,000 in performance royalties across its run. Meanwhile, if it was something closer to Shakespeare's *Antony and Cleopatra* that audiences wanted, they could see George Vining's heavily cut but spectacular production at the Princess's Theatre (1867) – these being the years when the Suez Canal was being dug, when tourism to Egypt was becoming fashionable, when Egyptomania was rampant and when the theatre was staging Egypt to the London gaze. Vining's Cleopatra was Isabella Glyn, who'd been playing the part for twenty years.

Some seventy years later, while Howard Carter was writing *A Report upon the Tomb of Tut 'ankh Amun*, the monumental multi-volume account of his excavations in the Valley of the Kings, the vaudeville act 'Wilson, Keppel & Betty' was 'Doing the Egyptian' for another generation of popular audiences in 1930s Britain.[1] Dressed identically in short togas, Arab-style headdresses, Groucho Marx eyebrows and droopy moustaches, Wilson and Keppel (one from Lancashire, the other, Cork) performed an 'authentic' soft-shoe shuffle on sand (including poses and hand gestures parodying hieroglyphics) against a painted backdrop of the Sphinx and pyramids. Betty followed on in bedazzled 'Cleopatra' costume, undulating to the orchestral accompaniment of the 'Egyptian Ballet' in an impression of 'exotic dancing' that revealed bits of the female body not seen in (respectable) public. In the winter of 1946 the trio was playing the London Palladium on Regent Street, a run of 466 performances, 'two shows daily'. For the 800,000 or so theatre-goers who saw them, it was Wilson, Keppel & Betty, not William Shakespeare, who identified 'the Egyptian'; though if they'd wanted something closer to Shakespeare, they could have caught Glen Byam Shaw's pseudo-Elizabethan production of *Antony and Cleopatra* (his first shot at the production he would stage seven years later in the Shakespeare Memorial Theatre) further down Regent Street at the Piccadilly Theatre that December, with Edith Evans as Cleopatra in a farthingale and red wig.

By now, of course, the new-model 'mechanic slaves' (5.2.208) of Cleopatra's imagination were mostly seeing Antony and Cleopatra in the movies. In 1917 there was a silent film *Cleopatra* starring Theda Bara, to which, as the *Exhibitors Herald* reported, the Chicago Board of Censors attached a string of objections requiring cuts: 'all front views of Queen showing her breasts outlined by snake breast plates'; 'three scenes of Queen in leopard skin costume with one breast exposed'; 'Queen walking to throne in costume exposing body' ('Official Cut-Outs' 1918). In 1934 there was an epic *Cleopatra* directed by Cecil B. DeMille with Claudette Colbert as a big-eyed, wise-cracking Queen of Egypt in a series of flesh-baring costumes. In 1963 Joseph L. Mankiewicz's extravagant blockbuster *Cleopatra* reproduced the 'scandal' of Antony and Cleopatra on set in the adulterous goings on between the film's stars, Richard Burton and Elizabeth Taylor, reported in the 'thick breaths' (5.2.210) of the local *paparazzi*. The wink Taylor's Cleopatra gave Caesar when the seemingly endless procession of her orientalism into Rome finally brought them face to face (a full nine minutes of screen time that culminated with Cleopatra and the boy Caesarion delivered to the Roman emperor atop a monument-sized Sphinx dragged by hundreds of harnessed slaves) might have been the actor tipping the wink to film-goers, subverting the high seriousness of the spectacle's signifiers with that low comic gesture, iconoclastically revealing the whole 'show' as camp farce.

A year later, and as though locating that wink in every frame, the British spoof masters of the *Carry On* film series released *Carry On, Cleo* with Kenneth Williams, Sid James and Amanda Barrie as Julius Caesar, Antony and Cleopatra – and with second-hand sets and costumes, all the fabulous stuff that Mankiewicz had abandoned in Britain when he moved his shoot to Rome. (Ironically, relying on these hand-me-downs, *Cleo* was produced to a budget and schedule that meant it was actually released before the blockbuster it parodied.) The 'lowest of the cultural low', as Colin MacCabe calls them, the *Carry On*s were entertainment-after-Bakhtin (*Guardian*, 29 January 1999). *Cleo* gave a pleb's-eye view of Plutarch in a script laden with saucy innuendo (one sequence has the Egyptian queen, bathing in asses' milk in Caesar's Rome, handed a foot-long stiff loofah), derisive gags and atrocious puns (viz. Williams's camp Caesar wailing as the assassins Antony has organised to get him out of the way of his love life close in: 'Infamy, infamy, they've all got it in for me'). Its targets were class pomp, pretension and authority, the *Carry On*s showing authority, MacCabe writes, as 'little more than a ridiculous attempt to deny the reality and presence of the body'. *Cleo* made a meal of Barrie's body.

From Burnand to *Carry On*, this burlesque tradition had nothing to do with Shakespeare's *Antony and Cleopatra* – and everything to do with it. Anarchic, carnivalesque, burlesque was both iconoclastic and restorative. It swiped a kipper across the po-face of bardolatry, knocking the bloated BARD off the elitist plinth where high culture maroons him to allow him to be again a playwright who speaks to the people. It took as its whole irreverent subject the farcical matter that's there in Shakespeare's script and that so startles the play generically: Cleopatra mauling the messenger; Antony botching his suicide; the Asp Man arriving with a delivery. It looked steadily and lubriciously at the bawdy body that Shakespeare's script puts in view, the body that the 'legitimate' theatre and mainstream reviewers frequently find so embarrassing. In terms of what Joseph Roach calls 'genealogies of performance' (Roach 1996, 28), burlesque versions of the infamous love story are the distant relatives of two 'straight' (but seriously unconventional) British productions of *Antony and Cleopatra* that reframed the play's meaning by bending expectations, staging alternative interpretations – aimed at very different audiences – to those then on offer at the RSC.

### 'Gimmick theatre'

Shortly before rehearsals began for Trevor Nunn's *Antony and Cleopatra* in Stratford-upon-Avon in late spring of 1972, another *Antony and Cleopatra* opened, at the Citizens' Theatre in Glasgow.[2] This coincidence means that all the national current events rehearsed in Chapter 4 which contextualised Nunn's production – from the miners' strike to the three-day week and gay pride march – likewise informed Giles Havergal's production, while not at all accounting for its particular location in the cultural life of Glasgow, a cultural life that the theatre was instrumental in radically re-imagining by using Shakespeare as material to do so.

The Citizens' stands at 119 Gorbals Street, on the fringe of what, well into the 1950s, was the most notorious slum not just in Britain but in Europe, in a city that had been vertiginously on the skids for thirty years. Three minutes' walk away is the mighty Clyde, the river that was called the 'grey anvil' of Britain's industrial revolution, the metaphoric hammers that fell upon it beating Glasgow into shape as the super-prosperous, shining 'Second City of the Empire' by the end of the nineteenth century. A hundred years earlier, more than half of the British tobacco trade – which depended on the trans-Atlantic African slave trade into the Americas – was already concentrated on the Clyde. Glasgow's population surpassed Edinburgh's by 1821; by 1900 the city was producing more than half of Britain's tonnage in shipping and a quarter of all locomotives in the world (according to W. Hamish Fraser's account in *The Glasgow Story*, 2004). Accelerating industrialisation in shipbuilding, engineering (of everything from machinery to bridges to theatre structures), manufacturing (furniture, textiles, carpets, cigarettes, explosives) and all the support industries necessary to sustain industrialisation on that scale led to a population explosion in the city's workforce, housed in once-handsome tenements built in areas such as Gorbals that, even before the end of Victoria's reign, were simply overwhelmed. Glasgow took a double economic hit during the recession that followed the Great War and, a decade later, the Great Depression. By the 1930s Gorbals tenements made the housing that Sean O'Casey was writing about in *The Plough and the Stars*, in destitute Dublin of about the same period, look like luxury accommodation: whole families crammed into single rooms stacked four storeys high; shared lavvies on the stairs; middens out the back; a population density of 40,000 per square kilometre.

Gang warfare was rife, some of it territorial (the 'Beehive Boys' controlling Gorbals), some of it structured on deadly sectarian rivalries imported with the immigrant workforce from Ireland, 'Taigs' v. 'Proddies', 'Norman Conks' v. 'Billy Boys', the weapon of choice the flick razor. By the 1950s the toxic combination of unemployment, drug and alcohol abuse, crime and casual street violence made Glasgow the most dangerous city in Britain – some achievement, given that it sustained its reputation in the 1960s against competition from cities under military occupation such as Belfast and (London)Derry. Even attempts at urban regeneration produced ironic effects: the festering Victorian tenements cleared from Gorbals in the 1950s left behind wastelands, while what replaced them on other urban sites in the 1960s, modern high-rises, 'cities in the sky' designed by Basil Spence after Le Corbusier, and housing estates, such as the infamous Red Road estate (all since demolished), became ghettos, home to the latest generation of Glasgow gangs.

The Citizens' Theatre at 119 Gorbals Street defied the urban ruin that surrounded it. Built in 1878 and shortly thereafter named the Royal Princess's Theatre, it stood on the south side of an elegant Victorian square, one of four thriving theatres in the immediate area, its neo-Greek façade topped with statues of William Shakespeare and Robbie Burns looking down from its Parthenon-style entablature. By the time the slum clearances of the 1950s had levelled Gorbals, the Royal Princess's had passed through conversion into a cinema while the Palace Theatre, next door, had become a bingo hall. They, along with the public swimming baths and a single tenement, were all that was left standing of the Victorian square, which today is still empty scrubland. In 1945 the Royal was taken over by James Bridie, whose vision of a 'Citizens' Theatre' had been inspired by a 1909 manifesto along the lines of Yeats's and Lady Gregory's declaration for an Irish theatre. It called for a repertory theatre that would be 'Glasgow's own theatre … a citizens' theatre in the fullest sense of the term'. Established 'to make Glasgow independent from London for its dramatic supplies', it would produce 'plays which the Glasgow playgoers would otherwise not have the opportunity of seeing'.[3]

Bridie had ambitions for the cultural life of Glasgow's citizens. His theatre would not be a glorified music hall offering the stodge fare of pantomimes, farces and low-comic burlesques (although there would be an annual Christmas pantomime). Rather, it would be a national theatre that staged new plays on Scottish themes while mining the European tradition. It would give audiences plays such as *Paradise Enow*, *John Knox* and *The Baikie Charivari* alongside Ibsen's *Hedda Gabler*, Molière's *The Misanthrope* and Molnár's *Liliom*. And at prices Gorbals residents could afford. Bridie and his team beat down ticket prices to undercut the Palace Bingo Hall next door, an aim finally achieved by the young turks Giles Havergal, Philip Prowse (both up from London) and Robert David MacDonald (a Scot), who took over the theatre in 1969. A hoarding (circa 1971) at the foyer entrance advertises the current shows, *A Country Wife* and *The Importance of Being Earnest*, below signage six feet high: 'ALL SEATS 50P'.

Under the triumvirate's auspices, this people's theatre got its popular name: the Citz. The actor Ian McDiarmid, who arrived at the Citz from across town in 1971, straight out of Glasgow's Royal Scottish Academy of Music and Drama and aged twenty-seven (which made him the old man in that year's company), remembers Havergal running the place 'as a temple of Dionysian excess'. While most British theatre 'was Apollonian: rational and ordered, with the emphasis on clarity' – an excellent description of the theatre that Peter Hall had introduced in Stratford-upon-Avon and that his successor Trevor Nunn was now busy institutionalising – the Citz, said McDiarmid, 'was spontaneous, passionate, intuitive'

(*Guardian*, 4 March 2014). The institutional hierarchies that structured other companies, in which actors worked their way up from spear-carrying to bit parts to (if they were lucky) major roles, didn't obtain at the Citz. Everyone in the eighteen-strong company of twenty-something-year-olds who performed across the three or four plays produced each season got a crack at the leads. The repertoire was challenging, international. The casting ignored age and gender. In that 1971 season, McDiarmid played both the title part in Brecht's *Galileo* and Rebecca Nurse in Arthur Miller's *The Crucible*.

Any artistic director who described himself 'as the madam of a brothel, parading his creatures of the night six times a week for public delectation' was likely to prove controversial (*Guardian*, 4 March 2014). And Havergal *was* controversial.[4] He set *Woyzeck* in a bathhouse; flaunted nudity in an all-male *Hamlet*; advertised *The Changeling* with a poster that featured Shakespeare as 'Sheila', the head from the Droeshout portrait (its features enhanced with rouge and mascara), the body in drag (corset, suspender belt, stripper's elbow-length gloves).[5] 'Some', says McDiarmid, 'were appalled and outraged' by what critics called 'gimmicks'; but 'Most were seduced', particularly the young. By 1979 75 per cent of Havergal's audience was under thirty-five (see MacDonald *et al.* 1980, 53).

All this provides the surround story for Havergal's *Antony and Cleopatra* in 1972. The production itself is under-documented. The production file contains only two rehearsal and eight production photographs and the twelve-page programme. Only one metropolitan newspaper, the *Guardian*, reviewed the production. *The Times*, *Daily Telegraph*, *Daily Express*, *Daily Mail* and all the Sunday broadsheets that regularly covered the UK's theatrical map from Exeter, Bristol and Chichester to Oxford, Coventry, Birmingham, Nottingham, even Colchester, Stoke-on-Trent and, in Scotland, both the Edinburgh and Pitlochry festivals, stayed away. The review file, then, is woefully thin, eight notices amounting to a couple of dozen column inches and a pair of letters to the editor (one from 'Disgusted' of Kingswood Drive; the other from a pensioner who looked at the number of young people in Havergal's audience and suggested that readers of the *Glasgow Herald* should 'Cheer up' since 'We may be on the verge of a new renaissance').[6]

Thin on the ground they may be, but even these few reviews give instant access to Havergal's production – and its shock. The headline that screams 'Cleopatra as a Zulu – in drag!' was pointing to only what was most alarmingly conspicuous on the surface of this *Antony and Cleopatra* (alarming, that is, to the *Jewish Echo*'s reviewer, 18 May 1972). The actual challenge Havergal offered was much more deeply structural than that.

The production used only seven actors. Jonathan Kent, cross-cast, played Cleopatra as 'she' in an Alexandria that Havergal and his designer, Philip Prowse, saw belonging to Africa, not Europe. The key to the design concept (which functioned also as political interpretation) was clearly visible in the production's twelve-page programme. All of the bodies that illustrated the 'Facts' and 'Fictions' of Antony and Cleopatra's story were black. Although no reviewer mentioned it except in coded language – reviews called Cleopatra 'Zulu', 'Tahitian', and described her face as 'dusky' or 'gilded' – Kent wore dark body makeup to embody a Cleopatra who was 'with Phoebus' amorous pinches black' (1.5.29). Plenty of that body was on display. Naked to below the waist except for the ropes of beads strung around her neck like so many snakes and the woven leather bands knotted around her arms that fell in long tails, she was boyishly torsoed like one of Ovid's youths. Below the waist she was 'woman-ed' in a sarong that wrapped around her hips and fell to the ground, some leather macramé weaving covering 'her' private parts – or teasingly enhancing them, drawing attention to what had to be hidden.

The effect of this cross-gender casting was to re-charge the erotic batteries of Shakespeare's play, to give Cleopatra's sexual magnetism danger, to put squarely in view its destructive power. UK divorce courts had long since taken the sting out of what poisons a line such as 'What says the married woman … ?' (1.3.21). Adultery was hardly transgressive in 1972. But the Sexual Offences Act that decriminalised homosexual acts between consenting adult males had been passed only in 1967, the first 'gay studies' programmes wouldn't be launched in any university until the autumn of 1972 (and then only in the United States), and ten years later, in 1982, the normalising role that theatre played in the representation of such acts would still be so hotly disputed in the UK that the case of *The Romans in Britain* could bring a director at the National Theatre in London to court, prosecuted for 'procuring' a public act of gross indecency in a scene on stage that simulated male-on-male anal rape. In Havergal's *Antony and Cleopatra* the body represented was unambiguously female, but the body 'beneath' was undisguisedly male. It was the traffic between those bodies that provoked anxiety in some quarters – or outrage: 'a display of "high camp" that beggars description'; 'exactly what Cleopatra feared when she said: "I shall see some squeaking Cleopatra boy my greatness"' (*Scotsman*, 15 May 1972); 'Bizarre novelties ... heaped upon' the play (*Glasgow Herald*, 19 May 1972); 'deliberate provocation ... no valid reason for the sex-shuffle' (*Scottish Daily Express*, 13 May 1972).

But if it provoked outrage, then this 'sex-shuffle' also elicited an under-determined fascination from youthful spectators who didn't yet have a history or language to articulate their experience of a theatre where, not just in this *Antony and Cleopatra* but in *every* Citz production, 'there was', as one Citz spectator remembers of his adolescent theatre-going, 'a sense that there was something ostensibly "unusual" going on ... that might have something to do with sex', though 'that was probably too daring a thought for a wee Catholic boy from the east end' of Glasgow to entertain in 1972.[7] Given the theatre's demographics, there must have been hundreds of 'wee' ones, lads and lasses, Catholics and Protestants, from all sides of the city who, coming to Havergal's 'community theatre' in Gorbals as teenagers, shared this contemporary witness of a theatre that was bringing them, however haltingly, into social, political and sexual consciousness:

> I didn't think of the productions (or of Havergal himself) as gay; but that may have been ('may have been'? no, 'was') more due to my own lack of sexual precocity at the time, and my own parochial mentality. For me, it was probably a sense that there was an undercurrent running through, something 'dangerous' because it was subterranean and pertaining to a world that was unspoken – not fully 'out' as we might now say; the sense that that was a world inhabited by others – by people other than me, other than those I knew, and all the more seductive because of that; but also something that would not be openly addressed by 'conventional' folk like me. Or like the me of that time. Later, I knew more of all this; and it became again all the more exciting and – literally – charming.

(Is it fanciful – but perhaps permissible – to hear in this reaction an echo of the force of early modern performance, something of the danger, excitement and seductive charm that this play exerted upon its Jacobean audiences?)

In Havergal's *Antony and Cleopatra*, it wasn't just cross-cast Cleopatra who was 'unusual' and 'dangerous'. The single set designed by Prowse was a dark space for enacting 'barbaric ritual', its 'sultry, watchful atmosphere' created by 'light filtering down from far above through a high canopy of shredded hemp on to a sandy floor' where the Soothsayer sketched out prophetic hieroglyphs, where human skulls grinned, and where incense rose from an animal's skull (Cordelia Oliver, *Guardian*, 15 May 1972). The furniture on stage was minimalist. Ladders propped up against the back wall, stage left and right, gave elevation, places for observation, surveillance, comment. Octavius (Mike Gwilym) and Antony (John Duttine) were exotic barbarians more fully clothed from knee to ankle than from neck to knee, their crotches cased in leather jockstraps that spewed leather ejaculations like intimations of virility. Duttine's torso was naked, Gwilym's girdled in a network of leather belts and laces; both were necklaced with beads, arms braceleted shoulder to wrist, calves wrapped in shaggy leggings that made them animal-footed. Beyond the principals, four further actors (Cheryl Campbell, Angela Chadfield, Colin Haigh and Geoff Lerway) played all the remaining parts, a Chorus permanently on stage, drumming, flailing the earth, keening, punctuating speech with a flute underscore or percussive striking on bells, plucking of strings or beating on the wooden sides of the African drums, a single 'TING' regularly marking a speech's change of emotional direction. The two women wore dark cheesecloth knotted at the neck, necklaces, bracelets. Campbell's blonde mane was leonine; Chadfield's face was slashed by an African braid. One of her breasts was exposed. All of the actors played barefoot.

Reviewers complained that Kent's Cleopatra 'yelps and whimpers, sobs and shrieks, while flouncing around the stage in an ecstasy of petulance', while Gwilym's Octavius 'struts and strikes postures' and Duttine's Antony simply 'appears perplexed' (*Scotsman*, 15 May 1972). Such reactions ignored what the letter writer to the *Glasgow Herald* editor on 19 May wanted said: not just that such reviews 'fail[ed] to inform us of the overall effect of the production (which last night was quite something)' but that they failed 'to appreciate what is happening in the theatre today, both north and south of the Border, and that is the return of youth to the theatre, certainly for the first time in my 60-odd years'. Might it not, the writer concluded, 'be true to say that the proportion of under-25s to the middle-aged and elderly [in the audience] is higher today than at any time since Shakespeare's "Antony and Cleopatra" was first produced?' Even Christopher Small, whose *Glasgow Herald* review had ended with the dire comment 'the asp bite can't come too soon' (15 May 1972), found 'remarkable effects' in Havergal's production: 'the sight of Cleopatra as a kind of sorceress, gazing through the flames of a sacrificial fire at her own dark future, her face half-visible in the flickering light'; the 'stunning visual coup when Antony returns to surrender to her wiles and, taking him into her arms, she envelopes him in an enormous gauzy red cloak that also covers half the stage'.

Finally, however, Small had to dismiss as a 'false economy' what was Havergal's boldest directorial work on this *Antony and Cleopatra*, far beyond the cross-casting of Cleopatra or the flesh-baring on stage, and that was his reshaping of the text, compressing its sprawling structure into two parts, each under an hour long. Swathes of writing and production were cut: Ventidius in Syria; Pompey and the knees-up on his galley; the deaths of Lepidus, Pompey and Enobarbus; Eros's suicide. Parts were ruthlessly reduced: the Asp Man got one line, and all the parts beyond Antony, Cleopatra and Caesar were stripped of their names and characters and assigned to the onstage Chorus, called 'Acolytes', who sometimes spoke in unison, sometimes repeated lines, sometimes volleyed lines back and forth in speeches taken apart. The happy survival of the promptbook makes following Havergal's process possible.[8]

This *Antony and Cleopatra* began not with disaffected grousing about Antony's dotage but with a communal celebration of Cleopatra's camp self-representation, 'The barge she sat in …'. The speech was shared out among the full company, voice after voice picking up the narrative, cutting in ('For her own person…'; 'The city cast / Her people out …'; 'Rare Egyptian!'; 'Royal wench!': all marked with actors' initials in the promptbook). Then a lighting change after 'She made great Caesar lay his sword to bed; / He plowed her' [stage direction: 'new voice'] 'and she cropped' effected a scenic cut into 'Nay, but this dotage …' (2.2.201–235, *passim*, 1.1.1). Cleopatra's 'If it be love indeed, tell me how much' (1.1.14) was spoken twice, first by an Acolyte, then by the queen. Seconds later, when she was chivvying Antony about hearing the messenger – 'Fulvia perchance is angry … Perform't, or else we damn thee' (1.1.21, 25) – her speech was intercut with lines from later premonitory interjections by the Acolytes: 'In each thing give him way …' (1.3.10). (All of these intercuts are hand-written, inserted into the promptbook on pasted strips.) 'Why did he marry Fulvia, and not love her?' was answered first with the interpolated 'Tempt him not so far … / In time we hate that which we often fear', then with Antony coming in on 'Now for the love of Love ... What sport tonight?' (1.1.42, 1.3.12–13, 1.1.45, 48). With such interpolations, such anticipations uncannily serving retrospection, audiences heard, as Lady Macbeth might put it, 'the future ... in the instant' (1.5.58).

Havergal achieved scenic compression – and speed of play – by layering scenes, by keeping actors permanently on stage so that subsequence made for presence. After she commanded an Acolyte to find Antony, 'See where he is', 'He was disposed to mirth, but on the sudden / A Roman thought hath struck him' (1.2.87–88), Cleopatra moved upstage and knelt as downstage Antony and an Acolyte entered with that 'News ... from Rome': 'Fulvia thy wife first came into the field.' The war report, the news of Fulvia's death, Antony's musing, 'Thus did I desire it ...', were superimposed upon the upstage image of the kneeling body of the 'enchanting queen' from whom 'I must break off' (1.1.18, 1.2.93, 129, 135). Intercut into this soliloquy came voices delivering urgent news, 'Menecrates and Menas, famous pirates ...'. These voices rose in a crescendo of overlapping lines repeated over and over – 'No vessel can peep forth', 'famous pirates', 'flush youth revolts' – as though going round and round in Antony's head before he silenced them: 'I shall break / The cause of our expedience to the Queen' (1.4.49, 54, 53, 1.2.184–185). But his next interpolated line, 'Would I had never seen her!', called up Enobarbus's savvy rejoinder, spoken by an Acolyte, 'O, sir, you had then left unseen a wonderful piece of work' (1.2.160–161). This prompted an exchange that ended with Antony brooking no further contradiction – 'I must away from hence' – then turning upstage to see Cleopatra approaching downstage, wailing, 'Help me away! I shall fall' (1.2.139, 1.3.16). This then segued into a farewell scene that was largely uncut, Shakespeare's 1.3.15–105, which moved straight into 'Ha, ha!', the promptbook indicating Cleopatra 'YELLING', not yawning: 'Give me to drink mandragora' (1.5.3–4), a segue made possible by bringing forward to just after the messenger's shocked reaction to his rebuff in 1.1 ('Is Caesar with Antonius prized so slight?') the damning report Caesar makes of Antony in Shakespeare's 1.4. In Havergal's edit this report began, 'It is not Caesar's natural vice to hate / Our great competitor' and had Gwilym on his knees invoking 'Antony' to 'Leave thy lascivious wassails', remembering 'When thou once / Was beaten from Modena ... famine ... strange flesh ... borne so like a soldier' (1.4.56–71, *passim*) while behind him Acolytes produced a soundtrack of moaning. Characters who, in Shakespeare, would have been 'off' in Havergal were 'on', having climbed the ladders, right and left, to survey the scene in progress or having retreated upstage, fixed as a silent tableau, the downstage scene superimposed upon it and playing off it.

Such were the 'gimmicks' Havergal employed. He reassigned speeches: stunningly, it was his Caesar who proposed Antony's marriage to Octavia (and who, at some point in the proceedings, buckled a dog collar and lead around Antony's neck which he used literally to jerk Antony into line). He used freeze-framing to capture the ironies that would doom politics: 'There's my hand', said Caesar, 'bequeath[ing]' a 'sister' 'To join our kingdoms and our hearts' (2.2.157–160). At Antony's response, 'Happily, amen', the promptbook marked a lighting cue and stage direction, 'NOISES STOP FREEZE' while Acolyte voices came in: 'Now Antony must leave her utterly'. 'Never. He will not' repeated twice, then a rush of single voices cutting in on each other, on lines and half lines in a dissident clamour, 'Age cannot wither her', 'nor custom stale / Her infinite variety'; 'Other women cloy / The appetites they feed, but she makes hungry / Where most she satisfies' (2.2.243–244, 245–248). This freeze dissolved with a lighting change and resumption of drumming after 'the holy priests / Bless her when she is riggish' as the Roman generals returned to preparations for war: 'I did not think to draw my sword 'gainst Pompey' (2.2.249–250, 162). Havergal used overlapped entrances to insist on bitter juxtapositions: the words hardly out of her mouth, Cleopatra's interrogation of the messenger who delivered 'infectious' news of a new wife whose new marriage she might yet thwart ('Why, methinks, by him, / This creature's no such thing') brought Antony downstage, complaining to Octavia of her brother and giving her leave to return to Rome to be their 'reconciler' (3.3.39–40, 3.4.30). 'Make your soonest haste' (3.4.27) cued a crescendo of drums, a lighting cue, and a stage direction for a 'Dumb show – Antony returns to Cleopatra – Octavia moves towards Caesar'. 'CLOAK!' written in inch-high capitals across the top of the page indicates the 'stunning visual coup' that wowed the *Glasgow Herald* reviewer, Antony returning 'to surrender to her wiles' and Cleopatra 'taking him into her arms' and 'enveloping him in an enormous gauzy red cloak that also covers half the stage' (15 May 1972). Acolytes observed, and commented in lines from Shakespeare's 1.1: 'Behold and see, the triple pillar of the world transformed into a strumpet's fool'. Blackout. Interval.

The lights came up after the interval on 'Dumb show as end of Act I', the positions enacting the shifted allegiances. In this second half, Actium was staged as a 'Battle Collage' with Caesar and Antony directing things ('Strike not by land'; 'Set we our squadrons on yond side o'th' hill') from atop the ladders (3.8.3, 3.9.1). The forward momentum of war, Shakespeare's three scenes staged simultaneously, was punctuated by pared-down scenes of reflection and twisted diplomacy that reduced these scenes to their essence (Antony's rage, 3.11, Thidias's attempt to corrupt Cleopatra into colluding with Caesar, 3.13, and Antony's musing upon the shape-changing clouds and his botched suicide, alone on stage in 4.14, Eros's death having been cut). Antony was not lifted into a monument to die; rather, he stood, held upright in Cleopatra's arms before sagging to the ground (see 5.1). Dead, his corpse was propped up against a ladder in the background. As the Queen's end came, pressed on by her treasurer's (heavily cut) betrayal, and she called for 'the

5.1 'Noblest of men, woo't die?' (4.15). Cleopatra (Jonathan Kent), Antony (John Duttine).

5.2 'My resolution's placed, and I have nothing / Of woman in me' (5.2). Cleopatra (Jonathan Kent), Acolyte (Angela Chadfield), Antony (John Duttine), dead (behind).

pretty worm of Nilus there / That kills and pains not', an Acolyte on a ladder held up the asp as another Acolyte wished her 'joy o'th' worm' (5.2.242–243, 278). Her women dressed her in robe and crown to prepare her for death, a solitary death, everything around Iras's and Charmian's final moments having been cut (see 5.2). After 'Dost thou not see my baby at my breast / That sucks the nurse asleep?' her last words were 'As sweet as balm, as soft as air, as gentle – / O Antony!' (5.2.308–311). Most of the final 'discovery' sequence was cut, the speeches that remained re-ordered to give Caesar the last words in lines compiled from 5.2.334–357):

> She looks like sleep.
> As she would catch another Antony
> In her strong toil of grace. Bravest at the last,
> She levelled at our purposes and, being royal,
> Took her own way.
> She shall be buried by her Antony. [Blackout]

This *Antony and Cleopatra* closed the second full season of Havergal's work at the Citizens', work (as he wrote in the programme) that aimed to give audiences 'a "theatrical experience"', to make 'each performance an "event" in which you participate'. At the Citz, theatre was 'no longer' to be 'a place where you sit at one end of the building in the dark and watch us acting at the other end in the light'. 'Doing what we should be doing within this community' meant offering 'an experience which will entertain in the fullest sense – amusing, enlightening, moving, shocking, upsetting, angering, delighting, and above all astonishing you – the audience.' According to Thomas Docherty's contemporary witness, Havergal's commitment to 'doing what we should be doing within this community' succeeded:

> We always expected to be surprised, engaged and 'addressed' or 'called out' by what was going on in the productions. They were always structurally thoughtful, original and likely to invoke strong reactions in the thinking that they generated. The plays never 'finished' when the lights went down because the foyer and streets outside were always alive with discussion of what we had just seen; and those conversations persisted for ages. They made me think of theatre in ways that were very different from just having an audience performed to by actors on a stage. The productions spoke to us – and I think they expected us to speak back, in various ways.

Havergal's production was the first UK *Antony and Cleopatra* since Byam Shaw's at the Memorial Theatre in 1953. As I argued in Chapter 3, while that earlier production flirted with the blackness Shakespeare writes for Egypt, it put on stage a Cleopatra who was utterly English, even 'too English'. At the Citz, Havergal exploded the notion of the 'English' *Antony and Cleopatra*. He made the play about Africa. It was not about 'civilisation', as Nunn's production for the RSC, which would open only some weeks later, would claim to be. It was about 'Dionysian excess': bodies erotically on display, primitive rhythms underscoring primitive passions, the cross-casting of Jonathan Kent recuperating the sexual shock and political threat of Shakespeare's writing for Cleopatra. Distancing the play, Havergal made it about difference. He 'called out' the audience, deeply unsettling Shakespeare, especially the Shakespeare of those reviewers who suggested that Havergal's work belonged in some dubious 'Carry On' tradition ('Cleopatra ... in Drag'; 'Camped up Cleopatra'; 'a hysterical schoolfellow of [Frederic William Farrar's] Eric': *Jewish Echo*, 8 May 1972; *Scotsman, Glasgow Herald*, both 15 May 1972). Havergal's outrageously cross-dressed 'Shakespeare as Sheila' outfaced any who would dismiss 'burlesque' as merely out-of-date

Victorian seaside sauce or (following on from Burnand's *His-story*) another era's colonial condescension. Havergal's seriously travestied 'Sheila' planted a Glasgow fist on the jawbone of cultural authority. His airy manipulation of Shakespeare's playtext asserted the right to exploit Shakespeare the way Shakespeare exploited his sources, to use Shakespeare as material for re-performance. Perhaps most significantly, Havergal located theatre in the community, for the citizens who were now queuing outside 119 Gorbals Street not to play bingo but to watch 'a happening' called 'Shakespeare'.

### 'Proudly provincial'

Like Havergal's, Barrie Rutter's ambition was to establish a community theatre, but his was a community identified by voice, not venue, or by voice first and venue afterwards. Like Havergal, he was waging war on history, a history that had, as it happened, an even longer back-story in the UK than the miserable history of Glasgow's urban decline, a history epitomised in the cultural exclusion voiced by Tony Harrison's 'Them & [uz]'. The poem has Harrison's schoolboy self remembering reading Keats aloud in class in his native Leeds accent and getting only three words out – '*mi 'art aches*' – before he's stopped by his English teacher's mockery. Ignorant 'barbarian'! Doesn't he know that 'Poetry's the speech of kings'? And that 'You're one of those / Shakespeare gives the comic bits to: prose!'? A voice like his had to learn its place, and that place wasn't at any top table or in any 'establishment' position in church, civil service, Parliament, university, military, classical theatre or broadcasting. *Those* places belonged to the tribe that, since Dr Thomas Arnold began introducing 'Public School Pronunciation' to Rugby School boys in 1828, was identified by the common linguistic marker of what later was termed 'Received Pronunciation' (RP) or 'talking posh'. Where other state interests used race, Britain employed accent to effect political and cultural apartheid. No longer heard as a regional marker (as in Shakespeare's day), accent now registered class, dividing the privileged and educated from the working class and the socially excluded, the 'toffs' from the 'plebs'. It would have surprised no one in 1950s Britain that the Shakespeare part the schoolboy Harrison 'played [was] the drunken Porter in Macbeth'.

The cliché that Shakespeare's kings speak poetry, his plebs, prose, is, of course, utter tosh, as a swift glance at *Hamlet* or *Richard II* demonstrates. But it's remarkably tenacious tosh that, attached to notions of accent as class indicator and Shakespeare as increasingly the property of the culturally elite, meant that in the twentieth-century British theatre, what Harrison's English teacher wrongly attributed to Shakespeare was rightly attributable to producers, directors and casting agents. It was *they* who typecast regional actors as plebs. Cockneys, Scousers, Loiners, Geordies: these were voices directors gave 'the comic bits to'.

Forty years after the schoolboy Harrison suffered his humiliation, Barrie Rutter was ready to challenge the cliché (see Rutter 2003). A Northerner, he'd refused to erase his Hull accent or become bilingual in RP at the Royal Scottish Academy of Music and Drama in Glasgow (where, exiting, he just missed the entrance of Ian McDiarmid, who did adopt RP: Havergal's Shakespeare, for all its radicalism, never spoke to Glasgow spectators in their native voice). In the mid 1970s Rutter spent two seasons with the RSC playing parts 'naturally' suited to his accent: First Citizen in *Coriolanus*, Dick the Butcher in *Henry VI*, Lollio in *The Changeling*. But when his director suggested that a voice like his should be looking for a future in television soaps and variety, not 'serious' work on the classics, he decamped to the National Theatre, where Harrison – now equipped with knowledge of the classics by a grammar school education not unlike Shakespeare's four hundred years earlier – was emerging, after Shakespeare, as England's most serious theatre poet. His *Mysteries* (1977–81) adapted and new-scripted fragments from the medieval York, Wakefield and Chester mystery plays into a three-part cycle that took spectators from *Nativity* to *Doomsday*, all voiced, like the originals, in Northern accents. The following year his stunning translation of *The Oresteia* opened at the National. Scripted for masks and an all-male company, *The Oresteia* specified Northern voices, which alone, insisted the playwright, would be able to produce the percussive, consonant-heavy sound required to 'carry the traffic' his Aeschylus script had to deliver, in imitation of the original, through the open mouths of the tragic masks. That was the formal argument. But politically, Harrison was doing something else. Putting his Northern *Oresteia* on the National Theatre stage, he was 'inserting his "marginal" barbarian voice into the very centre of elite Establishment culture' and rousing 'the ghost of humiliated memory once again – this time to mock it. For in *his* theatre poetry, *Northern* voices produced "the speech of kings". Of course, they also produced "the comic bits", but in Harrison, 'the "comic bits", too, were poetry' (Rutter 2003, 241).

If playing in Harrison's *Mysteries* and *Oresteia* gave Rutter a crash course in the politics of his voice, his education culminated in *The Trackers of Oxyrhynchus* (1988), a modern satyr play written specifically for him, Harrison building out of a fragment of Sophocles a contemporary story of cultural vandalism in the UK as depressing as anything wreaked forty years earlier (and still in process) upon the human geography of Glasgow. Seeing the story of the flaying of the satyr Marsyas, ordered by Apollo, as an appalling metaphor for current cultural practices, *Trackers* critiqued the status quo that ten years of Thatcher government had normalised by limiting public subsidy of the arts and 'privatising' funding: the division of art into 'high' and 'low', and the mystification of culture by an Apollonian elite bent on excluding the 'plebs' from 'patrician' pleasures including theatre, opera, ballet – and Shakespeare.

The part Harrison wrote for Rutter was the satyr Silenus. Taking the play and its politics 'home' to Yorkshire two years later, putting it in front of audiences who heard the satyrs speaking not as 'Them' but as '[uz]', audiences who occupied the very ideological space of conflict the play explored, provoked Rutter to his next move. He issued a UDI – Unilateral Declaration of Independence – on RP. He founded his own theatre company, Northern Broadsides, to give Northern audiences a Shakespeare who talked *to* them by talking *like* them. Two principles underpinned the company that was launched in 1992 with *Richard III* – a canny choice, since Richard himself was a Northerner who lived most of his life in Middleham and was, therefore, the one Shakespeare role that could be claimed to talk like '[uz]'. First, that the actors would all use their 'real' Northern voices where 'North' meant 'north of Derby', and 'voice' meant, as Geoffrey Wainwright perceptively put it in the *Independent* (16 June 1993), 'emphatically not Shakespeare with a northern *accent* but Shakespeare in a northern *voice*, with all the bodily depth, personal and cultural rootedness the word implies'. And he might have added, with its linguistic habit of collapsing grammar, of condensing pronouns and connectives, so that the weight in a line of Shakespeare is thrown upon nouns and verbs, upon the formal stress points that drive the argument of a speech and the pace of the play as a whole. The Northern voice, as Gillian Reynolds observed of Broadsides in action, is a vehicle for 'speeding the mind to meaning' (quoted in Rutter 2003, 249). Second, that this touring company would tour to what Rutter called 'non-velvet spaces': a derelict underground viaduct in a repurposed carpet factory in Halifax, a boatshed in Hull, the Skipton cattle market, 'rough' places that restored Peter Brook's 'rough theatre' to give Shakespeare back to the groundlings. (From the first, however, concessions were made to velvet-ish venues: the company played the RSC's Swan, Shakespeare's Globe and the Warwick Arts Centre. And from the first, it toured internationally.)

*Antony and Cleopatra* (1995) was Broadsides's fourth production, its first tragedy and, thus, its first serious challenge to the history of vocal stereotyping. Rutter, who both directed and played Antony, took the challenge head-on. He staged the opening as if to shove down their carping throats the elitism of reviewers who'd savaged *Richard III* in Northern voices as 'karaoke theatre' (*Sunday Times*, 13 December 1992) and sneered that Broadsides's attempts 'to destroy the hegemony of Oxford vowels' put 'regional actors back where they began: as comic relief' (*Evening Standard*, 11 December 1992). In a front-of-cloth scene (though without the cloth) Rutter gave them an ironic prologue, gave them what the 'toffs' anticipated they'd be seeing in this production: *Antony and Cleopatra* as if stepped out of Burnand; *Antony and Cleopatra* staged by Octavius Caesar; *Antony and Cleopatra* imagined in Cleopatra's worst fantasies; *Antony and Cleopatra* performed by 'mechanic slaves' in 'funny voices' as burlesque.

A young man walked into the empty space. He was a black hole of human chill, his features as sharp as the CEO's suit he wore. Dead-eyed, he took in the audience before turning his back on them. A cabaret drum-roll began. As it crescendoed, a bare-chested bowler-hatted MC in bowtie, braces and spats bounded on squawking 'Nhe'bu'this doootage of'uh gen'ral's …' (1.1.1) while he pointed offstage, smirking, as a scrawny drag-queen Cleopatra in lurex bra, suspender belt and flapper's 'fascinator' was wheeled in atop a mortuary gurney-cum-dodg'em (see 5.3). 'If it be luuv …' (1.1.14), she squealed, sprawled under a banner that proclaimed 'Ægypta Capta', then giggled hysterically as her drunken Antony, wearing red Doc Martens, a cartoon-Roman skirt and quivering chest-wig, launched head first into her crotch to demonstrate 'the nobleness o'life …' (1.1.37). Wheeled out as the silent spectator who'd watched it (now discovered to be Octavius) turned on his heel and exited, this travesty (one got the sense that Octavius had it performed every morning after breakfast, a ritual of magical thinking as solipsistic

5.3 'Nay, but this dotage …' (1.1). A 'squeaking boy' 'Cleopatra' (Andrew Whitehead) and drunken 'Antony' (David Fenwick) 'Extemporally … stage … / Our Alexandrian revels' to Octavius Caesar (Andrew Cryer).

inspirational team-building for a team of one) passed the 'straight' Cleopatra entering, taunting her Antony, 'If it be luv …'.

This production had Broadsides's signature stamped all over it. It put sixteen actors on stage. This meant multiple doubling, with actors working also as stage crew to keep the action in continuous play and all of them, men and women, mustering as soldiers: Roy North was Lepidus and Thidias; John Gully, Pompey, Eros and Dolabella; Deborah McAndrew, Iras and Octavia. Stephen Anderson (Agrippa), Andy Wear (Messenger), David Peacock (Mardian) and David Findlay (Soothsayer) doubled parts that did most of the fetching and carrying and heavy lifting. Players in the front-of-cloth cabaret returned in 'straight' roles: Andrew Whitehead's 'Cleopatra' came back as Ventidius, David Fenwick's 'Antony' as Maecenas, Gerard McDermott's MC as Menas and Proculeius.

But it also meant spending the company's lean budget on actors' salaries, not production. This company carried practically no baggage. Cleopatra's monument was a length of wire mesh security fencing, Alexandria, sunset-red cloth hung from whatever passed for the 'flies' in the non-velvet spaces that were passing for a theatre.

A couple of low benches strewn with cushions were Cleopatra's only furniture, these commandeered for the gaudy night on Pompey's galley where they were set with crates of bottled ale and the instruments of a skiffle band that thumped out 'Plumpy Bacchus' to a rowdy crew of assembled caterwaulers who'd clearly fronted dozens of gigs in working men's clubs (a scene that started with genial mockery but got dangerous as alcohol settled moroseness on Octavius). Costumes were modern, basic and uncomplicatedly significant: Andrew Cryer's Octavius and his sister both in prim suits, like senior accountants or market traders; Ishia Bennison's Cleopatra and her 'girls' (McAndrew as Iras, Julie Livesey as Charmian) in slack 'hostess' trousers, their shapelessness doing nothing to expose or eroticise the Egyptian body. Antony (Rutter) in Alexandria had 'gone native' in Egyptian scarves and sandals, but at the Roman summit, in a white linen suit, he managed to acknowledge both the buttoned-up Roman dress code *and* suggest he'd rather be dining with crocodiles, for both he and Enobarbus (Dave Hill) wore their waistcoats flapping. Egypt was colour-coded orange, yellow and red and lit for heat; Rome, ice-blue.

But for radicalism, what really counted was none of this production's separate elements; rather, their coincidence, the revelation it offered audiences and reviewers alike by matching 'poor theatre' production values to the Northern voice. That voice was discovered here to produce a 'great travelling language' which punched out the story with the urgency of ticker-tape, urged on by Rutter's directorial policy of honouring Shakespeare's writing, refusing to apologise for his poetry or to treat it naturalistically as though it were a slightly embarrassing version of prose – or indeed, to put speaking on 'hold' while an actor performed some item of 'business'. As Robert Butler reported in the *Independent on Sunday*:

> There is no elaborate staging ... There's a rostrum at one end, some cloth, a couple of cushions and that's it. The conference between the triumvirate ... is a few guys in suits sitting in chairs, two of whom look as if they stepped off the commuter train an hour before. (15 October 1995)

Then he asked rhetorically:

> Who needs scenery, props, background music or lighting cues? None of them can rival the visual grandeur of Antony spelling out to Cleopatra as a matter of fact why he had to follow her from the battle: 'Egypt, thou knew'est ...'

For Butler, Broadsides's gift to audiences was a 'vigorously acted version of the text' delivered at a cracking pace that placed audiences to attend to what characters were saying, not to what actors were 'feeling'; story direct, that is, not elaborated with actorly interpretation overlaid onto text:

> No one lingers. If the actors get dressing rooms on tour, you imagine there are signs up, saying: 'Get On With It'; 'No Acting'. In this fresh, abrasive context, there's no room for displays of sensibility, which so often slide in, like double-glazing, between us and the play. We act like jurors. Argument is prized so highly, that in this flinty atmosphere, the poetry suddenly takes flight.

And flight, he might have added, as if via Concorde, for after years of hearing Shakespeare played at half speed, like Mozart on a wound-down gramophone, audiences were finally getting him at tempo. Nunn's production in 1972 came in at just over three hours playing time, or three and three quarter hours running time, counting the two intervals he felt it necessary to introduce; Rutter's, making internal cuts equivalent to Nunn's but retaining three scenes that Nunn axed entirely, ran for two hours and twenty-five minutes plus a ten-minute interval. (As a London reviewer marvelled, 'It takes the actors just 70 minutes to get to the battle of Actium, ... and they reach Cleopatra's Monument faster than I sometimes do when I take the Tube to the station of the same name' (Benedict Nightingale, *The Times*, 5 October 1995).) But it wasn't speed for speed's sake. What the pace of this playing made unmissable was the sheer relentlessness of the story of Antony's power, energy, soldiership and manliness draining into the sands of Egypt as though rushing down a sump hole.

Opening this *Antony and Cleopatra* by looking through the warped frame of Octavius's mean-minded desiring imaginary and seeing the aspiring autocrat needing to cut his great opposites down to size allowed Rutter, by inverting them in the burlesque, to dispose of 'received ideas' of these characters as 'epic' or 'mythic' (a disposal job Peter Brook had attempted; see Chapter 4). Broadsides's *Antony and Cleopatra* wasn't exactly a tale of 'everyday folk'. But it certainly wasn't about iconic figures (as in Nunn's opening procession in 1972) or hieroglyphs (as in Jackson's performance in 1978).

Hook-nosed, olive-skinned (the actor, half Egyptian), squat, her 'salad days' long gone, Bennison played a Cleopatra closer to Plutarch than Hollywood. It wasn't 'her beauty' that 'did enamor men with her', wrote Plutarch, but her 'company and conversation', her 'talk and discourse', 'her tongue' and the way she 'taunted [Antony] thoroughly', spinning around herself a cyclone of unpredictability that threw out lightning storms of passion or violence (North 1579, 981–982). Jeffrey Wainwright commented on Bennison's way with Shakespeare's writing: 'In the superb early scene where the queen accuses [Antony] of dissembling his love', she and her 'girls' 'interrupt his fumbling explanations with bursts of mock applause before Bennison transforms the moment with that amazing piece of theatrical sincerity, "O, my oblivion is a very Antony / And I am all forgotten!".' This Cleopatra showed 'no regard for queenliness in the high English fashion'. (In support, Wainwright might have quoted her line, 'Can Fulvia die?' (1.3.59) which combined wide-eyed amazement with a lewd snigger and throaty, wise-cracking lasciviousness.) 'Yet', Wainwright continued, 'in such lines as "my honour is not yielded but conquered merely", we hear in that "merely" that not only can she match them all man for man in pride and energy [but that] she inhabits a different sphere – "fire and air" indeed' (*Independent*, 6 October 1995). Bennison's Cleopatra swaggered her matronly hips imitating Antony's gait. She ran full tilt at the messenger who brought news of a marriage in Rome, belting him in the solar plexus, smothering him with cushions, then drawing a knife on him before observing in her archest accent (like *Coronation Street*'s Elsie Tanner, trying to talk 'posh'), 'Though it be honest, it is never good / To bring bad news' (2.5.85–86). This Cleopatra had watched Antony betray her, agreeing his politic marriage to Octavia. She and her girls retreated upstage behind the mesh fence and looked on, their faces, masks, while downstage the Romans parleyed and made their opportunistic matches. Later, in a visual echo of the betrayal, the women would watch Antony in defeat talking idly to Eros of clouds and shape-changing, and would continue watching as he set about performing what was 'left us': 'Ourselves to end ourselves' (4.14.21–22). Thus she watched the botched consequences of her own betrayal.

Later, fussing over Antony's dying body, making Antony's 'I am *dying*, Egypt' a laugh line, a last gasp of high Roman exasperation set against her 'No, let *me* speak' (4.15.43, 45), she wasn't just comically 'natter[ing] his ear off' (Michael Coveney, *Observer*, 8 October 1995). She was, heartbreakingly, attempting to delay the inevitable: her Antony, her 'man of men', couldn't die so long as she stopped him speaking his last word.

Her own death came simply. Sitting on a plain bench set against the wire mesh 'wall' of her monument, surrounded by candles that cast light upwards from the floor to throw deep shadows behind, crowned with a wreath of flowers and robed in white, this Cleopatra pulled from the asp basket a jewelled necklace, its links like the articulated vertebrae of a snake. She clasped it around her neck. Her eyes emptied. Livesey's Charmian made her last 'chare' of closing those eyes an act of supreme love. Her final gesture towards the Roman guard who rushed in as she herself died ('Ah, soldier!' (5.2.327)) was a mingle of erotic tease and wicked laughter: Octavius had been trounced by her mistress's triumph. Shortly, he'd know it. Entering upstage, looking into the scene from behind the wire and seeing that he'd been robbed of his trophy, 'her life in Rome' (5.1.65), Cryer's Octavius hurled himself against the fence, a snarling beast, his face twisted in a grimace of fury and pain, his fingers clutching the mesh but really snatching only at empty air (see 5.4).

For his part, Rutter played Antony in Shakespeare's play as a further iteration of work he was developing on the Hercules myth in Tony Harrison's *The Kaisers of Carnuntum* and *The Labourers*

5.4 'Caesar's beguiled!' (5.2). Cleopatra (Ishia Bennison), Iras (Deborah McAndrews), Charmian (Julie Livesey), Octavius Caesar (Andrew Cryer) behind.

*of Herakles* (both 1995). In Shakespeare's source, Plutarch reports how Antony groomed himself to imitate the hero from whom his family claimed descent, wearing his beard like Hercules, and 'also his garments', a rough tunic, belted low around his hips (North 1579, 971–972). Shakespeare twins the two. His Antony is mocked by Cleopatra as 'this Herculean Roman' (1.3.85), and in his rages against her he's 'Hercules furens': 'You have been a boggler ever' (3.13.115); 'Triple-turned whore! 'Tis thou / Hast sold me to this novice' (4.12.13–14). Betrayed into defeat, as he thinks, by a woman, he feels 'The shirt of Nessus' on his back (4.12.43); and his soldiers, hearing strange 'Music ... / Under the earth', know its meaning: "Tis the god Hercules whom Antony loved / Now leaves him' (4.3.16–17, 21–22). Of course, the super-hero of Plutarch's citation is also the murderous madman of Euripides's *Herakles Furens* and boorish guest of his *Alcestis* as well as the alias the blustering coward Dionysus takes in Aristophanes's *Frogs* – that fools no one. Hercules, then, is a figure as much buffoonish as awesome, and as Wainright in the *Independent* observed, 'Buffoonery [was] always fascinatingly and dangerously close' in Rutter's Antony, 'a blunderer' in a 'realm of female sovereignty' (6 October 1995).

Running to fat, grey and bristly as a badger around the chops, he was a wide-gesturing, sozzled lord of misrule in that carnival of male-bonding on Pompey's galley, and a dangerously glittering, goggle-eyed maniac when savaging Cleopatra, as though the rage exploding in his brain was pushing his eyes out of their sockets. This Antony's big speeches were poised on a rhetorical knife edge between high oratory and bombast, sublime poetry just missing flipping into bluster, while one-liners such as "M'treasure's in't'harbour – tek it!' (3.11.11) came out like rattling thunder. When he realised he'd botched his tragic suicide ('How? Not dead? Not dead?' (4.14.104)) his eyes went wide in comic amazement, the repetition ('dead', 'dead') coming out like a stand-up comedian's patter. That was followed, when he learned that Cleopatra was alive, with a huge laugh of relief, a laugh that was a kind of love letter.

He'd gone to the Battle of Actium dressed like Hercules, draped in a lion skin, its head a mask he wore like a bizarre hat. He was fearsome. But also ridiculous. It was as though Snug the Joiner had suddenly pitched up in Egypt to play the lion's part. This battle sequence showed the production at its best. The two armies lined up side by side in double rows behind steel oil drums, facing out, Romans in blue boiler suits, Egyptians in orange, Cleopatra wearing her horned Isis crown, Antony, his lion pelt. Drumming began, slowly at first, then picked up tempo, rose to deafening noise, and then dropped to a near hush as words leaped from the battle. This war, pounded out as percussion, emerged as a story told by a Chorus throwing out dispatches across a 'field' of play. When one drummer put down his sticks and crossed to the other side, an orange body among the blue, spectators saw Antony's army defecting, their betrayals materialised. The rout happened when Cleopatra threw down her sticks and ran. The Egyptian drumming missed a beat, then stumbled into arrhythmia, and finally, when Antony went after her, fell silent – while Rome drummed its thunderous triumph.

Broadsides produced ensemble acting that gave every part its focus. Returned to Rome, McAndrew's Octavia stood alone, downstage, facing out as her brother's harangues ('That ever I should call thee castaway!'; 'Where is he now?' (3.6.41, 65)) fell relentlessly on her little shoulders, her only emotion registered in the tears that silently slid down her face. Hill's Enobarbus (*Independent*, 6 October 1995), his Northern 'muck-and-nettles' working-class vowels so flat they might have been scraped off a mill room floor, applied 'a head-shaking cynical decency' to Cleopatra's barge speech that placed 'the larger personal and political tragedy in a completely fresh perspective. He's seen it all and watches it happen again' (*Observer*, 8 October 1995). You 'could hear a pin drop' (*Daily Telegraph*, 13 October 1995). Even the soldiers who stormed Cleopatra's monument got a moment of stunning theatricality. When the production played in Broadsides's home venue, the underground viaduct at Dean Clough, they came bursting through a brick wall in an SAS commando-style raid. On the one hand, this production's Northern voices gave full throat to the play's rammies: Enobarbus and Cleopatra going at each other ('Your presence needs must puzzle Antony'; 'Sink Rome, and their tongues rot / That speak against us!' (3.7.10, 15–16)) were like fishwives on Hull docks in full vitriolic flood. On the other, they made lines such as 'Let th'Egyptians / And the Phoenicians go a-ducking' (3.7.63–64); 'The jack of Caesar's shall / Bear us an errand to him' (3.13.108–109); 'No, my chuck' (4.4.2); 'A lass unparalleled' (5.2.315) sound contemporary, colloquial, as if just written and written for 'our' time.

Robin Thornber in the *Guardian* (5 October 1995) wrote of the production's anti-heroism, the way in which the 'star duo' at its centre (she with her 'tawny, tempestuous intemperance'; he with his 'brazen *braggadocio*') 'still suggest a flawed, failing couple past their passionate best but desperately inflating their own and each other's egos and dignifying as world domination what is really no more than glorified gangsterism'. Michael Coveney in the *Observer* (8 October 1995) caught its unexpected –because so immediate – power. 'Until last week in Halifax', he confessed, 'I had never really enjoyed *Antony and Cleopatra*.' He'd sat through it 'dutifully' but 'never experienced the full blast of its poetic majesty and brilliance'. Now, he averred, 'Shakespeare's most insistently glorious and beguiling text' – spectators would 'have to catch Barrie Rutter's Northern Broadsides on tour to test that not too controversial opinion' for themselves – 'is fully restored.' 'This', he concluded, 'is the production Peter Brook never achieved when he went minimal at Stratford-upon-Avon in 1978.'

Like Giles Havergal in Glasgow, Barrie Rutter in Halifax produced Shakespeare for a local audience. Like Havergal, he inserted a narrative of Cleopatra's blackness into the play, though reviewers, with other things on their minds – like trying to transliterate the Northern voice in print – rarely noticed it except when they used their standard coded language to describe Bennison as 'tawny'. And like Havergal, he wasn't afraid to introduce burlesque, though neither of them put it to its original, conservative Victorian purpose of appearing to satirise hegemonic cultural values while in fact confirmimg them. The lads in the North used burlesque like an offensive weapon, an explosive, an incendiary device. They produced Shakespeare for a theatre that didn't need an elite audience. 'Boying greatness' they demonstrated that the so-called 'plebs' had come of age.

### Notes

1 A 1933 performance of this 'Sand Dance' can be viewed at https://www.youtube.com/watch?v=j2fqjsijaMM (accessed 16 December 2019).
2 It should be noted that at some point in its history the theatre's name lost its apostrophe. Today is it known as the 'Citizens Theatre'.
3 James Bridie, the pseudonym of Glasgow University graduate and physician Osborne Henry Mavor, was one of the leading playwrights of his generation as well as the founder of the Citizens' Theatre. He was instrumental in establishing what became Glasgow's Royal Scottish Academy of Music and Drama. See: https://

www.universitystory.gla.ac.uk/biography/?id=WH0204&type=P and https://en.wikipedia.org/wiki/Citizens_Theatre (accessed 16 December 2019).

4  Lest it be imagined that controversy was imported to Gorbals Street from the racy London metropolis, it should be remembered that the Citizens' Theatre was already home-growing 'shock' performances in its studio space, The Close Theatre Club. Born 'from rumblings' from both patrons and press that the Citizens' should 'produce more new work', The Close was opened in 1964. Once a dance hall, most recently a 'notorious pitch and toss club', it served as a space for experiment, a place 'for trying out new actors, new plays and new playwrights', a place that staged the risqué and didn't duck controversy. Charles Marowitz's 1965 *Dr Faustus* made front-page news in the national press, having introduced a character wearing a mask of the (reigning) queen's face. Later, a naked photo call put Artaud's *The Cenci* in the headlines. See Knotts 2015. Havergal and Prowse, then, were continuing work that was already in progress.

5  For an account of the theatre's 'queer' aesthetic and more on 'Sheila', see Thomas 2015.

6  The production records for this *Antony and Cleopatra* are held among the Special Collections in the University of Glasgow Library, catalogued as STA E.x22 (Programme), STA 2G.i.34 (Production File), STA E.e.1 (Photographs), STA TP 47/8f (Newspaper Cuttings), and STA E.a. Box 4/17 (Press Cuttings). I am grateful to Bryony Rutter for accessing the archive and providing me with digital copies of these materials.

7  The first-person memories I quote throughout this chapter, not specifically of *Antony and Cleopatra* but of the Citz repertoire across the years, I owe to my colleague Thomas Docherty who grew up in Glasgow in the 1970s.

8  This promptbook is held (with the other materials belonging to the production) in the University of Glasgow Library's Special Collections department, catalogued as STA 2G.i.33 (Script). I am grateful to the Special Collections archivist for making a photocopy of the promptbook available to me. Some discrepancies between the Arden text I've been citing throughout and lines quoted in this chapter are due to Havergal's edits.

6

# 'Back to Basics': Peter Hall, Olivier Theatre, National Theatre, 1987

### Rehearsing returns

The party-political slogan 'Back to Basics' wouldn't be coined for another few years by post-Thatcherite UK Tories anxious to unify the nation under a nostalgic appeal to so-called 'traditional values', but it aptly summarises the cultural politics of Peter Hall's *Antony and Cleopatra* at the National Theatre (London) in 1987. The 'basics' he was returning to – and returning the play to – were theatrical, textual, critical, nationalist: this *Antony and Cleopatra* would be decidedly *English*. They were also deeply personal, for this production would be Hall's self-declared swan song. The director who'd begun his professional life as a radical young turk aged twenty-five 'discovering' Beckett's *Waiting for Godot* for English audiences in 1955; who'd gone to what was then the Shakespeare Memorial Theatre in Stratford in 1956, taking over the artistic directorship of what he radically re-conceived as the Royal Shakespeare Theatre in 1960; who'd fought tooth and nail for public subsidy of the arts throughout the 1960s and 1970s, fashioning himself into the UK's chief theatre spokesman, impresario, fixer, politician and machiavel; who'd left the RSC in 1968, accepting in 1973 the artistic directorship of the National Theatre, where he'd watched himself steadily dwindling into conservatism, partly a result of having to take on the increasingly entrenched Labour-led trade unions that he saw holding governments, right and left, to ransom and wrecking the theatre with strikes and walk-outs; who'd slid into an establishment figure he bewailed (and confirmed) by accepting a knighthood in 1977 ('I don't want it, I really don't: I'm too young to be labelled a member of the Establishment. Yet there's no doubt it will help combat all the mischief-makers and the horrors'): this was the man who was waving goodbye to all that in 1987 (Goodwin 1983, 295). He announced after the press night of *Antony and Cleopatra* that he was resigning from the National Theatre and that this production would be 'the last large-scale production' he'd direct 'in the Olivier auditorium'.[1] 'The rest of the plays' would be 'in the smaller Cottesloe Theatre' (*Evening Standard*, 10 April 1987). This *Antony and Cleopatra* would be Hall's valedictory piece in the theatre that bore the name of the Herculean theatrical elder statesman he'd ousted, Octavius-style, from the National Theatre's top job to plant himself as 'Sole sir o'th' world' (5.2.119) on London's South Bank. Now aged fifty-seven, the politick English empire-builder might have mused that he was already four years older than the clapped-out 'old ruffian' Antony (4.1.4), whose decline into what Hall called 'paranoia', an 'unbalanced "bunker mentality"', he was directing in a play he described as 'more than a play about middle age ... a menopausal play' (Lowen 1990, 76). How much was this production about Hall himself? Given that it would be Hall's last chance to stamp his artistic signature on the Olivier Theatre, was it any wonder he'd have a number of 'returns to basics' in his sights?

For starters, he'd ignore every modern edition of the play. For his working script, he'd return to the earliest printed version of *Antony and Cleopatra*, Shakespeare's Folio text of 1623. Hall's production promptbook would mark not a single line cut. He would direct every line Shakespeare wrote – even ones the Oxford editor Stanley Wells thought Shakespeare himself might have 'tightened up in rehearsal' (Wells 1989, 176). Next, he would ignore the 'alarums and excursions' that had been convulsing academic Shakespeare scholarship over the previous fifteen years via the discourses of French theory, American New Historicism and British Cultural Materialism (including anything any of the theorists had to say about *Antony and Cleopatra*) and instead situate his production inside a 'traditional' conceptual framework retrieved from sixty years earlier. His production programme would offer ten 'expert' 'Sightlines', none later than 1971, four of them quoting that most

English of Edwardian theatre-makers, Harley Granville-Barker. During rehearsals Hall would return over and over to Granville-Barker's 'Antony and Cleopatra' in his *Prefaces to Shakespeare* of 1930 for basic practical insights on everything from staging to scenic construction to characterisation – including the suggestion that Enobarus's sudden death is not in consequence of a breaking heart but of malarial fever – or as Granville-Barker put it, ague (Granville-Barker 1951, 151).

Along with so much else, Granville-Barker would give Hall and his designer, Alison Chitty, their design concept, one that would eschew the 'orientalism' (more or less approximately inhabited) of every *Antony and Cleopatra* seen on the English stage since 1953 and would return the visual conceit to Elizabethan basics. Harley Granville-Barker knew 'how Shakespeare saw his Roman figures' and told readers in 1930 that they, too, could see them as Shakespeare saw them. They were there, on display in London's National Gallery, in 'Paolo Veronese's "Alexander and the wife and daughter of Darius"', an authentic early modern mash-up of 'Renaissance view' and 'Classic subject' (Granville-Barker 1951, 168). In 1987, Chitty's design sketches would quote Granville-Barker, would show a design based on 'a concept of the classical world as seen through Elizabethan eyes' and costumes that were not 'historical Egyptian or Roman but Renaissance, with suggestions of both, as in the paintings of Mantegna, Veronese and Titian' (Lowen 1990, 4, 10).

And this idea of the classical gazed at through the Elizabethan would be carried over into the production's publicity – the place, that is, where a production first encounters its audiences and conditions their looking. Hall would have Veronese's *Mars and Venus Bound by Cupid* (circa 1570) featured on the production poster and the programme cover. That image (reproduced in 'antique' sepia) would offer Veronese's immortals as visual proxies for Shakespeare's Antony and Cleopatra: Venus, near-naked, milk-white (one nipple flowing white maternal abundance), blue-eyed, her neck wreathed in dazzling white pearls threaded also through her courtesan-crimped golden hair; Mars, rough-bearded, fully armed and 'plated', using his cloak modestly to drape the goddess' private parts while a curly-headed infant Cupid knotted the lovers' legs with a silk scarf. Inside, the programme would declare 'Cleopatra VII' a 'Greek from Macedonia', as though she'd just stepped off the boat, while her family tree on another page would show those Macedonian origins dating thirteen generations back.

Clearly, if the return to Veronese epitomised how Hall imagined Shakespeare's characters, casting Judi Dench and Anthony Hopkins as his principals signalled another attempt to get back to basics. Hall hadn't directed Dench in a Shakespeare role since Titania in *A Midsummer Night's Dream* in 1962 when she was still in her twenties. When he left the RSC, she stayed behind, maturing her craft under Hall's 'heirs', principally Trevor Nunn, and giving celebrated performances in *The Winter's Tale* (1969), *The Merchant of Venice* and *The Duchess of Malfi* (1971), *Much Ado About Nothing*, *The Comedy of Errors*, *Macbeth* and *King Lear* (all 1976) and *Cymbeline* (1979). Later at the RSC Dench would play *Juno and the Paycock* (1980), *Façade* (1982), *Mother Courage* (1984) and *Waste* (1985). Of Nunn's 1976 *Lear*, in which Dench played Regan, Hall would complain to his diary of the actors' 'slow, over-emphatic, line breaking of the text', and of their being 'so busy telling us the ambiguities and the resonances that there is little or no sense of form' (Goodwin 1983, 302). Of Nunn's *Macbeth* in which Dench played Lady Macbeth at TOP, Stratford's studio venue, he would observe that while it was 'magnificent: refreshing, invigorating, utterly clear and original', still, 'by doing Shakespeare in a tiny room you do actually sidestep the main problem we moderns have with Shakespeare – rhetoric. We don't like rhetoric, we mistrust it … So how on earth do you do a great deal of Shakespeare?' (Goodwin 1983, 314–315). Was bringing Dench to the National in 1982 to direct her first in Pinter's *A Kind of Alaska* and then in *The Importance of Being Earnest* an attempt to answer his own question? Was it a first step in remedial training, using the materials of those non-Shakespeare parts as a way of limbering up old muscles and actorly behaviours, re-engaging with the 'outrageous sexuality', 'decorum' and 'extraordinary wit' that he'd seen first in Titania twenty years earlier, sexuality and wit that would make Dench his ideal casting for Cleopatra five years hence? (quoted in Prince 2013, 184). Was Hall's goal to re-train her textual delivery, to re-route her way into Shakespeare via the very different rhetorics of Pinter and Wilde?

For his part, Anthony Hopkins in 1987 was doubtless a candidate for remedial training. Aged twenty-eight in 1965, he'd been hand-picked by Laurence Olivier to join the National Theatre that year when the company was still bivouacked at the Old Vic. Like his Welsh compatriot Richard Burton, ten years his senior (and someone who gave his career a generous nudge with advice and moral support), Hopkins brought to performance a dark brooding quality that could flip from warm Celtic virility to maudlin misery. Built square and more like a rugby prop forward than Burton but, like his compatriot, composed of strange metal, he could be explosive on stage. (He once walked off mid-performance in *Macbeth* enraged at audience behaviour.) But he was also liable to sinking into alcohol-induced moroseness. The memory of alcoholism that he finally kicked in 1975 stayed with him, permanently green. Were these qualities that might fit him for Mark Antony? By 1987, though, he hadn't been on an English stage for nearly twenty years. His career had been largely in the United States, making films like *A Lion in Winter*, *Young Winston* and *A Bridge Too Far*. When he was lured back to London, to the National and to live theatre in 1985 to play the sleazily monstrous newspaper tycoon Lambert Le Roux in David Hare's and Howard Brenton's smash hit industry satire *Pravda*, then the following year to be directed by Hare at the National Theatre as King Lear, he hadn't played any Shakespeare for decades. In Hall's hands, Hopkins might be said to be returning to text classes at drama school.

Thereafter, his principals in place, Hall would cast his *Antony and Cleopatra*-after-Veronese with a company of all-white actors (only excepting, possibly, the Turkish-born Hus Levent) – casting that cannot have been unconsidered. (In Bridget Escolme's diplomatic understatement, this production 'erase[d] problems around ... otherness' (Escolme 2006, 122).) By 1987 plenty of black actors were being seen in Shakespeare at the RSC and in regional theatres up and down the UK. Black actors had been prominent in Trevor Nunn's 1972 *Antony and Cleopatra* in Stratford and in Jonathan Miller's 1981 filmed production for the BBC, a film that reached a global audience, normalising inter-racial Shakespeare (and gesturing towards, even if not fully embodying, a black Egypt). Indeed, on site at the National in 1987 an all-black 'Studio Night' production of *Macbeth* was rehearsing in parallel to Hall's *Antony and Cleopatra*.[2] Bizarrely, however, and without, apparently, any discussion of Egypt's racial configuration taking place during Hall's thirteen-week-long rehearsal period, on the day of the technical rehearsal, two days before the production was put in front of its first audiences, Alison Chitty left for Hall's all-white company 'sticks of burnished colour in the dressing-rooms', 'some questions about makeup for those in Egypt' having arisen: 'How dark should it be?' (Lowen 1990, 120–121).

Without doubt, however, the most cherished 'basic' returned to in this *Antony and Cleopatra* was what Hall saw as an 'almost religious attention to the text' and 'to the correct speaking of the verse' (Lowen 1990, 6, 3). In later years actors would affectionately (though not entirely gratefully) call Peter Hall an 'iambic fundamentalist' (Holland 2008, 140), and rehearsal photographs would show him, half grammar school 'magister', half orchestral conductor, seated on a high chair behind a lectern, eyes riveted upon his open 'score', oblivious to his actors. He'd settled into this habit over years. In 1973, he'd disclosed in a diary entry that his 'proudest' theatrical achievement to date was to 'have brought back a standard of speaking and of understanding Shakespeare by actors'. He went on to confess that in 1956 when he arrived at the Shakespeare Memorial Theatre he'd been 'very worried by the absence of any tangible tradition of speaking Shakespeare' – a claim that surely must be paused over since during those years, when he had virtually no Shakespeare under his belt, he'd been mentored by that directorial genius of verse speaking, the company's then artistic director, Glen Byam Shaw, who'd specifically given him Shakespeare productions in each season so he could come to grips with Shakespeare's writing. And thereafter, the acting companies in Hall's first three seasons as artistic director included Peggy Ashcroft, Laurence Olivier, John Gielgud, Michael Redgrave, Maxine Audley, Rachel Kempson, Mark Dignam, Patrick Whymark, Alan Badell and Harry Andrews – actors, surely, who knew *something* about 'how Shakespeare should be spoken' (Goodwin 1983, 31).

Still, by 1987 Hall's 'unashamedly pedantic' insistence that 'You cannot play Shakespeare without a sense of line', that 'every single line in Shakespeare will scan', and that the actor's 'business is to find and keep as close to the five beats of the iambic pentameter as possible', always 'marking the end of each line' 'where the verb usually is [sic]' while treating the line ending 'not [as] a hold-up but a release of energy': these articles of religion had settled into the credo that would underpin all the actor training in verse speaking that Hall would conduct across his *Antony and Cleopatra* rehearsal period (Lowen 1990, 27–28; Goodwin 1983, 302). Such training amounted to a 'required style of speaking Shakespeare', a 'system' built on 'absolute rigidity', 'taught [to] his actors and demanded of them' (Holland 2008, 149). Oxymoronically, this 'new discipline' was not to be seen, Hall told his actors, 'as a frightful imprisonment' but rather as 'the very opposite': 'it frees you' to relish the play's 'extrovert writing', writing that never traffics in subtext but always 'says what it feels' (Lowen 1990, 29).

Later in rehearsals, Hall's 'religious attention to the text' and its coercive 'clues and signposts' would produce some surprising, and certainly debatable, extra-textual notes to actors: on Enobarbus as 'the man Shakespeare [sic, for Antony?] loves, blunt, honest, without guile'; on Antony after Actium (prefaced by 'I don't want to impose this on you' addressed to the actor), 'I think he's past great feeling for her'; on the Schoolmaster as Ambassador in 3.12, 'He botches it, out of nerves'; on Antony in 4.12, 'I believe he gets the shakes on "The shirt of Nessus is upon me"'; on Cleopatra in 3.3, that since she 'received the news [of Antony's remarriage] a full five scenes before [that is, in 2.5], 'by now she would have pulled herself together' (Lowen 1990, 16, 76, 35, 87, 107). But that last note to his actor is patently absurd, defying both the narrative and structural logic of Shakespeare's dramaturgy, since no time at all elapses for Cleopatra between 2.5 and 3.3. The so-called 'messenger scene' performs a single continuous action, 3.3 picking up where 2.5 left off, the action only being intercut with 'noises' from elsewhere. Receiving such notes, one actor first said he would absorb 'Hall's guidance on the verse with the fervour of a novitiate'; another declared it would be 'emblazoned on his heart' (Lowen 1990, 30). Later, however, resistances would niggle. Hopkins balked at several of Hall's line readings. Dench 'wrestled' with Hall's conviction that she should address 'I must stay his time' directly to Antony despite the line's third-person 'his' (Lowen 1990, 80). Basil Henson playing Agrippa quietly insisted on cutting his own path through the later scenes of the play, scenes that he thought showed Agrippa disgusted by Octavius's small-minded plotting, an interpretation that he based on his own reading of the text in modest defiance of his director – an interpretation that came up trumps in performance, reviewers noticing it admiringly.

The schizophrenic tension between Hall the 'iambic fundamentalist' and Hall the '"structure sets you free" textual liberationist' was evidently constitutional. Hall had quoted Trevor Nunn in 1972 on his style of directing: 'Nunn ... says that I am a "political" director – not in the sense of political commitment, but because from the beginning I know what I want the play to mean and how I want the actors to do it, and by persuasion and diplomacy I nudge them into doing just that'. (Another word for Nunn's 'political' might have been 'machiavellian'.) This view Hall found 'interesting' but 'too simple' (Goodwin 1983, 15). He saw himself as rather (or also) going on 'voyages of discovery' in rehearsal and 'find[ing] things' he 'didn't know were there'. In 1987 the observer who recorded Hall's *Antony and Cleopatra* rehearsals wrote (retrospectively, from the point of view of the first read-through) of the rehearsal room politician v. the intrepid explorer: 'Much later on, Hall [would] say that he had no particular vision of the play when he started – to have had one would, he feels, have been limiting'. Yet 'with hindsight' it was clear that 'in his first talk to his actors, and in his comments during their first read-through, he prepared the ground for virtually everything that was to be fleshed out, in dramatic terms, in the weeks ahead' (Lowen 1990, 6).

The production, then, would enact a return (via actorly 'discovery') to what Peter Hall knew – and disclaimed knowing – about the play from the beginning. It was a return that, when the first night notices came in, had reviewers raving: 'RENAISSANCE OF THE GOLDEN AGE' (*Sunday Times*, 12 April 1987). If two days earlier Michael Billington in the *Guardian* had been worrying about a 'decline in verbal culture' in the theatre and about 'actors … losing the ability to relish Shakespeare's irony, ambiguity and play of imagery', which had been 'a cardinal feature of Peter Hall's policy in creating the RSC all those years ago' (10 April 1987), the press night of Hall's *Antony and Cleopatra* restored Billington's confidence in at least one director's ability still to 'do' Shakespeare's language (*Guardian*, 11 April 1987). 'Hall reminds us', wrote John Peter in the *Sunday Times*, 'and we do need reminding, that the bedrock of classical theatre is the text: that the life of the play is first and most essentially in the words of the play' (12 April 1987). What Hall's production achieved, wrote John Peter, was a return to 'a golden age'. A return evidently to 'basic values' – or to what the maestro had known all along, and known it with the conviction of the conservative politician returning 'us' to 'shared [English] values'.

### 'Electrifying detail' and the 'true sound of Shakespeare'

Hall's production opened almost conspiratorially, in near dark, with a massive door in an even more massive wall, like the wooden postern to a gated city, opening, and two men, both in early modern doublet and hose, slipping through one after the other then silently closing it, and coming downstage to stand in shadows and break the silence, talking in urgent whispers. On the wide-open stage of the Olivier, a theatre modelled architecturally on the *orchestra* of the ancient open-air Greek theatres at Delphi and Epidaurus where the audience sits in a fan-shaped spread, Alison Chitty designed a set to pull in focus by inscribing a circular playing space inside the circular *orchestra* and setting on its back rim three interlocking pieces of monumental masonry, two storeys high, rough-plastered, though some of the mortar had fallen away to reveal the stone blocks beneath. The façade was fissured with deep cracks running jaggedly down the surface – intimations of ruin, but in technical design terms, where the interlocked pieces could pull apart to stand alone. Opened, they left a gap behind which racks of weapons would be seen when Pompey and his pirates conspired or through which Romans strode into a summit meeting. Closed, they presented a solid blank face or, the pieces joined by a heavy metal gate, made this façade, at the end, the foot of Cleopatra's monument.

The whole set was mottled red, the colour of dried ox blood (though lighting would flood scenes in Egypt with dazzling sun-gold heat while sinking Rome into blue gloom). Occasionally walls would retreat, leaving the full playing space to the actors. Behind them, far upstage, an ox-blood-red cyclorama dressed the open void space above stage level that makes the Olivier Theatre feel cavernous, filling emptiness with a sense of something vast and epic. Furniture on this stage was reduced to almost nothing: three chairs for the summit (into which the subalterns would settle when, politics of state giving way to erotic politics, the story of a queen and her barge was recounted); a long table on Pompey's galley; a banner to back Octavius's first entrance. Deafening sound effects after the interval (taken at 3.6, Octavia's return to Rome) produced the Battle of Actium (scored by Dominic Muldowney), and the wars were conducted by banner-waving troops, their numbers made up with every available actor in the company, not excepting Octavia cross-dressed in doublet as well as recruits grabbed from other productions in the building, marching down the aisles and through the auditorium, criss-crossing the stage, producing bewildering mayhem that gave a sense of this conflict as a global convulsion (but that also felt dated, harking back to Hall's staging of battle sequences in *The Wars of the Roses* in 1963).

Otherwise, actors would carry this production's spectacle on their backs. Chitty's pre-production 'costume bible' is stuffed with snippets of taffetas that change colours as the light hits them and translucent saree fabric embroidered with sequins or appliqued with gold thread, the colours burnt red and gold, deep purple, violet, indigo, Mediterranean blue. They're pinned to costume sketches that show Antony in Egypt as an oriental and Octavius wearing a rich Jacobean satin doublet with slashed sleeves while his sister appears gowned, corseted, neck demurely filled in with linen, as a figure from Tudor portraiture. For Alexandria, Chitty designed layered clothing, on one sketch writing, 'Cleopatra? poss. Veronese under N. African'.[3] Elsewhere, over what she described as an 'Egyptian undergarment', she would put a richly embroidered over-dress, long-sleeved and tasseled, giving the effect of the female body as cultural palimpsest, the body that is on display in, for example, that early modern portrait known as *Lady Ralegh as Cleopatra*.[4] Heading for Actium, the Egyptian queen's 'war outfit' would comprise a 'Fine Leather Warring Cloak' with 'Gold Leather Binding' and 'Laced Tiny gold kid gloves + boots' over a stiff, Chinese-style imperial tunic robe, loaded with decoration at the shoulders and trailing long sleeves. Not for this Cleopatra military trousers or metal breastplate. She would go to battle fully rigged, like a ship in sail.

This, then, was the design spectacle sketched proleptically in Chitty's costume bible which came explosively to life when, on Philo's line about a 'gipsy's lust' (1.1.10), the upstage doors swung open. Through it launched a rowdy procession, half carnival, half ritual, Judi Dench's Cleopatra in gold, with auburn curls only a shade off the red of her palace walls tumbling down her back almost to her waist, held in place by a gold coronet, tugging reins lashed to Mardian's waist. Mardian (Iain Ormsby-Knox), naked-chested, wearing Egyptian trousers, was half man, half beast. He wore a Ptolemaic Apis bull's head and swaggered under the weight of Anthony Hopkins's Antony, aloft on his shoulders, who looked like an Asian satrap playing at Bacchus. Antony flourished a sloshing goblet and wore a gown that materialised the antithesis of soldier-ship in its voluptuous 'girly' embroidery (see 6.1).

Behind them crowded a mass of jubilant on-lookers, eunuchs waving palms, Cleopatra's girls moving to the noise of flutes, drums, bombards, archcitterns and ouds (all of the instruments 'authentic' to North Africa and Europe of 1607). Told of 'News from Rome', Cleopatra threw down her reins. Antony dismounted. But as she taunted him, 'Nay, hear them' (1.1.20), they began weaving around each other, Cleopatra 'pushing him'. Then 'in the jostles' – moves

6.1 'Look where they come!' (1.1). Cleopatra (Judi Dench), Antony (Anthony Hopkins), Mardian in mask (Iain Ormsby-Knox).

that the promptbook records in present tense – Antony 'goes down to the floor C[entre]', 'Cleo bestrides him', and Mardian, Antony's goblet in his hand, 'emptys [sic] some wine on Ant's head'. 'Wrestling' as she mocks him with hearing the ambassadors, 'Antony turns Cleo over and now kneels astride her. The "court" enjoys all the horseplay, encircling and encouraging. The Romans s[tage] r[ight] look on disdainfully', stunned into silence by the 'paroxysms of lascivious giggles' they're hearing (Irving Wardle, *The Times*, 11 April 1987). Then, the messengers' attempts to interrupt cut off by 'Speak not to us' (1.1.56) 'the entire court' exit 'swiftly u[p]/s[tage] doors'. Left alone, the two Romans 'exit separate ways'.

The management of this gaudy circus showed Peter Hall the producer at his showy best. But for all his attention to the *speaking* of the text, particularly in the main roles, perhaps it showed the limits of his attention to the details of the *performances* suggested by Shakespeare's writing, blind spots that muddied the narrative. Here, for instance, marking no visual distinction between Philo and Demetrius, he emptied the opening exchange of its shock. (But isn't one man just arrived from Rome with messages in his hands, a member of that diplomatic suite, bright and 'correct' – an *ambassador*, as Cleopatra calls him, deserving the protocols of embassy so insolently daffed aside by Antony? Isn't the other man a weary veteran of this Egyptian tour of 'duty', digging the dirt on what would soon hit the new boy in the face?) And at the end of the scene having the Romans 'exit separate ways' down slips into separate 'nowheres', wasn't that a theatrical expedient? It made no sense in the narrative.

That said, the moves recorded in the promptbook's opening scene suggest the Cleopatra that Dench would play and the Cleopatra that reviewers would find entrancing, a Cleopatra constantly on the move, volatile, prowling, the human equivalent of the tigress' lashing tail. Like so many Cleopatras before her, Dench was not obvious casting, even to herself, a self-declared 'menopausal dwarf', a mock much quoted, and perhaps the origins of Hall's notion of *Antony and Cleopatra* as a 'menopausal play' (quoted in Prince 2013, 184). But if Hall in 1987 was, like Peter Brook in 1978, thinking back twenty years to cast Cleopatra as his wish-fulfilment of an actor's early suggestiveness – Glenda Jackson/Charlotte Corday; Judi Dench/Titania – the interim decades had been kinder to Hall's fantasies. By the time Jackson got round to Cleopatra, the 'infinite variety' Brook had seen in her sensualist and mercurial Corday had hardened under the pressure of subsequent parts like Gudrun Brangwen and Elizabeth R. Meanwhile, while Dench's Fairy Queen may have metamorphosed into the Lady Bracknell of Hall's 1982 National Theatre production of *The Importance of Being Earnest*, she wasn't Bracknell the braying old trout. Rather, she was Bracknell self-constituted of wit; a Bracknell, moreover, for whom wit was not a verbal flourish but a way of thinking and ordering the world; a Bracknell who placed Wilde's lines with the precision, deep seriousness and dangerous intent of a picador landing lances in a bull's neck, but with comic effect.

There was plenty of the picador in Dench's Cleopatra. ('A gnat buzzing around a bull' would be her own image (Lowen 1990, 33).) Critics found her embodying 'an extraordinary range of emotion and temperament' against the grain of what they'd come to expect from this actor: 'She's restless and she's flighty and she's violent and she's sexy and histrionic' (Margaret Walters, *Critics' Forum*, BBC Radio 3, 18 April 1987); 'vivacious, provocative, tempestuous, always moving about ... much better than I had dared to think that Judi Dench could be in the part' (John Carey, *Critics' Forum*, 18 April 1987), not least because she was able to manage not just 'the comedy and the mischief' but 'the *balefulness* of the part'

(Adrian Poole, *Kaleidoscope*, BBC Radio 4, 14 April 1987). After Antony's death, her dream of 'an emperor Antony' (5.2.75) was given 'quietly', an 'incredibly intelligent and ... very moving rendering' that made the audience 'really think about ... the glamorous image' as against 'the reality' (Walters, *Critics' Forum*), a reality that contained the 'real fear ... and anxiety' of a 'very powerful woman', a '*middle-aged woman*', whose 'power is now on the wane' and who 'feels things going out of control' (Poole, *Kaleidoscope*, 14 April 1987). Adam Mars-Jones captured the complexity of Dench's performance for readers of the *Independent*: 'Recognising that the play is both sumptous [*sic*] and satiric', Dench 'does rich justice to the luscious speeches dripping with hyperbole, sensuous excess and gorgeous perversities of syntax and imagery but also keeps you aware of Cleopatra's tawdrinesses – the peevish insecurity of the mistress behind the swagger of the Queen, the crafty calculation and occasional panic, the stagey luxuriatings in her own performances'. This was a Cleopatra who postured 'before her court like the amorous star-turn of the Mediterranean Basin' but bristled 'with rage at the thought of being defamed in Rome'; a Cleopatra who 'never lets you forget the play's concern with public image' (11 April 1987).

Where Shakespeare's Cleopatra sees Antony anamorphically constituted of monster and marvel – one way 'painted ... like a Gorgon', 'The other way[ ] a Mars' (2.5.116–117) – it was Dench's Cleopatra that reviewers saw as the anamorph. The dazzling shifts in perspective she achieved in the role are suggested in the one minute of film recording that exists of this production.[5] It sees a golden Cleopatra at the top of 3.3 crashing open her palace door at the head of a panicky retinue swarming around her like a flock of flapping geese rising at gunshot as she shoots 'Where is the fellow?' (3.3.1 and *passim*). Caustically silencing Alexas's intervention about Herod of Jewry with 'That Herod's head / I'll have', she lapses into near silence, plumbing the depth of her political impotence with a voice that catches: 'But how, when Antony is gone, / Through whom I might command it?' Like a Gorgon turning the hapless Messenger into stone in her sight, she is arch: 'Come thou near'. (This Messenger is recognisably Antony's Eros, Jeremy Flynn, unaccountably haring between his master currently in Rome and his queen abandoned in Alexandria, a double that's one of those director-imposed decisions presented to the actor with 'satisfying logic' [*sic*, Lowen 1990, 19] – that is, that Antony's closest personal servant *would* be his personal messenger – that for the audience only muddies the narrative.) Interrogating the messenger, she's as barbed as Lady Bracknell punctiliously quizzing Cicely's suitor: 'Didst thou behold Octavia?' She's dangerously poised on 'Guess at her years, I prithee'. Then she turns, nearly collapsing into the arms of Charmian (Miranda Foster) with laughter that is half mocking guffaw, half a lascivious burst of relief on 'Widow? Charmian, hark!', only for her face to freeze into a mask when the Messenger volunteers, 'I do think she's thirty'. Instantly, every age-line scored in her flesh is appallingly visible in a revelation that hardens her, that she hears as a premonition of death. Enraged, she charges for the door, then sweeps her skirts back, the sartorial equivalent of the lashing tiger tail, and turns – she will not be routed – to eyeball the Messenger, to put more loaded demands to him: to note Octavia's 'face' (spoken acidly) and 'hair'. That last word is almost a caress which yields to her reward for information that the Messenger has now learned to deliver diplomatically, information that appeals. She reaches around the young Messenger's head and draws him into a lingering kiss before dismissing him.

Reviews of Antony Hopkins's performance were much more mixed. John Peter wrote poignantly of the 'searing, wounded intimacy' projected by the 'fleshy, ageing people' at the story's centre, Hopkins giving Antony 'a moving and painful honesty' (*Sunday Times*, 12 April 1987). Irving Wardle thought that 'for the first time in living memory, the English stage' had 'two actors capable of doing full justice' to a 'last tango' that 'would take you by the throat even played on a windy day on Brighton pier', with Hopkins strikingly choosing to 'resist[ ] all the invitations to rage and despair' that the part of Antony holds out for the actor, playing instead a man 'with too much dignity to exhibit his real despair to his followers' (*The Times*, 11 April 1987). Michael Billington thought Hopkins's grizzle-haired, grey-bearded Antony 'magnificent': 'a real old campaigner (you can believe that he ate "strange flesh" in the Alps) for whom Alexandria represents escape and fantasy', an Antony who, recalled to Rome, externalised the conflict between the soldier and the lover by prowling 'the stage hungrily like a lion waiting to get back in the arena'. He was an Antony, wrote Billington, whom he would remember most for his 'false gaiety – and overpowering inward grief – in the short scene where he bids farewell to his servants'. From that point on, 'the knowledge of death sits on Antony; and when Mr Hopkins says he will contend even with his [that is, death's] pestilent scythe it is with a swashbuckling bravura that moves one to tears' (*Guardian*, 11 April 1987).

But other reviewers savaged the performance. They found Hopkins's Antony 'inert ... wooden' (*Independent*, 11 April 1987); a 'velvet suited pultroon [*sic*]' 'stumbling around the stage speaking in a slurred voice' (*Critics' Forum*, 18 April 1987). Like Michael Redgrave in 1953, Anthony Hopkins found learning the part of Mark Antony a nightmare: 'I couldn't remember the lines', the 'chopped up, short sentences, short phrases' that Redgrave complained of. 'Normally', said Hopkins, 'they go in and there is no problem. But this time it wasn't happening' (*Evening Standard*, 10 April 1987). His difficulties may have had something to do with the fact that he'd just opened as King Lear at the National as rehearsals for *Antony and Cleopatra* began. The actor was trying to consolidate one huge part while he learned another. But they may also have had to do with differences of opinion between actor and director. The director demanded more from the actor of what Hall called Hopkins's 'dark, Welsh side'. The actor balked. Hall wanted 4.2, Antony's farewell to his followers – 'usually done as a touching scene' – to be 'in fact' 'maudlin and disgusting' (Lowen 1990, 37), a far cry from the heart-wrenching scene in performance that Billington would find memorable for Antony's 'false gaiety' and 'overpowering inward grief'. But to play 'maudlin', Hopkins said he needed to play drunk, to play 'acute self pity' arising 'out of a far-gone inebriation'. By the time they were several weeks into rehearsal, however, Hall had concluded 'that the scene works best' if Antony is 'sober and tragically self-aware' (Lowen 1990, 113). Still, he directed the actor along that self-defeating line for another two weeks, until just days before opening, before challenging 'the drunkenness: "It's exciting, but does it help ...?"' and allowing Hopkins to shed both the maudlin and the drunk (Lowen 1990, 141). The 'new' Antony was incomplete on press night. One critic complained that Hopkins's Antony 'never sobers up enough to make you feel what a disaster the Battle of Actium was' (*Kaleidoscope*, 14 April 1987). It would take him weeks of playing the play in the repertoire before he could put Hall's rehearsal room behind him and play his own Antony.

Despite such complaints, there was plenty of 'electrifying detail and tragic exhilaration' (*The Times*, 4 April 1987) for some reviewers to find satisfying in the Dench–Hopkins partnership on opening night. Some of it is recorded in Tirzah Lowen's account of 3.13.90–207. Having sent Caesar's treacherous ambassador Thidias (Desmond Adams) to be whipped, Hopkins's Antony rounded on Cleopatra, making her a 'boggler', a 'morsel' leftover shoved to the side of a dead man's trencher, a verbal beating that turned into physical abuse: 'he pushes, prods and shoves at her, and, for all her spirit, Cleopatra suddenly seems powerless .... Mimicking how she let Caesar's ambassador kiss her hand, Antony also kisses it – then spits'. When Thidias was dragged back in, 'Antony lies down beside him, luxuriating in his power to punish'. Finally, 'when Cleopatra kneels ... to protest her love for him, Antony strolls out of the room. Just when one thinks he has gone forever, he returns to stand behind her and at last accepts her words: "I am satisfied" ... Cleopatra collapses into helpless sobs. He kneels to comfort her, cradling her in his arms' (Lowen 1990, 158–159).

Such detail characterised the central performances throughout. Michael Bryant's 'Cockneyfied soldier' Enobarbus, 'like something out of Kipling' (*Independent*, 11 April 1987), made John Peter in the *Sunday Times* see 'this blunt, cautious man' as 'the moral touchstone of both the politics and the emotions of the play' (12 April 1987). Standing just off Antony but always familiarly to hand, he produced the 'very, very painful' 'perspective on Antony that makes you feel the shame of Antony's dishonour, his dereliction of all that it has meant to be a Roman' (*Kaleidoscope*, 14 April 1987). Bryant began the barge speech 'in the casual tones of an old sweat reporting what he has seen', plonking himself down in the chair Octavius had just vacated, swinging a leg over the arm as if to kick carelessly into touch the negotiations the Roman summit had just concluded. Marriage with Octavia? Pshaw! But when he came to describe Cleopatra's 'own person', he seemed to recede into 'an imaginative trance', rubbing a hand across his eyes 'as if to dispel a mirage' as he 're-dreams' Cydnus (*Guardian*, 11 April 1987; Lowen 1990, 158; *Kaleidoscope*, 14 April 1987).

Tim Pigott-Smith's Octavius occupied the other end of familiarity. He'd been a footsoldier to Corin Redgrave's martinet Octavius in the Trevor Nunn *Antony and Cleopatra* at the RSC in 1972. By contrast, Pigott-Smith played not Redgrave's lemon-sucking emotional anorexic but a man of superficial punctiliousness whose impassivity of face betrayed itself in the twitchy knotting of his ankles and the way his fingers picked at the arm of his chair.

'Devious', 'self-righteous', able by the end to 'steer Rome towards an arid stability', he was almost silly in his callowness to begin with, a glowering youth simply out-classed by the devious statesmanship of his elders (*Sunday Times*, 12 April 1987). A man who shrank from human contact, his Octavius was blind-sided by Agrippa's proposal of the marriage between Antony and Octavia, for this sister was the only person he adored, the only person who thawed the ice-water in his veins. This sister now would be sacrificed to the womaniser – and it would be she who fueled Octavius's deadly revenge when Antony cast her off. Reviewers spotted in his affection for, perhaps even his incestuous attraction towards, Sally Dexter's Octavia an interpretation new to the play. They *noticed* Octavia's part as if for the first time, and not only noticed, but were 'magnetised by her', a figure in Jacobean costume presented 'almost as a woman out of a Fuseli painting … very pale, ghostly, sepulchral' moving 'almost as if without feet' (*Critics' Forum*, 18 April 1987). Putting the interval at the end of 3.6, Octavia's return to Rome, which first had Pigott-Smith's Octavius roaring at her, 'No, / My most wronged sister', then hotly embracing her and promising revenge ('You are abused / … and the high gods, / To do you justice, makes his ministers / Of us and those that love you' (3.6.65–91, *passim*)), this production located the interval to mark a sharp reversal in the narrative, but also to announce that, one way or another, a woman would be responsible for bringing down the world.

In 5.2 Dench's Cleopatra rapidly discovered she had no room for manoeuvre with this Octavius. In 3.13 her 'Oh!' responding to Thidias's corrupt embassy from Caesar ('He knows that you embrace not Antony / As you did love, but as you feared him' (3.13.59–60)) had been ambiguous. She'd heard a life line being thrown her, and she'd lassoed it with her 'Oh!', a woman, a queen, keeping her options open. Later, early in 5.2, dreaming an emperor Antony to a Dolabella (Michael Bottle) who'd entered swaggering, cocky, but melted, 'discandied' like so many greater men before him in her presence, she – guilelessly 'cunning past man's thought' (1.2.152) – got him to divulge the information she needed. Told the part she'd play in a Roman triumph, Dench's Cleopatra was resolute for death. But then she appeared to renege. When Caesar entered, asserting imperial command by striding into the monument in an act of triumphalist male penetration, at the head of a military procession that came with trumpets blaring down the main aisle of the auditorium to fill the female monument with soldiers' bodies, she faced him head-on and coolly presented to him the 'huge ornate accounts book' that Charmian handed her, laying 'it at his feet' (promptbook), the 'brief' of all her 'money, plate and jewels' she was 'possessed of' (5.2.137–138), now Caesar's booty. Seleucus (Daniel Thorndike), the treasurer she summoned to verify her accounts, like Antony's Schoolmaster (Peter Gordon) before him, knelt to Caesar. His revelation that she had 'kept back' 'Enough to purchase what you have made known' (5.2.146–147) was a betrayal. But it was also the truth. Dench's Cleopatra *was* a queen who'd secretly bankrolled a future.

Her servant's betrayal simply confirmed that after Antony, after the death of magnanimity and her dream-sized 'Noblest of men', this 'dull world' really was 'a sty' (4.15.61, 63–64). It was peopled with 'Mechanic slaves' (5.2.208) whose 'Caesar' was a 'paltry' 'ass / Unpolicied' (5.2.2, 306–307). Why survive to live in a sty? Handing the account book – and the concealed treasure – back to her ('Still be't yours'), Pigott-Smith's Octavius smoothly guaranteed the future she had planned for: 'Bestow it at your pleasure'. Gone was the unpractised youth of the opening scenes. This Octavius was now the consummate smiling politician: 'we intend so to dispose you as / Yourself shall give us counsel' (5.2.180–181, 185–186). Dench's Cleopatra appeared won. She not only prostrated herself, but as he turned to exit, she reached out to clasp his hand, gesturing her abjection. Seconds later, though, holding the treacherous account book in her hands, she snarled, 'He words me, girls, he *words me*' (5.2.190; Dench's emphasis), and with a mighty rage hurled it from her (promptbook). Dolabella, entering just then, crossed Charmian en route to fetch what had been 'provided' (5.2.194). His last exchange with the queen ('I shall remain your debtor'; 'I, your servant' (5.2.204)) ended with him kissing her hand and (marked in the promptbook) a 'Moment of eye contact. Aha!' This Cleopatra, heretofore the mistress of the comic quip, the witty come-back, the devastating mock, the girlish giggle and deep-throated, lascivious chortle, all played with exquisite comic timing, was going to have the last laugh. What a joke it was going to be to 'fool' the Romans' 'preparation' and to 'conquer' Caesar's 'most absurd intents' (5.2.224–225).

For this last great arc of the narrative, Dench's Cleopatra, who'd appeared always in gold as if embodying the Greek etymology of her name, 'glory of the father', now wore blue, the colour of Rome. Was it a sign of capitulation? A ruse to fool Caesar, or perhaps to enrol her among – like Octavia – the legitimate married matrons of the city? For her death, however, her 'BEST ATTIRES' (as the costume bible records) re-inscribed her as 'EGYPT', in radiant gold, a voluminous 'Ptolemaic gown', pleated around the hem and down the sleeves, a triple-layered gold collar lying flat on her shoulders, a crown twice the size of the coronet she'd worn throughout. Hers was a body on the way to becoming an icon, its dazzling magnificence doubled in the mirror image that the polished surface of her golden throne threw back into the eyes of spectators. Caesar encountered this last performance-into-final-becoming head-on, in a three-pronged massed entrance down the centre and side aisles that filled the stage and surrounded the throne – but too late. The scene momentarily stopped him in his tracks. His recovery first belittled it: 'O noble weakness' (5.2.343). But then he couldn't help wondering at it: 'she looks like sleep, / As she would catch another Antony / In her strong toil of grace' (5.2.345–347). Foiled of his Roman triumph, he ordered an Egyptian triumph. On 'Take up her bed' (5.2.355), as the promptbook recorded, '4 soldiers go to each corner of the throne', 'the soldiers raise Cleopatra – 2 others move in + they hold her aloft bearing her horizontally', to 'process through audience followed by Caesar' and his men. A follow-spot traced her journey. The Cleopatra who'd tumbled into this production like a gipsy to the jangling accompaniment of the equivalent of authentic Egyptian street music left it to the sounds of funeral. The 'lass unparalleled', her 'bright day' 'done', was 'for the dark' (5.2.315, 192–193). Oxymoronically, however, in her exit she carried 'glory' through the auditorium. Triumphant Caesar walked in her shadow.

## Of 'mechanic' tackle and 'fallible' worms

As a coda to this large-scale production and as a salutary reminder to those of us who aim to write performance criticism that we need also to attend to the work of production that's going on *beyond* 'the performance', it is worth considering the degree of technical difficulty Shakespeare poses for his actors in *Antony and Cleopatra* and how such difficulty is dealt with on 'subsequent' stages. These technical challenges are mostly made invisible, covered in actors' performances, but they get written up night after night in stage managers' show reports (here, the job of Ernest Hall) that can be read as documents of theatre labour. For Anthony Hopkins, the lift of Antony's dying body into Cleopatra's arms 'above' posed the technical difficulty that threatened to wreck his performance on a nightly basis. Alison Chitty had designed the monument as two high walls connected by a heavy grilled iron gate whose lintel formed the pediment of a platform some eighteen feet above stage level. It looked like the service entrance to the monument, the gate, bolted, and the platform equipped with pulley and tackle, of the sort used in docklands warehouses for hoisting cargo out of ships' holds, which Cleopatra and her girls now took in hand to haul the body up into the redoubt where they would make their last stand against Caesar's assault. The original design had Hopkins's Antony hoisted in a sling; but when on the first preview the tackle tangled, the hoist stuck, and Antony's anguish was wrecked with audience laughter, the actor demanded changes. Overnight the sling was replaced with a net and the hoisting mechanics re-jigged. Thereafter, the 'S[tage]M[anager's] ACTIVITY PLOT' indicated the nightly routine with 'BE' standing in for Hopkins:

> PRESHOW CHECK LIST
> NET & HOIST (BE HOISTED UP IN THE NET ON THE
>   RESET).
> ...
> CALL THE HALF
> OPEN THE HOUSE
> TELL MR. HOPKINS THE NET HAS BEEN CHECKED

Without that check, Hopkins wouldn't go on.

For Dench's part, it might be thought that her chief technical difficulty, once the hoist was sorted, would be negotiating the business Peter Hall devised for reconceiving the spatial dynamics of the monument scenes. For 4.16, Hall wanted the activity located 'above'; 5.2, however, he wanted transferred 'below'. Clearly the narrow platform where Antony would die in Cleopatra's arms could not contain the spacious action of Cleopatra's face-off with Rome. That needed to happen on the main stage. The challenge was how to get her down. Hall decided to enact the shift in full view of the audience – while interpolating a significant death that, *inter alia*, would define Caesar's new regime. The promptbook records the moves. At the start of 5.2, the monument was trucked downstage 'with actors aloft'. When Proculeius and his assault team entered around the sides of the monument, 'Mardian [on sentinel duty inside the monument] descends within to be enclosed twixt the gates below'; the soldiers 'enter in shadow', one 'with crowbar'. Proculeius's 'This I'll report' (5.2.32) was the 'signal' for the soldiers to 'climb over the rear gate – kill Mardian, open gate run up the stairs come around the sides of the monument to prize [*sic*] open the gates Cleo is held by the arms + jerked over the side'. Then 'dropped [eighteen feet] onto the crowd below'. The promptbook records the stage manager's dry parenthesis: '(steadied on the way for safety)'. Evidently, this stunt was performed without incident throughout the run.

But as it happened, something even more challenging than an eighteen-foot drop faced Dench, the actor, while Cleopatra, the role, was busy preparing 'again for Cydnus' to 'meet the curled Antony' (5.2.227, 300). She had to play straight man to a snake. Shakespeare sensationally improves on Plutarch by having his Cleopatra apply the killing serpent to her breast, to make the asp a suckling infant who makes Cleopatra a mother even as her crown makes her a queen, while her answer to Antony's summons, 'Husband, I come!' makes her 'the married woman', his wife, all three fixing the final image of Cleopatra in death as a *female* 'triumvir' routing Rome's (5.2.286, 1.3.21). Hall's production employed real 'asps', two baby garter snakes. The 'understudy' was a diffident performer who hid at the bottom of the Asp Man's basket and needed a great deal of unseemly scrabbling about by Dench to fetch him out while Cleopatra was dreamily imagining a rapturous encounter: 'Come, thou mortal wretch …' (5.2.302). The 'principal' asp was of an entirely different character. Dubbed 'Keppel', after the famous music hall act of the 1930s, 'Do the Egyptian' starring 'Wilson, Keppel, & Betty', he was an extrovert who made a habit of shooting vertically into the limelight the moment the lid came off the basket.[6] Dench needed the skills of a cricketer at silly point to field Keppel – who, off stage, was occasionally given to the temperamental behaviour of a 'luvvie'. The stage manager's report on 31 October 1987 recorded:

> The snake was not present tonight (we used the dummy). The real one had a turn just before going on and leapt out of its basket and bit a propman. We could not use the live substitute in Stage Control

because the only master key was with a security officer who was on the roof because someone was trapped in a lift. It seems a shame that, when so much could have gone wrong tonight and didn't, we were let down by the shortage of keys.

The following night:

> The hoist was silent.
> The snake behaved impeccably.

As actors remind us (and as Keppel demonstrates), there is always much more going on on stage than the play.

### But yet

It is an irony of the critical reception of this production that the 'hacks' and the 'pundits' who reviewed it were divided by opinions poles apart, opinions centred on the subject of nostalgic returns that happen to express the deep ambivalence that I, for one, felt about this production. Like John Peter in the *Sunday Times*, most newspaper reviewers saw in it a marvellous return to a 'golden age', a triumph of 'Hallstyle' (Lowen 1990, 100) that produced the 'True sound of Shakespeare' (Charles Osborne, *Daily Telegraph*, 11 April 1987), 'the most intelligently spoken Shakespeare' Michael Billington had 'heard in years' (*Guardian*, 11 April 1987), with actors, wrote John Peter, speaking 'this soaring voluptuous, difficult text with the finest of techniques' (*Sunday Times*, 12 April 1987). English Shakespeare at its spoken best. As in the olden days.

By contrast, the 'pundits' – Barbara Everett in the *Times Literary Supplement* (14 April 1987) and John Elsom, Margaret Walters and Nigel Andrews on BBC Radio 3's *Critics' Forum* (18 April 1987) – saw in it a return, alright, but (wrote Everett) to a place of redundancy, to 'that image of Shakespeare's tragedy which a century ago made it seem unplayable', one 'sumptuous picture succeed[ing] another as if we were seeing the work of a distinguished Victorian antiquarian painter of the Renaissance'. Unwittingly quoting back at Hall his own moans about the 'slow, over-emphatic' verse speaking at the RSC in 1977, 'the pundits' complained of Hall's theatrical pedantry as a director in 1987, the 'very, very slow and deliberate' speaking (Walters) of 'people' who stand 'around the stage delivering the arias of familiar speeches' with 'a sort of pedantic attention to getting the words across' (Elsom). Sometimes those words 'were even explained for you' (Elsom), all of which made for 'a very good O-Level production': a production, that is, for sixteen-year-olds sitting school exams (Andrews). But in Peter Hall's 'sumptuous nostalgia for the grand style' (Elsom), 'something vital to Shakespeare [had] got lost', something Everett found in the much rawer, rough-and-ready productions of the *Henry IV* plays currently at the Old Vic directed by Michael Bogdanov with the English Shakespeare Company. Was that 'something' a 'profound respect for, a deference to, Shakespeare's intelligence' (Everett), including the 'intelligence' of Shakespeare speaking always to the present, *to the moment*? The problem with nostalgia, with any campaign to take 'us' 'back to basics' is that 'we' don't live there any more. And we certainly don't talk like that any more. What Peter Hall gave spectators, Everett concluded, was 'a major rendering of something curiously like Dryden's Restoration *All for Love*'.

**Notes**

1 In fact, his last Olivier production would be *The Tempest* the following year, staged in repertoire opposite, in the Cottesloe, *Cymbeline* and *The Winter's Tale*.
2 This 'workshop production' of *Macbeth* played a single performance in the Cottesloe on 14 April, just days after Hall's production opened. Hall habitually cast Shakespeare white. In 1988 when *Tempest*s at the RSC, Old Vic and Cheek by Jowl were casting black actors as Miranda, Caliban, Ariel, Adrian, Francisco and all the spirits, Hall's *Tempest* had no black presence. Neither did his *The Winter's Tale* or *Cymbeline* in 1988. The only black actors Hall cast during his twenty-three years directing the Peter Hall Company (1988–2011) were Kammy Darweish (unnamed servant) and Jeffrey Kissoon (Prince of Morocco), both in *The Merchant of Venice* (1989). Astonishingly, Morocco's servants in that production were played by blacked-up white actors – a decade after Donald Sinden was the last white actor to play a blacked-up *Othello* at the RSC.
3 Production records, including the promptbook, photographs and Chitty's costume bible, are held in the archives of the National Theatre, London.
4 Yasmin Arshad (2011, 2019; Arshad, Hackett and Whipday 2015) has persuasively argued that the sitter in this portrait is not Elizabeth Throckmorton, Lady Raleigh, but Anne Clifford, Countess of Dorset. Publicly known today only by a photograph held by the National Portrait Gallery (London) that was taken for reproduction in the sale catalogue when the painting was last sold at Christie's in 1948, the

portrait is oil on panel, by an unknown artist. Its current whereabouts are unknown.
5 Available at https://www.youtube.com/watch?v=wZ_xoXWhW5o (accessed 17 December 2019). A montage of still images made into a short film can be seen at https://www.youtube.com/watch?v=9dZ0TkxHLZs (accessed 17 December 2019).
6 Dench profiled her co-actors for me in 1987 – a conversation I've never forgotten.

7

# 'Some squeaking Cleopatra': Shakespeare's Globe, 1999

### Authenticity and its discontents

Sweltering in the sun of an uncharacteristically hot English August, the theatre-goers who weren't using their programmes for fans but were flipping through them looking for the plot synopsis and cast list for the just-opened *Antony and Cleopatra* they'd come to the Globe to see, encountered an advertisement. In bold capitals it told them that the previous year's

> 7 TIMES ACADEMY AWARD WINNER
> INCLUDING
> BEST PICTURE
> *Shakespeare in Love*

was now 'available to rent' for home entertainment.[1] The central conceit of this dizzyingly and uproariously inauthentic bio-pic, a supposed 'documentary' of the everyday working life of one Will Shakespeare, up-and-coming playwright (except that, since his writerly debut with *The Two Gentlemen of Verona*, he's been paralysed with writer's block), is 'authenticity'. Or, better said, authenticity and its discontents. The aristo Viola de Lesseps, home from having seen Shakespeare's play at court, performed for Queen Elizabeth, complains as she undresses for bed that the lad who acted Silvia just wasn't persuasive as a woman. He had 'fingers' 'red from fighting' and 'spoke like a schoolboy at lessons'. Oh, she sighs, referring to the 'authentic' state of affairs in the all-male Elizabethan playing companies, 'stage love will never be true love while the law of the land has our heroines being played by pipsqueak boys in petticoats'. Later, cross-dressed in doublet and hose as one of those 'pipsqueak boys', she auditions for a part in the play Shakespeare still can't write, *Ethel, the Pirate's Daughter*. And later still, she stunningly stands in for Sam, whose voice has broken overnight and dropped two octaves, impersonating a 'boy' to walk on, 'cross-dressed' in (her own) women's clothes, in the play Will has written instead, as Juliet. And the goofy lessons this story teaches (tongue firmly in cheek) are two. First, that 'only' women can play women authentically. Second, that when Shakespeare sees a 'real' woman in the woman's part, he starts writing parts for women differently: next up, Viola in *Twelfth Night*, and further down the line, Cleopatra.

Any theatre-goers who paused over this advertisement in the 1999 *Antony and Cleopatra* programme for a film that performed, critiqued and confounded 'authenticity' might have been struck by an irony, for they were there at the Globe to see exactly what the film lampooned: 'original practices Shakespeare'; *Antony and Cleopatra* in a retro-version of Shakespeare's play. This was a production that said it aimed to restore the very 'authenticity' the film so comically mocked: to play the play 'as if' in Shakespeare's day, in a theatre promoting itself as an 'authentic' reconstruction of an Elizabethan playhouse and with 'authentic casting' using an all-male company: Toby Cockerell as Octavia; Danny Sapani, Charmian; James Gillan, Iras; and the Globe's self-styled 'actor-manager', Mark Rylance, Cleopatra.

'Authenticity' had been one of the Globe's legitimating fictions since the 1960s when Sam Wanamaker conceived the project of building a facsimile of Shakespeare's playhouse on London's South Bank. A draft artistic policy from 1988 called for 'at least one play each season' to be 'presented as authentically as possible' (Purcell 2017, 22) on a stage – yet to be built but constructed (notionally) to the specifications of the original Globe's platform stage – whose *raison d'être* was imagined by the project's academic consultants as 'a machine' for testing 'current ideas about the original staging of the plays' (Purcell 2017, 20, quoting Gurr). Now occupying that stage and produced in the Globe's third season (fifth, if the 1995 'Workshop' and 1996 'Prologue' seasons were counted), the 1999

*Antony and Cleopatra* was sticking to the 'authenticity' brief even as it admitted playing fast and loose with it. On the one hand, as the Globe's in-house *Research Bulletin* reported, the 'main rope' used to haul dying Antony into Cleopatra's monument would be 'made of hemp', thus 'scoring points in terms of authenticity'; on the other, as 'a safety measure', Antony would wear 'a nylon wrist strap' (issue 14, March 2000).[2] Meanwhile, the company manager admitted that the organisation tended 'to ignore aspects of original staging that don't suit us', making this admission right around the time that Mark Rylance began calling 'authenticity' a 'big misconception' and substituting for it the term 'original practices' (Purcell 2017, 21, 23). By 'original practices' was meant 'work with all-male companies, the use of early modern music and instruments, research into the accurate reconstruction of Elizabethan and Jacobean costume using "original" materials [right down, audiences were told, to the underwear in the 1997 *Henry V*], research into early design elements, a direct relationship between performer and audience' and, at the end, a final 'jig' (Escolme 2008, 409).

What evaded the specifics of such 'practices' was, first, casting. On the one hand, the decision to cast an all-male company supported 'authenticity' since, according to the *Guardian*, which told readers this as a matter of fact ahead of *Antony and Cleopatra*'s opening, 'all Shakespeare's plays' were 'written for and performed by men', except for 'the female parts' which 'were played by boys' (8 December 1998). But on the other hand, having cast himself, just shy of forty, and certainly no boy, in one of those female parts, Mark Rylance was (by July) back-pedalling on 'fact', now asserting (without offering evidence) that 'popular belief' was wrong; that Shakespeare's 'big female roles' were actually 'played by strong young actors, not boys with unbroken voices'; and that 'the boy actors – the good ones, anyway – played women long after their voices had broken' (*Observer Review*, 25 July 1999). No 'boys' were cast in the Globe's *Antony and Cleopatra*.

What *was* cast, however, was a racially diverse company. This, of course, was conspicuously, even ridiculously *inauthentic*. Given Jacobean demographics and the organisation of the London playing companies, cross-racial casting – Benedict Wong was cast in 1999 to double Scarus and Menas – was hardly available to the early modern playhouse. However, the particular 'diversity' of this casting was, in one respect, depressingly familiar from post-imperialist English productions of *Antony and Cleopatra* since Glen Byam

Shaw's: while Cleopatra was cast white (even, cosmetically, whiter than white), Charmian was black. 'Historically researched theatre practice' of the kind the Globe claimed was underwriting their productions (Escolme 2008, 407–408) hadn't extended so far, however, as to discover from Shakespeare's sources and writing just how 'right' the opportunistic exceptionalism of that black casting was. Indeed, to be *really* 'authentic', his Egypt *should have been all black*.

Another evasion had to do with that claim about the 'accurate reconstruction of Elizabethan and Jacobean costume'. Jenny Tiramani, quaintly called 'Master of Clothing and Properties', not designer, among the Globe's creatives (where no director or composer was listed either, but a 'Master of Play' and a 'Master of Music'), researched 'original' fabrics, dyes and fashions to mock up 'authentic' material facsimiles of period costumes for this *Antony and Cleopatra*. But then she dressed these early modern clothes on post-modern bodies, bodies that, wearing them, performed – standing, moving, gesturing – resolutely post-modern behaviours.[3] This was a discrepancy Stephen Purcell spotted. Querying how Giles Block, 'Master of Play', had used improvisation, with its 'method-like insistence on lived memory as raw material for Shakespearean performance' in rehearsals for this *Antony and Cleopatra*, Purcell points out that such improvisation 'elides both historical difference (how can a modern actor, with modern habits and impulses, improvise accurately as a sixteenth-century person?) and Shakespearean form (these are poetic dramas, often in verse, not naturalistic plays)' (Purcell 2017, 68).

The same elision happened between bodies and costumes, which operated here as a kind of semiotic mirage. (To daft effect: Octavius (Ben Walden) appeared dressed for the Battle of Actium in Act 3 in the same gorgeous purple silk and satin suit he wore when greeting Antony at the Act 2 summit in Rome.) Moreover, their status as material artefacts that had absorbed huge tranches of budget and had issued from a department ('a veritable hotbed of authenticity') where a 'team of devoted experts' 'painstakingly stitched, hemmed, embroidered' (*Observer Review*, 25 July 1999) meant that these costumes could not operate as standard theatrical 'stuff' – the way they clearly did 'originally' in Shakespeare's playhouse, where costumes may have been ordered for named parts but then found themselves absorbed into wardrobe and continuously recycled (Rutter 1984, *passim*). The Globe's fabulously costly costumes had to be protected and preserved rather than allowed to do 'real', grubby theatrical work, for, as Mark Rylance explained, answering objections from spectators who complained that everybody in 'original practices' productions looked, bizarrely, as though they wore nothing but new clothes, 'The clothing [*sic*, for cloth?] that made up the costumes was so expensive [that] you wouldn't have broken it down' (Escolme 2008, 410) – 'breaking down' being the theatrical term for distressing a costume, roughing it up to make it look worn and lived-in. The clothes that Shakespeare-the-designer puts on stage carry history and story. Here, 'original practices' design gave spectators a parade of glossy fancy dress (Rutter 2001, 104).

A third evasion stared everyone full in the face in the open-air, full daylight Globe. Spectators were looking at the stage at characters in doublet and hose – but also across the yard and galleries at each other, in T-shirts and jeans, waving mobile phones. So where were these spectators located conceptually in the 'original practices' scheme? They might be listening to shawms and bagpipes and looking at facsimiles of early modern costumes, but they were looking and listening with post-modern eyes and ears – and sensibilities. Perhaps they'd bought standing tickets in the yard in order to have an 'authentic' Elizabethan experience as 'groundlings'. But how could they 'look' like Elizabethans? How was the much-touted 'direct relationship between performer and audience' to be constituted across what was visible in that discrepancy between stage and yard, a four-hundred-year gap in time? And if Rylance 'wanted the reconstructed theatre building, and the audiences that came to it, to play a primary role in "directing" the meanings that were produced there', how was that 'directing' to be informed (Escolme 2008, 407)?

As Robert Butler wrote in the *Independent on Sunday*, the Globe posited 'an imaginative world' that relied 'as much on the participation of the audience' as it did 'on the actors' (30 May 1999). But what kind of 'participation' and what kind of 'audience'? Back in 1995 during the Workshop Season, Rylance (who'd been named artistic director in early 1994 following the untimely death of Sam Wanamaker) told *The Times* that he wanted the Globe to be a theatre that brought together the high with the low, the 'classical Greek' with the 'bear-baiting pit', the 'bordello ... circus ... carnival' (2 August 1995), a theatre where he 'would be very happy for people to throw [and] shout things' – to behave perhaps like authentically 'robustious' 'nut-cracking Elizabethans' of the variety Hamlet scorned, 'groundlings ... capable of nothing but inexplicable dumb-shows and noise' (3.2.10–12). With this sound bite Rylance licensed 'authentic' audience participation at the Globe as bad behaviour. He created 'a monster', as Alan Dessen wrote in *Shakespeare Quarterly*, that needed 'feeding, a monster that can elicit the worst from some actors' (quoted in Purcell 2017, 45). In 1997 audiences jingoistically booed the French in *Henry V.* In 1999 'drunken groundlings' – as the stage manager reported – took a 'dislike to Cassius from his first entrance' in *Julius Caesar*, that season's companion play to *Antony and Cleopatra*, 'pre-empting lines *from their own copies of the play*' to sabotage the performance (quoted in Escolme 2008, 412; my italics).

That last is significant. It underscores the fallacy of any experiments with 'original practices'. They can't hope to reproduce the terms of the original encounter between audience, theatre practice and play. In Shakespeare's original playhouse, the conventions of performance (starting with the all-male company) were entirely ordinary, known, unremarkable, 'the universe of what is taken for granted' as Pierre Bourdieu might put it (quoted in Stallybrass 1986, 142). It was the play – the new writing – that was extraordinary. It was the new writing – radical, iconoclastic, culturally challenging writing; writing that brought a world of new histories and thoughts into the audience's ken – that went on, in performance, to put pressure on, even to trouble, the very conventions of performance the early modern playhouse had inherited, and to trouble, too, in consequence, the audience's spectatorship. At Rylance's Globe, the terms of encounter were reversed. The 'new writing' was no longer 'new'. The play had become 'ordinary'. Groundlings could quote from 'their own copies' of *Julius Caesar* brought into the theatre with them. Now the 'extraordinary' was the unfamiliar mechanics of early modern play production – and how to respond to them. Whatever 'trouble' the Globe offered spectators lay there: not in anything that was being performed with the writing but rather in the merely mechanical delivery of the writing.

As Robert Hewison wrote in the *Sunday Times*, it was impossible in 1999 to 'normalise' the all-male company. (Edward Hall's Propeller theatre company, which would go on to do just that for Shakespeare, was barely three productions old. Its *Twelfth Night* in 1999, and its commitment to *all* acting of men *or* women's parts as role-play, not impersonation, would retrospectively expose as nonsense most of what Rylance-the-actor claimed for his cross-gender performance of the Egyptian queen: 'I will be a woman. I will be Cleopatra' (*Daily Telegraph*, 30 July 1999).) 'The English', Hewison observed in a review that reveals a great deal about the state of British attitudes towards sex and gender in 1999, 'have a funny thing about men dressing up as women. They laugh at it, but they also fear it', 'that uniquely English theatrical creation, the pantomime dame' embodying 'both a hatred of women and a fear of homosexuality that can only be defused by the camp excesses of drag'. 'Cross-dressing', he concluded, was 'a risky business' (8 August 1999). It was, perhaps unsurprisingly, the women reviewers of the Globe's *Antony and Cleopatra* who most nearly called out both the misogyny and homophobia of the 'risky business' that Rylance performed as he attempted to 'be Cleopatra'. They'd had nearly a decade, tutored by Judith Butler in *Gender Trouble* (1990) and Marjorie Garber in *Vested Interests* (1992), to rethink both 'gender' and 'identity', to theorise the location of the transvestite in a cultural world that no longer defined itself sexually as 'binary', and, taking on the paradigm-shifting argument that both sex and gender are not essential but performative, to dispose of the whole notion of an 'identity' and its presumed 'authenticity'.[4] The time was ripe to interrogate, as women reviewers of theatrical representation, the stereotyped 'essentialist' performances they regularly saw imposed on women's roles by cross-dressed men. Their male colleagues – who perhaps weren't reading the same books – were largely won over by Rylance's 'risky business', though for the most part they were only reluctantly, grudgingly won over. Meanwhile, spectators were left gazing at Jacobean costumes on turn-of-the-millennium bodies – and trying to know what to make of the kind of mash-up on stage that Tom Stoppard's screenplay for *Shakespeare in Love* had so wittily entertained and shrewdly dismantled.

### 'Show me like a quean'

A consort of cornets, bagpipes and shawms played from the balcony over the stage as spectators filled the Globe's yard and galleries, a soundscape that put them aurally into an early modern world. A trumpet flourish announced the entrance of Philo (Timothy Davies) and Demetrius (Terence Maynard). They crossed the empty space of the Globe's wide platform on a long diagonal and took up positions in front of the stage left pillar within touching distance of the groundlings who leaned in on them. Dressed not as soldiers but as Jacobean courtiers in court-fashioned doublet, hose, starched ruffs and the kinds of hats Osric flourishes in *Hamlet*, they struck poses like those caught in Jacobean portraiture, one hand at waist, the other held up in a balletic flourish (uncanny look-alikes for Proteus and Valentine performing to the queen in Stoppard's *Shakespeare in Love*). The stance announced 'authenticity' – which evaporated the instant 'Look where they come!' (1.1.10) cued the painted cloth across the central double door entrance in the upstage *frons scenae* to be pulled aside for Cleopatra's entrance. Outpacing an Antony (Paul Shelley) who panted after her, costumed in 'exotic' Eastern robes, she came skipping in, simpering, flouncing, throwing pillows, lifting her skirt to flash her thighs, sprawling gap-legged on the ground, busy with scarves, restless as a gadfly, trailing the rest of the court – and barefoot.

Were these fitful behaviours meant to say something about 'infinite variety', a queen whom 'everything becomes' (2.2.246, 1.1.50)? Or were they meant to register as the 'authentic' performance of an 'authentic' Jacobean portrait of the (inevitably, essentially constituted) 'inconstant woman', the culture's misogyny starkly visible on the portrait's surface? That is, was the performance meant to reproduce a facsimile of the early modern period's degrading stereotypes of female inconstancy, as Rob Conkie would ingeniously argue (Conkie 2008, 189 and *passim*)?[5] Or when Rylance 'pranced on like a lissome girl, swaying his hips, toying with his wig of long gipsy curls, and glancing with a naughty smile' at Antony (Kate Bassett, *Daily Telegraph*, 31 July 1999), was he actually performing a caricature of *contemporary* misogynist tropes of stereotyped 'feminine' behaviour and 'authentic female subjectivity' derived from a redundant history of ideas that Butler's *Gender Trouble* had blown out of the water a decade earlier? In the *Mail on Sunday* Rhoda Koenig described Rylance's performance as running 'the gamut from Lady Bracknell to Mrs Andy Capp' (8 August 1999), via, she might have added contemporaneously, the Spice Girls and the television sitcom *Friends*. So was Rylance citing the past opportunistically and fraudulently to pass off these current stereotypes under cover of the period costume 'as if' they were period representations, representations knowingly to be laughed at like some 'horrible histories' visitors from a 'long ago' we could gaze at smugly, a 'foreign country' where they did 'things differently'? (Such smugness suggested that we, of course, were now vastly superior, and doing these 'things' so much better.) In short, if Rylance was 'performing' gender (along lines Butler proposed), whose tropes of performance was he playing with? Politically, what was he playing at?

His queen was dressed like a direct quotation of the Jacobean painting Alison Chitty may have been only alluding to when she designed Judi Dench's costumes at the National Theatre in 1987, *Lady Ralegh as Cleopatra* (see 7.1).[6] Here – approximating period 'authenticity'? – Tiramani appears to have raided the painting directly: Rylance's Cleopatra was uncannily look-alike. She had the same long dark corkscrew curls flowing across her shoulders, a version of the same high headdress holding her hair off her forehead, the same embroidered bodice exposing a wide expanse of chest (though Rylance's paps, unlike Ralegh's, weren't quite on view); the same sense of the louche, braceleted, necklaced, scarved, bangled 'oriental' gipsy, but with a cosmetically enhanced chalk-white English face, unwittingly reproducing the same 'cultural

7.1 'Tonight we'll wander through the streets and note / The qualities of people' (1.1). Cleopatra (Mark Rylance), Antony (Paul Shelley).

tourist' appropriation of Cleopatra in 1999 as Ralegh's portraitist had done circa 1607.

But in 1999 it was Cleopatra's bare feet (alone among the Egyptians) that registered the semiotic incoherence of this production, exposing the gap between 'authentic' costume and actorly behaviour – and the fraud being perpetrated upon any spectators who imagined themselves watching 'original practices'. For no early modern queen, no aristocrat would have appeared in public in bare feet – unless she were being exposed to shame, doing public penance like the disgraced Eleanor, Duchess of Gloucester, in *2 Henry VI*, sentenced to walk through London's streets 'in a white sheet' with 'papers' on her 'back', her 'tender feet' 'cut' with the 'ruthless flint' while jeering crowds mocked her (2.4.16, 30–34).[7] Reviewers spotted the deception. Punning headlines abounded. 'Playing fast and loose with a queen' (*Sunday Times*, 8 August 1999); 'Everything but the girl' (*Independent*, 3 August 1999); 'Drag queen barges on' (*Observer Review*, 25 July 1999); 'A dreadful carry-on by clumsy Cleo and co' (*Mail on Sunday*, 8 August 1999). As reviewers saw it, this production gave spectators not so much an Antony 'transformed / Into a strumpet's fool' (1.1.12–13) as a strumpet Cleopatra playing the fool.[8]

She entered at 1.2.83 ('Saw you my lord?') as if coming from a raid on her dressing-up box out of which she'd chosen a get-up for the 'sports' Antony was proposing for 'Tonight', to 'wander through the streets' of Alexandria and 'note / The qualities of people' (1.1.54–55). Plutarch's account of these 'sports' has Antony and Cleopatra going abroad incognito, but no one in this Cleopatra's city could have failed to recognise her, ostentatious in an over-sized red feathered Roman helmet and big-boy's war cloak, a look that raised laughs from the audience. But was she, in this outfit, in fact wearing 'borrowed robes' (*Macbeth*, 1.4.109)?[9] Antony's from Philippi? In that season's *Julius Caesar* (as Robert Smallwood reported), Antony's battle dress had 'long red feathers sticking out of the top of his helmet, fatally reminiscent of an ambitious Costard's presentation of Pompey in the Pageant of the Nine Worthies' in *Love's Labour's Lost* (Smallwood 2000, 245). Was Cleopatra doing a bit of memorial reconstruction, camp cross-dressing to present herself as her general's general? She played 2.5 (the savaging of the messenger) for laughs, pulling a knife out of her knickers, cooing 'I will not hurt him' in a little girl's voice, pronouncing 'it is never good / To bring bad news' as though to an idiot child while stroking the cringing messenger's hair. She collapsed on 'I faint', instantly recovered on "'Tis no matter', and sent her 'girls' to pump the messenger for the low-down on Octavia ('Bring me word how tall she is') (2.5.81, 85–86, 110, 118). Then, as if in extravagant over-compensation for her anxieties, she entered at 3.3.1 ('Where is the fellow?') clomping across the space in four-inch high chopines under a head-tire that elevated her stature to a giant. 'Is she as tall as me?', asked coyly, and 'What majesty is in her gait?', asked as she cat-walked the width of the stage, raised gales of audience laughter (3.3.11, 17). As did her entrance dressed for Actium: 'like Britannia on an old penny' (Smallwood 2000, 246); 'like a cut-out figure from Pollock's toy theatre' (*Sunday Times*, 8 August 1999); or like next casting for Bottom-as-Pyramus in a golden breastplate, plumed helmet, boots designed for an Inigo Jones masque, and a 'girl'-sized spear, as decorative as her bangles, that left one hand free to flick her hair then to park petulantly onto a thrust-out hip. In Cleopatra's self-refashioning caricatures, the 'royal occupation' (4.4.17), the masculine enterprise of war, masculinity itself as a subject position worthy of being taken seriously in history or by actors on this stage, was utterly trashed – along with the serious role women play in warlike majesty.

Other characters struggled to 'vie' with the 'strange forms' produced by this Egyptian queen's 'fancy' (5.2.97) in a production that Robert Smallwood thought handed 'the play entirely to Rylance's Cleopatra' (Smallwood 2000, 246). As Bridget Escolme has observed with devastating (though gracious) understatement, Rylance 'has sometimes dominated the Globe stage': a stage which, she writes, he understands 'demands a kind of honourable showing off, a theatricality centred not only on the generous giving of focus but also the shameless taking of it'. Shamelessness – 'clearest in his performance of female roles' – was front and centre here (Escolme 2008, 415). Certainly the production budget had been lavished on Cleopatra. She had six full changes of Jacobean costume. Shelley's Antony had only one, shedding his white Egyptian tunic pyjamas and silk robe for doublet and hose to attend the summit in Rome, attire he wore across the next three acts, and going into battle at Actium 'plated' only in a ceremonial sash. His 'armour' was reserved improbably but literal-mindedly to 4.4.1, long after one might have thought he'd needed it ('Eros! Mine armour, Eros!'). Octavius's wardrobe didn't get even that much attention. Unchanged across five acts, his costume gave the bizarre sense of everyone save Cleopatra living in a single-suited time warp. For their part, Danny Sapani's 'statuesque Negress' Charmian and James Gillan's 'wan wench' Iras (*Sunday Times*, 8 August 1999) served mostly as human wallpaper – with one stunning exception, when Sapani, answering Cleopatra's 'Did I, Charmian, / Ever love Caesar so?' with 'O that *BRAVE* Caesar!' (1.5.69–70; Sapani's emphasis), did a wicked impression of Cleopatra fluttering across the forestage (or was it not Cleopatra but Rylance who was being mocked?). Sapani brought the house down.

More tellingly, Giles Block's direction appeared to rush through any scenes that took the focus off Cleopatra. Perhaps under pressure from the much-touted 'verse work' Block had done in rehearsals, this production went for 'pace and volume', which produced little nuance and still less attention to 'the exquisite poetry begging to be recognised in Shakespeare's dialogue' (*Daily Telegraph*, 31 July 1999). Block wanted 'clarity, momentum, and audibility' (*Research Bulletin*, 14 March 2000). What he got was certainly Shakespeare spoken at speed – but by actors straining to throw their voices across the open space of the Globe's yard, producing sound high in their throats, stridency and a generalised wash of high emotion but not line-by-line intelligibility. Aspects of the narrative simply went missing. The global politics of the play were so underplayed that Walden's Octavius came across as 'strutting, prissy ... a petulant, silly little man, accepting power with a kind of apology' (Smallwood 2000, 246). The deep treachery of his instructions to Thidias in Act 4 to 'win' Cleopatra was lost in adenoidal gabble. The revelry on Pompey's galley was desultory: the Bacchanals, a conga-line that wove around the stage pillars as a 'Boy Singer', dressed like an adolescent Dionysus in lurid green chiton and mask, danced on a tabletop. The encounters of armies were perfunctory passings over of the stage by drums and flags, squadrons squaring off like drill teams on parade before disappearing. The sounds of battle that came from off stage behind the closed doors of the *frons scenae* suggested to Michael Billington 'kids fighting in a broom cupboard' (*Guardian*, 2 August 1999).

## 'A machine to test ... original staging'

The question to be asked about a production that ranged in reviewers' estimates from a 'shambles' to the high praise of 'run-of-the-mill' (*Mail on Sunday*, *Sunday Times*, both 8 August 1999) is whether, played in something like 'original' performance conditions on a stage designed as a 'machine to test' theories about early modern performance practice, it earned its keep by teaching us anything not already known about *Antony and Cleopatra* from conventional stagings (Gurr, quoted in Purcell 2017, 20).

Michael Billington thought it did, in, conspicuously, the male casting of Cleopatra. The 'chief gain' was 'not any spurious "authenticity"' but the way a man in the role 'highlights the character's histrionic excess' (*Guardian*, 2 August 1999). Paul Taylor agreed, pointing to the 'beguiling persuasiveness and compelling mercuriality' [*sic*] in the transvestite performance that enhanced the sense of the queen 'as a fluid and compulsive actress' (*Independent*, 3 August 1999). For Robert Smallwood, 'what Rylance's performance achieved', 'showing an actor shadowing, or paralleling, the role, rather than identifying with it', was a demonstration of 'the extent to which Cleopatra is constantly performing, deliberately presenting theatrical displays, never identifiable as herself' (Smallwood 2000, 246).[10] But surely it needed no reconstructed Globe sprung up on the South Bank to tell us any of this. Such 'shadow' play, such 'compelling mercuriality' in 'transvestite' performance may perhaps have been new news in 1972 when played to such culture shock at the Citz in Glasgow, but was hardly a news flash in metropolitan London in 1999. As for 'histrionic excess', was it located in the character – or in the actor?

Meanwhile, and as dubiously, Bridget Escolme thought the all-male casting allowed Rylance 'to develop techniques for playing female' that showed what 'rarely emerges in modern production' when women's parts are played by women: that these roles can be 'ludicrous as well as vulnerable, comical figures as well as funny women'. For Escolme, 'In playing, rather than being, a woman', viz. Smallwood's notion of 'shadowing the role' rather than 'identifying with it', Rylance 'explored the comic vulnerability of the female', actresses, Escolme thought, being 'more inclined to discover their strengths'. Performance by a man seemed 'to allow this Cleopatra a comedic enjoyment of sex and sexuality' (that eluded women actors?) – to wit, as Rylance made Cleopatra's jokes about horses happy to carry the weight of Antony, he groaned with outsized orgasmic pleasure (Escolme 2006, 129).[11]

There is more than a little to dispute here.[12] Anyone who'd experienced Suzman's or Mirren's RSC Cleopatras, or Dench at the National Theatre, or Bennison at Northern Broadsides had seen plenty of 'comic vulnerability' on stage and racy 'comedic enjoyment of sex', sexuality made seriously erotic and raunchily sublime, but not, like Rylance, coarse. That said, at the generous heart of Escolme's appreciation of Rylance's Cleopatra is a significant observation, that performing vulnerability, he performed 'the vulnerability of the modern clown' (Escolme 2008, 417).

Was this, then, the great discovery of 'original practices' staging? That Shakespeare's Cleopatra is a clown? That the play 'should be placed on the Shakespeare transfer-list and moved from the tragedies to the comedies' (Michael Billington, *Guardian*, 2 August 1999)? That in making 'her a comic turn' (Robert Hewison, *Sunday Times*, 8 August 1999) and cocking a snook at reviewers' expectations of a 'long adagio' building tragically to 'Cleopatra's end' (Billington), Rylance was revealing the 'authentic' Cleopatra?

Reviewers had objected that playing so much for laughs predisposed the audience to laugh where they shouldn't – as they did at Antony's death. Spectators had already found the botched suicide in 4.14 comic: first Eros spectacularly wrong-footing his master by cutting his own throat; then Antony wrecking his heroic death with anti-climax ('How? Not dead?' (line 104)); the soldiers rushing on, refusing to finish him off, then rushing off; the entrance of Diomedes sent by Cleopatra, answering Antony's 'When ...?' with the monosyllablic laugh line, 'Now, my lord' (line 121); the bizarre relay of body images, the interruptions, the timing: this was a scene the audience reacted to as they would to stand-up comedy. As wounded Antony was carried off to Cleopatra's monument, she and her 'girls' appeared aloft on the gallery over the stage where one section of balustrade had been removed. A bed-like piece of furniture was shoved forward into the gap while, from the heavens, rope tackle fell, the women manhandling it into position. Below, soldiers dumped Antony into a cargo-net sling, whereupon 'a big, muscular Charmian' proceeded to 'haul [him] up to the monument' and wrestle him onto the bed so 'beefily' that the audience broke out in 'unseemly giggles' (*The Times*, 2 August 1999); 'a piece of pantomime which solicits laughter', wrote John Gross, 'and receives it' (*Sunday Telegraph*, 8 August 1999); a scene that should go down 'in the annals of the art of coarse acting as one of the great examples of its kind' (Smallwood 2000, 247).

But if, as Billington saw it, 'Block's production implie[d] that even the business of pulleying Antony up to the monument was meant to raise laughs as well as a body', perhaps that was exactly right (*Guardian*, 2 August 1999). Perhaps Block knew exactly what he was directing in the scene, finding – as Deborah Warner had at the end of *Titus Andronicus* at the RSC in 1987 – Shakespeare staging human actions so grotesque as to make laughter the only sane reaction. Perhaps spectators were seeing this scene authentically performed for the first time in memory. What Antony absurdly claims for his death ('a Roman by a Roman / Valiantly vanquished' (4.15.59–60)), what Cleopatra cravenly makes as excuses ('I dare not / Lest I be taken' (23–24)); the high-mindedness ('former fortunes' (55)); the pettiness ('Your wife Octavia …' (28)); the slapstick exchanges ('let me speak a little', 'No, let me speak' (44–45)) and one-liners ('I am *dying*, Egypt, dying' (19); 'How heavy weighs my lord!' (33)): what the audience hears in the scene is perhaps Shakespeare exploding the idea of the heroic male death.

If the function of clowns is to enact parodic inversions, by the time the Clown arrived in Act 5 with his basket of asps, Rylance's Cleopatra was more clown than he. Rylance modelled the queen's final entrance ('My desolation does begin to make / A better life' (5.2.1–2)) on Plutarch's description of Cleopatra's self-mutilation in the face of Antony's death and her parley with Caesar soon after: 'she rent her garments … clapping her brest, and scratching her face & stomake'; she 'fell downe at his feete maruelously disfigured: both for that she had plucked her heare from her head, as also for that she had martired all her face with her nailes' (North 1579, 1006, 1008). Rylance's Cleopatra looked as if she'd hacked off her hair with a blunt nail file, pulling it out by the roots when it wouldn't cut, leaving bloody patches on a near-bald pate.[13] (Rylance, however, held back from 'martir[ing]' Cleopatra's face, presumably to avoid spoiling the prettiness of the *actor's* face.) Oddly, since in Plutarch this performance of self-mutilation is calculatedly put on for Caesar, Rylance concealed it when Caesar approached. He wrapped Cleopatra's shorn head in a white turban, yanking it off only on 'He words me, girls, he words me' (5.2.190).) The effect was shocking, but also ludicrous. Like the botched suicide that made a mockery of the heroic death, the botched self made a joke of the performing diva.

Rylance's Cleopatra relied on a standard histrionic repertoire in this final scene, dressed in a plain white shift, her 'monument' now relocated from the balcony to the main stage where Antony's death bed was re-set as her throne. She was being ritually washed by her women when a deafening pounding on the door froze them, a pounding that covered the sounds of the soldiers who surprised her, abseiling ('authentically'?) into the space. Taken captive, she was hysterical; dreaming an Antony, she sobbed ostentatious grief; performing their future in Caesar's Roman triumph to Iras, she skipped around the stage then posed in the discovery space, arms outstretched like one of the 'quick comedians' (5.2.215). Hearing of the 'rural fellow' who 'brings you figs' (5.2.232, 234), she responded in her little girl's voice with an interpolated 'Oh'. But now she was a doddering old woman who'd wearied her audience. These performances were clownish recalls, shadow play of former fascinations – and disgusting, inhabiting this ridiculously wrecked body.

But other than perhaps discovering an 'authentic' Cleopatra, this 'original practices' production told audiences little that was new. The empty stage, unobstructed with furniture and set changes, might have been expected to demonstrate something about the forward movement of the play, its fluidity and relentless pace, the acceleration of Act 4's cross-cut war scenes, the theatrical and narrative meanings foregrounded in Shakespeare's scenic juxtapositions (exit Rome, enter Egypt). But such demonstration was lost, not least because the performance was twice interrupted with (wholly inauthentic) intervals. No light was thrown on Seleucus either. (Was he a traitor, or a human shield?) The sequence was cut, Giles Block calling it a 'red herring' – Shakespeare's deliberate stagecraft of distraction at this point evidently eluding the director (*Research Bulletin*, 14 March 2000).

Moments of performance, if telling us nothing new about *Antony and Cleopatra*, did remind audiences what glorious potential this script holds for actors. While reviewers found Paul Shelley's 'bluff, grey-bearded, sombre and ultimately uninteresting Antony' (Smallwood 2000, 246) an Antony who 'offered neither a sense of past grandeur nor ... present passion', 'not a has-been but a never was' (Rhoda Koenig, *Mail on Sunday*, 8 August 1999), he did reveal a 'hawk-eyed canniness' in agreeing to marry Octavia 'to mollify her stroppy brother' (Kate Bassett, *Daily Telegraph*, 31 July 1999), but a canniness flawed by dreary lubricity. Traipsing after Octavia as she exited from their first introduction, Shelley's Antony was yet again in thrall to a woman – and trying to look up her skirts. Yet, later, his Herculean rages were magnificent: when he bellowed 'The witch shall die!', he meant it (4.12.47).

Equally, if reviewers thought John McEnery as Enobarbus 'attempted nothing beyond the hard-bitten soldier caricature', dying 'kneeling upright, with a sort of unsurprised resignation' (Smallwood 2000, 246), he did show spectators first an Enobarbus who, alone in Egypt, troubled Cleopatra's narcissism. He stopped her dead in her tracks in 3.13 as she was flitting after Antony who was exiting with the Schoolmaster to write his ludicrous challenge to Octavius. Enobarbus addressed 'Yes, like enough high-battled Caesar will / ... be stag'd to th' show / Against a sworder!' not aside, but directly to Cleopatra. 'I see men's judgements are / A parcel of their fortunes ... / ... Caesar, thou hast subdued / His judgment too' (3.13.36–*passim*) expressed a cynicism that was as deep as a grave. When Caesar's ambassador was announced and the women rushed around to set the scene for a 'performance', kneeling on cushions downstage and facing upstage at Thidias's entrance, McEnery's Enobarbus lounged against a pillar: 'Mine honesty and I begin to square. / ... Yet he that can endure / ... earns a place i'th' story' was addressed out to the audience (3.13.42, 44–47).

His Enobarbus had no doubt about what he was seeing in Thidias's embassy. And he was right. This Cleopatra's 'Oh!' opened a loop-hole into a survivor's future. She took the audience in as conspirators before running to Thidias on 'He is a god', then backing him across the stage while leeringly quizzing him, 'What's your name?' (3.13.60, 63, 76). She allowed him not just to kiss her hand; she stroked his head suggestively while he did so. Antony caught this betrayal *in flagrante*. When Cleopatra tried to intervene to save Thidias, Antony shoved her brutally away. No one protested when he savaged her – 'You have been a boggler ever'; 'I found you as a morsel, cold upon / Dead Caesar's trencher ...' (3.13.115, 121–122) – or moved to support her. Charmian turned away. But then another performance – 'Not know me yet?' – yet again reduced Antony to 'I am satisfied'. This performance, which ended with more blustering folly ('I and my sword ... / There's hope in't yet') and with the couple entwined in each other's arms, left Enobarbus mute, frozen at the downstage pillar. As he stood gazing out at a bleak nothingness, it was clear that something in Antony's lieutenant had broken (3.13.162, 172, 180–181). Cleopatra ducked out of Antony's embrace, crossed to Enobarbus and touched his cheek. He pushed her hand away. As Antony kept talking, she couldn't take her eyes off Enobarbus. Even as the couple exited to another gaudy night, her head was turned, her gaze swivelled back over her shoulder, eyes fixed on him. But the witness said nothing. And saying nothing, said everything.

It was just such another mute witness who constructed Cleopatra's death in 5.2 and made that death finally, miraculously, a move that transformed this Cleopatra from clownish diva to icon. While Rylance's queen herself rushed towards death on a rising tide of flapping hysteria, Danny Sapani's silent Charmian dressed her in gold – robe, veil, crown – and settled her on her golden throne, finishing her dying sentence: 'What should I stay –'; 'In this vile world?' (5.2.312–313). She mended her mistress's crown. She pronounced her eulogy, fixing her as 'A lass unparalleled' (line 315). The dignity and the high seriousness of Sapani's performance at the end were that actor's greatest gift to this production. Yet it was ironic, too, that his Charmian should have appropriated Cleopatra's voice. For in Danny Sapani, spectators saw the actor who *should* have been playing Cleopatra.

### Notes

1 Screenplay by Tom Stoppard in collaboration with Marc Norman; directed by John Madden (Universal Pictures, 1998).
2 This, and other performance materials for the production including an archive video of a live performance, are held in Shakespeare's Globe Library & Archive, London.
3 In fact, as Escolme writes, a certain amount of research and rehearsal time went into establishing early modern 'behaviours' – 'bowing, curtseying, shaking hands and doffing hats', the 'carefully socially encoded gestures' of the period (2008, 418). In performance, however, these 'behaviours' were only promiscuously introduced, so the social texture of the play was disconcertingly uneven. More significantly, the codes were totally illegible to audiences in 1999 as productive of any particular social meanings, meanings that in their original Jacobean context would have been instantly interpretable. Take, for example, that 'deepest of historically researched curtsies' that Rylance's Cleopatra made, bidding Antony farewell ('all the gods go with you!' (1.3.101)). Was this gesture (and its ostentation) to be read as typical of Jacobean courtesy, a sign of settled submission and gracious sincerity? Or was it ironic, given its (to post-modern eyes) stagey exaggeration? Was this curtsey the early modern equivalent of sticking two insulting fingers up to Antony, giving him, as Americans in the audience would say, the finger?
4 Before Butler, most feminist theory had made a distinction between sex and gender: sex, a biological given; gender, a social construction.

But that formulation, Butler argued, meant having to accept that 'identity' exists and is constituted of an 'essence' (the biological given) that can then be 'represented' in various ways (under the pressure of social construction or conditioning). Countering, she explodes the very notion of 'identity', calling into doubt the essence, the presence that is supposed to be re-presented. All that we have are representations – which she refigures as 'performances'. Thus 'identity' itself is and always has been a performance; and this means that there is no essence of male or female that can be 're-presented'. As a theorist, then, and for the women who were following her, Butler exposed the nonsense of Rylance's 'authentic' Cleopatra. For Shakespeareans, however, there was nothing very radical in Butler's theorisations. 'Identity' is alien to early modernity, where instead the 'self' is thought of as a mosaic or palimpsest, as a function of a series of rhetorically and socially managed role-plays. See Smith 2000. Or see the Lord's instructions to Bartholomew, his page, in *The Taming of the Shrew*, that, 'dressed in all suits like a lady', he is to play the woman's part in the deception of Christopher Sly: 'Tell him' to 'bear himself with honourable action / Such as he hath observed in noble ladies / Unto their lords by them accomplished. / ... With low soft tongue and lowly courtesy ... [to] usurp the grace, / Voice, gait and action of a gentlewoman' (Induction 1, lines 105, 108–111, 113, 130–131, in Hodgdon 2010).

5 Quoting Paul Taylor's review in the *Independent* (3 August 1999), Conkie argues that 'for [Taylor] and for Rylance, in an authentic production, "the queen's capricious *volte-faces*" are spontaneous, unpremeditated, and natural eruptions of an authentic female subjectivity, not the calculated performativity enacted by [say] [Helen] Mirren and [Frances] de la Tour' (then currently playing Cleopatra in productions at the National Theatre and the RSC). Conkie's 'argument is that Rylance is "right", however inadvertently. For in portraying ... [the female] stereotype, Rylance's Cleopatra represented a simulation of the early modern ideological constructions that [Mark] Breitenberg calls the [period's] "misogynistic caricatures of women" and [Michael] Shapiro labels "the culture's most blatant female stereotypes"'. For Conkie, then, 'this production represented a number of caricatured feminine subject positions traceable across history to early modern crises of masculinity' (Conkie 2008, 202, 205). But at the heart of those observations is surely a question about whether those 'caricatured positions' are being staged (in Shakespeare and elsewhere) in order to instantiate and affirm them or to expose, explode and dismantle them. For me, it's the latter. To see what Shakespeare is up to in *Antony and Cleopatra*, we might consult *The Taming of the Shrew* as a case

study in the performance of male anxiety and of the 'most blatant female stereotypes' circulated by the playwright's culture. After the Hostess exits at line 10, *Shrew* is a play played by, to and for men only. Its plot conceit hangs on 'misogynistic caricatures of women' (shrew v. mute) and on what the play shows to be the equally caricatured subject position of the patriarchy's authority, including the patriarchy's executive ability to 'tame a shrew'. At the end, when the all-male company that has acted the play exits, when the Lord and his all-male suite who have managed the performance disperse and when Christopher Sly returns to consciousness (and, in some productions, into performance), what is the result? The final score in the war of the sexes? Hardly an affirmation. Not only has the 'subject position' of the 'shrew' been thoroughly interrogated and re-gendered ('he is more shrew than she' (4.1.76)) but the power of the patriarchy has been exposed to ridicule: if one 'shrew' is 'tamed', two others have sprung up to take her place. A study in male anxiety, indeed.

6 See Chapter 6 n. 4.
7 All quotations of *2 Henry VI* are from Knowles 1999.
8 An index, perhaps, of how little they took this Cleopatra seriously registers in the number of critics who reviewed her as 'Cleo' as though she were featuring in a *Carry On* film, including Koenig, *Mail on Sunday* (8 August 1999); Holden, *Observer Review* (25 July 1999); Billington, *Guardian* (2 August 1999); Nightingale, *The Times* (2 August 1999).
9 All quotations of *Macbeth* are from Clark and Mason 2015.
10 It has been observed that 'these thinly veiled and lazily predictable misogynistic accolades to the male who is performing "the female" presume that located in the female is a hysteria (connected to the "histrionic") from which the female herself can never wholly disassociate herself in performance – and which can only be "truly" rendered by the male able to *authenticate* the female experience'. 'Which is', my commentator continues, 'A REPRESENTATION THEY HAVE BEEN CLAIMING FOR THOUSANDS OF YEARS, LEST WE FORGET.' I owe this note (and the capital letters) to Rowan Rutter, whose critical intelligence informs my writing on the gender politics of this production.
11 Escolme appears to head off the critique she anticipates by admitting that Rylance's performance of 'carnivalesque sexuality should, perhaps, be disturbing or distasteful, like laughter at a misogynist drag-act'. But then she immediately absolves him of the 'disturbing' and 'distasteful' with an apparent *non sequitur*, saying that he is a 'powerful presentational performer who knows how to ride the laughs' (2006, 129).

12 Not insignificantly for the performances that women give as Cleopatra, this play has no history in the UK of being directed by women. What the women of my book *Clamorous Voices: Shakespeare's Women Today* observed thirty years ago (in a book that is still a core text for women in the industry in the UK) remains the case for many women in the theatre. Today, 'A lot of what actresses feel they can do in performance is administered to them by a director. And if Cleopatra is read as somehow contained within her own hysteria/histrionics – what actress wants to play that? That's a minefield. So the actress plays it straight, unfunny, unself-aware. The male performer and the male director do not fear self-awareness, and therefore male actors can play the part objectively. Because they are being self-aware of something that is *not* their self. The actress cannot do that'. I owe this observation to Rowan Rutter.

13 Both the washing ritual and the exposed scalp were familiar tropes from earlier productions: Helen Mirren (RSC, 1982), Clare Higgins (RSC, 1992). In the production then playing at the RSC in Stratford, Frances de la Tour's Cleopatra, her wig gone, her head bald, ritually washed her servants. Robert Smallwood parenthetically remarked that this 'production opened before the Globe's so any influence had moved in a southerly direction' (Smallwood 2000, 249). But he also recorded a 'dignity' found 'in death' in the RSC production that only Sapani was able to offer at the Globe: 'Wig-less ... make-up-less, wearing something between a dressing gown and a monk's habit, her ashen face made to look two hundred years old through defeat and grief, [de la Tour's] Cleopatra moved, via a strangely beautiful ritual of anointing her attendants' necks to the final performance: slowly and ritualistically she applied ghostly white make-up to her face and painted her eye-lids, then her servants dressed her in golden cope and splendid oriental crown ... we watched it being created as we would in an actor's dressing room' (Smallwood 2000, 249).

# 8

# Estranging the crocodile: foreign *Antony and Cleopatra* in Britain and abroad

### Locating 'it self'

In 2.7, bleary-eyed yet with the persistence of the drunk buttonholing his subject even as he's sliding off the barstool (and in this case, out of the frame of Shakespeare's history), Roman Lepidus quizzes Antony on a place very different from Rome: 'What manner o' thing is your crocodile?' (2.7.41). Antony replies:

> It is shaped, sir, like it self, and it is as broad as it hath breadth. It is just so high as it is, and moves with it own organs. It lives by that which nourisheth it, and the elements once out of it, it transmigrates. (2.7.42–46)

The crocodile is knowable, that is, only as 'it self'.[1] So, too, by extension, are Egypt and the gipsy queen proxied in the crocodile. It is, Lepidus concludes, 'a strange serpent' (2.7.51).

This soddenly idiotic exchange, the inebriates' scrutiny of cultural difference discovering cultural difference to be literally inscrutable, offers me an initial paradigm for seeing how the foreign productions of *Antony and Cleopatra* considered in this chapter have been treated on British stages. The foreign 'thing' watched with the boggled Lepidian eyes of the 'native' who's half curious, half suspicious of what 'Johnny foreigner' is making of 'our' Shakespeare turns out to be, like the crocodile, knowable only as 'it self' – and 'strange'. (See, for example, the English newspaper headline to Peter Zadek's 1994 Berliner Ensemble *Antony and Cleopatra* at the Edinburgh Festival, a production it touts as 'Playing lip-service' to Shakespeare. That's the kind of clever-while-condescending pun the English language delights in, and delights in mobilising against the 'Other', emerging as it did from the reviewer's bemused opening comment that this 'must be the first account of Shakespeare's great play in which the hero, prior to the final battle, is seen applying lipsalve' (Paul Taylor, *Independent*, 19 August 1994).) But while foreign productions have played on British stages, the play, both in translation and in versions of Shakespeare's original, has also 'transmigrate[d]' to non-British stages. What 'self' does the crocodile show in Amsterdam in Dutch, or in Washington DC, and Stratford, Ontario, in trans-Atlantic English? And for that matter, how do Shakespeare's Romans 'play' on foreign stages?

In this chapter I look at Peter Zadek's 1994 German production and its reception, playing to British audiences at the Edinburgh Festival, where it was surtitled with Shakespeare's English text (while the actors were speaking a new German translation commissioned for the production). Then I consider Toneelgroep Amsterdam's *Antony and Cleopatra*, which I saw in Amsterdam in 2018 in one of the final performances of a production that had originated in 2007 and toured the world for the next decade, twice visiting London for limited runs. Both in London and in Amsterdam this *Antony and Cleopatra* was played in Dutch with surtitles that gave the English translation of the modern, demotic text the actors were speaking. Finally, I cross the Atlantic where, in Washington DC, and Stratford, Ontario, Shakespeare's play was performed in English but was nevertheless 'estranged' by cultural difference that naturalised *Antony and Cleopatra* to a local racial politics. Everywhere, I found the 'foreign' to be a problematic concept: 'foreign', it turns out, figures the gaze of Lepidus who can only see the crocodile with Roman eyes. I start, however in England, locating 'foreign Shakespeare' as an aspect of home-grown xenophobia.

## Imported crocodiles on English stages

It was Richard Findlater in the *New York Tribune* in 1930 who pronounced a legacy of doom upon foreign productions of *Antony and Cleopatra*, writing that while 'no English player ... can act Cleopatra', 'no actress of any other nation can speak it' (quoted in Neill 1994, 64).² He meant, of course, 'speak it' in English. That was certainly the message critics gave Theodore Komisarjevsky in 1936.³

Komisarjevsky had worked in British theatre since 1919 (having fled Moscow ahead of the Cheka). He became a citizen in 1932. In reviews, however, he was never naturalised. He was always 'the Russian' or 'the foreign director'. His Chekhov trilogy – plays virtually unknown in England at that time – performed in a tiny theatre in west London in 1926 astonished spectators and revolutionised acting for a generation that included John Gielgud and Peggy Ashcroft. This foreigner introduced foreign ideas and put them into practice on the English stage, theories he'd been absorbing, contesting and refining out of Stanislavsky over the past three decades. He introduced startling innovations, such as the notion of 'continuous acting'. English actors, he observed, lived 'their parts only when they speak'. On his stage, he kept every actor and actress 'continuously and simultaneously acting' (Rutter 2013, 119 and *passim*). Two further innovations also astonished: his acting company was an ensemble, and his texts, largely uncut (against the English practice of 'star' casting and scripts drastically cut to present the star in splendid isolation). His was an actor-centred theatre where 'the first place belongs to the actor' (Borovsky 2001, 289). He directed his actors to work not 'from outside' but 'from within' in order to absorb the 'atmosphere and background of the play', to locate a play's 'particular reality', the whole point of acting being to 'reveal the "philosophical meaning of the work"' (Borovsky 2001, 289). As Peggy Ashcroft recalled, the 'Russian magician' who was 'Komis' taught her things actors weren't learning in English drama schools: 'how to approach a part, how to analyse a role, how important it was to understand the director's whole conception of a play', and 'that the whole is more important than the individual part' (Borovsky 2001, 318). That is, he introduced 'director's theatre' *avant la lettre* into England in his notion of 'total concept' theatre, where the 'concept' was *his*: the design, costumes, music, lighting. 'Apart from the author', said the actor Anthony Quayle, 'his was the only other single creative brain' at work on a production (quoted in Borovsky 2001, 319).

When Komisarjevsky was summoned to Stratford-upon-Avon in 1932 he had never directed a professional Shakespeare production in England.⁴ Ironically, this 'foreign director' took up his guest appointment in the season in which the modernist-designed, newly constructed Shakespeare Memorial Theatre opened (the original *faux* gothic building having been destroyed by fire in 1929) with the Prince of Wales reminding the assembled crowd that 'Shakespeare was above all an Englishman' (quoted in Beauman 1982, 118). Komisarjevsky was being recruited to Stratford, the theatre's artistic director W. Bridges-Adams frankly told him, as a *'machine de guerre'* to put a rocket up the settled backside of English Shakespeare (quoted in Mennen 1979, 387). It was about time. Komisarjevsky found it staggering that 'Shakespeare is performed and staged here in the way [Russians] do it in the backwaters of Chukhloma' (quoted in Burt 2016, n. 15). And no wonder. Given that the Memorial Theatre festival organisers allotted only six rehearsals to each of the seven to ten plays that would feature in the season, the repertoire was heavy on revivals, some of them, deadeningly, reappearing year after year.

Komisarjevsky hit Stratford like 'an invasion' (Mennen 1979, 388). Declaring no interest in 'tradition' of the kind that hung around the Shakespeare Memorial Theatre in the form of the stuffed stag that was trundled on in countless *As You Like It*s or of 'digging artistic corpses out of cemeteries', not least because that 'business' has 'no value as far as the *living* theatre is concerned', he likewise registered 'his scorn for those upper-class English for whom the theatre was merely a "form of hospitality"' (Kenneth Tynan, *Evening Standard*, 30 June 1953). 'Ahead, ahead, ahead' of his time, as Quayle put it (Billington 1988, 52), he 'shook our drama like a dog worrying new juice out of an old bone', wrote Tynan. In 1932 his *Merchant of Venice*, the first rethinking of the play the since 1879, erased the version that had held sway ever since Henry Irving (and after him in Stratford, Frank Benson) played Shylock as the tragedy of the tricked and humiliated Jew. Komisarjevsky's *Merchant* was a romantic, but acerbic, comedy, played on a set that gave Venice as a wonky city of leaning towers, crooked houses, and bridges constructed on the back of too much prosecco, a city permanently in carnival mode, its citizens out of *commedia dell'arte*, its lads, said Komisarjevsky, 'dissipated, fast, bright young people like the crowd we have in London today' (quoted in Mennen 1979, 391). The casket scenes were played 'with heartless vivacity' (Berry 1983, 74).[5] The trial was conducted in a courtroom where the on-lookers were a mob wearing sheep masks.

The following season Komisarjevsky produced a *Macbeth* that removed the play from Scotland into a 'futurist, dehumanised setting'. This world, constructed entirely of aluminium, stood as 'an apt metaphor for the action, a metallic nightmare' but also conjured the recent past (Berry 1983, 75). The three hags who scoured the battlefield at the beginning, rolling bodies for booty, might have been scavengers looting the dead after Passchendaele. In 1935 came a *Merry Wives of Windsor* that trained Bridges-Adams's *'machine de guerre'* on home territory, on the most English of Shakespeare's comedies, and, with breathtaking irreverence, cut the play free from its Elizabethan moorings. 'For the setting', wrote the *Yorkshire Post* reviewer,

> imagine a series of ice-cream kiosks on a seaside pier each enamelled in a different tint ... Imagine ... balconies ... on ornate houseboats, with steps and companion ways of a millionaire's yacht. Then think of a highly decorated birthday cake of many tiers and conjure up the impressions of all the French farces with their multitude of doors and cubby holes that you have ever seen. (20 April 1935, quoted in Berry 1983, 77)

Falstaff looked like Franz Josef, his henchmen like Corsican bandits. The Wives wore Victorian crinolines. Ford was 'a villain out of Edwardian melodrama'. And the louts 'who took away the buck-basket were American express delivery men' (Berry 1983, 77). Throughout, music cued this deliciously eclectic and time-travelling romp as part melodrama, part Viennese opera. All of it worked as effectively as a wildly swinging wrecking ball to dismantle 'the Windsor of tradition' (Berry 1983, 77).

But Stratford's *enfant terrible* and iconoclastic 'prankster' (epithets given him at the time) did not get away with his innovations without protest (Berry 1983, 73). The *Birmingham Mail* headlined 'Shocks for Stratford' (20 April 1935), and the *Birmingham Gazette*, 'Russian Producer's Dominating Work' (19 April 1933). The *Daily Express* called his *Merchant* a 'miserable' failure of 'confusion': the company 'tried to make it Shakespeare, but Komisarjevsky made it Stratford's crazy night'. A glowing review in the *Spectator* ended by souring its praise with a dismissive facetious question, 'It's pretty, but is it Art?', an echo of what the *Daily Express* had earlier implied in that phrase, 'tried to make it Shakespeare' (26 April 1935). For such critics, it wasn't just tradition Komisarjevky was insulting; it was national pride. Unconcealed Russophobia (as Philippa Burt has found and analysed in terms of British jingoism and anti-immigration legislation in the decade after World War I, including the passing of the first British nationality law in 1914 (Burt 2016, 378–379)) emerges in numbers of reviews, like the one from the *Yorkshire Post* that sympathised with Shakespeare Memorial Theatre actors in *Wives* who 'were asked to carry out "business" and distort familiar characters in a manner that comes natural only to players such as those who people Russian Art Theatres'. 'This production', it concluded, 'should be renamed "The Merry Wives of Moscow"' (quoted in Burt 2016, 384). Even more ominous, given the direction European history was taking in the 1930s, were the sentiments that the actor Oscar Asche – not at the time in the Memorial Theatre company – set down in a letter to the *Stratford-upon-Avon Herald* in response to *The Merchant of Venice*, that 'Shakespeare's plays should be presented without freak scenery and costumes, the products of foreign minds' (quoted in Burt 2016, 384). Of comments like this, Ralph Berry understatedly remarks that 'One must, I think, postulate a deep-seated antipathy to the new as permeating the English theatre world of the 1930s' and, even more drily, that for chauvinists like Asche, 'The playing of Shakespeare was not to be revolutionized by a Russian émigré' (Berry 1983, 84).

Komisarjevsky could look to his box office to deflect such barbs, but their sting made him always aware of himself as the outsider.[6] He had no institutional standing in Stratford and was always the 'guest director' (Berry 1983, 73). And he saw himself working in a theatre culture that treated 'all continental stagings of Shakespeare with orgulous contempt'. Why? Because Shakespeare was 'an Englishman', and because Shakespeare productions were 'an English tradition'. So an *Englishman* might break with tradition and 'be forgiven. But a foreigner – never' (quoted in Burt 2016, 378).

All of this stands as back-story to Komisarjevsky's production of *Antony and Cleopatra* in 1936, which can in turn stand as backdrop to all subsequent 'foreign' productions of the play on the British stage. There is practically no record of this *Antony and Cleopatra*.[7] Unlike Komisarjevsky's seven other Shakespeares, all produced at the Shakespeare Memorial Theatre, this one was aimed at the commercial theatre in the West End, but its commercial ambitions failed dismally. It opened in Glasgow on 5 October, transferred to London's New Theatre on the 14th and closed after four performances.

Its first insult to critics was how it presumed to begin the action not with Shakespeare's 'Nay, but this dotage ...', but with 'a scene of small-scale comic bawdy – the Soothsayer's prophecies of Iras and Charmian' (Lamb 1980, 127). Critics took this as textual desecration rather than as the striking of a deliberately 'off' keynote to a 'whole conception' of the play that would go on to expose the 'tragedy' of Antony and Cleopatra as a grand but shabby game of human pitch and toss (though by offering this speculation on the maestro's 'conception', I'm second-guessing Komisarjevsky from a distance of eighty years). Komis, we remember, was 'ahead, ahead, ahead' of his time, as we see by fast-forwarding to future productions that unwittingly reproduced his innovations. In 2014 Gary Griffin's production in Stratford, Ontario, would open not with the soldiers but with Antony and Cleopatra rolling dice. In 1995 a 'scene of small-scale comic bawdy' would aptly have described Northern Broadsides's opening. Critics didn't much like Komisarjevsky's fixed, open-stage set with its 'blue-curtain backdrop' lit 'both alternately and consecutively' to represent 'the Mediterranean and the sky' (Lamb 1980, 127) – that is, precisely the set Glen Byam Shaw and Motley would present to such acclaim in 1953. How, wailed the critics in 1936, were the audience to know where they were if traverse curtains didn't open and close to mark the shifts between Rome and Alexandria, as they had done thirty-three times in the productions Robert Atkins staged in Stratford in the 1920s (Lamb 1980, 127, 130)?

But the main trouble was Cleopatra. As other English productions had done and would do, this one cast an American Broadway star in the role. But a star with a difference, because like Theodore Komisarjevsky, Eugenie Leontovich was a Russian émigré. Like him, she'd studied at the Moscow Art Theatre; like him, she'd fled Bolshevism, arriving in New York in 1922 and immediately embarking on a stage career. She'd been naturalised as a United States citizen in 1929. In 1935 London critics had found her wonderful – and perfectly comprehensible – starring alongside big-name Cedric Hardwicke in *Tovarich* at the Lyric. But that was a comedy about a pair of exiled Russian aristocrats-in-Paris who survive politics by going incognito as domestic servants. A year later, when the script was by William Shakespeare, critics found her 'unintelligible', capable of neither 'English' nor 'verse' (*Stage*, 22 October 1936; *The Times*, 15 October 1936). It was bad enough that this Cleopatra 'skipped around the stage, "clad", as her Antony recalled, "in the scantiest draperies and surmounted by a fireman's helmet adorned with large white plumes"' (quoted in Lamb 1980,

128) – a performance that might have predicted Mark Rylance's at the Globe in 1999. But what was 'beyond excuse' was Leontovich's 'slaughter of the matchless poetry which Shakespeare poured into *Antony and Cleopatra*' (Ivor Brown, *Observer*, 18 October 1936). Devastatingly, Charles Morgan reproduced that 'slaughter' for readers of *The Times*. He lampooned Leontovich's rendering of 'O withered is the garland of the war' (4.15.66) as 'O weederdee de garlano devar' (15 October 1936).

Almost nothing besides Morgan's parody is remembered of Komisarjevsky's production – except perhaps James Agate's keep-your-foreign-hands-off-Shakespeare review in the *Sunday Times*. He, who'd just five months earlier seen Komisarjevsky's *The Seagull* in the same theatre, with Ashcroft as Nina and Gielgud as Tregorin, and had called it 'endlessly beautiful', a 'triumph' (24 May 1936), now wrote a piece headlined 'Anton and Cleoptrova, a Tragedy by Komisphere'. 'I do not think', he intoned solemnly, 'that foreign producers, however distinguished, should permit themselves to take such liberties' – with, he didn't need to add, '*our*' Shakespeare (*Sunday Times*, 18 October 1936).

Strictly speaking, Komisarjevsky's *Antony and Cleopatra* doesn't belong in this chapter. It was hardly 'foreign'.[8] It played Shakespeare's script in English. Its actors, except for Leontovich, were English heavyweights: Donald Wolfit, Antony; Leon Quartermaine, Enobarbus; Margaret Rawlings, Charmian. Yet it was savagely estranged in reviews that could have been signed 'John Bull', a mark of residual cultural supremacism barely disguising its anxious English protectionism, a kind of scramble for identity in the interwar years as the British Empire crumbled and England clutched tightly the national icons that made England England.

Such chauvinism persisted. Echoes of the Leontovich lampoon were heard sixty years later in Kenneth Hurren's comments on the 'funny accent' of the Québécoise Angela Laurier, who played Puck in Robert Lepage's *A Midsummer Night's Dream* at the National Theatre in London 'with all the nimbleness of Inspector Clouseau' (*Mail on Sunday*, 12 July 1992). Two years after that, London critics hostile to the RSC's internationalist initiative, 'Everybody's Shakespeare', complained of having to sit through Shakespeare in German and Japanese. In translation, wrote Jeremy Kingston, productions 'come without the poetry' and so the actors 'must fall back on plot and fancy dress' (*The Times*, 1 November 1994). Charles Spencer in the *Daily Telegraph* admitted that while it might be 'stimulating to be exposed to different views on Shakespeare', he wasn't much stimulated. Indeed, there was 'something coals-to-Newcastle-ish about importing foreign-language productions to England: there we sit, following an edited version of the script in surtitles while listening to the performers delivering matchless poetry in an incomprehensible tongue' (30 October 1994). Incomprehensible, that is, to mono-lingual Brits and Euro-sceptics. The terms of the rebuttal to such 'little England-ism' that was published by the festival's organiser, Michael Kustow, are instructive. The critics were behaving 'with fury and betrayal at foreign fingerprints on the family heirlooms'. In post-Thatcher England where 'Everything else is turning to dust', they were howling, '"can't they at least leave our Shakespeare alone?"' (Kennedy 1997, 34–35; *Independent*, 19 November 1994).

But attitudes were also changing – or at least running neck-and-neck with the cultural xenophobes'. The Berliner Ensemble, whose visits the British Foreign Office had done everything to block in 1956 (unsuccessfully) and 1963 (successfully), was finally given official Home Office 'leave to appear' in 1965 following an avalanche of protest by the likes of Kenneth Tynan. The ensemble played a three-week season at the Old Vic of three Brecht classics – and Shakespeare's *Coriolanus*.[9] Now, a German import of Shakespeare was hailed as 'the revelation of the theatrical year'. Its politicised thrust (it 'sets out to destroy the legend of the hero') and Marxist rewriting of Shakespeare's ending simply 'confounded expectations': Caius Martius was 'broken, not by a mother's tears, but by the tidings that the people of Rome – and in Brecht's view that means the "workers" – were prepared to do battle with him, regardless of life or death'. This was Shakespeare 'not easily bettered anywhere' (Herbert Kretzmer, *Daily Express*, 11 August 1965).

A year earlier a 'World Theatre Season' (WTS) had been launched. It was the brain-child of (another) German émigré, the impresario Peter Daubeny, who back in 1956 had been pressured into withdrawing support for the Berliner Ensemble's first tour. Now working in association with the RSC at the Aldwych Theatre, Daubeny brought to London productions from around the world. They included from a South Africa still suffering under apartheid Welcome Msomi's Zulu reworking of *Macbeth*, *uMabatha*. Where WTS led, LIFT (London International Festival of Theatre) and WSF (World Shakespeare Festival) followed. The first, a still-running biennial event, in 1999 brought Romeo Castellucci's shocking *Giulio Cesare* to London, its Mark Antony played by a cancer patient who spoke 'Friends, Romans, countrymen' (3.2.74) through the blowhole of his post-tracheotomy neck. The second, attached to the London Olympics of 2012, staged among much else Belarus Free Theatre's provocative counter-cultural *King Lear*, an oblique satire on the tyrant back home whose 'democratic mandate' meant that this 'free' theatre company lives in permanent exile. Its Lear was a sexy brute who wore on one fist an elbow-length metal gauntlet and who divided his kingdom by dumping dirt into the skirts of his daughters that they lifted up like buckets – waddling away, 'pregnant' with dad's endowment. Such imported Shakespeare made home-grown Shakespeare look gutless.

Meanwhile, if since the 1960s the RSC had been working to John Barton's specification, that 'Shakespeare *is* his text' (quoted in Brown 1993, 24), textual editors like Stanley Wells had been troubling Barton's dictum by asking questions about exactly what constituted Shakespeare's text. And writers on performance like William Worthen, James C. Bulman and Barbara Hodgdon were challenging readers to think beyond Shakespeare's-words-as-text, to see the writer as also a 'wrighter' of physical performance texts that, released by enactment, would always exceed the scripted text. If, then, performance studies argued that 'a non-logocentric Shakespeare' was 'still ... Shakespeare' (Kennedy 1997, 33[10]), weren't the carping criticisms about 'foreign' Shakespeare swept away? If all performance requires spectators to 'read' Shakespeare without the words, does it matter if the words are in English – or German?

Enter Peter Zadek, yet another German émigré. Raised in England from 1933, the son of Jewish refugees, he later left Oxford University after only a year to work in theatre. His world premiere in 1957 of Jean Genet's *The Balcony* at the Arts Theatre, its status as a private club theatre allowing it to evade the Lord Chamberlain's censorship, which meant it could put on stage what would close down other theatres, was a measure of things to come. Genet attacked the director for turning the play's 'ideal eroticism' into 'vulgar sex acts'. The playwright was so enraged that he arrived 'on stage with a revolver in hand and threatened to shoot Zadek' if he didn't cancel the production (Engle 1993, 94). An *enfant terrible* in Komisarjevsky's mould, well on his way to establishing himself, like Komis, as a 'prankster', Zadek perhaps felt, like Komis before him, that his radical wings were clipped by the establishment that dominated English theatre in the 1950s: this English-speaking émigré who flatly stated in interviews that 'I am English' re-emigrated, returning to Germany in 1958 to establish himself over the next twenty years as among the most provocative of (West) Germany's post-war theatre-makers.[11]

By 1994, the year he directed *Antony and Cleopatra*, the Berlin wall was down, Germany was unified, and Zadek was one of the five artistic directors appointed to run the theatre Brecht had founded, the Berliner Ensemble, and specifically to represent the 'West' in the 'East'. (One wonders what sense terms like 'native' and 'foreign' made in the context of German reunification.) He had some dozen major Shakespeare productions behind him, all of them one-offs but consistent in their inconsistency: all of them contested the reigning idiom of German theatre production, which depended on 'scholarly interpretation and historical accuracy'. Zadek's object was 'instead to popularize the plays through comedy, grotesquerie, eroticism, brutality, and highly visual imagery' (Engle 1993, 94). An iconoclast and provocateur who frequently staged productions in vacant cinemas or factories, Zadek considered the 'element of provocation ... essential' to what he called *Volkstheater*, 'people's theatre', a theatre aimed at a new audience, at the '90 percent who do not attend theatre' (Engle 1993, 95). Like Komisarjevsky, Zadek scorned theatre as a form of 'hospitality'. Like Komisarjevsky's, Zadek's Shakespeares played to full houses. In 1972 his Shylock was 'a shouting, spitting Jew' from Nazi propaganda films, Portia, 'a furious Marlene Dietrich on the war-path in a Wild West film' (Engle 1993, 95). In 1974 Gloucester was blinded when his signature top hat was rammed down over his eyes. In 1976 Othello looked like a castaway from *Treasure Island*, in pirate boots, breeches and wide-brimmed hat over straggling shoulder length black hair, his face a grotesque smear of black Christy Minstrel greasepaint that made no attempt to hide the white actor beneath, blackface that rubbed off on Desdemona. She, dressed for Cyprus beaches, wore a bikini and carried a straw bag decorated with camel and pyramid motifs. Iago, a 'stud beach boy', concealed her handkerchief by shoving it down the front of his speedos, swelling the bulge into a fantasy of potency that only a rival male would credit (Engle 1993, 100). In 1977 costumes for *Hamlet* 'were a conglomeration of mixed periods and styles ranging from baroque to modern dress'. (One wonders if, as a lad, Zadek was ever taken to Stratford to see Komisarjevsky's Shakespeares.) Gertrude wore 'a crinoline skirt with red bull's eyes painted on her bare breasts', and the 'gay' couple, Rosencrantz and Guildenstern, turned out to be trans-women (Engle 1993, 98).

By the 1990s Zadek had outgrown his more outrageous 'frantic assembly' productions. *Antony and Cleopatra* was mellower.[12] Indeed, Dennis Kennedy called it comparatively 'rather tame' (Kennedy 1997, 34). But it had Zadek's signature written all over it. Like *Othello*, *Antony and Cleopatra* was minimal in concept and 'devoid of conventional set pieces' (Engle 1993, 100). Like *Othello*, it was backed by a three-metre-high curtain stretched the full width of the stage (that one red, this one the colour of desert heat haze). Partially tucked up teasingly like the hem of a skirt or pulled aside for big entrances, it allowed glimpses beyond into the deep recesses of the stage where (gesturing towards Brecht's practice) a notional life was going on elsewhere. Like *Othello* it played with the house lights fully up to dis-illusion the space, and it used scarcely any props: a few bentwood chairs (Enobarbus would stand on one of them to survey the rout at Actium), a cafe-style table, a collapsible tripod podium, a billiard table and (most substantially) a compact wooden scaffold structure on wheels. Zadek's Cleopatra would die not on a throne but as if slumped sideways after one too many aperitifs, her crown clattering to the ground and spinning slowly. As usual, Zadek commissioned a new, production-specific translation of Shakespeare's script (from his long-time partner and collaborator, Barbara Plessen, of which more later).[13] As usual, he cast actors he'd worked with before: Gert Voss (Antony) had been Zadek's Ferdinand in *The Duchess of Malfi* (1985); Shylock in a fully reimagined *Merchant* (1988) where the caricature Jew of the 1970s production was transformed into a suave, genial financier who could perform a mocking impersonation of that old-world grotesque; and Ivanov in Chekhov's comedy (1990). Eva Mattes (Cleopatra) had a history with Zadek going back twenty years, being first directed by him as Hedwig in *The Wild Duck* (1975) when she was nineteen, then as Desdemona (1976), Gertrude (1977) and Portia opposite Voss's Shylock in 1988.

This production was not without Zadek's signature anachronism. There was the lipsalve which the *Independent* reviewer found so remarkable. Roman breastplates next to service revolvers. Sounds of aeroplanes flying over the heads of soldiers carrying Roman *gladii*. The newly-weds in Athens (3.4), already on the marital skids, appeared in a scene set on a holiday beach – were they still on honeymoon? – with Antony in towel bathrobe, sand shoes, straw Borsalino and shades, and Octavia like a 1950s swimsuit pin-up posed with a giant plastic beach ball. But to look at, this production had a consistency not seen in Zadek's earlier, wildly eclectic post-modern mash-ups of visual, cultural, and political signifers. A source-book of 'Materialien zur Aufführung' published by the Berliner Ensemble to support the production documents what had informed the director's thinking.[14] It collects writing from the ancient world – Lucan, Horace, Virgil, Ovid – but even more from all sides of the Great War: Klemm, Adler, Hecht; Buzzi, Kavafis; Owen, MacLeish, Sandberg; T. E. Lawrence. And Bertolt Brecht (who, we remember, faced expulsion from school in 1915 for writing that 'Dulce et decorum est' was 'Zweckpropaganda' and later evaded conscription by enrolling in medical school). This book-of-the-production is illustrated with photographs dating from the Great War. They show soldiers dug into some European trench crowding around a honky-tonk piano. Soldiers in khaki shorts marching across some Egyptian desert. Soldiers in some winter-bound field shovelling frozen bodies into a mass grave. Winston Churchill in top hat and morning suit striding (down Whitehall?) alongside Admiral of the Fleet John Fisher.

It was this war, this Egypt campaign, this generation of donkeys-leading-lions that grounded Zadek's production, Wilfried Minks's design and Norma Moriceau's costumes. And it was the acerbic dissidence this war provoked at the time in the likes of schoolboy Brecht, followed by the profound disillusion experienced globally in its aftermath, that gave this *Antony and Cleopatra* its political edge. The suicidal folly of 1914–1918 troped Actium. The monstrous egotism of the politicians who made Europe (and beyond) a battleground troped the narcissism of Antony and Cleopatra.

This production opened with two legionnaires in desert khaki, pith helmets and knee socks grousing. 'Da kommen sie' turned attention upstage. The curtain was pulled aside, and behind it was revealed a full-blown orientalist fantasy. There stood Antony as Lawrence of Arabia in burnous, a Bedouin keffiyeh startlingly framing his European face. Cleopatra was a thing of gold. On her head the horned crown of Isis sat atop a mass of dark hair that tumbled to her waist. The skirt of her cloth-of-tissue dress, pleated tight à la Fortuny, shimmered like running water. When she was stretched out on the ground in her 'ready-for-love' pose, torso raised on arms set for pouncing, this costume turned her into a living Sphinx or human crocodile. (*Die Zeit*, 14 May 1994, reported a bored Antony 'looking past her ... body in disgust'.[15]) From the first, wrote Michael Coveney of the production in Edinburgh, 'sensuality' came off these two like 'rising damp' (*Observer*, 21 August 1994). Crowded behind them was a retinue stepped off a hieroglyph, heads covered in masks that made them Horus, Anubis, Seth. Watching the spectacle, Benjamin Heinrich in *Die Zeit* saw Zadek ironising his material from the outset:

> It's the end of the world and, what's worse, the end of a love. But Zadek's production doesn't seem to realise this. We're in the East, and the beds are soft, and so Zadek's end-of-the-world drama starts out like an oriental operetta. The stage is vast and empty ... There is a lot of light – on stage, in the auditorium, in the heads of the heroes.

He cued his readers: 'Think *Arabian Nights* and *Sons of the Desert* by Laurel & Hardy' (14 May 1994).

This opening showed an Egypt where the principals would always be performing – to their public, to each other, to themselves. Their 'conversation', said *Die Zeit*, was 'Whisper[ed] fast like conspirators, but also shamelessly, wantonly'. For while Antony and Cleopatra made 'their most intimate confessions', the entire stage was 'filled with public goings-on' (14 May 1994). In this oh-so-public private space, display would be calculated to meet the needs of the moment, to produce immediate effect. 'Performance' in the instant wasn't pretence, but the opposite. It was the only means these 'selves' had for making meaning. Foregrounding 'the vanity rather than the grandeur of these historical figures', wrote Michael Billington, Zadek gave his audience not 'a romantic epic celebrating doomed love' but a 'deeply political study' of characters 'who use war as a means of sustaining personal vendettas' (*Guardian*, 18 August 1994).

This opening, too, gave German-speakers their first taste of Plessen's translation. It was not, as Dennis Kennedy would later state, written in a 'highly colloquial and informal prose' (Kennedy 1997, 33); rather, it was a line-for-line verse translation that 'reads like Friedrich Schiller'.[16] Where Shakespeare's first word is 'Nay', Plessen's was 'Ja':

> Ja, die Affenliebe unsres Generals
> Geht zu weit. Seine schönen Augen
> Die beim Aufgebot der angetretnen
> Truppen funkelten wie gestählter Mars,
> Verdrehen sich jetzt, wenden den verliebten

>Blick an eine braune Stirn ... einer Zigeunerin.
>Da kommen sie ... Da, sieh nur hin. (1.1.1–6, 10, 18, 20)[17]

Quite deliberately employing archaic idioms and heightened language, this translation frequently used a lexicon that distanced it from contemporary German: *Wurm* instead of *Schlange*; *Knabe* not *Junge*. Some text couldn't or didn't translate. The German Cleopatra couldn't imagine any 'squeaking Cleopatra' 'boy[ing]' her 'greatness' because 'boy' can't function as a verb in German. At the end, Charmian didn't get her wonderfully enigmatic final line, 'Ah, soldier!' (5.2.327).[18]

That said, Kennedy's mistake about the writing is understandable given that, directed by Zadek, the *speaking* of Plessen's text everywhere undercut its formality. 'The lovers make conversation', wrote Benjamin Henrichs in *Die Zeit* (14 May 1994). So, too, the Roman politicians. Figured as English colonial rulers, they didn't 'declaim their lines'; they '[made] conversation', conversation that combined 'British nonchalance with German gloom'. Zadek's stage was 'filled with chatting, strolling bantering', with an 'incessantly carefree conversational tone' in which 'Shakespeare sounds like Shaw, Shaw like Ayckbourn' so that, for *Die Zeit*, the 'most audacious contradiction of the text is completely lost, i.e., that Cleopatra and Antony desperately try to halt the waning of their physical passions by means of deeply passionate speeches', a contradiction, it should be said, that is there in Plessen's text as well as in Shakespeare's (14 May 1994). Under Zadek's direction, such passionate speech-making fell victim to myth-destroying chat.

From the point of view of performance, what is perhaps most impressive about Plessen's translation is that it cut practically nothing, Charmian's final line excepted. Nor did it mark up the play into acts and scenes, but, like the Folio, delivered a continuous text. (In Plessen's published edition, the 'through line numbering' (TLN) ends at line 3637, one line later than in the Folio.) More staggeringly, the Ensemble played what no English company had ever done, the play's full text. Zadek kept his audiences in the theatre for just under four hours. With no interval.

But reviewers didn't complain. 'Light, fast, witty, ironic' and 'stripped of its usual archaeological clutter', the play raced by 'on the wings of Mercury', telling a 'queasily anti-heroic' story by 'emphasising those elements that undercut the lovers' word-drunkenly glorified estimate of themselves' (*Guardian*, 18 August

1994). To one reviewer, this *Antony and Cleopatra* had more in common with *Troilus and Cressida*, that disillusioned play of 'Lechery, lechery, wars and lechery' (5.2.201–202), than with earlier productions of itself (*Independent*, 19 August 1994).[19]

Billington in the *Guardian* saw Mattes's Cleopatra as 'less the grandiose Egyptian queen than a restless nympho who eyes up every man she sees and lives in a state of deluded fantasy about her affair with Antony'. Like Shakespeare's Cressida as Ulysses describes her, this Cleopatra was a 'wanton' whose 'spirits' looked out 'At every joint and motive of her body' (4.5.57–58). Her Egyptian wardrobe was a fashion parade of stunningly coloured and exquisitely appliqued gowns in floating diaphanous fabrics that revealed the naked body beneath. Her court, 'rampant with the most pleasurable idleness', hot with 'oriental fever', smacked of the harem (*Die Zeit*, 14 May 1994). Her 'girls' (Charmian: Deborah Kaufmann; Iras: Gaby Herz), who would 'belly dance for the triumphalist potentates', wore see-through harem trousers and midriff-baring tops (*Observer*, 21 August 1994). Backing them, from a distance, a clutch of male minders in robes and turbans – those 'eunuchs' specified in Shakespeare's (and Plessen's) opening stage direction? – kept the women's antics under surveillance (Mardian: Nino Sandow; Servants: Thomas Wendrich, Christoph Müller). For these Egyptians, Actium was 'largely an excuse for dressing up': it was clear how completely she'd prevailed with Antony to 'fight … by sea' (3.7.28) when Mattes's Cleopatra came on in an *haute couture* version of naval officer's uniform complete with captain's peaked hat, her look-alike 'girls' tilting bowlers on their heads while they ogled Antony's soldiers during a pre-mobilisation press call that they treated as cabaret. Given more to 'infinite caprice' than 'variety', this Cleopatra's performances-in-the-instant were literally uninterpretable (*Guardian*, 18 August 1994). When, exiting to Actium, she stopped to kiss the old campaigner who'd objected to the folly of fighting by sea, did that kiss tell him he had nothing to worry about? *Or the opposite?*[20]

In the end, this Cleopatra achieved a certain dignity. If earlier she'd wasted time playing shuttlecock, if earlier she'd been so petty that she couldn't pronounce Octavia's name, if earlier 'at a crucial time in their fortunes' she'd indulged Antony's 'cackling prank' of 'spitting wine in virtuosic arcs' into her mouth, at the end, invested by her girls in a flowing white robe in place of the scarlet number she'd worn to her (failed) seduction of Octavius, she achieved 'an impressive, hushed majesty in her suicide' (*Independent*, 19 August 1994). Even so, in Zadek's 'myth-revising production', she had nothing more than a cafe chair for a throne and, dying, couldn't even keep possession of her crown, 'awry' or not. For *Die Zeit*'s reviewer, a production that started as 'oriental operetta' 'taking a holiday from Shakespeare', then 'halfway through … instead of falling for oriental fever', sent Shakespeare 'to Tuscany for therapy', finally wound up in some kind of fairy-tale 'Vienna' in the hands of 'Shakespeare, the inspired rake' with that 'long epilogue that belongs to no one but the queen' (14 May 1994). For him, Mattes was 'miscast' as Cleopatra, but was 'the most beautiful miscast imaginable'. She was rather 'the confidante, the good companion than the woman you must flee to prevent her from swallowing you alive'. But she was a woman who found it 'impossible to pretend' since all of her performances, what others called her 'state of deluded fantasy', were enactments of real present selves. So now she played 'Cleopatra's death not as a high priestess of Eros and Death but in all its fairy-tale seriousness':

> There is no reason to cry, for love will triumph in the end: Cleopatra is not going to Rome. The queen places the snake on her breast. (*Die Zeit*, 14 May 1994)

As compelling as reviewers found Mattes's Cleopatra, for them the stunning revelation was Gert Voss's Antony. Voss was a big man, a highly tactile actor, expressive in both mobile facial and detailed physical gesture, capable of absolute stillness and then a sudden move that tripped an emotional switch, flipping jocularity into menace, a conversation into a grilling. He was also a brilliant mimic – sending up, not least, himself. He can be seen in filmed clips of *Richard III* where he is a palimpsest of Shakespeare's twisted butcher overlaid with a grotesque parody of Adolf Hitler. A sequence from *Othello* in 3.3, the so-called 'seduction' scene, shows *him* seducing Iago, sitting knee to knee opposite Iago, enticing him, drawing out revelation, then suddenly kicking one foot after the other onto Iago's shoulders, gripping his throat in a scissor lock.[21] Playing Antony, he achieved what, historically, had eluded English actors. He played both sides of the Roman coin, Mars and Gorgon, Antony great and Antony ruined.

If he'd been kitted out like some character in an oriental operetta to star in that over-blown spectacle that opened this *Antony and Cleopatra*, minutes later he'd changed. Still wearing his Yasser Arafat head gear but now in a three-piece suit evidently shipped from Savile Row in London, its double-breasted waistcoat the kind worn by King George V, he seemed 'suddenly shattered and withered. Too much intercourse – and far too much alcohol'. He lounged 'sullenly' in a deck chair 'taking comfort from a hip flask', 'old and bitter', 'tired of the endless feasting and lechery'. He'd 'started lying to Cleopatra'. When Enobarbus probed his commitment ('the business you have broached here / Cannot be without you …' (1.2.180–181)) Voss's Antony 'shrug[ged], suck[ed] on his cigarette, then just chat[ted] the big words away'. Fixed permanently to his face was a 'spellbound idiot's smile' (*Süddeutsche Zeitung*, quoted in *Der Spiegel*, 16 May 1994). For this sex-weary machine – too often bellows, too often fan – 'A small battle' would have been 'rather restorative'. 'Indifferently, he listen[ed] to news of the goings-on in the Roman Empire, and at the same time' was 'annoyed at his own indifference' (*Die Zeit*, 14 May 1994). One moment Gorgon, the next, Mars.

His costume changes tracked his personal progress through history. He met Caesar (Veit Schubert) in Rome in his Savile Row suit (without the head gear) – but he was distinctly down-dressed against the Romans' pinstripes, tails, top hats and gloves. Marrying Octavia (Gaby Herz), he put on the white tie, boiled shirt and toff's hat of the Establishment; in Athens, the beach wear of the playboy; back in Alexandria, khakis, a naval overcoat and his Arafat headdress. Before his last stand – the battle itself would be presented as an infantile game, the rival armies marching in opposite directions past each other across the forestage like mechanical toy soldiers around a clock face – his costume anticipated the vacuity of the show he'd be putting on. Dressing for war (when the production first opened in Vienna) to look once again like T. E. Lawrence, Voss's Antony had 'makeup and powder applied' as if he were getting ready for 'a TV appearance' (*Die Zeit*, 14 May 1994). In Edinburgh, 'Egyptian' Antony layered himself with Western kit, dressing himself in 'breast plate, binoculars, and lipsalve in front of vanity mirrors as if creating his own legend' (*Independent*, 19 August 1994) – or perhaps as if 'debunking his own myth in a spirit of despairing, reckless jocularity' (*Guardian*, 18 August 1994).

As *Die Zeit* observed, if 'Every death is a tragedy', 'every hero's death is also a farce' (14 May 1994). Magnificently, Voss captured both for Antony. Swinging between the 'lover as a cynic, the hero as a ruin', he proceeded to 'illuminate and corrode the colourful, bright images' that had been the garish human currency of Alexandria. One moment he was tossing brandy into the open wounds on Thidias's scourged back; the next, collapsing in self-disgust at such brutishness: 'he squats babbling, pointing his gun at his head, the image of a desperate man, more womanish than any woman' (*Die Zeit*, 14 May 1994).

Voss's Antony needed a good death. He didn't get it. Failing even to fall on his sword in 'the high Roman fashion' (4.15.91), he lay on his back, 'wailing, his weapon ... in his belly rising up like a ridiculous phallus' (*Die Zeit*, 14 May 1994). Yet even the 'grim farce' of his lifting into the monument contributed to the awed sense reviewers had of the tragedy of this Antony's ending. Voss, wrote Paul Taylor, took spectators 'deep inside the frustrations of having Antony's complicated, fatally self-indulgent nature, so you feel that, deep down, he too pays the price of even his pettiest actions' (*Independent*, 19 August 1994). Like Macbeth, like Othello, Voss's Antony was a man who realised 'too late, precisely what he has lost' (*Guardian*, 18 August 1994).

That Antony died tragically, however, did not let him or this play off Zadek's anti-romantic, anti-sentimentalist hook. The one scene that epitomised this production, that condensed its anti-heroic political content, that burned onto spectators' retinas, featured neither Antony nor Cleopatra. Rather, it was the scene that's so frequently cut, set in Syria (3.1); the one that Shakespeare butts up against the drunken revels on Pompey's galley (2.7). In it, Ventidius has slain King Orodes's son in a tit-for-tat killing. Here, while a lone harmonica played in the distance, Ventidius sat casually leaning against the struts of a wooden scaffold, chatting to the son's corpse, holding an entirely redundant revolver to the head that swung only inches away from his own face. Filthy, bloody, mutilated Pacorus had been strung up by his ankles from the apparatus that would later serve as Cleopatra's monument. Antony, spectators might have reflected later, had always been heading to the same end.

### Foreign crocodiles on foreign stages: take 1

Ending his review of Zadek's *Antony and Cleopatra*, Michael Billington noted that he'd 'often argued that Shakespeare in a foreign tongue' became 'an analogue to the original that gives the director new freedom'. Zadek, he wrote, had used 'that freedom brilliantly.' And now Billington dropped the bombshell: 'After this startling, radical, Brechtian re-appraisal, it will be hard to go back to traditional productions in which the ageing lovers are accepted at their own self-satisfied evaluation' (*Guardian*, 18 August 1994). Thus Richard Findlater from 1930 was swept clean away. Now, it appeared, *only* foreigners could do justice to *Antony and Cleopatra*.

Billington wasn't wrong. Over the next dozen years, RSC productions in 1993, 1999, 2002 and 2006 had nothing at all 'radical' to say about *Antony and Cleopatra*, their only 'startling' contribution some dire miscasting of the principals. Then, in 2007, an extraordinary theatrical event opened in Amsterdam. Radical? Startling? Ivo van Hove's *Romeinse Tragedies* recalibrated the words in a production that would continue to tour for more than a decade.

Played by the Toneelgroep Amsterdam, led by van Hove at the head of a permanent ensemble (twenty-two actors in 2007; twenty-three in 2018), the *Romeinse Tragedies* began life at their home theatre, Stadsschouwburg Amsterdam, before being released into the world on a tour that would finish up back in Amsterdam at the Theater Carré in 2018. The same actors would be playing the same parts they'd created eleven years earlier.[22] A trilogy, the *Tragedies* played Shakespeare's *Coriolanus*, *Julius Caesar* and *Antonius & Cleopatra* in sequence, in Dutch, with English surtitles,[23] with no intervals, in five hours and forty-four minutes – precisely. A hand-out given to spectators with their programmes clocked events against the playing time, which would also be clocked by timepieces running on stage, starting at '00min' with 'War' in *Coriolanus*. Caius Martius's 'Death' came at '88min'. Cassius was quizzing Brutus at '90min'. The assassins hit Caesar at '138min'. The funeral orations came at '153min'. Twelve minutes after Brutus's death at '185min', Antony was in Egypt, then in Rome at '211min'. Actium was fought at '244min', the final battle, '275min'. Antony died at '317min', and Cleopatra at '340'. On tour – the *Tragedies* went twice to London's Barbican, in 2009 and 2017, on both occasions given only three performances, all of them sold out – surtitles provided a direct English translation of the colloquial Dutch script the actors were speaking. The only Shakespeare spoken was incidental: 'My salad days, / When I was green in judgement, cold in blood' (1.5.76–77); 'The bright day is done / And we are for the dark' (5.2.192–193). For the rest, the surtitles flashed up lines like 'Do not anger me. Be silent'; 'Even wild boars have less foam on their snouts'; 'How are you, my women? Cheer up!'[24] Vast swathes of Shakespeare were compressed almost to sound bites: 'I dreamed of an emperor, Mark Antony. / Oh, for another dream like that, that I might see such another man! / With a face like heaven / his voice, the music of the spheres. / Do you think there was or could be a man such as I dreamed of?'

This was Shakespeare for a tech-and-media savvy 'Generation Y', not a rendering of a text but an interactive event, a live expression of installation art, immersive theatre with a capital I; a project, said the *Volkskrant* (quoted in publicity) that showed Toneelgroep Amsterdam writing 'a new and impressive chapter in their ongoing quest for a new theatrical language'.

Like the two plays before it, *Antonius & Cleopatra* was dressed in suits and ties and stiletto heels and located in something that looked like today's office world, the crowded open-plan floor of the BBC in London, for instance, or any high-end tech company doing global business. But where the first two plays repeatedly set up scenes as press calls in front of banks of microphones (Caius Martius v. Tribunes; the funeral orations), *Antonius & Cleopatra* occupied the sort of company lounge space where potential clients or contributors are schmoozed. There were sofas of the squared-off IKEA kind. Armchairs (ditto). Work stations. Potted plants. LED screens. Monitors. On the back wall, clocks told the time in Athens, Rome, London (but weren't synchronised; were out of kilter). Cameras (roving and stationary) that could zoom in on individual faces and relay them to monitors that displayed them in screen-filling close-up. Some of the screens flashed up silent film images of current events from around the world (footage of some desert warfare somewhere; interviews with Donald Trump, Hillary Clinton, David Cameron) bizarrely intercut with a children's cartoon. There was no single focus, no single point of view; a welter of the extraneous insisted on attention. (This barrage of the undifferentiated, the random: was it equipping a polity with information that needed sifting, ordering, prioritising for action? Or in its sheer overwhelmingness, randomness, was it mocking democracy, rendering our political impotence as information over-kill? Did it tell us we were living now in a world of mass, undifferentiated mediatised content, where intervention was hopeless? Did the flat-screen presentation of this 'news' flatten reaction, betray our ability to achieve perspective, to discriminate the superficial from the profound?) Overhead, a rolling strip of news-feed gave headlines: the day's football scores;

progress in the Brexit talks; another immigrant boat capsized in the Mediterranean.

The set's oddest feature was an apparatus placed upstage, centre. It looked like a version of the screening devices airport passengers walk through, made of high Perspex panels set parallel to each other; but instead of a walkway between them, it had a low roll-out surface that could shunt forwards and backwards. Spectators had seen its use in the earlier two plays, a bizarre souvenir of the ancient Greek theatre, a modern *ekkyklema*. Shunted out, it was where the bodies were dumped and the wounded went to die. Not laid out. Not ceremonially presented. But left as if thrown from a car by mafiosi or tangled in a foetal knot like a joke after-birth. Whereupon the shunt shifted back into place while overhead a suspended camera took a screenshot of the corpse. Like a mug shot or police forensics photo, the grainy image was relayed to the projection screen that hung the full width of the proscenium above the stage, captioned underneath on a red LED display with the deceased's name, d.o.b., d.o.d. Shockingly magnified, this death 'shot' looked like the crude images of atrocities that cover the front pages of today's tabloid press. Kate Kellaway in London saw what van Hove was up to, trafficking in the topical. There was 'no mistaking the buzz', she wrote in the *Guardian*; 'This production turns Shakespearean tragedy into news' (26 March 2017).

But it also located tragedy as news self-consciously *staged*, made in a theatre where the materials of production were smack in front of spectators, with the narrative constantly reminding them that it was exactly that. 'Ten minutes until the death of Antony', announced one monitor. 'Scene change 5 minutes', another told the audience, instantly flashing up a digital clock counting down the minutes. If 'office world' occupied the clearly marked-out central stage space where (almost like a stage upon a stage) playing spaces for individual scenes were established, 'theatre world' flanked it, framed it. There was no 'off stage' in this theatre. Rather, running the depth of the stage, along the wall stage right, a notional/actual/ functional 'backstage' was set up as if just 'off stage' in a row of dressing room make-up stations, littered with cosmetics, tattered scripts, empty coffee cups. When actors were 'off', out of character but still fully visible, they retreated to check themselves in mirrors, glug water, eat a banana, have their lipstick or hair repaired by the make-up crew. Mirroring this visible 'backstage' and running the depth of the stage down the stage left wall, a notional/actual/

functional 'front of house' was set up: a bar where spectators could buy beer and crisps as the performance continued. And they did.

Creating a totalising theatre space where 'front' and 'back' of house had no meaning, this production went a step further. It exploded the separation between 'stage' and 'auditorium'. Half an hour into *Coriolanus* when the first 'Scene change 5 minutes' appeared on the monitors and the action paused as stage crew got busy rearranging the furniture, a voice on a Tannoy told spectators they could leave their seats, take a break – or come up on stage. (In Amsterdam, this announcement produced a thunder of feet as the balconies emptied.) After that, until the final half hour of *Antonius & Cleopatra*, spectators were free to make the stage space their own: to move about, put themselves inside the action on the sofas next to the actors where their faces became part of the media show, watch the action from different positions (live; screened), post comments on social media, visit the bar, take time out or, indeed, watch the whole thing from out front. In van Hove's theatre, the audience doubled as Shakespeare's 'Romeinse' crowds. The people *were* the people, a conceit, as Lyn Gardner observed, that took 'new meaning' in the contemporary political world 'in light of the rise of populist movements across the US and Europe'. Van Hove's 'masterstroke' was to cut 'all the scenes depicting war'. Instead, the action was 'punctuated by the cacophonous clash of drums and cymbals to denote the conflicts that endlessly ensue from the strutting and decisions of leaders – mostly men in suits. It's the audience that is cast in the role of the Roman citizens' (*Guardian*, 19 March 2017). In *WhatsOnStage* Matt Trueman saw van Hove and his permanent collaborator, the designer Jan Versweyveld, using 'the semiotics of auditoria to make meaning, asking us to examine not just what we're watching, but how we're watching it':

> Turning us, the theatre audience, into the play's people, Rome's citizens, they fuse the real and the fictional space together ... It matters that the doors are open and that we can come and go as we please. This isn't a separate space, but a continuation of the world.[25]

The theatre itself, then, troped the politics it was performing, spatially blurring the physical depth of field spectators normally experience in a theatre that keeps its 'fiction' separate from its 'real life'. Like those flat television screens that literally flattened spectators' ability to put things in perspective, the theatre rendered the *Romeinse Tragedies*'s in-yer-face politics shockingly superficial. In *Antonius & Cleopatra* those politics were sexual. In the opening beat of the third play in the trilogy, in our first sight of Egypt, Charmian (Marieke Heebink) was insistently groping one of Antonius's men for prophetic knowledge, for reserved knowledge, *mystified knowledge* of 'secret things' – which turned out to be the name of the future husband she'd be cuckolding. Meanwhile, Antonius (Hans Kesting) lay sprawled on a sofa in his boxer shorts, scanning through images on an iPad propped on his belly, oblivious to the actual news around him.

Spectators had seen this man, at about 'min. 170', crumpled in front of the lectern where he was supposed to be delivering Caesar's funeral oration. He'd been a furious ball of rage and grief. He'd stammered into the microphone, stopped, tried again, stopped again. Then he'd thrown away his prepared speech and started to talk from the heart, words that roused Rome to mutiny and put him back on his feet. Now, in Alexandria, he'd been laid – literally. Hearing news from Rome, though, he began struggling into trousers, pulling on a jumper, shoving sockless feet into shoes. (Those sockless feet would be indicative: in Rome, Caesar and the rest were dressed in Armani; Antonius would look like some Venetian gigolo.) He was nearly dressed when Cleopatra (Chris Nietvelt) appeared, slicing through his preparations with verbal acid: 'I read in your glance that there is good news'. She was a long tall sally, stringy, not voluptuous, a red-head in a clingy strappy dress, but fascinating in her volatile movements, folding her long, long legs under her like an articulated stick insect or flinging them over the back of a sofa in a gesture of contemptuous dismissal, then leaping up, collapsing, attacking, retreating. To get his exit, Antonius had literally to capture her in an embrace. But then this man who'd seconds earlier stopped Enobarbus's raunchy comment ('No vulgar jokes') shoved his hand up Cleopatra's skirts. His fingers found no resistance. And as he made his final 'political' speech ('Our separation does not divide us …') he was pleasuring her to orgasmic climax – undercut when he yanked out his hand with a loud vocalised 'POP'. He exited to Rome, 'doing' the Egyptian, with struts and hand gestures like Wilson and Keppel in the 1930s.

The playing out of the suicidal sexual politics of this relationship was probably something spectators had seen before in *Antony and Cleopatra*. Here, what gave it edge was the way, by comparative viewing alongside television footage, it was made topical. As the television screens demonstrated, just such narcissists, just such celebrities and ethical bankrupts whose vacuity is covered with the glamorous veneer of mega-wealth are manipulating today's political institutions. Thus the same sort of egotism and devastating narcissism Zadek had located in the politics of 1916 were found to be alive and well – and still in the driving seat – in the consumerist celebrity politics of a hundred years later. What was new and impressive here was the way van Hove used his cameras, monitors and screens to multiply the frame of such political reference, to show those 'personal' politics (the fiction extrapolated to 'real life') impacting other lives – and global politics. Thus in Rome, while Octavius Caesar (the role re-gendered: Maria Kraakman's Caesar was always 'she') bartered her sister away in a marriage to Antonius in a scene that was set on the downstage playing space, the hand-held roving camera found Octavia (Hélène Devos) sitting anonymously upstage among the crowds on the sofas. A close-up produced her image on multiple screens. Her red curly hair was pinned up in an explosive knot. She was chewing gum and reading a fan-zine, its cover a lurid pink. The camera zoomed in even further on her face as her ears pricked up, hearing that word 'sister', to make her listen, all ears, to the negotiations about her future that spectators were also watching, played out 'in person' downstage. Then she was brought forward, threaded through the onstage crowd to meet Antonius in the flesh and to make the marriage. The camera looked at him looking at her. She was just a kid. Antonius stared goofily into the lens in close-up. Did the old geezer's comic expression register 'I can't believe my luck!' or something more cynical about this clueless fresh-faced girl? Was his brief comment to her, 'I haven't always behaved well, but in future I will play by the rules', reassuring, a wedding vow? He turned instantly back to business: 'We must make haste and take on Pompey'. Exiting the scene, he was well off the playing area when he came running back – he'd forgotten his bride. Now he tugged her away by the hand. She kept chewing her gum.

All experience in our contemporary world, this production suggested, was simultaneously lived in real time and mediated, turned into virtual experience for mass consumption and vicarious affect. That we could see both frames playing out simultaneously in this theatre only intensified the impact of this existential duplicity. When the scrub-faced eager-beaver Thidias (Harm Duco Schut) was caught paddling Cleopatra's palm, Antonius's violence was 'virtualised', taken out on the spruce lad's classy briefcase. Earlier, delivering his treacherous 'get-out-of-jail-free' speech to Cleopatra ('They know that you have embraced Antony out of fear rather than love'), Thidias was sitting opposite her on a sofa. Between them, perched on the back of the sofa, sat Charmian, knees primly clamped together, eyes fixed on Thidias, a clipboard on her lap, ready to take notes. When this corrupt ambassador made his offer ('What is your desire? Caesar begs the favor of granting your wish …'), Charmian swung her entire body to stare at Cleopatra, whose long, drawn-out 'O' was the sound of political thinking going on in a top-notch political brain. Twice Cleopatra offered her hand to Thidias, then snatched it away, talking about conditions, before allowing him to grasp it. When she finally conceded her hand, kisses that first were courtly got hotter and hotter, Thidias evidently experiencing something like oral sex. Caught in the act, his expression was merely curious when he looked up to hear Antonius ordering 'whip him'. There was no dragging away, no ripping off of costume, no bloody back or sign of flogging written on the lad's body. Instead, the camera was fixed in close-up on his face, seeing the growing terror registered there as Antonius's threats entered his brain while his precious briefcase was hurled across the space and kicked. Watching the monitor watching this face was like watching a terrorist snuff film.

To tell the story-beyond-the-text that van Hove, Versweyveld and their percussionists, camera operators, technicians and actors wanted to tell, it mattered, as Matt Trueman put it, that the theatre's 'doors' were 'open', that this stage was 'a continuation of the world', that the narratives it was hosting spilled into, were being lived in, the 'real' world. These ideas were literally registered in the death of Enobarbus (Bart Slegers). He'd deserted Antonius. Now sitting on Caesar's sofa, he heard Caesar's order to 'put the deserters in the front line' against Antonius in the next day's battle 'so that it will seem that Antony spends his fury upon himself'. He'd learned that Antonius had 'sent on all [his] treasure with more gifts added'. When he'd retorted to the messenger, 'I give it to you', the messenger's rebuke, 'Don't mock, Enobarbus. Your emperor remains a generous god', had stunned him into soul-destroying remorse: 'I am alone the villain of the earth'. This was grief, guilt and humiliation that couldn't be contained, and when this Enobarbus said he'd 'go seek a ditch to die in', he headed for that destination, leaping off the stage, running through the auditorium, across the lobby and out into the Amsterdam night, followed by the cameraman, who filmed both him, as he died in words and close-ups relayed to the monitors back on stage, and passers-by on the street who, inhabitants of the 'real' world, paused to watch what they couldn't know was a fiction and had no way of making sense of except as 'real' anguish. Should they do something? Intervene? Nobody did. This Enobarbus died alone in an Amsterdam gutter.

Shortly thereafter, Antony needed to die. And he tried to, wounded, groping towards the *ekkyklema*, attempting to clamber up on it so his end would be fixed in that final screen shot. But he wasn't dead. So he just sprawled there, a grim joke, while Cleopatra frantically talked to him through the Perspex panel. Then finally, *finally* (as if operating like some *deus ex machina* to put him out of his misery) the LED screen displayed its latest capture: Antonius 'shot' dead (see 8.1).

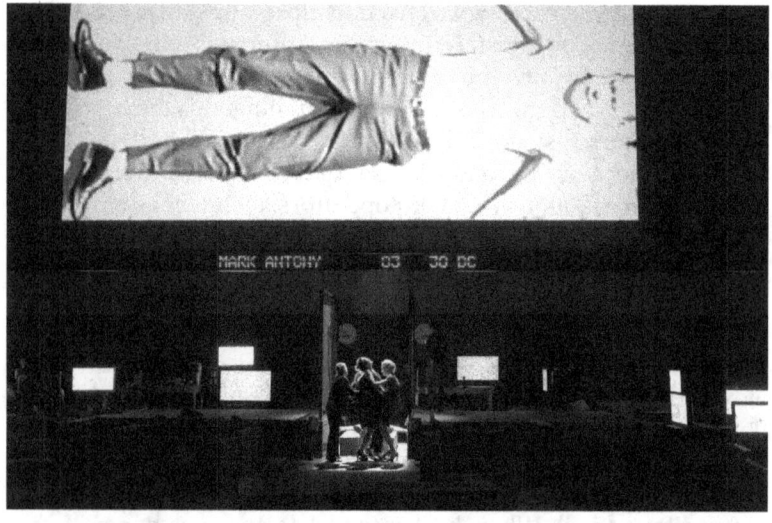

8.1 'Most noble of all men, will you die? / Do you care nothing about me? Must I remain here in this dull world / that without you is no better than a pig sty?' Photo capture of Antonius's corpse (Hans Kesting) projected onto video screen (above) while Cleopatra (Chris Nietvelt) collapses into the arms of Charmian (Marieke Heebink) and Iras (Frieda Pittoors).

Cleopatra's death re-performed the queen's constitutional voluptuousness. She did a long *pas de deux* with a langorous boa constrictor whose windings and turnings troped her wantonness, her 'infinite variety', her 'becomings', her final 'becoming' perhaps becoming what Antonius had made her, his 'serpent of old Nile'. Once she'd handed her out-sized 'asp' to Charmian, she stretched herself alongside Antony. The overhead camera flashed. The red LED display documented the event. She'd out-manoeuvred Caesar. The evidence: her post mortem photograph; d.o.b., d.o.d. Caesar was left looking on at Cleopatra's death, beating angrily on the Perspex panel while the medical crash team she had on call in case of emergency swarmed in, trying to resuscitate the corpse by applying cardiac shock paddles to her chest. Like all the deaths before hers, Cleopatra's death said nothing about heroics, apotheosis, mythography.

Bang on '334 min.', the *Romeinse Tragedies* ended. The soundtrack cut in. Bob Dylan sang 'The times they are a' changing', reprising the track that had opened the show, where it had played over a Dylan quotation projected onto the overhead screen: 'God, I'm glad I'm not me'. Then, that seemingly random comment was uninterpretable – even if you knew he'd made it after reading about himself in a newspaper interview where he'd confessed to smoking eighty cigarettes a day. Now, at '334 min.', for those who could retrospectively caption it, that quotation returned under pressure of the song lyrics as a joke about the experience of the past '334 min.', about whether, battered with relentless mediatised 'news', any of us could discriminate the 'real' from the 'virtual', the actual 'self' from the 'reported', the 'I' from the 'me', the superficial from the profound. How could any of us know the 'truth'? Was there any 'truth' to know?

As the audience gave a standing ovation, and the actors took it, overhead on the projection screen a series of questions started scrolling. There would be a hundred of them, questions that had arisen in rehearsal and that now became the last words spectators took away. The text was projected white on black, like rolling film credits:

Can politics change a person's opinion?

Should a politician tell the masses what they want to hear?

Are the masses susceptible to reason?

Is a politician allowed to be irrational?

Is the state responsible for all of its citizens?

How far should one go out of love for one's country?

How far should one go out of love for democracy?

How far should one go out of love for one's values?

Based on how politicians have organised the world, do you know how to act?

Is everything communication?

All over the theatre spectators stood and read. Numbers of them held up mobile phones, capturing these rhetorical 'credits' in digital images, perhaps to archive a mnemonic of the political thinking the *Romeinse Tragedies* had provoked them to; perhaps to prompt later postings on social media. Here, then, was the 'Generation Y' version of Glasgow's experience at the Citz in the 1970s, where 'The plays never "finished" when the lights went down because the foyer and streets outside were always alive with discussion ... and those conversations persisted for ages' (see Chapter 5). 'Live' discussion yields in the digital age to virtual conversation; bodies on the street in three dimensions yield to flat-screen imaging in two.

Back in March 2017 when van Hove's show was making its second swing through London, Matt Trueman had called the *Roman Tragedies* 'the most significant piece of theatre in Britain over the past decade'. But what was, what *is* its significance? For Trueman (in slightly hyperbolising mode) that significance had everything to do with the director's and designer's spatial imagination, the way their productions 'exist on stages, not on sets, not in settings ... [I]f van Hove and Versweyveld have had any one impact, it is this: the two of them have taught artists to use theatres as site-specific spaces'.[26] Here, Trueman touches on what has always been fundamental to the van Hove–Versweyveld partnership, work that for them took its first form in Antwerp in the 1980s 'with happenings', with 'pieces' made 'in old houses and factories'. 'From the beginning', said Versweyveld, 'we asked how we relate to the audience', a question the creative team has never stopped asking

(*Guardian*, 18 August 2015). It's as if the aims and methods and iconoclasm of Zadek's German *Volkstheater* in the 1960s had been reborn in Amsterdam two decades later.

Certainly, however, significance lies too in the creative organisation van Hove established when he was appointed artistic director of Toneelgroep Amsterdam in 2001: the sacred Grail and scarlet pimpernel of British theatre, the acting ensemble. The actors who make up Toneelgroep Amsterdam's permanent company comprise a 'pool of acting talent which enables us', says the group's 2018 programme, 'to develop distinctive and daring productions' and 'to continue reviving our successful productions at regular intervals'. The actors' hunger for new work is satisfied in the continuous stream of new projects the company takes on, much of it in collaboration with guest directors: productions such as *The Year of Cancer*, *Medea*, *The Maids*, *Ibsen House* and *Kings of War* (this last, compiled from Shakespeare's history cycle, *Henry V* to *Richard III*). But when these new projects pass into the company's repertoire as productions for revival, the integrity of the individual actor's original creative work is preserved as an effect of the ensemble: the actor who created the role will (usually) be the actor reviving it.[27]

Still, Trueman's further observation that Toneelgroep Amsterdam's 'mantra' is 'that any production ought to tap into the core essence of a play' returns us to the vexed question: what *is* the 'core essence' of a Shakespeare play? If his writing is disposed of, *once* his writing is disposed of, what's left? Can foreign Shakespeare, Shakespeare in translation, ever reach the 'core'? In the *Romeinse Tragedies*, perhaps Toneelgroep Amsterdam elided the difference between surface and depth suggested by that word 'core'. Using those flat television screens not just as apparatus but as presentational conceit, it gave us theatre as event. Now. It produced these plays in the format in which its spectators live their lives – perhaps a twenty-first-century analogue to early modern Shakespearean theatre viewing. Moving between live and mediated action, it made all acts a kind of performance, and it made us spectators 'voyeurs of tragedy' (Mee-Lai Stone, *Guardian*, 18 August 2015). Most certainly, it put proof to David Lan's statement quoted by Lyn Gardner in the *Guardian* (19 March 2017) that 'European productions aren't "infecting" our [British] theatre – they're telling [it] hard truths'.

## Foreign crocodiles on foreign stages: take 2

Meanwhile, on the other side of the Atlantic, where the big beast Shakespeare and the 'strange serpent' Cleopatra had both been naturalised to North America over decades, a different politics of representation was changing the look of theatre in the United States and Canada. In post-war Europe, as Dennis Kennedy observes, the move had been, in the wake of the Polish writer Jan Kott, to see Shakespeare as 'our contemporary', to 'discover contemporary themes' in the plays and to 'stress the spectator's inclusion in those themes'. Getting to grips with the theatrical implications of Brecht's Marxism and Kott's Existentialism, populist European directors, as Kennedy puts it, 'struck a bargain with Shakespeare: he delivered a Renaissance classic text, they overlaid it with a post-war social text' (Kennedy 1993, 7). Some of this effort crossed the Atlantic. In New York in 1954 Joseph Papp (the son of Russian Jewish émigrés) launched the New York Shakespeare Festival in Central Park, putting on productions that 'worked hard (though not always successfully) to find a progressive American expression equal to the excitement generated by the European theatre thinkers' (Kennedy 1993, 13). But elsewhere, the 'social text' went largely unnoticed, as in Stratford, Ontario, in Canada where, a year earlier, another Shakespeare festival had been launched. The Stratford Shakespeare Festival (SSF) was revolutionary in re-imagining the space of performance, in putting into bricks and mortar the kind of open stage Harley Granville-Barker and William Poel in England in the 1930s had argued that Shakespeare needed if the conventions of his playhouse were to be honoured, conventions that, observed, would release his writing in contemporary performance. The Festival Theatre in Stratford, Ontario, combined both Greek and Elizabethan design elements. It had a modified thrust stage and seating wrapped around it as in the ancient theatre at Epidaurus, architecture that brought 'the plays closer to their audiences in both the literal and figurative sense' while demystifying the dramatic event by stressing its non-illusionism. Shakespeare was thrust forward into the communal lap of his spectators, not trapped behind a proscenium arch in an illusory world apart. But because the festival director, Tyrone Guthrie, was largely apolitical, productions in *that* Stratford 'seemed devoid of social commentary', a legacy that has persisted (Kennedy 1993, 13). Five *Antony and Cleopatra*s have been produced in Ontario since 1967. None has made the play 'our contemporary'. In Ontario, Shakespeare's Romans wear togas. Still, something distinctly progressive and Canadian can be seen in them: in 1972 Maggie Smith was a porcelain-skinned Ptolemaic Cleopatra in a red wig; in 2014 Yanna McIntosh was a black African Cleopatra in beaded cornrow braids. North America was restoring Cleopatra's Shakespearean blackness in mainstream theatre long before Britain got around to it.

An important sign for the future of this play in particular and for the integrated racial casting of Shakespeare more generally turned up in a most unlikely (because so evidently backward-looking) place, the mock-Elizabethan theatre that had been built in 1932 as part of the Folger Shakespeare Library complex in Washington DC; built perhaps as a material reminder that much of the stuff in the Folger's stacks had once had a 'real' life on a 'real' stage. This replica had been made functional for performance in 1970 when Shakespeare Theatre at the Folger (STF) was launched, its object to develop an 'American style' of playing Shakespeare and his contemporaries that 'honors the playwrights' language and intentions while viewing their work through a 21st century lens'.[28] Michael Kahn took over as artistic director of STF in 1986.

Two years later, he staged *Antony and Cleopatra*. The script, he thought, was 'particularly appropriate for our city at this time when the whole nation will be focused upon the question of leadership': citizens would go to the polls to vote in the 1988 presidential election that would put George H. W. Bush in the White House while this *Antony and Cleopatra* was up and running (*Asides*, Fall 1988).[29] It wasn't a critical success. Reviewers didn't think Kahn made 'a lot of the symbolic conceit' of Robert Edward Darling's design, a set, wrote David Richards in the *Washington Post*, that came 'close to being an abstract, three-dimensional collage. With its large pyramidal forms tilted on edge, its obelisks wrapped in shrouds, and the canvas vistas in the distance, it looks like some forgotten museum, half buried in the sands of time' (28 September 1988). They mocked his decision to set the Battle of Actium in a paddling pool afloat with toy model ships where Antony and Cleopatra waded into each others' arms to share the kiss that meant more to them than their defeat. Reviewers didn't think much of Kenneth Haigh's Antony. He'd played the original 'angry young man' Jimmy Porter in John Osborne's *Look Back in Anger* at the Royal Court in London in 1956, but now he was much more squirrel than bear; 'heavy-lidded, puffy', an Antony who seemed

[ 255 ]

'to be nurturing a hangover rather than a grand passion'. The *Washington Post* tipped off its readers about Haigh's Antony: 'forget the battle. Just gearing up for it taxes him' (28 September 1988). But reviewers thought Franchelle Stewart Dorn's Cleopatra was magnificent. She 'looked ravishing', a Cleopatra of 'exotic appeal' who couldn't help eclipsing her co-star. 'As an actress', wrote Richards, 'she invariably leads from strength – with her grave voice, her uncluttered profile and what seems to be a deeply ingrained sense of purpose' (28 September 1988). The previous season she'd played a Lady Macbeth 'animated by a primitive Attic passion'; the year before that, she'd won the Helen Hayes Award for Best Supporting Actress for Paulina in *The Winter's Tale*, both productions directed by Kahn at the Folger (*Asides*, Fall 1988).

What was not mentioned in any pre-publicity, any reviews, any of the potted histories of the play on Shakespeare's stage that were wheeled out to inform Kahn's production, was Cleopatra's blackness, and *this* Cleopatra's blackness. (Was blackness coded in those references to Dorn's 'uncluttered profile' and 'primitive Attic passion'?) Nor did anyone mention what might have been taken as Michael Kahn's most significant human representation of the play's politics. It wasn't just Cleopatra who was black. *All* of Alexandria was black. For once, spectators saw Actium as a racialised battle for global supremacy, Europe v. Africa.

Or did they? Did the fact that no one mentioned the 'significant' casting mean that in 1988 it simply didn't register – a glorious, ironic spin on the state of affairs in Shaw's production from 1953? That it wasn't *meant* to register? That a black Egypt wasn't seen as any way 'significant' to the internal politics of Shakespeare's history play? That instead, the casting was participating, though nobody was talking about it, in a local politics of representation and inclusion that, ironically for a play that *needs* its racial politics re-instantiated, meant spectators to be colour blind? In the 1980s 70 per cent of the population of Washington DC was black. If theatre was going to make any headway in the city, it needed that population to see itself belonging to Shakespeare's audience, which meant seeing itself represented on Shakespeare's stage. In Washington DC finding a 'progressive American expression' for Shakespeare meant giving black actors an equal piece of the action, and Kahn at the Folger showed the way. He'd begun casting black actors in major parts in his first season at the STF. In 1990 he and the black director Harold Scott would cast Iago (Andre Braugher) and Emilia (Franchelle Stewart Dorn) as a black married couple opposite Avery Brooks in *Othello*. (It would take the RSC another twenty-five years to imagine a black Iago.) In 1997 Kahn's theatre would host the so-called 'photo-negative' *Othello* directed by Jude Kelly, a 'race reversed' production in which the Moor (Patrick Stewart) was the only white in the play.

If the significance of black casting in Washington DC in 1988 was its insignificance, by 2014 in Ontario there was no 'if'. As Liza Giffin, the SSF archivist, recalls, the ethnicity of Jamaican-born Yanna McIntosh and what it might 'mean' for Cleopatra wasn't 'discussed at the time, and doesn't come up in director's/programme notes, publicity, news cuttings or anywhere'.[30] Neither was the ethnicity of the supporting casting around her Cleopatra noticed. Jennifer Mogbock (Iras), Sophia Walker (Charmian) and E. B. Smith (Alexas) are black actors; Antoine Yared (Mardian) is Lebanese. For her part, Yanna McIntosh made her Stratford debut in 1992 – and 'it wasn't seen as odd', says Giffin, 'that she would understudy Lady Montague opposite [white] Antoni Cimolino's Romeo'. The following year she was Iras alongside Goldie Semple's Cleopatra, then Maria in *Twelfth Night* (1994). She returned to the SSF in 2008 as Helen in *The Trojan Women*, Lady Macbeth and Titania (2009), Hermione (2010) and Queen Elizabeth in *Richard III* (2011), a line of parts that demonstrates not just the actor's progression in the profession, hitting top women's Shakespeare roles that still in the UK were almost exclusively cast white, but the irrelevance of race to the casting.[31]

Meanwhile, actor training had been attached to the business of making theatre at the SSF when the Birmingham Conservatory for Classical Theatre was founded as its affiliate in 1998 by its then artistic director Richard Monet. It began by accepting eight students annually, requiring them to come with a couple of years' professional acting experience, paying them while they developed their practice in a year-long intensive course in the conservatory, then offering them a season of work in the festival. By the time McIntosh played Cleopatra, the conservatory had been developing actors and feeding them into the SSF company for nearly twenty years – and had been taking seriously a diversity agenda that Britain would *still* be struggling to put into place fifteen years later. The casting of *Antony and Cleopatra* in 2014, then, needs to be seen in that context, of a company that for two decades had been committed to actor training, to 'building an ethnically diverse classical company' and to sustaining a 'flowering of new diverse talent' that increasingly represented Canadian demographics, giving 'them parts', says Giffin, 'on our main stages year on year until they have the experience to take on major roles'. Case in point: Antoine Yared, Mardian in 2014, would play Romeo in 2017.

The production itself, directed by Gary Griffin in the festival's second thrust-stage space, the Tom Patterson Theatre, was the kind of production audiences at the 'original' Stratford long for when they leave the Royal Shakespeare Theatre grumbling, 'Why can't directors let Shakespeare speak for himself?' There were no gimmicks, no 'innovations'; no 'interpretation'; no over-determining 'concept'. It was dressed 'as if' from Plutarch, the Romans in sober linen togas, the Alexandrians in gorgeous modern takes on the signature Egyptian tube dress, the kalasiris (designer: Charlotte Dean) (see 8.2). The set was functional, minimalist and simple. Above, Octavius delivered his political speeches and struck his political deals from an iron railed balcony. Below, a keyhole-shaped dais placed at the centre of the thrust stage was frequently set with Cleopatra's sturdy four-square low-slung bed, but it also (enhanced by some strategic lighting) doubled as the monument. Two columns upstage seemed to support the balcony – intimations of both Rome in their solid mass and Egypt in their decoration. They were covered, like steles, in hieroglyphics. Concept-lite, this

8.2 'We stand up peerless'. Antony (Geraint Wyn Davies) and Cleopatra (Yanna McIntosh) surrounded by Cleopatra's Egyptians.

production wasn't blighted with the kinds of directorial decisions that had made the RSC's most recent *Antony and Cleopatra* (2010) a 'gobsmackingly bad ... clueless, pig's ear of a production' (David Jays, quoting Kate Bassett, *Guardian Theatre Blog*, 1 February 2011). Griffin staged Actium as a series of scenic cross-cuts, men swiftly passing over the space; Michael Boyd at the RSC had Cleopatra and her retinue in cute naval uniforms halt-stepping across the stage in half-time as in some cabaret number, holding aloft cute model ships. Best of all, with McIntosh's Cleopatra, Geraint Wyn Davies's Antony and Ben Carlson's Octavius, the casting at the centre of Griffin's production was equally weighted with actors who were clearly in the same show. (By contrast, at the RSC, the actors seemed on different planets. Kathryn Hunter's 'lightning mood-swings' from 'grotesque comedy' to 'black farce' made her Cleopatra 'near-certifiably psychotic', 'a crank in the grip of a Cleopatra-complex', an incomprehensible erotic partner for Darell D'Silva's 'rather middle-class and middle scale Antony' and an unlikely political game-player opposite the 'near-funny hysteria' of John MacKay's 'puritanical Octavius' (Paul Taylor, *Independent*, 12 May 2010).)

Where Antony in Shakespeare is a man who will 'stand the buffet / With knaves that smells of sweat' (1.4.20–21), Wyn Davies's Antony in Griffin's production was built for Rugby Union. He was broad-chested, broad-fronted, and his open face was a screen that registered volcanic reactions. When the lights came up on this production he was crouched with Cleopatra on her bed, the retinue crowded around them, rolling dice. Rome's 'News!' (1.1.18) was met with groans. He marked his 'space' (line 35), kneeling, by planting a kiss on Cleopatra's belly, figuratively and literally for him the womb of Egypt. He could be as teasing as the queen: when he was 'stirred by Cleopatra' (line 44), he fluttered the hem of his Egyptian robes, miming an erection. Later, proposing they spend the night 'wander[ing] through the streets and not[ing] / The qualities of people' (1.1.54–55), he wrapped a scarf around his head, transforming himself into a smirking girl. Getting Cleopatra's leave to go from Egypt ('Sir, you and I must part'), he experienced farewell ('Upon your sword / Sit laurel victory') as seduction, and the kisses she twice gave him as temptation he had to push roughly away ('Let us go!'; 'Away!') (1.3.89, 101–102, 103, 107) (see 8.3). He was an Antony who could play what's conventionally required of Cleopatra, the 'infinite variety' (2.2.246) of the part, its bluffness,

8.3 'I go from hence your soldier'. Cleopatra (Yanna McIntosh) and Antony (Geraint Wyn Davies).

its poisoned humiliation, its swoops into mindless Herculean rages, its reckless abandon (whirling like a dervish ordering one last 'gaudy night' (3.13.188)), but also its matchless magnanimity (sending the master-leaver's treasure after him together with that message that breaks Enobarbus's heart).

McIntosh's Cleopatra was a match for this 'Mars', this 'huge spirit' (2.5.117, 4.15.93). Her physicality produced a Cleopatra who was sensuous rather than sexual, who was fluid and mobile rather than jaggedly erratic, who could be the player queen but also royal Egypt (see 8.4). Dean's costume designs helped her. They gave an opulent female body but not a public body disclosed, so this Cleopatra's eroticism was an affect of speech, not of sensationalised carnality. A dazzling mimic, McIntosh's Cleopatra could go from impersonating Antony's horse (deliciously happy 'to bear the weight of Antony') to imagining herself a fish hook ("Aha! You're caught") (1.5.22, 2.5.15). She could be childish, flinging herself on her bed and covering her head with the bedclothes so she couldn't hear Antony's 'News ... from Rome' (1.1.18). But also expertly politick. Her 'Oh!' to Thidias knew exactly what game was afoot and how she would run it to ground (3.13.60).

Making some cuts (the soldiers at the beginning, 'Nay, but this dotage' ... 'approves the common liar' (1.1.1, 61); Ventidius in Syria, 3.1; Seleucus with his inventory, 5.2); compressing elsewhere

8.4 'He's married?' Cleopatra (Yanna McIntosh) eyeballs the Messenger (Andrew Lawrie) as Iras (Jennifer Mogbock), Charmian (Sophia Walker), Mardian (Antoine Yared) and Alexas (E. B. Smith) look on.

(Cleopatra's chat with the Asp Man did the business but cut out all the double-talking jokes); and delivering a 'straight' reading of Shakespeare's script, Griffin's production told a clear story that also repositioned the political narrative to locate it at the centre of things (which showed how habitually it's de-centred in British productions). Ben Carlson's beefy Octavius was no petulant hysteric but a serious political manipulator, credible in both toga and armour. 'Take your time' epitomised him, spoken evenly to Pompey who was mentally over-heating as he remembered Caesar's assassination and why Brutus and Cassius, those 'courtiers of beauteous freedom', had been moved to 'drench the Capitol', to prevent tyranny, to show 'that they would / Have one man but a man' (2.6.23, 17, 18–19). The political point Pompey was making passed Antony by. His retort was a *non sequitur*: 'Thou canst not fear us, Pompey, with thy sails' (line 24). But it was not lost on Octavius – he who was studying to become 'Sole sir o'th' world' (5.2.119). Astonishingly, after mourning dead Antony, hearing the message from captive Cleopatra, instructing Proculeius how to cozen her, sending other men on other missions, twenty items of business, he turned his full attention back to that flunky soldier who'd brought him Antony's sword, stained in Antony's blood, who'd been sitting miserable, shrunk, ignominious at the side since he'd made his delivery. 'Go with me to my tent', he invited the nobody, 'where you shall see / How hardly I was drawn into this war' (5.1.73–74). 'Go with me' the second time (line 76) was a command. It announced a new world order.

### Whose crocodile?

In chapter 5 of *The Portrait of the Artist as a Young Man* Stephen Dedalus in a classroom in University College Dublin ponders the ironies of linguistic colonisation. That thing his physics lecturer from England is calling a 'funnel' Stephen knows as a 'tundish', a word that Shakespeare used, a word imported into Ireland with the colonising Tudors, a word that had survived in Ireland while English in England had moved on, modernising, changing, replacing tundishes with funnels. There is perhaps an analogy to be drawn between this scene in Joyce's *Portrait* and Griffin's *Antony and Cleopatra* in Stratford, Ontario. Canada, a former British colony, manifestly having made a distinct Canadian 'self' over several centuries, yet appears to preserve intact certain cultural remnants of the mother country. These forms (if we're talking about Shakespeare) were deposited there back in the 1950s – Tyrone Guthrie, we remember, was an English import. But 'mother' has moved on, prodded in new directions by unruly European step-children who don't speak her language and so don't talk of tundishes *or* funnels. Still, while European *Antony and Cleopatra* goes rambunctiously, iconoclastically on its way in the wake of Komisarjevsky, Zadek and Toneelgroep Amsterdam, the solid, perhaps priceless value of SSF's *Antony and Cleopatra* is, almost counter-intuitively, its conservatism in the way it produces (in English) Shakespeare's words; the way, delivering Shakespeare's writing (in English) with such attention to the kind of verse speaking the RSC prided itself on in the 1960s and 1970s, it reminds spectators of how great the play is, *it self*, without interposing the white noise of what Kennedy terms a 'social text' (Kennedy 1993, 7).

In his programme note in 1994 Peter Zadek wrote of 'the fascination of this writer for me'. Shakespeare, he said, 'is an author who really does present the opportunity for a re-interpretation every five years. The stories which he tells have a kind of openness which allows one to produce the greatest rubbish, but also the greatest non-rubbish'. The point about the crocodile, then, is that she will constantly be on the move, migrating, naturalising to other habitats, picking up new habits, ways of being, then sloughing them off at a new address. Reflecting on the 'intercultural experiences' that foreign Shakespeare offers spectators 'in the innumerable ... productions throughout the world in which the name of Shakespeare is mentioned', Patrice Pavis wonders: 'is there anything that still might concern that little dramatist from Stratford?' And answers, 'Who knows, maybe!' (Pavis 1993, 286).

But then he continues:

> It's clear that the work of the classic of all classics is no longer a model to follow, nor a score to be performed; it is instead an entire culture of otherness, similar and different, unrepresentable and unattainable, ready to lead us on to an infinity of other cultural enterprises. The variable now is not the political teaching that the dramaturgy carries, nor the cultural and philological characteristics that all these foreign expressions discover in it, but rather the theatrical and aesthetic practices than can be manufactured out of it. In this sense, Shakespeare is now a machine to make theatre, to reveal other cultures, to observe their constant changes. As if the truth no longer came from Stratford-upon-Avon, but from cultures affected despite themselves by Stratford, cultures which have the strength to resist it and at the same time the longing to consult it. (Pavis 1993, 286–287)

It's almost as if, under the pressure of Pavis's metaphors, Shakespeare himself has become the 'strange' beast, my crocodile, 'unrepresentable and unattainable' but constantly represented; resisted yet irresistible; like the Cleopatra whom the crocodile tropes, 'an entire culture of otherness'. For the Anglophone world the 'little dramatist from Stratford', speaking to it in English, no doubt 'still' has things to say that 'concern' them, though they probably don't call it 'the truth'. It's much bigger than mere 'truth'. For 'other cultures' 'affected' by the crocodile 'despite themselves' – like Lepidus's Rome – it is entirely appropriate that in their local cultural 'triumphs' across the globe they have wonderfully transformed the living animal into a 'machine to make theatre', not unlike Octavius Caesar, who, cheated of Cleopatra alive to perform in his triumph, parades her body in Rome as a statue in gold, 'a machine to make theatre'. Translated, adapted, revised, put in 'foreign' clothes, in 'foreign' demotic, neither model nor score (for after all, Shakespeare-the-crocodile, 'shaped like it self', pipes to nobody else's tune), the beast who is Shakespeare is material for re-performance. He tropes an 'infinity of ... cultural enterprises', past and yet to come, on both British and on foreign stages.

**Notes**

1 I am consciously using a version of Folio's spelling of 'it selfe' at TLN 1381. Later English would elide the separate words into 'itself'. In contrast to what modernity will think of as 'identity', early modern English marks the emphasis on 'self'-hood as that which is consciously 'self-fashioned'. See Smith 2000, 7–9, 24–27.
2 Neill, however, wrongly supposes that Findlater was referring to Peggy Ashcroft (who would not play Cleopatra until 1953).
3 The essential, sometimes contradictory, sources for trying to piece together a picture of Komisarjevsky's work and an assessment of his influence on British theatre in the 1930s are provided by Ralph Berry (1983), Philippa Burt (2016), Richard E. Mennen (1979) and Victor Borovsky (2001). These should be read against Tony Howard (2000). I will be relying on these sources throughout this chapter.
4 Burt reports the 'lengthy battle' Bridges-Adams fought with Archibald Flower, chairman of the Shakespeare Memorial Theatre board, to get this first guest director appointed, even threatening to resign. But her further comment (Burt 2016, 384), derived from Borovsky (2001, 398), that relations between Komisarjevsky and the board remained strained thereafter needs to be put against Sally Beauman's, that it was 'Archie' who championed 'Komis' after Bridges-Adams resigned in 1934, appreciating 'the fact that Komisarjevsky productions attracted publicity and sold tickets' (Beauman 1982, 143). Evidently whatever scruples Flower had about the Russian 'invasion' were overcome by his business sense.
5 It was evidently Komisarjevsky who invented the mischievous business that has dogged this play ever since, making the song sung as Bassanio surveys the caskets a give-away. In his production, Nerissa batted away the hand Bassanio stretched towards the gold casket, then nudged him vigorously in the right direction by landing heavily on the 'bred/lead' rhyme. See Mennen 1979, 393.
6 As Berry points out, 'in box-office terms, Komisarjevsky never failed' in Stratford (1983, 73).
7 Margaret Lamb provides the essential source. She reports that when the Old Vic was bombed in May 1941, 'promptbooks, photographs, and other materials relating to the historic interwar productions of *Antony and Cleopatra* were apparently lost' (Lamb 1980, 129–30).
8 But that's not how it felt to Komisarjevsky at the time. Declining Antony Quayle's invitation to return to Stratford from yet another

emigration, this time to New York, to direct *Julius Caesar* in 1949, he wrote that 'during the seven or so years of my work at Stratford-upon-Avon' he'd 'had plenty of time getting a little tired of the fact that my productions in spite of their success with the British public, enhancing the reputation of the National British Memorial Theatre, had been constantly (to my mind quite senselessly too) labelled as "foreign", "Russian", and what not, by the majority of critics and other "knowing" people. I do not want to feel the soreness of yore all over again' (quoted in Burt 2016, 388). I see Komisarjevsky as the touchstone of the 'foreign' in this chapter.

9 For two fascinating accounts of this history of politics and performance, see James Smith (2006, 307–23) and Robert Ormsby (2014, 46–65). Brecht's adaptation of *Coriolanus* was incomplete at his death in 1956. The play brought to London in 1964 was an adaptation of his adaptation by its directors, Manfred Wekwerth and Joachim Tenschert, that restored some original elements. A copy of the promptbook is held at the Shakespeare Institute, University of Birmingham, in Stratford-upon-Avon. In it, every scene is photographed moment by moment, with the relevant speech placed beside each stage picture. This source shows how radically the end of Shakespeare's play was changed to deliver a Marxist message. In the penultimate scene, Martius is borne into the Volscian camp by a massed body of plebs. Aufidius turns the crowd against him; the mob rush forward, overwhelming Martius, then exits, now carrying *Aufidius* on their shoulders. (The irony was not lost. As Brecht's Galileo would retort to the slogan, 'Happy the land that has heroes', 'Happy the land that has no need of heroes'.) In the final scene, the Roman senators are discussing some civic matter having to do with the city's water supply. The news of Coriolanus's death is broken. They muse upon it momentarily. Then they return to the water problem.

10 Kennedy frames this as a 'paradox'.

11 I take this from the *Antony and Cleopatra* programme produced for the King's Theatre (Edinburgh) performances of 16–18 August 1994. It includes an edited interview with the director. Asked, 'You have worked in Germany for 30 years. Do you still possess a British passport? Which nation, which country do you feel you belong to?', Zadek answers, 'I am English. I was taken to England when I was five years old and was educated there. My experience of Germany was therefore not that great'. But then he goes on significantly to shift his sense of identity: 'Actually I feel myself to be Jewish rather than German or English'. In Zadek's obituary in *The Guardian* (3 August 2009) Hugh Rorrison wrote: 'Zadek remained an outsider in the closed world of London theatre. His friend Tom

Blumenau advised him to go abroad, and in 1957 [actually 1958] he appalled his Jewish friends by moving back to Germany'.

12 A co-production between the Berliner Ensemble and the Vienna Festival, the production had its first performance in Vienna on 7 May 1994. I quote German reviews of that opening.

13 I am extremely grateful to Betinna Boecker of the University of Munich for locating Barbara Plessen's translation of *Antony and Cleopatra* and to her research assistant, Johanna Stowasser, for scanning it and sending it to me. Having the text in hand has allowed me to correct errors that have appeared elsewhere in the performance history of this production.

14 While she was at it, Stowasser also sent a scanned copy of this invaluable source book, *Antonius und Cleopatra: Materialien zur Aufführung* (Berlin: Gemeinschaftsproduktion der Wiener Festwochen mit dem Berliner Ensemble, 1994). For this, much thanks.

15 I am grateful to Angela Ritter for the translations of German reviews that I am quoting here, and for talking me through Barbara Plessen's translation.

16 Ritter in correspondence, July 2018. The argument Kennedy builds on this mistake, then, needs to be revised. Where he sees for the audience in Edinburgh a disconnect between the Shakespeare text they were reading in the surtitles and the 'colloquial' acting they were seeing on stage and argues that for German audiences there would have been no such disconnect, in fact German audiences, too, experienced a collision between what they were seeing and what they were hearing.

17 'Nay, but this dotage of our general's / O'erflows the measure. Those his goodly eyes, / That o'er the files and musters of the war / Have glowed like plated Mars, now bend, now turn / The office and devotion of their view / Upon a tawny front ... / To cool a gipsy's lust. Look where they come! ... Behold and see' (1.1.1–6, 10, 18, 20).

18 I am grateful to Bernhard Klein for these readings.

19 Not all reviewers agreed. For two who panned the production (while contradicting each other in what they were objecting to), see Irving Wardle, a reviewer whose opinions should never be taken lightly, in the *Independent on Sunday* (21 August 1994), and Rudolf Augstein, one of Germany's most influential journalists, in *Der Spiegel*, 16 May 1994, 198–202. Wardle damned the production as uniting 'the worst habits of East and West German staging': 'this is tourist Shakespeare'. Augstein wrote: 'If the praise Gert Voss heaps on his director, Peter Zadek, is true – i.e. that he's only interested in what happens between two people – then Zadek ran his play into the desert sands. For there's hardly anything erotic

going on between the main characters. And that this love is always about politics as well becomes even less clear.'
20  I owe this observation to Rowland Cotterill, whose eye-witness of this production has informed my writing.
21  Footage accessed on *YouTube*, July 2018, https://www.youtube.com/watch?v=TYH4UE411xA (accessed 17 December 2019). No footage of *Antony and Cleopatra* appears to exist.
22  This is true for the most part but needs to be qualified. Maria Kraakman, who played Caesar in 2018, joined the ensemble in 2015. Hadewych Minis originated the role in 2007 but left the ensemble in 2011. I owe this information to Ben Fowler.
23  Even when performed in its 'native' city the production used English surtitles, an acknowledgement that its is an international audience.
24  I am very grateful to Johan Reyniers, head of dramaturgy at Toneelgroep Amsterdam, for providing me with a copy of the company's English script and giving me permission to quote from it.
25  *WOS* blog, 23 March 2017, https://www.whatsonstage.com/london-theatre/news/roman-tragedies-ivo-van-hove-barbican-significance_43186.html (accessed 17 December 2019). Ben Fowler observes that in fact spectators' 'navigation of the space was far more managed and controlled than Trueman's statement implies. People didn't come and go between the stage/auditorium outside of the official "breaks", and actors on stage gave lots of instructions to people to stand aside or move elsewhere – the actual playing spaces (marked out in tight areas of the set) were relatively clear of spectators. More crucially, the actors didn't really acknowledge the spectators when in role, other than as obstacles they had to navigate to play the scene. We were only "cast" in key moments – such as Antony's funeral oration' (personal communication, August 2018). Christian M. Billing's review (2010) discusses the strange proxemics of the living scenography and notes that in London most people on stage watched the monitors rather than the actors.
26  *WOS* blog, 23 March 2017.
27  This is largely the case, but for a list of actors and roles year by year see https://tga.nl/voorstellingen/romeinse-tragedies/cast (accessed 17 December 2019).
28  https://en.wikipedia.org/wiki/Shakespeare_Theatre_Company quoting The Mission of the Shakespeare Theatre Company. shakespearetheatre.org
29  Subtitled 'a quarterly publication of the Shakespeare Theatre at the Folger', *Asides* can be accessed at www.shakespearetheatre.org/_pdf/asides/88-89/88-89%20Antony%20Cleopatra.pdf (accessed 17 December 2019).

30 I am quoting Giffin from email exchanges in the summer of 2018, grateful to her for a steady stream of information and for suggesting what questions I *should* be asking.
31 Casting patterns in the UK can be examined via Howard and Rogers 2016. The *Database* demonstrates, according to Lyn Gardner in the *Guardian Theatre Blog* (13 January 2016), that 'there has been an increase in ethnic minority casting [in Britain] over the last 85 years', but it also 'suggests that casting directors and directors are paying lip service to colour-blind casting', often employing 'black or Asian actors to play smaller roles or servants' or developing 'concept' productions like Gregory Doran's 'African' *Julius Caesar* (2012) or Simon Godwin's 'West African' *Hamlet* (2016) that relocate the play to some 'black' geography in order to justify the casting.

9

# Restoring blackness: Josette Bushell-Mingo's Cleopatra, Royal Exchange, Manchester, 2005; Tarell Alvin McCraney's 'radical edit', Royal Shakespeare Company, The Public and GableStage, 2013

### 9 April 2005

An actor comes rushing barefoot across the massive stone flags of what was once an international commodities trading floor where, a century and a half back, brokers in top hats dealt principally in raw cotton imported from the slave states of America to feed the spinning mills of Lancashire. It's now the foyer of the Royal Exchange Theatre, Manchester. The self-contained theatre-in-the-round sits like a futuristic space pod inside the cavernous Victorian structure. The actor is bundled into a thick towelling dressing gown. She's just come off stage. She's clutching a copy of the Arden edition of *Antony and Cleopatra* that she holds out to me, open to an inscription dated November 1996, when she was at the RSC playing Death in the medieval morality play *Everyman*. I recognise my own handwriting. The inscription reads: 'I hope one day to see you play Cleopatra'. And now I have. For the past three hours I've been watching Josette Bushell-Mingo play Shakespeare's Egyptian queen, and play her as the playwright wrote her, a black Egyptian queen. It's a performance I've been waiting for since, a decade earlier, I'd begun engaging with Shakespeare's play through the writing of Edward Said and Martin Bernal in *Orientalism* and *Black Athena*, writing that opened my eyes to the 'whiting-out' of

[ 269 ]

African culture in Western imperialist representation, a 'whiting-out' whose politics I realised were put in view, reproduced, culturally authenticated and naturalised on the English stage under the coercively iconic signature of the national poet whenever *Antony and Cleopatra* was played with actors such as Peggy Ashcroft or Janet Suzman as Cleopatra – or Helen Mirren, Glenda Jackson, Sinead Cusack, Judi Dench, Vanessa Redgrave, Frances de la Tour, Harriet Walter, Kim Catrall, Eve Best or Katie Stephens (Rutter 2001, 57–103). Not to mention, most ostentatiously, given the cosmetic 'white face' he wore as simulating 'authentic' Jacobean practice, Mark Rylance. That is, all the Cleopatras I'd known in four decades of theatre-going – except for Ashcroft, her performance before my time.

Josette Bushell-Mingo (whose family history bears a distant relationship to the business originally conducted in Manchester's Royal Exchange, her ancestors imported as slaves to what became British Guyana before her parents immigrated to England in the 1960s in a second wave of the *'Windrush* generation') was not the first black British Cleopatra. That distinction goes to Doña Croll, directed by Yvonne Brewster in 1991 for Talawa, the 'all black' theatre company Brewster had co-founded five years earlier.[1] After Croll came Cathy Tyson (best known for playing up-market prostitutes on film and television in *Mona Lisa* and *Band of Gold*), directed by Michael Bogdanov for the English Shakespeare Company in 1998. Neither production was located remotely near the power centre of British Shakespeare performance. One played in the student theatre at University College, London, the other in a former East End music hall. Neither attracted much attention from reviewers or audiences. Talawa's might have been 'a ground breaking-venture', as Michael Billington wrote in the *Guardian*, but on opening night it played to only a 'devoted handful' (21 May 1991). At the Hackney Empire, actors stared out into 'dark corners' at 'Rows of empty seats' (Jeremy Kingston, *The Times*, 19 October 1998).

Meanwhile, it was evident that mainstream British theatre had institutionalised the practice first seen on the post-war stage in Shaw's 1953 *Antony and Cleopatra*, that of placing black bodies alongside white Cleopatras as if, by juxtaposition, to annex to her elite body atavistic ideas of orientalism, exoticism, ideas that could be simultaneously aroused by proxy and denied in the body of the queen herself. Joe Marcell, Calvin Lockhart, Loftus Burton,

Joseph Charles, 'genuine dark-skinned servants and lieutenants' – as the *Oxford Mail* noticed them (16 August 1972) – back-lit Janet Suzman's Cleopatra in 1972; Josette Simon played Iras opposite Helen Mirren in 1982; Claire Benedict, then Noma Dumezweni, then Golda Rosheuvel were Charmian to Clare Higgins (1992), Sinead Cusack (2002) and Harriet Walter (2006). All at the RSC. The only time any of Cleopatra's black side-kicks stepped into the lime light was on those occasions when Charmian-as-understudy went on for her 'mistress': Benedict played Cleopatra a handful of times across the 1992 run; Dumezweni, once, in a closed company understudy run.[2]

This history of shadow play, of playing on the periphery, perhaps accounts for an odd comment Doña Croll made in an interview in 2011. She was reflecting upon challenges she'd faced in the industry and observing that it had 'all got a lot easier' for black actors: 'it's so common now to see black actors playing different parts', such as 'a German officer' in *War Horse*, and even 'playing Kings' in 'RSC productions' (*Afridiziak Theatre News*, 15 May 2011). But, she went on, she'd 'yet to see a black actress play Cleopatra' – making no mention of the fact that twenty years earlier *she'd* played Cleopatra. Didn't Talawa's 'ground-breaking venture' count? Was it too marginal to count? Was it forgotten because it produced no sudden recognition, no revolution, no *change*? Or did its significance for the casting of a black Cleopatra and her Egyptians fail to register (even in Croll's memory) because it was obscured by the fact that *all* the parts in that production were played by black actors – which meant, too, that Egyptian blackness failed to register the ultimate signifying power Shakespeare assigned it in 1606, racial difference from white Rome? Would a breakthrough count as a breakthrough only when a black Cleopatra appeared opposite a white Antony on a *mainstream* stage? On the RSC stage?

Perhaps Croll missed Bushell-Mingo in 2005. Or perhaps the Royal Exchange in Manchester was, in Croll's terms, the regional equivalent of London's Bloomsbury Theatre, too provincial to grab the national attention, to pack the kind of theatrical punch that would knock the girl in the white corner out of the ring – and permanently out of contention when it came to casting Cleopatra on the English stage, Such speculations aside, Bushell-Mingo's performance in Braham Murray's production came at a moment when racial and cultural politics were interestingly aligned – and set on a collision course with national politics. Even while books as recent as those by Arthur L. Little, Jr (2000), Imtiaz Habib (1999) and Joyce Green MacDonald (2002) showed academic Shakespeare criticism focusing theorised, historicised attention on the racial politics of his plays and specifically on Cleopatra's blackness,[3] and even as black actors were more frequently crossing the 'colour bar' to play those English 'Kings' Croll referred to, daily headlines in the broadsheets and tabloids showed race politics firmly back on the UK's national agenda. 2005 marked the fortieth anniversary of the UK's first Race Relations Act. That legislation aimed to end the kind of discrimination regularly encountered in Britain by people like Bushell-Mingo's parents, a nurse and a bus driver, citizens of the Commonwealth who'd been called 'home' after the war to help rebuild the 'mother country' – citizens who, arriving in London, read signs in windows of lodging houses: 'No blacks. No dogs. No Irish'. The Act made it illegal to bar access to public places or to refuse rental accommodation on racial grounds. It made 'incitement' of racial hatred a criminal offence. Cause to celebrate, forty years on.

But 2005 also produced signs that race relations hadn't changed all that much in four decades. It was an election year. For the third time Tony Blair was leading Labour into the election, four years after he'd launched his controversial 'War on Terror', two years after he'd made his deeply divisive (some said criminal, being based on claims about non-existent 'Weapons of Mass Destruction') decision to invade Iraq. The massive popularity that Blair's governments had enjoyed since 1997 nose-dived. Back-benchers were in open revolt. Forty years earlier, the Tories had fiercely opposed Labour's Race Relations Act. In 2005 they used the election to stoke up racial animosity, first by suggesting to the public imagination some connection between race and the new fear of terror and then by eliding terror with immigration, to campaign on what, in the previous two elections, hadn't even featured as a 'resonance issue'. 'Immigration', wrote Gary Younge in the *Guardian*, was 'back' on the agenda, 'immigration' being 'a code word for non-white people, regardless of where they are from', and 'back' in 'an ugly manner reminiscent of the racially-charged 1960s'. In 1964 a Conservative had won a by-election 'with the slogan: "If you want a nigger for a neighbour, vote Labour"'. Now in 2005 another Tory campaign poster asked, 'What bit of "send them back" don't you understand Mr Blair?' (*Guardian*, 25 April 2005).

For her part, rehearsing *Antony and Cleopatra* to open in February 2005, Josette Bushell-Mingo refused to be drawn on the racial politics of the play. 'Cleopatra's colour is completely irrelevant', she told a *Guardian* interviewer: 'I'm not going to be judged on whether I'm white or black', just on 'whether I've been any good or not' (28 February 2005). She was probably wrong, not least because her casting *made* Cleopatra's colour relevant. She was hardly an actor to be disassociated from race politics, for she brought into any rehearsal room she entered a long personal history both of representing race and of advocating for racial representation on British stages. Her training with Lecoq, Kaboodle and Complicité had equipped her as an actor to exploit those physical 'things' that Doña Croll attributed to black 'earthiness and movement', 'things' that 'European actors' were 'not very good at' (*Guardian*, 19 May 1991). At the RSC in 1996, directed by Complicité's Marcello Magni and Kathryn Hunter, Bushell-Mingo both astonished and beguiled reviewers with her physicality. Her Death, sent to call Everyman to account, was 'a stunning femme fatale' who, transforming a wedding knees-up into a *danse macabre*, took Everyman into a 'slinky embrace' before revealing 'her true identity', a revelation that left him in a 'panicky terror' that was, wrote Charles Spencer, 'a wonder to behold' (*Daily Telegraph*, 23 November 1996). More recently, her production of Langston Hughes's classic Harlem musical *Simply Heavenly* had transferred from the Young Vic to the West End; she'd directed a Yoruba make-over of Brecht's *Mother Courage* and Rhashan Stone's debut play, *Two Step*; she'd been nominated for an Olivier, Best Actress, for Rafiki, the witch doctor baboon in Julie Taymor's *The Lion King*, and on the back of that experience, working, she told the *Guardian*, with 'so many brilliantly gifted black artists who weren't being given the time of day by mainstream arts institutions' (28 February 2005), she'd founded PUSH, to foreground talent in a black-led arts festival, which is still going strong more than a decade later.

In the event, her Cleopatra found herself in a production that certainly stretched the play in some directions, but too often fell back on the predictable. Michael Dobson in *Shakespeare Survey* called it 'a qualified success' (2006, 330). She was attended by black Egyptians – Sarah Paul (Charmian), Gugu Mbatha-Raw (Iras), Ali Sichilongo (Mardian), Everal A. Walsh (Soothsayer). Alexandria, then, presented what most audiences had never seen before, a black culture. But the designer, Johanna Bryant, had dressed them apparently out of one or other of the Eastern bazaar fabric outlets in Manchester's garment district as if they were extras in a Bollywood film. And she'd piled wigs on their heads that were fabulous constructions out of Africa, styles that had become a fashion rage as the hair extension industry hit the UK: cornrow plaits gilded with gold, intricate box braids bunched into cascades or sculpted into pompadours, high-maintenance hairstyles that made them women who spent hours immobile being 'dressed'. Cleopatra's hair was fashioned into gold-laced weaves pulled tight off her face, woven into a long tail down her back and bound in a coil that suggested a sleeping serpent; perched on top, a cobra-headed gold crownette that screamed cliché. The Egyptians' space was a low golden platform. On it sat a giant gold sculpture of a beady-eyed scarab. Set opposite were small plinths, cast (predictably) in silver, where Rome's power plays, wrote Lyn Gardner, were 'directed like a human chess game' (*Guardian*, 2 March 2005). On one side, the floor was etched with Roman numerals; on the other, Egyptian hieroglyphics. As for the central casting, Tom Mannion was too much the shaggy, scraggle-bearded, drug-blown hippy to make Antony's reputation as Mars credible, and Steven Robertson too much the single-toned martinet, improbably kitted out in toy soldier uniform backed by Romans in what looked like ski boots, to give access to Octavius the political thinker or Rome as imperially ambitious. In this production, it was Cleopatra and her Egyptians in her 'camp ... showbizzy' court who were the star attractions, Bushell-Mingo's Cleopatra, for Gardner, 'a drama queen', a 'woman so used to playing a part – majesty meets celebrity – that she is no longer sure what is real'; a woman who, 'in other circumstances ... could be Medea'; 'exotic, other, and very dangerous' (*Guardian*, 2 March 2005).

I, however, saw another Cleopatra than the one Gardner reviewed on press night, a Cleopatra who'd apparently fired her designer, dumped the stereotyped 'exotic' and transformed the part. A week into the run, Bushell-Mingo had stripped off Cleopatra's wig.[4] From then on, she wore her own hair, copied, she said, from a black woman she'd seen in Brixton who'd cropped her hair within half an inch of her scalp.[5] This stripped-back Cleopatra was no 'Egyptian dish' (2.6.128) concocted from expectation and served up to feed the desiring white imaginary. Where other Cleopatras (Higgins, de la Tour, Rylance) had shed the queen's iconic head of hair in her desolation – revealing it to be a wig, the icon, a deceptive construction, and the dazzling diva only an ugly chancer – before putting on robe and crown to mark her apotheosis, Bushell-Mingo's Cleopatra asserted from the outset that she was 'e'en a woman' *who was also* 'Royal Egypt' (4.15.77, 75). This Cleopatra escaped visual cliché: Nina Simone, not Elizabeth Taylor. She was all eyes – and mouth, a woman who didn't waste hours sitting still being plaited, who had a country to run. Modern, strong, powerful, she looked as though she'd have no trouble hopping 'forty paces' through a 'public street' – or indeed, through Brixton market.

Ironically, Doña Croll missed seeing this Cleopatra – and what she claimed for the body who performed the queen, a body who achieved so many of Croll's aspirations from 1991. Still, remarking upon those 'black actors playing Kings' in 'RSC productions', Croll half-predicted a black Cleopatra on the RSC stage: 'it will come – it will have to happen' (*Afridiziak Theatre News*, 15 May 2011). In 2013 it did.

## 13 November 2013

I'd never sat in a white minority audience at the RSC before. Tonight, I did. Around the Swan auditorium, I spotted a scattering of other white faces – among them the RSC's latest, newly appointed artistic director, several members of the current ensemble, reviewers from a couple of broadsheets, tabloids and the local rag. But for the rest: black actors, dancers, musicians, producers; black RSC veterans from across three decades; black university and drama students, at least one politician, black theatre-goers from London and Birmingham. The atmosphere was more carnival than press night, high more on celebration than on nerves. We were there to see *Antony and Cleopatra*, but also to see history being made by the first black director to be in full charge of his own production at the RSC in one of its main houses, Tarell Alvin McCraney, and by the first black Cleopatra to appear on the RSC stage, Joaquina Kalukango. Did it indicate some measure of progress in multi-racial casting that not a single reviewer noticed these firsts? In 2000 it was headline news when 'The Royal Shakespeare Company ... claimed to have broken the mould by casting a black actor in the role of an English monarch for the first time in its history', David Oyelowo as Henry VI (*Guardian*, 19 September 2000). After thirteen years had the (white) journalists who still dominated review discourse in Britain simply learned not to act surprised seeing black bodies on Shakespeare's stage?

Over the following days the notices that appeared were lukewarm; one was an outright pan. But the audience knew better than the hacks what they'd seen. As the stage manager's show report records on 13 November there were 'Cheers at the curtain call'. And these didn't stop on press night. On 15 November: 'whistles and cheers at the curtain call'. On 20 November: 'an engrossed audience and marvellous response ... with whoops and cheers'. On 25 November: 'tremendous response'; 'a splendiferous show'. On 30 November: 'An AWESOME show'; 'A phenomenal response at curtain call', 'whistles and cheers'.[6] No *Antony and Cleopatra* I'd ever seen had brought the house down. This one did.

It had its origins quite a while back from that opening night. One of the assignments that students in Yale University's graduate playwriting programme are set by the chair of dramaturgy is to produce 'a radical edit of a Shakespeare play', the cast 'limited to 10 actors, the running time to two hours'.[7] Tarell McCraney graduated from Yale's programme with that assignment under his belt in 2007, so a year later he had a shrewd idea what the current RSC's artistic director, Michael Boyd, was after when he asked him to make a 'bold adaptation' of *Antony and Cleopatra* for the 'long ensemble' Boyd had been directing in Stratford across three seasons while the company's iconic main stage was demolished and the company was camping out in the Courtyard Theatre, the prototype for the reconfigured thrust-stage new-build Royal Shakespeare Theatre. McCraney was still only twenty-eight years old. But he'd already achieved an international reputation as a 'theatrical road warrior' (Hirschman 2014). His militancy as a playwright was expressed in dialogue written in black demotic, his narratives fusing the ancient (and the erased) to the contemporary (and the repressed), West African Yoruba mythology to the legacy of slavery in America, where the Yoruba were among the three highest slave populations in the Caribbean. His semi-autobiographical *The Brothers Size* (2007), which premiered at the Young Vic in London and garnered for him numbers of prizes, relocated to a Louisiana bayou aspects of McCraney's life growing up poor, black and gay on the streets of a Miami housing project dulled by drugs and violence that finally claimed both his mother and his brother. Currently embedded in the RSC as international playwright in residence, a post funded by the University of Warwick that allowed him to work with both actors and students, he was writing *American Trade*, the sequel to *Choir Boy*. But at Boyd's behest, he'd also produced a 'radical edit' of *Hamlet* for the company's 'Young People's Shakespeare' outreach initiative. Clocking in at an hour and ten minutes, with a cast of nine and Dharmesh Patel as Hamlet (a prince 'young people' in the audience could recognise because he looked like them), McCraney's edit showed love letters wafted to Ophelia on air currents produced by a flapping umbrella; cut Yorick; but brought on the pirates in that scene Shakespeare 'forgot' to write. It had children sitting on the edges of their seats, hanging on every word.

Ultimately, in a decision he may have regretted, Boyd didn't go with the 'bold adaptation' of *Antony and Cleopatra* he commissioned from McCraney in 2008. Instead, the following year he directed a more-or-less uncut version of Shakespeare's script in what the theatre reviewer Kate Bassett called a 'gobsmackingly bad … clueless, pig's ear of a production' that had Cleopatra (Kathryn Hunter) walking out of the show mid-run (quoted in *Guardian Theatre Blog*, 1 February 2011). But as Boyd later blandly wrote in the programme note to the eventual 2013 production, 'while we didn't use Tarell's vivid vision of the play for that [long ensemble] repertoire' in 2008, his 'radical edit' was 'clearly a wonderful and important piece of work'. So he 'later asked Tarell if he would lead an intimate ensemble' and direct it, and Tarell, 'a brilliant young theatre-maker who wanted to equip himself to establish a repertoire company that could speak to the whole of the community in his native Miami … said yes'.[8] That's not quite how McCraney remembers it. As savvy, even wily as the Yoruba trickster Elegba in *The Brothers Size* (and as stunningly graceful in even the most cunning of his 'road warrior' moves), McCraney says he 'tricked' the RSC to get what he wanted: 'Uh, sure', he told Boyd, he'd direct his cut, 'but only if I can take it to Miami' – to put Shakespeare in front of the projects' current street kids (Hirschman 2014), maybe to capture some of them for life and theatre as he had been captured.[9]

Embarking on his 'radical cut', McCraney perhaps read Shakespeare the way Shakespeare read Pluratch: one eye, the historian's, gazing backward at 'ago', at what was done and dusted; the other, the playwright's, seeing everything 'right now', present, unaccounted for and potential. Thus read, the history of Antony, Cleopatra and Octavius is the story of a world-shifting struggle between (superior) East and (upstart) West, black culture and white, oriental opulence and imperialist ambition, where the outcome of Actium is by no means inevitable nor white supremacism a foregone conclusion; a suspenseful story playing out 'now' that holds in tension with it what we know retrospectively from history, that Rome won – and at what cost. Aiming, he said, to 'do it with race and ethnicity' (quoted in Hirschman 2014), to make visible the politically charged racial contours of Shakespeare's play, McCraney relocated *Antony and Cleopatra* to somewhere *something like* Shakespeare's imagined version of Plutarch's Egypt. He set it in Saint-Domingue, a French Caribbean colony as fabulously valuable to eighteenth-century Europe for its sugar production as Egypt was to Augustan Rome for its wheat. He set it at the time of the slave uprising of 1791, a revolt philosophically fuelled by the slogan that had crossed the Atlantic into this French colony from Paris and the 1789 Revolution, 'liberté, égalité, fraternité' – and ignited on a night in August by the Vodou priest Boukman, in a ritual that gave insurrection spiritual legitimacy from deities who'd travelled into slavery with Africans for whom Vodou was not just religion but resistance. The French had been unable to crush it. Thereafter, unnerved as black military power in the Caribbean gained traction under the leadership of the 'black Spartacus' who'd read French Enlightenment political tracts, Toussaint l'Ouverture, and his incredible (to white imperialist eyes) successes, France first declared the abolition of slavery in part of Saint-Domingue in 1792. Two years later a vote in the assembly of the First Republic led by Robespierre extended that decision across France and all French colonies, granting freedom to their black populations and political and civil rights to all black men. But this only provoked international war in the region, and on Saint-Domingue white resistance that was met with continuous black revolt. Given the driving forces of their economies, neither Britain, Spain nor the newly independent United States of America could tolerate a political philosophy that argued – and legislation that enacted – the abolition of slavery.

Besides, in a France bankrupted by the Republic, Napoleon Bonaparte – his *coup d'état* only months old – was secretly making plans to recapitalise the mother country's economy by restoring the plantation system to the Caribbean, a scheme that depended entirely on the re-enslavement of 'the mother's' (colonial) 'citizens'. It would take another decade of war, with sickening atrocities piling up on all sides, before Napoleon admitted defeat, sold France's vast territories in continental North America to the United States government, and withdrew from the hemisphere. On New Year's Day 1804, on the back of one final massacre, Saint-Domingue declared independence, naming the new nation 'Haiti', a black republic under black governance. (An engraving published in 1805 showing these last throes, the gruesome 'Revenge taken by the Black Army for the cruelties practised on them by the French', blacks stringing up whites, all of these men in the same Napoleonic uniforms, illustrated McCraney's production programme.) But the subjection that French military action couldn't achieve, French political chicanery did. France demanded 'reparations' before the French state would recognise the new nation. Haitians were required to compensate former plantation owners for 'loss of property' – that is, for themselves as slaves. While the United States paid France 50 million francs for the 827,000 square miles of the Louisiana Purchase, territory stretching from the Canadian border to New Orleans, from the Mississippi River on the east to the Continental Divide on the west, France demanded of Haiti 90 million gold francs to purchase freedom. Haiti didn't finish paying up until 1947.

By relocation translating and mobilising a black history that Europe knows little about and America mostly chooses to ignore, McCraney was re-igniting the race politics of Shakespeare's play that every production of *Antony and Cleopatra* in post-war Britain had marginalised, whited out.[10] Citing black history in the Caribbean, putting in view the spirit-craft of the Yoruba and the death-and-resurrection cult of Vodou with its attendant rituals of song, dance and destructive soul-tying that binds human emotions to inordinate affections, McCraney was making space for what frequently embarrasses 'white' productions: the supernatural, the soothsaying, the soul-tied dotage that reduces Roman Antony to a sex tool, the strange perambulations of deities abandoning their avatars, the primitive explanatory recoil to witchcraft and, particularly in Antony's rages, the recoil from 'white' reason to 'black' fury. McCraney's 'radical edit' reduced Shakespeare's thirty-four named parts to eighteen, and the acting company – a 'radical' riposte to Trevor Nunn's comment from 1972 that 'You can't really do [*Antony and Cleopatra*] with fewer than 50 people' – to just ten, five Yankees, five Brits. Swathes of Shakespeare's script were cut; scenes were re-ordered, speeches reassigned; but as in McCraney's 'Young People's *Hamlet*', scenes Shakespeare 'forgot' to write were introduced. Spectators would see shockingly enacted in a wordless torture ballet – captioned 'Caesar's Triumph' – the whole history of what is passed over in a single line in Shakespeare's script when tight-lipped Enobarbus observes that, having torn up their treaty, 'Caesar and Lepidus have made wars on Pompey' (3.5.4). As was his practice, borrowed from Suzan Lori Parks, McCraney wrote into his script stage directions to be spoken, here, by Enobarbus, who emerged as the story's Chorus, its master of ceremonies and last voice ('Enter a Messenger', 'Octavius Caesar's House'; 'An Interlude'; 'At sea. Aboard Pompey's ship').

McCraney's production opened on a Swan stage lit so blue that it was almost black. Upstage (designer: Tom Piper) stood three monumental arches that filled the proscenium below the musicians' gallery. These perhaps troped the 'wide arch / Of the ranged empire' (1.1.34–35). Drapes that would later curtain the arches (minimalistically signalling scenic relocations) were now pulled back in swags, allowing spectators access to a space beyond, a blank vista that would blaze gold in the heat of Egypt, sink to black and dark umber for the senate meeting in Rome, return to Mediterranean blue for Actium. In front of this back wall was sunk a shallow pool that stretched the width of the stage. Otherwise, there was no set, and almost no properties. Except for a fold-up camp stool and an unconventional asp basket, the Swan's thrust stage would remain empty, a space to privilege people and their stories.

Entering upstage against the stage left pillar, a female body stood long in black silhouette, curvaceously naked, then stepped into the pool, wading languorously through the shallows. Centre stage she stopped, turned her back and sat, spreading her legs wide as though ceremonially bathing or symbolically enwombing the water. Shadowy figures, shapes as if in black cut-outs, began assembling on the forestage poised for what McCraney's director's script described as 'a ritual expression of music, movement, and call/response'. He detailed his instructions to his actors in a list of bullet-points that also gives a sense of the occult mysteries that he wanted summoned in this production to be channelled through actors' bodies:[11]

- This is the ritual. They are waiting for something to happen and change.
- They shouldn't underestimate the power of just watching.
- Drop into full breathing.
- This is tribal, transforming. They are in orbit around Cleopatra.

- There is a submitting and a waiting. You go with it because that's your expectation.
- Don't stay anywhere – movement can be continuous.

A keening voice, half animal, half banshee, called out, a call accompanied by two 'STOMPS'. An explosive, drawn-out response of 'Deeeyy!' got 'Oohhhhh!' shouted in return, with 'More stomps'. Then:

- This is the peak of the event horizon.
- This is the moon rise.
- Antony & Cleo are two completely different heavenly bodies in the exact same position.
- This shouldn't feel like a show.

More feet began a rhythmic stomp. Drumming cut in. Bodies lunged, stretched, rose like animated sculpture from the ground. Moves were measured and poses looked as if struck from martial monuments. Upstage, the body in the water rose, turned, started slowly downstage, discovering its blackness as it entered the light. (Behind her, a figure robed the body's nakedness in white; in front of her a male body, stripped to the waist, white, dressed only in buff breeches, moved to meet her, to kneel before her.) Meanwhile, upstage, another male body (black, in buff cavalry breeches and shirt, high-polished boots) disengaged itself from a woman's voluptuous embrace, strode centre stage and took on the audience:

> I will tell you.

Enobarbus (Chukwudi Iwuji) was no hard-bitten campaigner, no weary cynic delivering reportage, but rather an Ariel 'flaming amazement'. He *danced* the memory, like a street rapper directly addressing the story to every spectator's listening, 'to us' as McCraney's stage direction has it:

> The barge she sat in, like a burnish'd throne,
> Burned on the water …

His voice was 'white'. For the Romans in this production would speak with English 'RP' accents. But his body and its rhythms were black, underscored (upstage) by he-who-would-be-revealed-as-the-Soothsayer calling in a haunting counter-tenor voice 'Oom da dee day oh da dey!' getting back from all those other bodies on stage the response 'La dee day oh la de ay!' (This song of black exile, memory, mourning and loss – 'Dey' – which fuses rural Haitian and Vodou themes, was borrowed from Toto Bissainthe, who wrote and performed it as an unofficial national anthem. It would return at significant moments throughout McCraney's production.)

Opening with this back-story relocated from Shakespeare's Act 2, what Enobarbus was doing felt like Vodou, as though he were Elegba, first cousin to Shakespeare's Autolycus, spirit-guardian of the crossroads, ushering 'us' along the corridors of memory into history's present. When he finished, telling of impossibilities, of fans

> whose wind did seem
> To glow the delicate cheeks which they did cool,
> And what they undid did,

a lighting change discovered Antony (Jonathan Cake) and Cleopatra (Joaquina Kalukango). They exchanged only four lines, out-mocking each other ('If it be love …'; '…new heaven, new earth') before they clasped hands and raced off. But those four lines spoke a world of difference. His voice was Roman. Hers, Creole. Enobarbus was left to fill in what happened next: at Cydnus, 'Upon her landing, Antony sent to her, / … she replied …'. So Antony went 'to the feast' and 'for his ordinary' paid 'his heart / For what his eyes eat only'.

Cut to Charmian (Sarah Niles), Alexas (Ash Hunter), Iras (Charise Castro Smith) and the Soothsayer (Chivas Michael); to a Creole Egypt bathed in orange and gold light; to women in simple white cotton reminiscent of 'house nigger' wear, heads wrapped in turbans, weaves cascading down backs; men in white sarongs or tunics that remembered both 'native' Africa and the Caribbean (see 9.1). Cut to laughter. To Creole voices, talking Shakespeare like street corner gossip. Chivvying. Lewd. Until the Soothsayer's 'You shall outlive the lady whom you serve' silenced them all. That instant switch from ribaldry to gravity, the light joke to its dark underbelly, would be characteristic of this production, making the *volte-face* reversals of the original even more pronounced by McCraney's stripping-down of Shakespeare's writing. So the initial eighty lines of Shakespeare's 1.2 were cut to twenty, then attached by a spoken stage direction ('Enter a Messenger') to some forty lines from 1.1 that caught Antony literally with his pants down, Charmian pulling back a curtain on 'News, my good lord, from Rome' to show him emerging from the upstage pool bare-arsed. Egyptian hilarity played

9.1 'O Charmian, / Where think'st thou he is now? ... /... is he on his horse? / O happy horse, to bear the weight of Antony' (1.5). Cleopatra (Joaquina Kalukango), Charmian (Sarah Niles), Iras (Charise Castro Smith).

off against the Messenger's Roman shock and was intensified with Cleopatra's quips about 'scarce-bearded Caesar' and 'Fulvia's process' before Antony's 'Speak not to us' swept the carnival off stage, leaving behind the Messenger stunned nearly to silence: 'Is Caesar with Antonius prized so slight?' It was Enobarbus who answered, 'Sir, sometimes, when he is not Antony / He comes too short of that great property / Which still should go with Antony'. And it was Enobarbus who, when the Messenger exited dully intoning 'I am full sorry / That he approves the common liar, who / Thus speaks of him at Rome', stepped forward to interpret what we'd just seen, 'Nay, but this dotage of our general's / O'erflows the measure ...' and to instruct us: 'Look where they come!': 'Take but good note, and you shall see in him / The triple pillar of the world transform'd / Into a strumpet's fool. Behold and see'. This Enobarbus, then, played along with Antony – but with eyes wide open.

What 'we' saw in Cake's Antony was, from the first, a doting mallard, a big man stupidly besotted who, to embrace his tiny Cleopatra, had to crouch, literally weak-kneed, in a stance that made him appear always thrusting towards her crotch. In a lightly cut 1.3, driven to distraction by her swerves from 'rare' to 'riggish' as he furiously attempted to stuff arms into his epauletted Napoleonic Roman uniform to dress up for a return to duty while she mocked how 'this Herculean Roman does become / The carriage of his chafe', he finally lunged at her, grabbed her, violently and deeply kissed her, then threw her down and strode off, raging 'I'll leave you lady', only to be stopped in his tracks with 'Courteous lord, one word.' One part of his brain really did believe 'I must from this enchanting queen break off', the same part that, shortly, really would believe that marrying Octavia would save his life by breaking the Creole witch's spell.

In Rome he faced a Caesar (Samuel Collins) who had stepped out of Jacques-Louis David's 1801 portrait *Napoleon Crossing the Alps*: lean, chisel-featured, eyes fixed on destiny, dainty feet tucked primly under him, right hand clenched in a fist held behind him in the small of his back, standing a full two heads shorter than Antony and, resplendent in scarlet uniform, backing down not an inch while standing him off. The eighty lines of Shakespeare's 1.4 were cut to some forty and, with a neat transition borrowed from elsewhere (Lepidus dismally opining, 'I cannot hope / Caesar and Antony will well greet together'), led straight into 2.2, the meeting of the triumvirs. Lepidus (Henry Stram), a slightly addled bureaucrat in a black frock coat and moth-eaten *ancien régime* periwig, flapped anxiously between the two tyros during their gritted-teeth exchange of the perfunctory: 'Welcome to Rome'. There was nowhere to sit. Antony guffawed at sniggering jokes from Enobarbus ('men might go to wars with the women!') while he himself, jiggling his hips, attempted to ingratiate himself to Octavius ('neglected rather'), who returned stinging accusations ('You have broken / The article of your oath') and stiff silence. Lepidus feebly clutched at diplomatic straws ("Tis noble spoken'). Then Agrippa (Ian Lassiter) stepped forward with his 'studied ... thought', the plan to 'hold' these 'brothers' in 'perpetual amity' with a marriage between 'widower' Antony and 'Admired Octavia'. Enobarbus's head whipped round. He stared at the generals' dead silence while Antony gazed into the distance and Caesar stood rooted. A deep pause dug a trench in Antony's response: 'What power is in Agrippa, / If I [pause] would say, "Agrippa, be it so" ...' Then his assent – 'May I never / To this good purpose ... / Dream of impediment!' – washed over him like relief. He gave Octavius his hand; then pulled him into a bear hug that embraced Lepidus as well, laughing, a man saved from enchantment, absolved of delinquency, squarely 'Roman' again.

This marriage? Cake's Antony hesitated only for the space it might take a man to catch his breath on the word he used for it, 'business' ('dispatch we / The business...'), a suggestive metaphor for a wedding. But he really meant it. And spectators saw it performed, McCraney staging the marriage as an elegant, artful participation dance (in marked contrast to the 'natural' body language of Egypt, dancing). Octavia (Charise Castro Smith) in a white empire gown moved from resplendent dress-uniformed partner to resplendent dress-uniformed partner in a choreography learned in elite imperial ballrooms until she reached Antony. The steps, like all the voices in Rome, were 'white'. Disconcertingly, though, the soundtrack was 'black', Egypt somehow present at this nuptial: it was the Soothsayer's countertenor voice that scored the dance with a strange music fitting his strange appearance in 'native' sarong and headwrap, a reprise of 'Dey' carried on the breath, beyond words. More disconcertingly, the wedding was pre-emptively framed with redundancy. Alone with him on stage even as the others exited to the 'business', Enobarbus doomed it to the man who'd proposed it, quashing Agrippa's certainty, 'Now Antony must leave [Cleopatra] utterly' with an even more certain 'Never. He will not.' As the dance 'Interlude' finished with Octavia delivered into Antony's hand, the wedding music hardly out of his ears, his earnest vows to his new-married wife hardly out of his earnest mouth ('I have not kept my square; but that to come / Shall all be done by the rule'), Antony turned from her exit on 'Good night' to a question he put to his Soothsayer ('Now, sirrah; you do wish yourself in Egypt?'). Even as Antony spoke the Soothsayer was furiously stripping off his 'white wedding' gear ('Would I had never come from thence, nor you thither!') as Antony, more deliberately, was shedding his too. Twenty lines later, rehabilitated Antony had relapsed, already en route 'to Egypt', to 'the east' where 'my pleasure lies'.

Cut to Alexandria. Downstage, Pompey (Ash Hunter) and Menas (Sarah Miles, cross-dressed) knelt, conjuring into action 'all the charms of love' that 'Salt Cleopatra' had stocked in her armoury of 'witchcraft', a 20–line exchange repositioned from 2.1. Upstage, 'Egypt' appeared in the person of Mardian (Chivas Michael), who, enacting those 'charms', began a ritual soul-tying, binding together dolls dressed like Antony and Cleopatra. So was the 'pleasure' offered by Joaquina Kalukango's Cleopatra Vodou? Black magic? Or something only a little more prosaic, this woman's ability to fascinate, to keep Antony's 'brain fuming' not with 'cloyless' cookery but with words in a voice that carried the seductive dark tang of molasses? A good decade younger than any Cleopatra who so far had appeared on the RSC stage, and pint-sized compared with, say, Suzman, Jackson or Mirren in the part, Kalukango had little that was conventionally regal about her. The corn-row weaves that hung down her back were no fashion statement but just ordinary Caribbean 'cane chopper's' hair. Her white cotton dresses did little to distinguish her from her women. Even dressing for death she underwent no spectacular metamorphosis: a simple white robe, a gold fillet for a crown. Once she emerged from the water in the opening vignette, this Cleopatra was earth, not fire or air. Her bare feet anchored her to the 'dungy'. Taunting, bad-mouthing Antony in that Creole voice that doubly mocked not just the subject matter but the sound of Roman pretentiousness, she was a spitting fishwife. Imagining him 'on his horse', she was deep-throatedly lewd ('O happy horse, to bear the weight of Antony!'). The sass that came out of this Cleopatra and her 'girls' as they cackled over their erotic jokes or batted away Caesar's circumlocutions like hover flies knocked RP off its po-faced linguistic pedestal, claiming for a black vocal demotic what Northern Broadsides in 1995 had claimed for the northern demotic. This was a Cleopatra and an Egypt that school kids in London's Southwark, Coventry's Foleshill or Miami's Liberty City could identify with.

Reviewers didn't see her embodying politics. Ian Shuttleworth in the *Financial Times* called her 'pert and peremptory without being imperious', a woman 'used to getting her own way, but not on a global scale'; Andrew Dickson in the *Guardian* couldn't 'quite believe' she was 'a political operator' (both 15 November 2013). Neither acknowledged what stared them in the face and hit them in the ear, the body politics of Kalukango's casting, the raced politics attached to her voice. Nor did they register the larger politics that McCraney's production put in view *beyond* bodies and voices, a textual politics. With his 'radical edit', McCraney was liberating Shakespeare performance from the straitjacket of Shakespeare's text. He was using Shakespeare the way foreign Shakespeare has always used him and as Giles Havergal had used him at the Citz, Glasgow, in 1972: 'a machine to make theatre', material for re-performance.[12] A playwright collaborating with another playwright, wanting like John Dryden centuries earlier to lift aspects of the source text's political discourse – in his case, to make spectators see, *really see*, the imperialist project that drives Rome's white supremacism in Shakespeare's play – McCraney made choices that re-made that play and re-politicised Shakespeare's writing. Starting with 'I will tell you. / The barge she sat in ...' rather than 'Nay, but this dotage ...' McCraney turned the narrative gaze around.[13] He put Egypt's magically generative body – a human Nile – at the centre of the visual field, not Rome's ruin. He choreographed strikingly beautiful (and painful) sequences that translated Shakespeare's dense speech-craft into movement: the opening 'primitive' dance sequence accompanied by drums, shouts, stomps that was remembered in the 'elite' marriage dance that (with no sense of irony) literally handed Octavia from brother to husband, which itself was later distantly recapitulated in 'An interlude. Caesar's Triumph over Pompey'.

This 'Triumph' sequence, its caption announced by Enobarbus, replaced the scene marked in Folio's stage direction '*Enter Ventidius as it were in triumph the dead body of Pacorus borne before him*' (TLN 1494). In McCraney, Pompey had just exited, maudlin drunk like the rest, getting Caesar and Antony – irony of ironies – safely off his galley, calling them 'friends' while Menas exited with Enobarbus 'to my cabin'. Almost instantly, to a drum tocsin, Menas reappeared, half undressed, dragged in by soldiers in French uniform. Forced to stagger the perimeter of the stage, hands tied to the end of a long rope that was used to jerk his body onto his knees while his back was flogged (by a soldier who brutally beat the stage floor with a thick knotted rope as Menas mimed the assault with screams), he was then yanked up, forced to stagger further, thrown down again, flogged again, yanked up again, over and over before being shoved centre stage to kneel looking upstage. A curtain whipped aside. Pompey was revealed, captive and noosed. A soldier yanked his head back and slit his throat – Menas's last sight before his throat, too, was cut. This 'ballet' enacting Caesar's treachery read also as a slave narrative – doubly brutal given the casting of Menas, cross-cast by a black actor. Chillingly, the bodies weren't fully off before Caesar entered for a 'triumphal' walk-down, in purple, wearing a gold laurel crown, now Napoleon-after-Gérard.[14]

Later, just this sort of inventive choreography made stunningly clear who was to blame for the rout at Actium. 'We are women's men', Enobarbus flipped over his shoulder, exiting behind Scarus while, drums beating, 'Cleopatra's War Suite' – Cleopatra, Iras, Charmian, the eunuch Mardian – took the stage. This battle was Egypt's gig (see 9.2). 'Dressed in war garb', skirts hiked up, cane chopper machetes in hand, they war-danced the attack into the distance upstage. Cleopatra waded out in front into the pool and stood disappearing in a haze while the throbbing drums beat faster and faster. Suddenly she twisted, plunged staggering out of the water and ran while behind her, on the far side of the pool, Antony appeared, splashing into the shallows, flailing after her, falling as Enobarbus entered, crying 'Naught, naught, naught!'

Doing *Antony and Cleopatra* 'with race and ethnicity', perhaps McCraney's boldest move, and the one least understood by (white) reviewers, was to replace playtext with performance text, speech with movement, which allowed him to devise a physical language that articulated blackness, not least in calling up the rituals of West Africa to make that language explicit. As Vodou was there at the beginning, so it presided over the play's ending, making mysterious sense of death as a first step into an 'after life', or what white culture calls 'immortality'. So the soldiers who bent over dead Enobarbus scattered terrified when the Soothsayer materialised out of nowhere to place an ashen hand over the corpse's face, then disappeared. Seconds later, the body jerked alive, turned, strode

9.2 'I never saw an action of such shame' (3.10). Cleopatra (Joaquina Kalukango) and her 'navy', Iras (Charise Castro Smith) and Mardian (Chivas Michael) flee the Battle of Actium.

upstage and through the water. Into forever. But then, as Cleopatra and her girls were ritually washing the body of Antony, chanting over him 'Dey-o. / Ayiti Cheri / Men Piti ou mouri', Enobarbus returned as a materialised 'after life' to lead Antony across the water. Finally, in a weirdly beautiful staging of Cleopatra's death, the asps were produced swimming in a round-bellied glass jar where they were brought to the surface as Iras poured in more and more water, filling it. Extending her arm to the asp's bite, Cleopatra seemed to be reaching for a 'forever' on the far side of the water.[15] And now as the sound of 'Dey-o' underscored the movement on stage, Caesar and his train massing around her body, Enobarbus once again returned, leaping like a Vodou loa into the centre of the scene, his face painted as a white skull, his chest, a skeleton, his movements, bones jigging. 'No grave upon the earth shall clip in it / A pair so famous', he called, and ordered, 'Come, all, see / The high order in this great solemnity'. With that, he put on a Bawon Samedi hat (see 9.3). We recognised him in his black tailcoat as the Baron indeed, the Vodou loa of the dead who is also the loa of resurrection. Around him, the sound of 'Dey-o' rose on a final swell of pain and longing. The dead walked. Upstage,

9.3 'No grave upon the earth shall clip in it / A pair so famous' (5.2). Enobarbus as Bawon Samedi (Chukwudi Iwuji) orders the funeral: 'Come, all, see / The high order in this great solemnity'.

in the water, Antony and Cleopatra appeared silhouetted. 'After lives', they turned to face each other. Blackout.

Staging rituals that white review discourse struggled to access, this *Antony and Cleopatra* enacted a sly parody of historical black exclusion from white hegemonic culture: McCraney 'tricked' the RSC into thinking black. More than that, and whatever it did for the play itself, his production operated as an institutional game changer. Commissioned from inside the company (as against arriving from outside, like the Wooster Group's 'experimental' *Troilus and Cressida* imported from the United States the previous year to howls of rage and mass walk-outs), McCraney's production gave the RSC permission – *challenged* the company – to treat Shakespeare as a working playwright and his plays as work in progress, work *for* progress, genuinely 'machines to make theatre'. This production took on squarely the rhetorical questions Lyn Gardner had posed a year earlier in a *Guardian* review of an Australian director's production of *Three Sisters* at the Young Vic in London when, under the headline 'Pickled Plays', she asked, 'Why won't British directors set classic texts free?' (27 September 2012).[16] Why do classic plays so often 'come with the side order of aspic when

British directors tackle' them? A 'classic play is simply one that is tried and tested', one that audiences and directors know 'works', so why don't British directors (as against, say, foreign directors working on British stages) take the opportunity of a new production to 'explore and play' with the classic, 'slicing through the musty layers of performance history in which it is cloaked'? 'If Shakespeare really is our contemporary', why are 'so many revivals so timid and reverential?'[17] A year later, McCraney de-pickled *Antony and Cleopatra*. Neither timid nor reverential, yet mightily respectful of the senior playwright who stood behind it (and withal, 'play-full'), McCraney's 'radical edit' aligned much more closely with Thomas Ostermeir's *Hamlet* (2008) and Katie Mitchell's *Ophelias Zimmer* (2015) than with either Gregory Doran's *Antony and Cleopatra* (2006) or Michael Boyd's (2010). It took on the job that Ben Fowler, writing about Mitchell, reminds us is implicit in that word 'radical', from Latin *radix*, 'root', signalling excavation but also 'a more generative sense of the term, pointing to the meanings and possibilities of creative practice that plays with the formal dramaturgical components of a production's construction' (Fowler forthcoming 2021). Offering such 'play', McCraney set Shakespeare's classic text free. That reviewers didn't see the freed play that audiences saw, that they could not be attentive to the black narrative McCraney drew out of it, perhaps speaks to the kind of politicised, culturally inscribed and historically determined and limited 'reading formations' or 'ways of seeing' that Barbara Hodgdon (1996) and John Berger (1972) have written about.[18] Baldly, some reviewers saw only what convention, cliché and ideology allowed them to see.

As for restoring blackness, after Kalukango, Cleopatra looks established as a black part on the British stage. At the RSC in 2017 she was played by Josette Simon (Iras to Helen Mirren in 1982),[19] and at the National in 2018, by Sophie Okonedo. Still, neither of these later productions saw Shakespeare's grand design for the play. Neither imagined Egypt black. Instead, casting 'colour-blind' (idiotically, at the RSC in 2017 the Egyptian Soothsayer was played by a whiter-than-white actor; at the National Theatre, Octavius Caesar was black), they erased the four-hundred-year-old gift that Shakespeare hands the theatre's current 'diversity agenda' on a plate, the opportunity not just to stage blackness but to politicise it, to mark the moment in history when hegemony shifted. To be blind to the colour that Shakespeare makes sensationally visible in this play is to operate a kind of miscegenation that, if restoring blackness of Cleopatra, 'whites out' the cultural field around her.

**4 May 2019**

Looking at performances of *Antony and Cleopatra* across four hundred years, performances that have used a Jacobean text to examine their own times, I want to end my history by rewinding, to remember the play in 1606 as it informs the present. Shakespeare gave us one answer to the question 'How did "we", globally, arrive at today's racial politics?', but only if 'we' observe the black/white binary that Shakespeare built into the play. Tarell Alvin McCraney's 'radical edit' gave us another. The audiences in Stratford-upon-Avon who leaped to their feet with 'whistles and cheers' at the curtain call in November 2013 heard him loud and clear. Even then, however, in the hands of other directors, other actors, other audiences, and under the pressure of other topicalities, the extraordinary crocodile that is *Antony and Cleopatra* was moving on, occupied as it always must be, as Barbara Hodgdon would put it, with a new 'now'.

**Notes**

1 An important *Guardian* interview with Croll and Brewster before opening night asked if this production 'could bring Cleopatra's whitewashing to an end' (19 May 1991). Brewster compared 'the backstage battle to establish Cleopatra as a black woman's part to the British theatre's blindness to Othello's blackness', wondering 'Why was it so difficult to imagine a black man *as a black man*?' Or, by inference, a woman, self-described, 'with Phoebus' amorous pinches black' (1.5.29), *as a black woman*. Croll insisted it was 'important that Cleo is black': she located in the role's blackness 'an earthiness and movement' not available to 'European actors [who] are not very good at using their bodies', while Croll's 'African side' equipped her to 'do these things' – 'things' not specified. But more than just playing Cleopatra, Croll wanted the production 'to cast a dark shadow over the whole Eurocentric portrayal of human history', to challenge head-on the 'unwillingness on the part of Europeans to acknowledge the contribution of Africa'. As for theatre practice, 'having [now] had a black Cleopatra', she hoped that 'the next time' the part was cast, 'that image will sweep across their brains'. Brewster's ground-breaking casting 'might just be the beginning'.

2  The stage manager's report for 7 November 1992 recorded 'Preview 4': 'After seeing a specialist it was decided that Miss Higgins should not perform this evening. After minimum rehearsal during the day Miss Benedict played the part of Cleopatra and Miss Russell played Charmian. Both were outstanding and it was truly a memorable evening for all involved. Director in attendance.' Benedict played Cleopatra twice more, on 19 November 1992 and 9 March 1993. Production records, including the promptbook, photos and show reports, are held at the Shakespeare Birthplace Trust, Stratford-upon-Avon.

3  It was Janet Adelman (1973) who touched off the debate twenty-five years earlier and Ania Loomba (1999, 2002) who thereafter applied post-colonial theory to the question. See too Geraldo U. de Sousa (1999), Sujata Iyengar (2005) and Rutter (2001). For a reading that aims to restore 'The Properties of Whiteness' to Cleopatra, see Pascale Aebischer (2013). But seeing textual 'contradictions' in how Cleopatra is physically imagined, her 'tawny front' at odds with 'the whiteness of her ladylike "white hand"' and her 'gypsyhood [with her] blue veins' – so that textually Cleopatra is now black, now white (and so 'beyond representation' because 'situated … in the gaps between the words the play consists of') – Aebischer is constructing false binaries. As the actor Rakie Ayola tells me, 'There's no contradiction between Cleopatra's "tawny front" and her "white hand". Look at our palms. A black woman's palms might be any shade from peachy/pink to bluish/black. Look at our wrists. We have VISIBLE blue veins. If you aren't aware of this, maybe it's because you've gazed at black women without truly seeing them' (personal communication, 14 January 2019). Shakespeare, I'd argue, was a man who did gaze at women's bodies and 'truly' saw them, to wit, observing the maternal detail (which any breastfeeding mother today could confirm) that the nursing baby frequently 'sucks the nurse asleep' (5.2.309). For the likelihood of Shakespeare encountering black women in London, see Miranda Kaufmann (2017).

4  By then, the photo-call had been held and the production had been photographed. The archive, possessing only these images, does not record the stunning look of the Cleopatra whom Bushell-Mingo actually played.

5  See https://www.thestage.co.uk/features/interviews/2017/josette-bushell-mingo-id-love-to-come-back-and-lead-a-company-or-run-a-building/ (accessed 6 January 2020).

6  These show reports, along with production records that include the promptbook, director's script, photographs and programme and a video of the production, are held in the RSC archive at the Shakespeare Birthplace Trust, Stratford-upon-Avon.

7 Yale's Catherine Sheehy writing in the RSC production programme, 'Barber'd Ten Times O'er' (2013).
8 RSC programme (2013), 'A New and Trusted Voice'.
9 McCraney's *Antony and Cleopatra*, commissioned by the RSC, was ultimately a co-production with the RSC, GableStage (Miami, Florida) and The Public (New York).
10 Calling this 'show' an 'utter dud', the 'arrogance' of its direction 'matched only by its incompetence', Charles Spencer in the *Daily Telegraph* (14 November 2013) dismissed it with a neo-colonialist waft of the hand: 'Everyone has some idea of the story [of *Antony and Cleopatra*], even if it comes from watching the immortal Carry on Cleo, but few of us have much idea of about [*sic*] the West Indies in the late 18th century'. Thus his crassness demonstrated that the ignorance and prejudice shown in 1948, when *Windrush* brought its first 'cargo' of black British 'aid workers' from the Caribbean to war-devastated England, ignorance repeated in 1965 when journalists on Spencer's conservative 'Tory-graph' editorialised against the Race Relations Act, and repeated yet again in 2005 when Tories campaigned on race fear, was still uninhibited in articulating its opinions. Andrew Dickson in the *Guardian* was slightly less dismissive, observing that while 'it's good to see the RSC treating the holy texts of its resident saint with a little less awe', and 'certainly exciting to see the RSC opening its doors' to experimentation, to allow us 'to watch McCraney tussling with the junk orientalism that often infects productions of the play', still, 'you wish they hadn't simply swapped one set of cliches for another', viz. 'the syrupy golden light that has apparently become Equity minimum for depictions of the exotic'.
11 All quotations are from the 'Director's Script' dated 'September 2013' held in the RSC archives at the Shakespeare Birthplace Trust, Stratford-upon-Avon. I am very grateful to Tarell Alvin McCraney for giving me a copy of his 'Prelim Draft' for the production's opening at the Public Theatre in New York in February 2014.
12 See Chapters 5 and 8 (where I'm quoting Patrice Pavis 1993). Dryden freely adapted Shakespeare – and Shakespeare ram-raided Plutarch for everything he could grab for his theatrical make-over of ancient history (which Plutarch himself had recounted with a distinctly Greek slant).
13 As Havergal had done at the Citz in Glasgow in 1972. See Chapter 5.
14 Spencer in the *Daily Telegraph* criticised this as 'a scene depicting slavery undreamt of by Shakespeare' (14 November 2013). Evidently, he'd never seen the Pacorus scene staged – or the scene that was its first draft, the opening triumph in *Titus and Andronicus*.

Or perhaps he didn't credit the visceral horror that Antony and Cleopatra imagine, being led in triumph in Rome, a 'slavery' that is by them nightmarishly 'dreamt of'.

15 The company ASM described this 'Snake Vassal [sic] with Calabash Gourd' thus: 'the gourd sits ontop of the vessal [sic]. The rubber snakes are fixed to the bottle [sic, for 'bottom', which the accompanying photograph shows?] of the vessal which is filled with water on stage making the snakes raise [sic] in the vase (trust me, it works)'. See production records archived at the Shakespeare Birthplace Trust.

16 Chekhov, Gardner thought, might have been 'surprised by his characters' extensive knowledge of swear words, or the way they leaped onto the tables to sing 'Smells Like Teen Spirit' in Andrews's production, 'but he would have recognised their damaged, yearning and fragile hearts that flutter and beat despite every setback'. And she thought Beckett would have recognised 'these girls too, given 'staging [that] leaves the sisters stranded – Winnie-like – on a mound of earth, not yet up to their necks but sinking fast'.

17 Why, we might wonder, wasn't Lyn Gardner sent by the *Guardian* to review McCraney's production?

18 Hodgdon writes: '[N]ot only are theatrical representations always produced within cultural limits and theoretical borders, but clearly spectators "read" performed Shakespeare (perhaps more so than other dramatic texts) through knowledges drawn from literary as well as theatrical cultures, knowledges which are necessarily implicated in particular economies of truth, value, and power, serving to mark one performance as a more acceptable interpretation than another'. I adopt Hodgdon to argue that review discourse – what it *doesn't* say as much as what it does – needs to be read 'not only as a struggle over the meaning of theatrical signs but as symptomatic of current cultural anxieties about gender, race, and nationality' (Hodgdon 1996, 70).

19 The *Guardian*'s assertion, 'that Simon will be the first black actor to play Cleopatra at Stratford's Royal Shakespeare *theatre*' (my italics), though smacking of institutional amnesia at best, repudiation at worst, is technically correct since Kalukango played in the Swan, not the Royal Shakespeare Theatre (David Jays, 21 March 2017). However, the Native American poet Jessica Mehta, a citizen of the Cherokee Nation who was then poet in residence in Stratford-upon-Avon, might have known better – or researched more thoroughly – before titling her poetic tribute to Simon, 'Stratford's First Black Cleopatra' (bloggingshakespeare.com/stratfords-first-black-cleopatra, 28 September 2017; accessed 26 March 2019).

# CAST LISTS

## The New Theatre (now the Noël Coward Theatre), London, 1936

Director: Theodore Komisarjevsky
Designer: Theodore Komisarjevsky

| | |
|---|---|
| *Cleopatra* | Eugenie Leontovich |
| *Antony* | Donald Wolfit |
| *Enobarbus* | Leon Quartermaine |
| *Charmian* | Margaret Rawlings |
| *Iras* | Vera Poliakoff |
| *Alexas* | Hubert Harben |

Other parts played by:
Lawrence Anderson
George Hayes
Ellis Irving
Vernon Kelso
Ion Swinley
Arthur Young

## Shakespeare Memorial Theatre, Stratford-upon-Avon, 1953

Director: Glen Byam Shaw
Designer: Motley (Margaret Harris)

| | |
|---|---|
| *Cleopatra* | Peggy Ashcroft |
| *Antony* | Michael Redgrave |
| *Octavius Caesar* | Marius Goring |
| *Lepidus, Diomedes* | Donald Pleasence |
| *Domitius Enobarbus* | Harry Andrews |
| *Octavia* | Rachel Kempson |
| *Sextus Pompeius* | Tony Britton |
| *Charmian* | Jean Wilson |
| *Iras* | Mary Watson |
| | |
| *Slave* | Anthony Adams |
| *Mardian* | Mervyn Blake |
| *Agrippa* | John Bushelle |

| | |
|---|---|
| *Nubian Slave Girl* | Diana Chadwick |
| *Dancing Girl* | Marigold Charlesworth |
| *Sailor, Soldier, Slave* | Dennis Clinton |
| *Slave* | James Culliford |
| *Soldier* | Nigel Davenport |
| *Dercetas, Sailor, Slave* | Peter Duguid |
| *Maecenas* | Donald Eccles |
| *Slave* | John Glendenning |
| *Gallus, Sailor, Slave* | Denys Graham |
| *Silius, Slave* | Charles Gray |
| *Old Soldier, Slave* | George Hart |
| *Ventidius, Soldier* | Michael Hayes |
| *Soldier* | Charles Howard |
| *Soldier* | Peter Johnson |
| *Seleucus, Soldier* | Gareth Jones |
| *Demetrius, Taurus, Soldier* | Bernard Kay |
| *Slave* | David King |
| *Slave* | Cavan Malone |
| *Soldier, Slave* | Richard Martin |
| *Canidius, Soothsayer, Soldier* | Philip Morant |
| *Sicyon, Messenger, Euphronius* | Peter Norris |
| *Eros, Slave* | David O'Brien |
| *Thidias* | William Peacock |
| *Soldier* | John Roberts |
| *Cabin Boy* | Robert Scroggins |
| *Dolabella* | Robert Shaw |
| *Slave* | Raymond Sherry |
| *Proculeius, Messenger* | Powys Thomas |
| *Alexas, Soldier* | Alan Townsend |
| *Philo, Sailor* | Michael Turner |
| *Menas* | Michael Warre |
| *Clown, Slave, Soldier* | James Wellman |
| *Scarus, Slave* | Jerome Willis |

## Citizens' Theatre, Glasgow, 1972

Director: Giles Havergal
Designer: Philip Prowse

| | |
|---|---|
| *Cleopatra* | Jonathan Kent |
| *Antony* | John Duttine |
| *Octavius Caesar* | Mike Gwilym |
| | |
| *Acolyte* | Cheryl Campbell |
| *Acolyte* | Angela Chadfield |

| | |
|---|---|
| Acolyte | Colin Haigh |
| Acolyte | Geoff Lerway |

## Royal Shakespeare Theatre, Stratford-upon-Avon, 1972

Directors: Trevor Nunn, Buzz Goodbody
Set designer: Christopher Morley
Costume designer: Ann Curtis

| | |
|---|---|
| Cleopatra | Janet Suzman |
| Mark Antony | Richard Johnson |
| Octavius Caesar | Corin Redgrave |
| Lepidus | Raymond Westwell |
| Domitius Enobarbus | Patrick Stewart |
| Octavia | Judy Cornwell |
| Sextus Pompeius | Gerald James |
| Charmian | Rosemary McHale |
| Iras | Mavis Taylor Blake |
| Alexas | Darien Angadi |
| Canidius, King | John Atkinson |
| Waiting Woman | Wendy Bailey |
| Demetrius | John Bardon |
| Lamprius | John Bott |
| Diomedes, Pacorus | Loftus Burton |
| Messenger | Joseph Charles |
| Gallus | Thomas Chesleigh |
| Ventidius | Constantin De Goguel |
| King, Soldier 5, Varrius | Hans De Vries |
| Eunuch | Michael Egan |
| Waiting Woman | Edwina Ford |
| Eunuch, Galley Servant 2 | Paul Gaymon |
| Maecenas | Patrick Godfrey |
| Guard 1, Servant | Peter Godfrey |
| Scarus | Don Henderson |
| Menas | Ian Hogg |
| Decretas | Jonathan Holt |
| Clown | Geoffrey Hutchings |
| Silius | Christopher Jenkinson |
| King, Silvius, Soldier 6 | Malcolm Kaye |
| Mardian | Sidney Livingstone |
| Thidias | Calvin Lockhart |
| Eros | Joe Marcel |
| Agrippa | Clement McCallin |
| Dolabella | Martin Milman |

| | |
|---|---|
| *King, Menecrates, Soldier 1* | Robert Oates |
| *Servant 1* | Tony Osoba |
| *Euphronius* | Lennard Pearce |
| *Proculeius* | Timothy Pigott-Smith |
| *Servant, Soldier 3* | Michael Radcliffe |
| *Eunuch, Seleucus* | Jason Rose |
| *Guard 2, Servant* | Simon Rouse |
| *Servant, Soldier 2* | Kevan Sheehan |
| *King, Taurus* | Desmond Stokes |
| *Messenger, Sentry* | Keith Taylor |
| *Galley Servant 1, King, Soldier 4* | Arthur Whybrow |

## Royal Shakespeare Theatre, Stratford-upon-Avon, 1978
Director: Peter Brook
Designer: Sally Jacobs

| | |
|---|---|
| *Cleopatra* | Glenda Jackson |
| *Mark Antony* | Alan Howard |
| *Octavius Caesar* | Jonathan Pryce |
| *Lepidus* | Paul Brooke |
| *Enobarbus* | Patrick Stewart |
| *Octavia* | Marjorie Bland |
| *Pompey* | David Suchet |
| *Charmian* | Paola Dionisotti |
| *Iras* | Juliet Stevenson |
| | |
| *Unnamed parts* | Alan Barker |
| *Philo, Scarus* | John Bowe |
| *Proculeius, Soothsayer, unnamed parts* | David Bradley |
| *Canidius, Gallus, unnamed parts* | Dennis Clinton |
| *Decretas, Taurus, Varrius, unnamed parts* | Alan Cody |
| *Clown, Messenger* | Richard Griffiths |
| *Demetrius, Maecenas* | David Lyon |
| *Mardian, Schoolmaster, unnamed parts* | Philip McGough |
| *Boy Singer, Eros* | Hilton McRae |
| *Menas* | Paul Moriarty |
| *Dolabella, Ventidius* | John Nettles |
| *Menecrates, Seleucus, unnamed parts* | George Raistrick |
| *Alexas, Thidias, unnamed parts* | Alan Rickman |

| | |
|---|---|
| *Agrippa* | Paul Webster |
| *Old Soldier* | Raymond Westwell |
| *Diomedes, Silius, unnamed parts* | Paul Whitworth |

## The Other Place, Stratford-upon-Avon, 1982

Director: Adrian Noble
Designer: Nadine Baylis

| | |
|---|---|
| *Cleopatra* | Helen Mirren |
| *Mark Antony* | Michael Gambon |
| *Octavius Caesar* | Jonathan Hyde |
| *Lepidus, Old Soldier, Proculeius* | Paul Webster |
| *Domitius Enobarbus* | Bob Peck |
| *Octavia* | Penelope Beaumont |
| *Sextus Pompeius, Dolabella* | Clive Wood |
| *Charmian* | Sorcha Cusack |
| *Iras* | Josette Simon |
| | |
| *Thidias, Alexas* | Ken Bones |
| *Mardian* | Michael Fitzgerald |
| *Maecenas, Euphronius* | David Glover |
| *Canidius, Seleucus* | Nigel Harrison |
| *Eros* | Michael Maloney |
| *Decretas, Menecrates* | Tom Mannion |
| *Taurus, Menas* | Niall Padden |
| *Agrippa* | George Parsons |
| *Clown* | David Troughton |
| *Varrius, Diomedes* | Albie Woodington |

## Olivier Theatre, National Theatre, London, 1987

Director: Peter Hall
Designer: Alison Chitty

| | |
|---|---|
| *Cleopatra* | Judi Dench |
| *Mark Antony* | Anthony Hopkins |
| *Octavius* | Tim Pigott-Smith |
| *Lepidus, Clown* | John Bluthal |
| *Domitius Enobarbus* | Michael Bryant |
| *Octavia* | Sally Dexter |
| *Sextus Pompey* | David Schofield |
| *Charmian* | Miranda Foster |
| *Iras* | Helen Fitzgerald |

| | |
|---|---|
| Silius, Thidias, Gallus | Desmond Adams |
| Scarus, Alexas, Diomedes | Robert Arnold |
| Soldier | Ian Bolt |
| Dolabella, Varrius | Michael Bottle |
| Soldier | Patrick Brennan |
| Decretas, Menas | Michael Carter |
| Eros | Jeremy Flynn |
| Menecrates, Schoolmaster | Peter Gordon |
| Philo | Mike Hayward |
| Agrippa | Basil Henson |
| Soldier | Hus Levent |
| Soldier | Simon Needs |
| Mardian | Iain Ormsby-Knox |
| Lady attending on Octavia | Frances Quinn |
| Egyptian, Soldier | Simon Scott |
| Maecenas | Graham Sinclair |
| Demetrius, Proculeius, Ventidius | Brian Spink |
| Canidius, Seleucus, Soothsayer | Daniel Thorndike |
| Boy | Peter Corey, Paul Vinhas |

## Shakespeare Theatre Company, Folger Shakespeare Library, Washington DC, 1988

Director: Michael Kahn
Set designer: Robert Edward Darling
Costume designer: Judith Dolan

| | |
|---|---|
| Cleopatra | Franchelle Stewart Dorn |
| Antony | Kenneth Haigh |
| Octavius Caesar | Michel R. Gill |
| Aemilius Lepidus, Schoolmaster | Emery Battis |
| Domitius Enobarbus | Jack Ryland |
| Octavia | Katrina Van Duyn |
| Sextus Pompeius, Dolabella | Edward Gero |
| Charmian | Gail Grate |
| Iras | Leah Maddrie |
| | |
| Messenger | Oliver Barreiro |
| Ensemble | Mark Douglas |
| A Rural Fellow, A Soothsayer | Charles Dumas |
| Thidias, Menas, Ensemble | Michael Forrest |
| Mardian | Carlos Juan Gonzalez |
| Ensemble | Steve Harley |
| Ensemble | Marvin E. Hart |
| Ensemble | James Huesz |

| | |
|---|---|
| *Alexas* | Robert Jason |
| *Attendant to Octavia* | Linda Khoury |
| *Agrippa* | Floyd King |
| *Ensemble* | Mykal Knight |
| *Canidius, Proculeius* | Barry Mulholland |
| *Demetrius, Ensemble* | Jan Notzon |
| *Maecenas* | K. Lype O'Dell |
| *Scarus* | Paris Peet |
| *Eros* | Andrew Land Prosky |
| *Attendant to Octavia* | Lisa Rhoden |
| *Menecrates, Ensemble* | D. Raymond Simonton |

## Wiener Festwochen and the Berliner Ensemble (co-production), King's Theatre (Edinburgh Festival), 1994

Director: Peter Zadek
Set designer: Wilfried Minks
Costume designer: Norma Moriceau
German translation: Elisabeth Plessen

| | |
|---|---|
| *Cleopatra* | Eva Mattes |
| *Antony* | Gert Voss |
| *Octavius* | Veit Schubert |
| *Lepidus* | Jaecki Schwarz |
| *Enobarbus* | Hermann Beyer |
| *Octavia, Iras* | Gaby Herz |
| *Pompey, Taurus, Diomedes* | Georg Bonn |
| *Charmian* | Deborah Kaufmann |
| *Eros* | Uwe Bohm |
| *Scarus, Messenger to Cleopatra* | Hans Fleischmann |
| *Menas, Schoolmaster, Soothsayer, Clown* | Urs Hefti |
| *Agrippa* | Dieter Knaup |
| *Proculeius, Thidias* | Rüdiger Kuhlbrodt |
| *Varrius, Egyptian Soldier* | Patrick Lanagan |
| *Canidius, Seleucus* | Stefan Lisewski |
| *Servant to Cleopatra* | Christoph Müller |
| *Old Soldier* | Hans-Peter Reinecke |
| *Servant* | Lothar Runkel |
| *Mardian* | Nino Sandow |
| *Maecenas* | Martin Seifert |
| *Dolabella, Alexas* | Götz Schulte |

| | |
|---|---|
| *Demetrius, Gallus* | Thomas Sicker |
| *Servant to Cleopatra* | Thomas Wendrich |
| *Ventidius, Menecrates* | Axel Werner |

## Northern Broadsides, Halifax, Yorkshire, and UK tour, 1995

Director: Barrie Rutter
Designer: Jessica Worrall

| | |
|---|---|
| *Cleopatra* | Ishia Bennison |
| *Antony* | Barrie Rutter |
| *Caesar* | Andrew Cryer |
| *Lepidus, Thidias* | Roy North |
| *Enobarbus* | Dave Hill |
| *Iras, Octavia* | Deborah McAndrew |
| *Pompey, Eros, Dolabella* | John Gully |
| *Charmian* | Julie Livesey |
| | |
| *Agrippa* | Stephen Anderson |
| *'Antony', Maecenas* | David Fenwick |
| *Soothsayer* | David Findlay |
| *Menas, Proculeius* | Gerard McDermott |
| *Mardian* | David Peacock |
| *Messenger* | Andy Wear |
| *'Cleopatra', Ventidius* | Andrew Whitehead |

## The Globe Theatre, London, 1999

Master of play and verse: Giles Block
Master of clothing and properties: Jenny Tiramani

| | |
|---|---|
| *Cleopatra* | Mark Rylance |
| *Mark Antony* | Paul Shelley |
| *Octavius Caesar* | Ben Walden |
| *Lepidus, Philo, A Schoolmaster, Proculeius* | Timothy Davies |
| *Enobarbus, Seleucus* | John McEnery |
| *Octavia, Thidias, Varrius* | Toby Cockerell |
| *Sextus Pompeius, Taurus, Diomedes* | Mark Lewis Jones |
| *Charmian* | Danny Sapani |
| *Iras, The Boy* | James Gillan |

| | |
|---|---|
| *Maecenas* | Jimmy Gardner |
| *Decretas, Soothsayer, Cleopatra's Messenger* | Roger Gartland |
| *Silius, Eros, Gallus, Menecrates* | Liam Hourican |
| *Demetrius, Agrippa* | Terence Maynard |
| *Dolabella, Mardian* | Quill Roberts |
| *Ventidius, Canidius, Alexas, Clown* | Michael Rudko |
| *Scarus, Menas* | Benedict Wong |

## Royal Exchange Theatre, Manchester, 2005

Director: Braham Murray
Designer: Johanna Bryant

| | |
|---|---|
| *Cleopatra* | Josette Bushell-Mingo |
| *Antony* | Tom Mannion |
| *Caesar* | Steven Robertson |
| *Lepidus, Thidias, Watch* | Will Tacey |
| *Enobarbus* | Terence Wilton |
| *Octavia, Iras* | Gugu Mbatha-Raw |
| *Charmian* | Sarah Paul |
| *Scarus* | Glenn Chapman |
| *Alexas, Seleucus* | Chris Hannon |
| *Agrippa* | James Howard |
| *Maecenas, Schoolmaster, Diomedes* | Jack Lord |
| *Philo, Clown* | Joseph Mawle |
| *Dercetus* | Fergus O'Donnell |
| *Mardian* | Ali Sichilongo |
| *Dolabella, Sentry* | Simeon Truby |
| *Soothsayer, Eros* | Everal A. Walsh |

## Royal Shakespeare Company, The Public and GableStage (co-production), Swan Theatre, Stratford-upon-Avon, 2013

Director: Tarell Alvin McCraney
Designer: Tom Piper

| | |
|---|---|
| *Cleopatra* | Joaquina Kalukango |
| *Mark Antony* | Jonathan Cake |
| *Octavius Caesar* | Samuel Collings |
| *Lepidus, Proculeius* | Henry Stram |
| *Enobarbus* | Chukwudi Iwuji |
| *Octavia, Iras* | Charise Castro Smith |

| | |
|---|---|
| Pompey, Alexas, Scarus | Ash Hunter |
| Charmian, Menas | Sarah Niles |
| Agrippa, Thyreus | Ian Lassiter |
| Mardian, Soothsayer, Eros | Chivas Michael |

## Tom Patterson Theatre, Stratford Festival of Canada, Ontario, 2014

Director: Gary Griffin
Designer: Charlotte Dean

| | |
|---|---|
| Cleopatra | Yanna McIntosh |
| Mark Antony | Geraint Wyn Davies |
| Octavius Caesar | Ben Carlson |
| Lepidus | Randy Hughson |
| Enobarbus | Tom McCamus |
| Octavia | Carmen Grant |
| Pompey, Clown | Brian Tree |
| Charmian | Sophia Walker |
| Iras | Jennifer Mogbock |
| | |
| Mecenas | Sean Arbuckle |
| Eros | Daniel Briere |
| Man from Sicyon | Ryan Field |
| Agrippa | Peter Hutt |
| Diomedes | Andrew Lawrie |
| Towrus | Jamie Mac |
| Dolabella, Thidias | Anthony Malarky |
| Varrius | André Morin |
| Scarrus | Karack Osborn |
| Ventidius | Andrew Robinson |
| Menas, Camidius | Brad Rudy |
| Soothsayer | Stephen Russell |
| Alexas, Proculeius | E. B. Smith |
| Mardian | Antoine Yared |

## Toneelgroep Amsterdam, Theater Carré, 2018

Director: Ivo van Hove
Set (and lighting) designer: Jan Versweyveld
Costume designer: Lies van Assche

| | |
|---|---|
| Cleopatra | Chris Nietvelt |
| Antonius | Hans Kesting |
| Octavius Caesar | Maria Kraakman |

| | |
|---|---|
| *Lepidus* | Fred Goessens |
| *Enobarbus* | Bart Slegers |
| *Octavia* | Hélène Devos |
| *Charmian* | Marieke Heebink |
| *Iras* | Frieda Pittoors |
| | |
| *Agrippa* | Gijs Scholten van Aschat |
| *Diomedes* | Janni Goslinga |
| *Proculeius* | Hugo Koolschijn |
| *Dolabella* | Alwin Pulinckx |
| *Thidias* | Harm Duco Schut |
| *Ventidius* | Eelco Smits |

# BIBLIOGRAPHY

Abbot, George, 1664. *A Briefe Description of the Whole World*, 5th edn (London: Margaret Sheares).
Addenbrooke, David, 1974. *The Royal Shakespeare Company: The Peter Hall Years* (London: William Kimber).
Adelman, Janet, 1973. *The Common Liar: An Essay on Antony and Cleopatra* (New Haven: Yale University Press).
Aebischer, Pascale, 2013. 'The Properties of Whiteness: Renaissance Cleopatras from Jodelle to Shakespeare', *Shakespeare Survey*, 65 (Cambridge: Cambridge University Press), 221–238.
Ansorge, Peter, 1970. 'Director in Interview', *Plays and Players*, September, 16–17, 21.
Arnold, Janet, 1988. *Queen Elizabeth's Wardrobe Unlock'd* (Leeds: Maney).
Arshad, Yasmin, 2011. 'The Enigma of a Portrait: Lady Anne Clifford and Daniel's *Cleopatra*', *The British Art Journal*, 11:3, 30–36.
Arshad, Yasmin, 2019. *Imagining Cleopatra: Performing Gender and Power in Early Modern England* (London: The Arden Shakespeare, 2019).
Arshad, Yasmin, Helen Hackett and Emma Whipday, 2015. 'Daniel's *Cleopatra* and Lady Anne Clifford: From a Jacobean Portrait to Modern Performance', *Early Theatre*, 18:2, 167–186.
Bakhtin, Mikhail, 1984. *Rabelais and his World*, trans. Helene Iswolsky (Bloomington: University of Indiana Press).
Barroll, J. Leeds, 1991. *Politics, Plague, and Shakespeare's Theater: The Stuart Years* (Ithaca, NY: Cornell University Press).
Barroll, J. Leeds, 2001. *Anna of Denmark, Queen of England: A Cultural Biography* (Philadelphia: University of Pennsylvania Press).
Beauman, Sally, 1982. *The Royal Shakespeare Company: A History of Ten Decades* (Oxford: Oxford University Press).
Beckerman, Bernard, 1979. 'Past the Size of Dreaming' in Philip C. McGuire and David A. Samuelson (eds), *Shakespeare: The Theatrical Dimension* (New York: AMS Press, New York), 209–223; first published in Mark Rose (ed.), *Antony and Cleopatra* (Prentice-Hall: Englewood Cliffs, NJ, 1977).
Berger, John, 1972. *Ways of Seeing* (London: Penguin). Also available on *YouTube* as the original four-part television series broadcast on BBC2 in January 1972, https://www.youtube.com (accessed 6 January 2020).
Berger, T., 1993. 'New Historicism and the Editing of Renaissance Texts' in W. Speed Hill (ed.), *New Ways of Looking at Old Texts: Papers of the Renaissance English Text Society, 1985–1991* (Binghamton:

MRTS in conjunction with Renaissance English Text Society), 194–197.

Bernal, Martin, 1991. *Black Athena: Afro-Asiatic Roots of Classical Civilization, 1785–1985*, vol. 1 (New York: Vintage).

Berry, Ralph, 1983. 'Komisarjevsky at Stratford-upon-Avon', *Shakespeare Survey*, 36 (Cambridge: Cambridge University Press, 73–84.

Bevington, David (ed.), 1998. *Troilus and Cressida* by William Shakespeare, The Arden Shakespeare Third Series (London: Thomas Nelson and Sons).

Billing, Christian M., 2010. 'The Roman Tragedies', *Shakespeare Quarterly*, 61:3 (Fall), 415–439.

Billington, Michael, 1998. *Peggy Ashcroft* (London: John Murray).

Boorde, Andrew, 1555. *The Fryst Boke of the Introduction of Knowledge* (London: William Copland).

Borovsky, Victor, 2001. *A Triptych from the Russian Theatre: An Artistic Biography of the Komissarzhevskys* (London: C. Hurst & Co.).

Bradley, David, 1992. *From Text to Performance in the Elizabethan Theatre: Preparing the Play for the Stage* (Cambridge: Cambridge University Press).

Bradby, David, Louis James and Bernard Sharratt (eds), 1981. *Performance and Politics in Popular Drama* (Cambridge: Cambridge University Press).

Brooks, H. F. (ed.), 1979. *A Midsummer Night's Dream* by William Shakespeare, The Arden Shakespeare Second Series (London: Methuen & Co.).

Brown, Horatio F. (ed.), 1900. *Calendar of State Papers Venetian*, vol X (London: Her Majesty's Stationery Office) [*CSPV*].

Brown, John Russell, 1993. 'Foreign Shakespeare and English-Speaking Audiences' in Dennis Kennedy (ed.), *Foreign Shakespeare, Contemporary Performance* (Cambridge: Cambridge University Press), 21–35.

Bulman, James C. (ed.), 1996. *Shakespeare, Theory, and Performance* (London: Routledge).

Bulman, James C. (ed.), 2016. *King Henry IV Part 2* by William Shakespeare, The Arden Shakespeare Third Series (London: Bloomsbury).

Burnim, Kalman A., 1961 *David Garrick, Director* (Carbondale: Southern Illinois University Press).

Burt, Philippa, 2016. 'The Merry Wives of Moscow: Komisarjevsky, Shakespeare, and Russophobia in the British Theatre', *New Theatre Quarterly*, 32:4 (November), 375–390.

Butler, Judith, 1999. *Gender Trouble: Feminism and the Subversion of Identity*, 2nd edn (London: Routledge).

Case, R. H. (ed.). 1906. *Antony and Cleopatra* by William Shakespeare, The Arden Shakespeare First Series (London: Methuen).

Chambers, E. K., 1923. *The Elizabethan Stage*, 4 vols (Oxford: Clarendon Press).

Clark, S., and P. Mason (eds), 2015. *Macbeth* by William Shakespeare, The Arden Shakespeare Third Series (London and New York: Bloomsbury).

Coleridge, S. T., 2004. 'Comments on *Othello*' in Edward Pechter (ed.), *William Shakespeare, Othello: A Norton Critical Edition* (New York and London: W. W. Norton & Co.), 230–234.

Conkie, Rob, 2008. 'Constructing Femininity in the New Globe's All-Male *Antony and Cleopatra*' in James C. Bulman (ed.), *Shakespeare Re-Dressed: Cross-Gender Casting in Contemporary Performance* (Madison, NJ: Fairleigh Dickinson University Press), 189–209.

Cowell, John, 1607. *The Interpreter* (Cambridge: John Legate).

Cromer, Evelyn Baring, first Earl of, 1908. *Modern Egypt*, 2 vols; reprint (New York: Macmillan, 2001).

Cuffe, Henry, 1607. *The differences of the ages of mans life together with the originall causes, progresse, and end thereof. Written by the learned Henrie Cuffe, sometime fellow of Merton College in Oxford. Ann. Dom. 1600* (London): Printed by Arnold Hatfield for Martin Clearke).

Daniell, D. (ed.), 1998. *Julius Caesar* by William Shakespeare, The Arden Shakespeare Third Series (London: Thomas Nelson and Sons).

de Sousa, Geraldo U., 1999. *Shakespeare's Cross-Cultural Encounters* (London: Macmillan).

Deats, Sara Munson, 2005. 'Shakespeare's Anamorphic Drama: A Survey of *Antony and Cleopatra* in Criticism, on Stage, and on Screen' in Sara Munson Deats (ed.), *New Critical Essays on Antony and Cleopatra* (New York: Routledge), 1–93.

Dobson, Michael, 2006. 'Shakespeare Performances in England, 2005', *Shakespeare Survey*, 59 (Cambridge: Cambridge University Press), 298–337.

Dunbar, Mary Judith, 2010. *The Winter's Tale*, Shakespeare in Performance (Manchester: Manchester University Press).

Engle, Ron, 1993. 'Audience, Style, and Language in the Shakespeare of Peter Zadek' in Dennis Kennedy (ed.), *Foreign Shakespeare: Contemporary Performance* (Cambridge: Cambridge University Press), 93–105.

Escolme, Bridget, 2006. *Antony and Cleopatra*, The Shakespeare Handbooks (Basingstoke: Palgrave Macmillan).

Escolme, Bridget, 2008. 'Mark Rylance' in John Russell Brown (ed.), *The Routledge Companion to Directors' Shakespeare* (Abingdon: Routledge), 407–24.

Eyber, Vitaliy, 2007. '"Let Rome in Moskva Melt": *Antony and Cleopatra* at Sovremennik', *Shakespeare Bulletin*, 25:4 (Winter), 147–152.

Foakes, R. A. (ed.), 1997. *King Lear* by William Shakespeare, The Arden Shakespeare Third Series (London: Thomas Nelson and Sons).

Foakes, R. A., and R. T. Rickert (eds), 1961. *Henslowe's Diary* (Cambridge: Cambridge University Press).

Fowler, Benjamin, forthcoming. *Beautiful Illogical Acts: Realism, Feminism & Artifice in the Theatre of Katie Mitchell* (London: Routledge).

Fraser, W. Hamish, 2004. 'Second City of the Empire', *The Glasgow Story*, https://www.theglasgowstory.com/story/?id=TGSD0 (accessed 6 January 2020).

Fuller, David, 2005. 'Passion and Politics: *Antony and Cleopatra* in Performance' in Sara Munson Deats (ed.), *New Critical Essays on Antony and Cleopatra* (New York: Routledge), 95–136.

Garber, Marjorie, 1992. *Vested Interests: Cross-Dressing and Cultural Anxiety* (New York: Routledge).

Gilliatt, Penelope, 1971. 'Making *Sunday Bloody Sunday*', https://www.criterion.com/current/posts/2524-making-sunday-bloody-sunday (accessed 6 January 2020).

Goodwin, John (ed.), 1983. *Peter Hall's Diaries: The Story of a Dramatic Battle* (London: Hamish Hamilton).

Granville-Barker, Harley, 1951. 'Antony and Cleopatra' in *Prefaces to Shakespeare Second Series* (London: Sidgwick & Jackson), 111–233; first published 1930.

Gurr, Andrew, 2004. *The Shakespeare Company, 1594–1642* (Cambridge: Cambridge University Press).

Habib, Imtiaz, 1999. *Shakespeare and Race: Postcolonial Praxis in the Early Modern Period* (Lanham, MD: University Press of America).

Herford, C. H., Percy and Evelyn Simpson (eds), 1941. *Ben Jonson*, vol. VII: *The Sad Shepherd; The Fall of Mortimer; Masques and Entertainments* (Oxford: Clarendon Press).

Herford, C. H., Percy and Evelyn Simpson (eds), 1950. *Ben Jonson*, vol. X: *Play Commentary; Masque Commentary* (Oxford: Clarendon Press).

Hinman, C., 1968. *The Norton Facsimile: The First Folio of Shakespeare* (New York: W. W. Norton & Company).

Hirschman, Bill, 2014. 'McCraney's Antony and Cleopatra is Referendum on Florida Theater', http://www.floridatheateronstage.com/features/mccraneys-antony-and-cleopatra-is-referendum-on-future-of-florida-theater/ (accessed 12 December 2018).

Hodgdon, Barbara, 1996. 'Looking for Mr. Shakespeare' in James C. Bulman (ed.), *Shakespeare, Theory and Performance* (London: Routledge), 68–91.

Hodgdon, Barbara, 1998. *The Shakespeare Trade: Performances and Appropriations* (Philadelphia: University of Pennsylvania Press).

Hodgdon, Barbara, 2002. '*Antony and Cleopatra* in the Theatre' in Claire McEachern (ed.), *The Cambridge Companion to Shakespearean Tragedy* (Cambridge: Cambridge University Press), 241–63.

Hodgdon, Barbara (ed.), 2010. *The Taming of the Shrew* by William Shakespeare, The Arden Shakespeare Third Series (London: A & C Black).

Hodgdon, Barbara, 2016. *Shakespeare, Performance and the Archive* (London: Routledge).

Holland, Peter, 2008. 'Peter Hall' in John Russell Brown (ed.), *The Routledge Companion to Directors' Shakespeare* (Abingdon: Routledge), 140–159.

Howard, Tony, 2000. 'Blood on the Bright Young Things: Shakespeare in the 1930s' in Clive Barker and Maggie Gale (eds), *British Theatre between the Wars* (Cambridge: Cambridge University Press), 135–161.

Howard, Tony, and Jamie Rogers, 2016. *British Black and Asian Shakespeare Database*, https://bbashakespeare.warwick.ac.uk/ (accessed 8 December 2019).

Iyengar, Sujata, 2005. *Shades of Difference: Mythologies of Skin Color in Early Modern England* (Philadelphia: University of Pennsylvania Press).

Kathman, David, 2004a 'Grocers, Goldsmiths, and Drapers: Freemen and Apprentices in the Elizabethan Theater', *Shakespeare Quarterly*, 55, 1–49.

Kathman, David, 2004b. 'Reconsidering *The Seven Deadly Sins*', *Early Theatre*, 7:1, 13–44.

Kathman, David, 2005. 'How Old Were Shakespeare's Boy Actors?', *Shakespeare Survey*, 58 (Cambridge: Cambridge University Press), 220–246.

Kathman, David, 2015. 'John Rice and the Boys of the Jacobean King's Men', *Shakespeare Survey*, 68 (Cambridge: Cambridge University Press), 247–266.

Kaufmann, Miranda, 2017. *Black Tudors: The Untold Story* (London: Oneworld).

Kennedy, Dennis (ed.), 1993. *Foreign Shakespeare: Contemporary Performance* (Cambridge: Cambridge University Press).

Kennedy, Dennis, 1997. 'The Language of the Spectator', *Shakespeare Survey*, 50 (Cambridge: Cambridge University Press), 29–40.

King, T. J., 1992. *Casting Shakespeare's Plays: London Actors and their Roles, 1590–1642* (Cambridge: Cambridge University Press).

Knotts, Jenny, 2015. 'A Short History of the Close Theatre Club', http://citizenstheatre.blogspot.com/2015/10/a-short-history-of-close-theatre-club.html (accessed 16 December 2019).

Knowles, R. (ed.), 1999. *King Henry VI Part II* by William Shakespeare, The Arden Shakespeare Third Series (London: Thomas Nelson and Sons).

Kott, Jan, 1965. *Shakespeare Our Contemporary*, trans. Boleslaw Taborski (London: Methuen).

Lamb, Margaret, 1980. *Antony and Cleopatra on the English Stage* (Rutherford: Fairleigh Dickinson University Press).

Little, Arthur L., 2000. *Shakespeare Jungle Fever: National-Imperial Re-Visions of Race, Rape and Sacrifice* (Stanford, CA: Stanford University Press).

Loomba, Ania, 1999. *Gender, Race, Renaissance Drama* (Manchester: Manchester University Press).

Loomba, Ania, 2002. *Shakespeare, Race, and Colonialism* (Oxford: Oxford University Press).

Lowen, Tirzah, 1990. *Peter Hall Directs Antony and Cleopatra* (London: Methuen Drama).

MacDonald, Joyce Green, 2002. *Women and Race in Early Modern Texts* (Cambridge: Cambridge University Press).

MacDonald, Robert David, Philip Prowse and Giles Havergal, 1980. 'The Citizens Company in Glasgow: "Four Hundred Miles from Civilization"', *Performing Arts Journal*, 5:1, 50–60.

Madelaine, Richard (ed.), 1998. *Antony and Cleopatra*, Shakespeare in Performance (Cambridge: Cambridge University Press).

McClure, Norman Egbert (ed.), 1939. *The Letters of John Chamberlain*, 2 vols (Philadelphia: American Philosophical Society).

McFarlane, Brian, 2003. *The Encyclopedia of British Film* (London: Methuen).

Mennen, Richard E., 1979. 'Theodore Komisarjevsky's Production of "The Merchant of Venice"', *Theatre Journal*, 31:3 (October), 386–397.

Mullin, Michael, 1996. *Design by Motley* (London: Associated University Presses).

Neill, Michael (ed.), 1994. *The Tragedy of Anthony and Cleopatra* by William Shakespeare (Oxford: Clarendon Press).

North, Thomas, 1579. *The Lives of the Noble Grecians and Romanes, Compared together by that graue learned Philosopher and Historiographer, Plutarke of Chæonea: Translated out of Greek into French by Iames Amyot, Abbot of Bellozane, Bishop of Auxerre, one of the Kings priuy counsel, and great Amner of Fraunce, and out of French into Englishe, by Thomas North* (London: Thomas Vautroullier and John Wight).

Novak, Maximillian E., George R. Guffey and Alan Roper (eds), 1984. *All for Love* in *The Works of John Dryden*, vol. XIII (Berkeley: University of California Press).

Odell, George C. D., 1966. *Shakespeare from Betterton to Irving*, vol. 2 (New York: Dover).

'Official Cut-Outs Made by the Chicago Board of Censors', 1918. *Exhibitors Herald*, 6:12, 29 (16 March), https://archive.org/stream/exhibitorsherald06exhi#page/n522/mode/1up (accessed 6 January 2020).

Olivier, Laurence, 1986. *On Acting* (New York: Simon and Schuster).

Ormsby, Robert, 2014. '*Coriolanus* and Brecht, 1951–71' in *Coriolanus*, Shakespeare in Performance (Manchester: Manchester University Press), 46–85.

Pavis, Patrice, 1993. 'Wilson, Brook, Zadek: An Intercultural Encounter?' in Dennis Kennedy (ed.), *Foreign Shakespeare: Contemporary Performance* (Cambridge: Cambridge University Press), 270–289.

Poole, Adrian, 2004. *Shakespeare and the Victorians* (London: Arden Shakespeare).

Prince, Kathryn, 2013. 'Judi Dench' in Russell Jackson (ed.), *Great Shakespeareans*, vol. XVI: *Gielgud, Olivier, Ashcroft, Dench* (London: Bloomsbury), 157–190.

Purcell, Stephen, 2017. *Shakespeare in the Theatre: Mark Rylance at the Globe* (London: Bloomsbury Arden Shakespeare).

Redgrave, Michael, 1983. *In My Mind's I* (New York: Viking Press).

Riche, Barnaby (trans), 1584. *The Famous Hystory of Herodotus* (London: Thomas Marshe).

Roach, Joseph, 1996. *Cities of the Dead: Circum-Atlantic Performance* (New York: Columbia University Press).

Rutter, Carol Chillington (ed.), 1984. *Documents of the Rose Playhouse* (Manchester: Manchester University Press).

Rutter, Carol Chillington, 1988. *Clamorous Voices: Shakespeare's Women Today* (London: Women's Press).

Rutter, Carol Chillington, 2001. *Enter the Body: Women and Representation on Shakespeare's Stage* (London: Routledge).

Rutter, Carol Chillington, 2003. 'Rough Magic: Northern Broadsides at Work at Play', *Shakespeare Survey*, 56 (Cambridge: Cambridge University Press), 236–255.

Rutter, Carol Chillington, 2006. '*The Wars of the Roses*: The RSC's *Henry VI* and *Edward IV* (1963–64)' in Stuart Hampton-Reeves and Carol Chillington Rutter, *The Henry VI Plays*, Shakespeare in Performance (Manchester: Manchester University Press), 54–79.

Rutter, Carol Chillington, 2013. 'Peggy Ashcroft' in Russell Jackson (ed.), *Great Shakespeareans*, vol. XVI: *Gielgud, Olivier, Ashcroft, Dench* (London: Bloomsbury), 110–156.

Said, Edward W., 1978. *Orientalism* (New York: Random House).

Sandys, George, 1615. *A Relation of a Journey Begun Anno Domini 1610* (London: Richard Field).

Shapiro, James, 2015. *1606: William Shakespeare and the Year of* Lear (London: Faber & Faber).
Shaw, Glen Byam. Notebooks, 1943, Shakespeare Birthplace Trust, Stratford-upon-Avon, MM/Shaw 6/8 and MM/Shaw/6/11 [NB 1943].
Shaw, Glen Byam. Notebooks, 1944, Shakespeare Birthplace Trust, Stratford-upon-Avon, MM/Shaw/6/2 and MM/Shaw/6/9 [NB 1944].
Siemon, J. R. (ed.), 2009. *King Richard III* by William Shakespeare, The Arden Shakespeare Third Series (London: Bloomsbury).
Sinfield, Alan, 1992. *Faultlines: Cultural Materialism and the Politics of Dissident Reading* (Oxford: Oxford University Press).
Smallwood, Robert, 2000, 'Shakespeare Performances in England, 1999', *Shakespeare Survey*, 53 (Cambridge: Cambridge University Press), 244–273.
Smith, Bruce R., 2000. 'Persons' in *Shakespeare and Masculinity* (Oxford: Oxford University Press), 7–37.
Smith, James, 2006. 'Brecht, the Berliner Ensemble, and the British Government', *New Theatre Quarterly*, 22:4 (November), 307–323.
Stallybrass, Peter, 1986. 'Patriarchal Territories: The Body Enclosed' in Margaret W. Ferguson, Maureen Quilligan and Nancy J. Vickers (eds), *Rewriting the Renaissance: The Discourses of Sexual Difference in Early Modern Europe* (Chicago: University of Chicago Press), 123–142.
Styan, John, 1979. 'Changeable Taffeta: Shakespeare's Characters in Performance' in Philip C. McGuire and David A. Samuelson (eds), *Shakespeare: The Theatrical Dimension* (New York: AMS Press), 133–148.
Thomas, Chad Allen, 2015. 'Queer Shakespeare at the Citizens Theatre', *Shakespeare Bulletin*, 33:2 (Summer), 245–271.
Thompson, A., and N. Taylor (eds), 2006. *Hamlet* by William Shakespeare, The Arden Shakespeare Third Series (London: Cengage Learning).
Thomson, Peter, 1974. 'Shakespeare Straight and Crooked: A Review of the 1973 Season at Stratford', *Shakespeare Survey*, 27 (Cambridge: Cambridge University Press), 143–154.
Tierney, Margaret, 1972. 'Direction and Design: Trevor Nunn and Christopher Morley', *Plays and Players* (September), 25–27.
Walton, Nick, 2008. 'Glen Byam Shaw' in John Russell Brown (ed.), *The Routledge Companion to Directors' Shakespeare* (London: Routledge), 37–53.
Warren, Roger, 1980. 'Shakespeare at Stratford and the National Theatre, 1979', *Shakespeare Survey*, 33 (Cambridge: Cambridge University Press), 169–180.
Wells, Stanley (ed.), 1978. 'Antony and Cleopatra; or, His-tory and Her-story in a Modern Nilo-Metre' in *Nineteenth-Century Shakespeare and Burlesques*, vol. IV (London: Diploma Press), 142–191.

Wells, Stanley, 1989. 'Shakespeare Performances in London and Stratford-upon-Avon, 1986–7', *Shakespeare Survey*, 41 (Cambridge: Cambridge University Press), 159–181.

Wilders, John (ed.), 1995. *Antony and Cleopatra* by William Shakespeare, The Arden Shakespeare Third Series (London: Routledge).

Worthen, William, 1997. *Shakespeare and the Authority of Performance* (Cambridge: Cambridge University Press).

Yachnin, Paul, 1991. '"Courtiers of Beauteous Freedom": *Antony and Cleopatra* in its Time', *Renaissance and Reformation*, 26:1, 1–20.

# INDEX

Note: page numbers in **bold** refer to figures.

*A Midsummer Night's Dream* 15, 33, 93, 112, 114, 131
Abbot, George 33
Actium, Battle of xix, 7, 15, 16, 46, 47, 52, 55, **56**, 87, 90, 107, 108, 110, 115, 124, 133, 140, 163, 172, 175–176, 185, 187, 188, 193, 206, 213, 235, 236, 239, 243, 255, 256, 259, 278, 280, 288, **289**
Adelman, Janet 293n3
Agate, James 231
*All for Love* (Dryden) 43–53
Anderson, James 59
Andrews, Harry 88
Andrews, Nigel 200
Antony xiii–xiv, 6, 13, 18, 32, 163, **170**, 181, 224–225, 235–236, 279
   Berliner Ensemble 235–236, 237, 240–242
   Cake's 282, 284–286
   casting 17
   character 14–16, 68, 171, 180, 185, 284
   death 7, 20, 21, 86–88, 109–110, ⏐ 125–129, 163, **163**, 173, 198, 216–217, 241–242, 250, **250**
   Dryden's 45, 47–48, 49–50, 50, 50–51, 53
   Duttine's 159, 162, 163, **163**
   Gambon's 134, 135, 139–140, 142, **143**
   Haigh's 255–256
   Hopkins's 182, 182–183, 188–190, **189**, 192–194, 198
   Howard's 113–114, 116–117, 119–121, **120**, 122, **123**, 124–128
   Jacobean 34–36
   James I as 25–26

   Johnson's 100, **101**, 102–103, 105, **105**, 109–110
   Redgrave's **76**, 78, 80–83, 86–88, 90
   Rutter's 174–176
   Sedley's 46
   Shelley's 210, **211**, 212, 213–214, 216–217, 218
   stage time 37
   Tree's 60
   Wyn Davies's **258**, 259–260, **260**
*Antony and Cleopatra* xiii–xvi
*Antony and Cleopatra; or, His-tory and Her-story in a Modern Nilo-Metre* (Burnand) 150–151
Arts Council 94, 146n5
Ashcroft, Peggy 65, 67, 69, 75–76, **76**, 78–81, 83–86, **85**, 88–89, 90–91, 107, 226
Asp Man 128–132, **130**, 261
Atkins, Robert 67, 230
Augstein, Rudolf 266–267n19
authenticity 203–209, 210, 212, 218, 220n3

Ballets Russes 73
Barber, John 98, 138
Barker, Felix 128
Barton, John 122, 137, 233
Bassett, Kate 277
BBC 183
Beauman, Sally 66n12
Beckerman, Bernard 92, 110
Belarus Free Theatre 233
Bennison, Ishia 172–174, **174**, 177
Benson, Frank 58, 61–62, 66n12, 81
Berger, John 291
Berliner Ensemble, the 94, 225, 232–242
   Antony 235–236, 237, 240–242
   Antony's death 241–242

background 232–234
casting 235
Cleopatra 236–238, 239–240
Cleopatra's death 235, 240
costumes 236, 240–241
opening scene 236–238
reviews 232, 237, 237–238, 238–239, 242, 242–243
set design 235
translation 237–238
Bernal, Martin 269
Betterton, Thomas 44
Billington, Michael 102, 115, 119, 129, 133, 139, 143, 192, 200, 214, 215, 216, 216–217, 237, 239, 242–243, 270
blackness and black representation xvi, 33–34, 90–91, 111–112, 157, 177, 183, 255, 256–258, 269–292, **283**, **289**, **290**, 292n1
Blair, Tony 272
Blake, Mervyn 77
Block, Giles 206, 214, 216–217, 218
body politics 157–158, 165–166, 287
Bogdanov, Michael 201
Boorde, Andrew 33
Borne, William 40n6
Boutell, Elizabeth 50
Boyd, Michael 259, 276–277, 291
Brewster, Yvonne 270, 292n1
Bridges-Adams, William 5, 62–65, 70, 227, 264n4
Bridie, James 155, 177n3
Brook, Peter 93, 112, 114, 128, 129–130, 131–132, 134, 137, 190
Brooks, Avery 257
Bryant, Johanna 273–274
Bryant, Michael 194
Burbage, Richard 31, 35, 36, 41–42n8
burlesque 150–151
Burnand, F. C. 150–151
Burt, Philippa 228
Burton, Richard 152
Bury, John 94
Bushell-Mingo, Josette 269–275
Butler, Judith 209, 220–221n4

Butler, Robert 171–172, 207, 210
Byam Shaw, Glen 13, 14, 21n2, 65, 92, 113, 128–129, 165, 230
character notes 68–69, 71–72, 78–79, 79–80, 84–85, 91n4
design concept 72–74

Cake, Jonathan 282, 284–286
Carey, John 190
Carleton, Dudley 30–32
Carlson, Ben 261
*Carry On, Cleo* (film) 152
Castellucci, Romeo 232–233
Cecil, Robert 26, 27, 31, 32
censorship 95
Chamberlain, John 27
characteristic trope 4–5
characters 13–19
Charles II, King 45–46
Charmian 19, 34, 76, 86, 91, 119, 132, 143–144, 196, 206, 214, 220, 282, **283**
Chatterton, Frederick 58, 59
chauvinism 231–232
Chitty, Alison 181, 183, 187, 188, 198–200, 211
Citizens' Theatre, Glasgow 153–166, 215
  Antony 159, 162, 163
  background 153–156, 178n4
  body politics 157–158, 165–166
  cast 157
  Cleopatra 157–158, 159–160, 160–161, 163–164, **163**, **164**
  costumes 157, 159
  opening scene 160–162
  promptbook 160, 178n8
  reviews 156–157, 158, 159–160
  scenic compression 160, 161–163
  set design 158–159
class divisions xv, 166–168
Cleopatra xiii–xiv, 1–4, 6, 7, 13, 15–16, 18, **170**, 181, 223n12, 292n1, 295n19
  1833 production 57
  Antony's death 86–88, 109–110, **163**, 173, 217

Ashcroft's 75–76, **76,** 78–81, 83–86, **85,** 88–89, 90–91
Bennison's 172–174, **174,** 177
Berliner Ensemble 235, 236–238, 239–240
blackness 255, 256–257
Bushell-Mingo's 269–275
casting 17
character 16–17, 71, 78–79, 79–80, 83, 91n4, 118–119, 185, 190–191
cinema versions 151–152
colour 273
death 20–21, 50, 88–89, 128–132, **130,** 144, **145,** 163–164, **164,** 174, 196–197, 199–200, 217–218, 220, 223n13, 235, 240, 251, 289–290, **290**
Dench's 182, 188–192, **189,** 193–194, 195–197, 198–200
Dorn's 256
Dryden's 45, 48, 50
Glyn's 57
Green's 61, 62–63
Jackson's 113, 115, 116–119, **120, 123,** 125, 126–127, 128–132, **130**
Jacobean 33–34, 36–38, 41n6
Kalukango's 275, 282, **283,** 284, 286–287, 288, 289–290, **289,** 291–292
Kent's 157–158, 159–160, 160–161, 163–164, **163, 164**
Komisarjevsky's 230–231
Langtry's 5, 59
McIntosh's 255, 257, **258,** 260, **260, 261**
Mirren's 134, 135, 138, 139–140, **140,** 142, **143,** 144, **145**
Rylance's 210–213, **211,** 214, 215–216, 217–218, 219–220
Sedley's 46
sexuality 17, 138
stage time 37
Suzman's 100, **101,** 106–110, 110–111, 111–112
whiting-out 270, 292
*Cleopatra* (film, 1917) 151–152

*Cleopatra* (film, 1934) 152
*Cleopatra* (film, 1963) 152
Collier, Constance 60
Collins, Samuel 284–285
colonialism 67–68, 106
colour-blind casting 268n31, 291
Conkie, Rob 221–222n5
continuous acting 226
Cooke, Alexander 37, 41n8
*Coriolanus* 94, 96, 97, 110, 232, 243, 246, 265n9
Coveney, Michael 136, 144–145, 177, 237
Croll, Doña 270, 271, 273, 275, 292n1
Cross, Richard 54
Cryer, Andrew 171, 174, **174**
Cuffe, Henry 36, 41n7
cultural background 23–32
cultural contradictions 75
cultural insights xvi
Curll, Edmund 50
Cusack, Sorcha 142–144
Cushman, Robert 112–113, 132

Daubeny, Peter 232–233
Davenant, William 44
deaths 19–21
DeMille, Cecil B. 152
Dench, Judy 182, 188–192, **189,** 193–194, 195–197, 198–200, 211
Dennis, John 51
Denshawai Incident, the 60, 66n11
Dessen, Alan 208
Dickson, Andrew 287, 294n10
Dietrich, Marlene 234
difference 165–166
Dignam, Mark 96
Dobson, Michael 273
Docherty, Thomas xv, 165
Dolabella 2–4, 21, 49, 89, 195
Doran, Gregory 291
Dorn, Franchelle Stewart 256, 257
double viewing 9–13, 39n4, 39n5
Douglass, John 58
dramatic structure 5–8

[ 318 ]

Dryden, John 4, 14, 65n2, 294n12
  *All for Love* 43–53, 54–55
Duttine, John 159, 162, 163, **163**

Edwardian theatre 60
Egypt 33–34
Egyptomania xiv, 44, 55, 58, 99–100, 147n6, 151
Ellis, Ruth 81–82, 88–89
Elsom, John 132–133, 200–201
emotional switchbacks 7–8
Enobarbus 18, 19, 20, 46, 63, 68, 88, **105**, 121, 133, 176, 185, 194, 218–219, 249–250, 280, 281–282, 284, 285–286, 288–289
Escolme, Bridget 183, 213, 215–216, 220n3, 222n11
Essex, Earl of 32–33, 41n7
Evans, Edith 69, 71
Everett, Barbara 200, 201
extemporal stagings 149–153
Eyber, Vitaliy xvi

Faucit, Harriet 55
Fenton, James 134
Fiddick, Peter 114
Findlater, Richard 225
First Folio 8, 21–22n6, 37, 43
Flecknoe, Richard 51
Fleming, Peter 79
Flower, Archibald 264n4
foreign productions 224–264
  Berliner Ensemble 225, 232–242
  Komisarjevsky 226–232
  Stratford, Ontario 230
  Toneelgroep Amsterdam 225, 267n25
foreignness, attitudes to xiv–xv

Gambon, Michael 134, 135, 139–140, **140**, 142
Garber, Marjorie 209
Gardner, Lyn 246, 274, 290, 295n16
Garrick David 4, 53–54
Gielgud, John 64, 67, 69, 226
Giffin, Liza 257
Gilliatt, Penelope 118

Globe theatre 8–9, 36
Globe Theatre, London, 1999 203–220, 214
  Antony 210, **211**, 212, 213–214, 216–217, 218
  Antony's death 216
  authenticity 203–209, 210, 212, 218, 220n3
  casting 205–206, 215
  Cleopatra 210–213, **211**, 214, 215–216, 217–218, 219–220
  Cleopatra's death 217–218, 220, 223n13
  costumes 206–207, 210, 211–212, 213–214
  Enobarbus 218–219
  Octavius Caesar 206
  opening scene 209–212, **211**
  reviews 210, 212, 214–216, 218–219, 221–222n5, 222n8
Goodbody, Buzz 96
Goring, Marius 77–78, 89
Goughe, Robert 37, 41n8
Granville-Barker, Harley 5, 60–61, 62, 70, 181, 254
Great Couple, the xiii–xiv
Green, Dorothy 61, 62–63, 64
Greville, Fulke 32
Griffin, Gary 230, 258, 261, 262
Griffiths, Richard 130–131, **130**
Guthrie, Tyrone 71, 254

Haigh, Kenneth 255–256
Hall, Ernest 198
Hall, Peter 93, 94, 106, 114, 155, 179–186, 190, 193, 201, 201n1, 201n2
*Hamlet* 32, 129, 156, 166–167, 291
Hands, Terry 136
Harris, Margaret 74–75, 77–78
Harrison, Tony 166–168, 174–175
Hart, Charles 50
Havergal, Giles 155, 156, 160, 164–166, 177, 287
Heinrich, Benjamin 237, 238
*Henry V* 208
*Henry VI* 212

Henson, Basil 185
Herbert, William 24
Herodotus 33–34
Hewison, Robert 208–209, 216
Hinman, Charlton 21–22n6
Hobson, Harold 98–99
Hodgdon, Barbara 5, 38, 60, 291, 292, 295n18
Holloway, Basil 62
homosexuality 141, 157
Hopkins, Anthony 87, 182, 182–183, 188–190, **189**, 192–194, 198
Howard, Alan 113–114, 116–117, 119–121, **120**, 122, **123**, 124–128
Hurren, Kenneth 231
Hyde, Jonathan 141

imperialism 53, 106
International Centre for Theatre Research 137
Iras 19, 34, 76, 86, 91, 132, **143**, **283**
Isham, Gyles 64

Jackson, Glenda 113, 115, 116–119, **120**, **123**, 125, 126–127, 128–132, **130**, 190
Jacobean performances 4, 23–38
  cultural background 23–32
  performance 33–38, 41n6
Jacobs, Sally 113
James I, King 5, 24, 25–28
jingoism 228–229
Johnson, Richard 100, **101**, 102–103, 105, **105**, 109–110
Jones, Inigo 28–29, **30**
Jonson, Ben 28–29, 39n4, 41n8
*Julius Caesar* 5–6, 7, 8, 16, 32, 94, 97–98, 103, 110, 208, 212, 243

Kahn, Michael 255–257
Kalukango, Joaquina 275, 282, **283**, 284, 286–287, 288, 289–290, **289**, 291–292
Kathman, David 39–41n6, 41–42n8
Kellaway, Kate 245
Kemble, John Philip 55

Kempson, Rachel 69–70, 104
Kennedy, Dennis 235, 237–238, 254, 266n16
Kent, Jonathan 156, 159–160, 160–161, 163–164, **163**, **164**
Killigrew, Thomas 43, 46
King, T. J. 39n5
*King Lear* 8, 20, 40n6, 64, 136–137, 233
King's Men, the 24, 26, 34, 39n5
Kingston, Jeremy 108, 231
Koenig, Rhoda 210
Komisarjevsky, Theodore 73, 226–232, 262, 264–265n8, 264n3, 264n4, 264n5
Kott, Jan 254
Kustow, Michael 232

Langtry, Lily 5, 59
Leontovich, Eugenie 230–231
Lepidus 19, 72, **105**, 224–225, 284–285
Levin, Bernard 113, 132, 133
Lewsen, Charles 102
linguistic colonisation 262
Loomba, Ania 293n3

*Macbeth* 3–4, 8, 129, 182, 183, 201n2, 227–228, 232
MacCabe, Colin 152
McCraney, Tarell Alvin 17, 275, 276–280, 282, 287, 290, 290–291, 292
McDiarmid, Ian 155–156, 167
MacDonald, Robert David 155
McEnery, John 218–219
McIntosh, Yanna 255, 257, **258**, 260, **260**, **261**
Macready, William Charles 57
Madelaine, Richard 5
Mankiewicz, Joseph L. 152
Mars-Jones, Adam 191
*Masque of Blackness* 27–32, **30**, 33, 39n4
Massingham, Dorothy 64
*Measure for Measure* 28
Mehta, Jessica 295n19

[ 320 ]

Memorial Theatre, Stratford-upon-
    Avon 5, 58, 61–62
*Merchant of Venice, The* 20, 227
*Merry Wives of Windsor, The*
    228–229
Miller, Jonathan xiii, 183
Mirren, Helen 134, 135, 136,
    137–138, 138, 139–140, **140**,
    142, **143**, 144, **145**, 148n21
Molino, Nicoló 26, 27
Monet, Richard 257
Morgan, Charles 231
Morley, Christopher 93, 94, 96, 99
Moscow xv–xvi, xvi
Msomi, Welcome 232
Murray, Braham 271
mythic figures 4

National Youth Theatre 137
naturalism 94
Neill, Michael 32, 50
new stagecraft 73–74
New York Shakespeare Festival 254
Nightingale, Benedict 118, 134
Niles, Sarah 282, **283**
Noble, Adrian 134, 136, 138–139,
    144–146
Northern Broadsides 166–177, 230
    Antony 169, **170**, 174–176
    Antony's death 173
    background 166–169
    Cleopatra 169, **170**, 172–174, **174**,
    77
    Cleopatra's death 174
    costumes 175–176
    opening scene 169–170, **170**, 172
    reviews 169, 171–172, 176–177
    set design 170–171
Nunn, Trevor 92–98, 99–100,
    101–102, 110–111, 112, 113,
    137, 155, 165, 172, 182, 183,
    185, 279

Octavia 10–11, 49, 71, 122, 176,
    285–286
Octavius Caesar xv, 13, 18, 21, 25,
    46, 72, 77–78, 86, 141, 159, 161,

162, 163, **170**, 171, 174, **174**,
    206, 214, 261, **261**, 284–285
character 14, 89
Dryden's 49
Goring's 77–78, 89
Pigott-Smith's 194–197
Pryce's 121–122, 124–125
Redgrave's 103–106, **105**
Odell, George 55
Olivier, Laurence 69
Olivier Theatre, National Theatre
    13, 179–201
    Antony 181, 182, 182–183, 185,
    188–190, **189**, 192–194, 198
    Antony's death 198
    attention to the text 184–186
    casting 182–183
    Cleopatra 181, 182, 185, 188–192,
    **189**, 193–194, 195–197, 198–200
    Cleopatra's death 196–197,
    199–200
    conceptual framework 180
    costumes 181, 187–188
    design concept 181, 187–188
    Enobarbus 194
    Octavius Caesar 194–197
    opening scene 186–187, 188–190,
    **189**
    promptbook 180, 190, 198–199
    return to rehearsal 179–186
    reviews 186, 189, 190–191,
    192–194, 200–201
    technical challenges 197–200
Orientalism 77, 91, 270
origins 23, 32–33
*Othello: The Moor of Venice* 28, 33,
    235, 257
Owen, Michael 109

pantomime 209
Papp, Joseph 254
Parkinson, Michael 148n21
Pavis, Patrice 263
Peaslee, Richard 113
Peter, John 186, 192, 194, 200
Phelps, Samuel 57

Phillips, Louisa Anne 57
Pigott-Smith, Tim 194–197
Piper, Tom 280
Plutarch xiii, 5–6, 17, 19, 32, 35, 173, 175, 199, 277, 294n12
Poel, William 254
point of view 9–13
politics xv–xvi, 32, 94
Poole, Adrian 190–191
Portsmouth, Duchess of 45–6, 65n2
Princess's Theatre 59
Prowse, Philip 155, 156–157
Pryce, Jonathan 121–122, 124–125
Purcell, Stephen 204, 206
Putin, Vladimir xv–xvi, xvi
Pyg, John 40n6

Quayle, Anthony 70, 71, 226, 264–265n8

race, racial politics and race relations xvi, 111–112, 205–206, 255, 272, 279, 287, 294n10
Radin, Victoria 140, 142
Received Pronunciation 166
Redgrave, Corin 103–106, **105**
Redgrave, Michael 65, 67, 69–70, **76**, 78, 80–83, 86–88, 90, 104
regime change 23, 51–52
Restoration, the 4, 43–53
reviews xvi, 62, 63, 64–65, 97–99, 228–229, 231, 255, 259, 266–267n19
*see also* individual productions
revival 53–55, **56**, 57–65
Reynolds, Gillian 168
*Richard II* 166–167
*Richard III* 168
Richards, David 255
Riche, Barnaby 33–34
Roach, Joseph 153
Roberts, Bronwyn 135
*Romans in Britain, The* 157
*Romeo and Juliet* 8, 33, 69
Royal Exchange, Manchester, 2005 17, 269–275

Royal Shakespeare Company, production, 1972 92–112
3rd Senate scene 104–106
Antony 102–103, 105, **105**, 109–110
background 92–98, 99–100
casting 111
Cleopatra 100, 106–110, 110–111, 111–112
costumes 100, **101**, 103
Octavius Caesar 103–106
opening procession 100–102, **101**
politics in 110–112
racial politics 111–112
reviews 99, 100, 101–102, 104, 107, 108, 110, 111–112
set design 99
Royal Shakespeare Company, production, 1978 112–134
Antony 113–114, 116–117, 119–121, **120**, 122, **123**, 124–128
Antony's death 125–129
Cleopatra 113, 115, 116–119, **120**, **123**, 125, 126–127, 128–132, **130**
Cleopatra's death 128–132
costumes 115, 131
Octavius Caesar 121–122, 124–125
opening scene 115–118, 119–121, 131
production team 113–114
reviews 112–113, 114, 118, 124–125, 132–134, 147n12
set design 114–115
Royal Shakespeare Company, production, 1982 134–146
Antony 134, 135, 139–140, **140**, 142
Cleopatra 134, 135, 138, 139–140, **140**, 142, **143**, 144, **145**, 146n4
Cleopatra's death 144, **145**
Cleopatra's girls 142–144
Octavius Caesar 141
opening scene 139–140, **140**
reviews 138, 141–142, 144–145
sexual charge 134, 135
spatial constraints 138–139

Royal Shakespeare Company,
  production, 2013 17, 275–292
  achievement 290–292
  Antony 279, 282, 284–286
  background 276–280
  Caesar 284–285
  casting 275
  Cleopatra 275, 282, **283**, 284,
    286–287, 288, 289–290, **289**,
    291–292
  Cleopatra's death 289–290, **290**
  costumes 284
  Enobarbus 280, 281–282, 284,
    285–286, 288–289, **290**
  opening scene 280–282, 284
  racial politics 279, 287
  reviews 276, 287, 294–295n14,
    294n10, 295n18
  set design 280
  setting 278–279
  Triumph sequence 287–288
  Vodou 288–290, **290**
Russia xv
Rutter, Barrie 166–169, 171, 172,
  174–176, 177
Rutter, Carol Chillington 39n5, 70,
  71, 74, 75, 79, 94, 111, 143, 167,
  168, 206, 207, 226, 270, 293
Rylance, Mark 205, 207, 209,
  210–213, **211**, 214, 215–216,
  217–218, 219–220

Sadlers Wells 55
Said, Edward 269
Saint-Domingue 278–279
Sandys, George 33
Sapani, Danny 220
scale 92, 112, 133–134, 135–136,
  144–146
scenic writing 8–13
Section 28 141
Sedley, Sir Charles 44, 45–46
Seleucus 12–13, 84–86
Serebrennikov, Kiryll xv, xvi,
  xvi–xviin2
sexism 148n21
sexual politics 49, 247–249

Shakespeare, William xiii–xiv, 4,
  5–8, 18, 23, 28, 32
Shakespeare Birthplace Trust 68
*Shakespeare in Love* (film) 203–204,
  209, 210
Shakespeare Jubilee celebrations,
  1769 54
Shakespeare Memorial Theatre,
  Stratford-upon-Avon,
  production, 1953 67–91, 104
  Antony's death 86–88
  character notes 68–69, 71–72,
    78–79, 79–80, 84–85, 91n4
  Cleopatra's death 88–89
  costumes 71, 74, 75–78
  cultural background 67–68, 75
  design concept 72–74, 75–78
  makeup 77
  opening scene 75–77, **76**, 80–81
  production team 69–70
  promptbook 67, 91n1
  reviews 78–80, 81–83, 86–87,
    88–89, 90–91
  Seleucus scene 84–86
  set 70–71
  Thidias scene **85**
  'Wogs' 67–68, 90–91
Shakespeare Theatre at the Folger,
  Washington DC 255–7
Shelley, Paul 210, **211**, 212,
  213–214, 216–217, 218
Shuttleworth, Ian 287
Small, Christopher 159–160
Smallwood, Robert 213, 215
Soothsayer, the 19, 34, 124, 282,
  286, 288
sources 5–6
Spencer, Charles 231–232, 294–
  295n14, 294n10
Stewart, Patrick **105**, 121, 133
Stratford, Ontario, Stratford
  Shakespeare Festival 230,
  254–255, 257–262, **258**, **260**,
  **261**, 262
Stratford-upon-Avon 54, 58, 61–65
Styan, John 13–14
Suchet, David 124

[ 323 ]

Suzman, Janet 100, **101**, 110–111, 111–112, 147n11

*Taming of the Shrew, The* 221–222n5
Taylor, Elizabeth 152
Taylor, Paul 215, 221n5, 242, 259
Tearle, Godfrey 71
The Other Place 135–136, 138–139
Theatre Royal, Covent Garden 46–47, 54–55, **56**, 57
Thornber, Robin 176–177
Tiramani, Jenny 206
*Titus Andronicus* 94, 217, 294–295n14
Toneelgroep Amsterdam 225, 243–253, 262, 267n25
   Antony's death 250, **250**
   Cleopatra 249
   Cleopatra's death 251
   closing sequence 251–252
   costumes 244
   death of Enobarbus 249–250
   interactive experience 243–244
   opening scene 247–248
   reviews 245, 253
   set design 244–247
   sexual politics 247–249
   significance 252–253
Tooley, Nicholas 37, 41–42n8
*Trackers of Oxyrhynchus, The* 168
Tree, Beerbohm xvi, 5, 60
triumvirate, the 72
   triumvir xiv, 8, 103, 284
   triumvirate 6, 17, 72, 99, 118, 155, 171
   triumvirate (female) 19, 114, 142
*Troilus and Cressida* 15, 24, 122, 137, 290
Truman, Matt 246, 249, 252, 253
*Twelfth Night* 208–209
Tynan, Kenneth 78–79, 80, 106, 227, 232
Tyson, Cathy 270

*uMabatha* 232
unstageability xv

van Hove, Ivo 243, 246, 248, 252
Versweyveld, Jan 246
Victorian theatre xiv, 4–5, 57–59, 150–151
Vining, George 58, 151
*Vision of the Twelve Goddesses* 28, 31
voice politics 166–169
Voss, Gert 240–242

Wainwright, Geoffrey 168, 173
Walter, Wilfrid 63
Walters, Margaret 190, 191, 200
Wanamaker, Sam 204
Wardle, Irving 98, 114, 121, 124, 137, 138, 141, 142, 144–145, 192, 266–267n19
Warner, Deborah 217
Watson, Mary 76
Wells, Stanley 138, 141, 180, 233
Westwell, Raymond **105**
white supremacism 106, 278, 287
whiting-out and whiteness 270, 292, 293n3
Williams, Harcourt 70
Williams, Stephen 90
Wilson, Jean 76
Wingfield, Lewis 58
*Winter's Tale, The* 8, 93
Women's Liberation Movement 95, 106
Wong, Benedict 205–206
Wooster Group 290
World Theatre Season 232–233
Worsley, T. C. 80, 81
wrong-footing 5, 9–13
Wyn Davies, Geraint **258**, 259–260, **260**

xenophobia 231–232

Younge, Gary 272

Zadek, Peter 225, 232–242, 242–243, 248, 262, 262–263, 265–266n11, 266–267n19

EU authorised representative for GPSR:
Easy Access System Europe, Mustamäe tee 50,
10621 Tallinn, Estonia
gpsr.requests@easproject.com

www.ingramcontent.com/pod-product-compliance
Lightning Source LLC
Chambersburg PA
CBHW051557230426
43668CB00013B/1887